PRESS

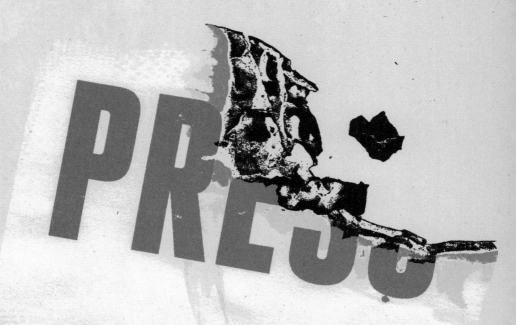

DMZ

HEARTS AND MINDS

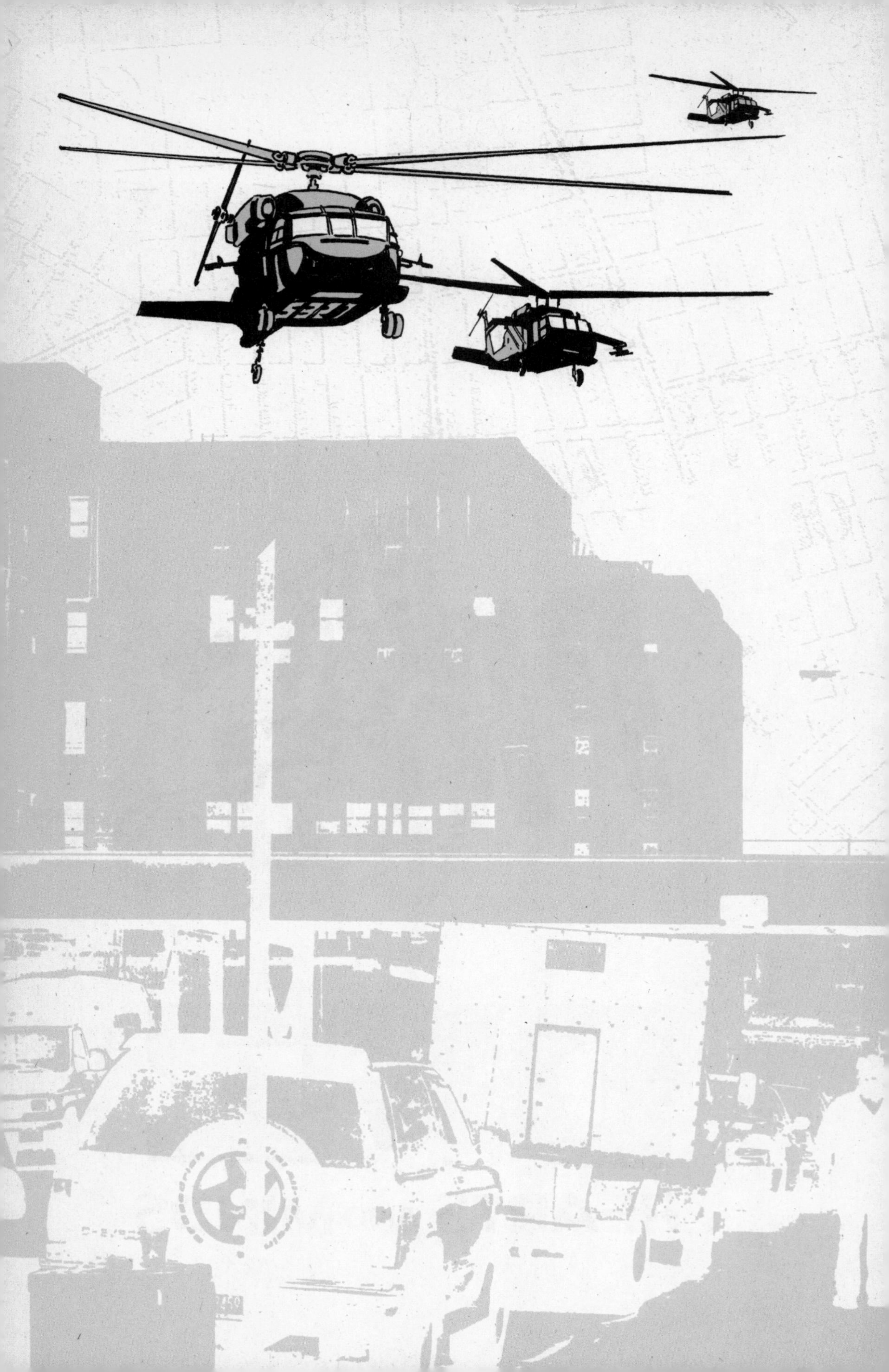

BRIAN WOOD
WRITER

NO FUTURE
RYAN KELLY
ARTIST

HEARTS AND MINDS
RICCARDO BURCHIELLI
ARTIST

JEROMY COX
COLORIST

JARED K. FLETCHER
LETTERER

ORIGINAL SERIES COVERS BY
JOHN PAUL LEON

DMZ CREATED BY **BRIAN WOOD**
AND **RICCARDO BURCHIELLI**

DMZ
HEARTS AND MINDS

Karen Berger SVP-Executive Editor **Will Dennis** Editor-Original Series **Mark Doyle** Associate Editor-Original Series
Bob Harras Group Editor-Collected Editions **Robbin Brosterman** Design Director-Books

DC COMICS

Diane Nelson President **Dan DiDio** and **Jim Lee** Co-Publishers **Geoff Johns** Chief Creative Officer
Patrick Caldon EVP-Finance and Administration **John Rood** EVP-Sales, Marketing and Business Development
Amy Genkins SVP-Business and Legal Affairs **Steve Rotterdam** SVP-Sales and Marketing
John Cunningham VP-Marketing **Terri Cunningham** VP-Managing Editor **Alison Gill** VP-Manufacturing
David Hyde VP-Publicity **Sue Pohja** VP-Book Trade Sales **Alysse Soll** VP-Advertising and Custom Publishing
Bob Wayne VP-Sales **Mark Chiarello** Art Director

Cover illustration by Brian Wood Logo design by Brian Wood Publication design and additional photography by Amelia Grohman

DMZ: HEARTS AND MINDS

Published by DC Comics. Cover and compilation Copyright © 2010 DC Comics. All Rights Reserved.

Originally published in single magazine form as DMZ 42–49. Copyright © 2009, 2010 Brian Wood and Riccardo Burchielli. All Rights Reserved. VERTIGO and all
characters, their distinctive likenesses and related elements featured in this publication are trademarks of DC Comics. The stories, characters and incidents featured in
this publication are entirely fictional. DC Comics does not read or accept unsolicited submissions of ideas, stories or artwork.

DC Comics, 1700 Broadway, New York, NY 10019 A Warner Bros. Entertainment Company. Printed in USA. First Printing. ISBN: 978-1-4012-2726-5

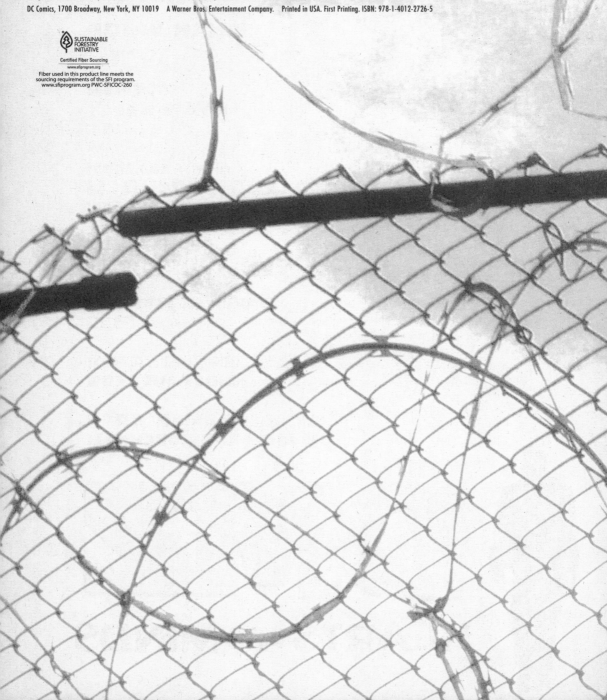

WE'RE LUCKY HERE IN THE UNITED STATES.

THERE HASN'T BEEN A WAR FOUGHT ON AMERICAN SOIL in more than 145 years. We've been distanced, protected, and made safe from the fear and horrors of war, especially from the possibility of having one in our own backyard.

When you go home tonight, turn on one of our Big 4 TV news networks and see how much coverage is actually dedicated to any of the ongoing struggles happening beyond our borders. In the United States, we have helped support and create a government and a media machine that puts us in a bubble, reinforces a xenophobic view of the world, and puts all of our troubles "out of sight and out of mind." But all that stops in DMZ—and I find that to be the bravest and most important part of this revolutionary series.

Insurgencies. Suicide bombers. Nuclear Armed States. These are all scary scenarios that could be ripped each day from the world's top stories, but in the hands of Brian Wood and Riccardo Burchielli, they create something much more frightening.

Rogue nations, outspoken dictators, private contractors and heartless mercenaries all find a place in the pages of DMZ. They open our eyes and our ears to events that, while fictional in the frames of this groundbreaking creation, are links in the chains of our global existence. Each story, each character and each page is undeniably tied to the world in which we live, and for me—that is DMZ's greatest triumph.

It would be easy to continue to go through life with blinders on to shield us from the ugly truths that, to this day, still send brave men and women to fight overseas. Soldiers who, we're told, are fighting "over there" so we won't have to here. By the time this hits the newsstands, more than 2,000,000 Americans will have fought either in Iraq or Afghanistan...a number that makes the stories of DMZ all the more terrifying, all the more plausible and all the more realistic.

What these books also do, especially the series that you are about to read, is bring into question the influence and power of hope. DMZ, like our own world, has been overshadowed with the beliefs that certain men and women, when given the chance, would reshape the course of human history. They would right the wrongs that had come before them and cut a clear path toward harmony. Citizens put their faith in these outspoken people, and now, as tensions mount both here and on the world's stage, we all stand poised to see if they will rise to the challenge we have given them, or if Icarus will fall to the ground.

When you read "No Future" and "Hearts and Minds," you will unquestionably draw parallels to questions in your own life, but what I hope happens more than anything else, is that in some small way, you actually start to find some answers.

MORGAN SPURLOCK

Morgan Spurlock is an American documentary filmmaker, television producer and screenwriter, best known for his Academy Award-nominated film Super Size Me. *He most recently finished directing an adaptation of the* New York Times *bestselling book* Freakonomics.

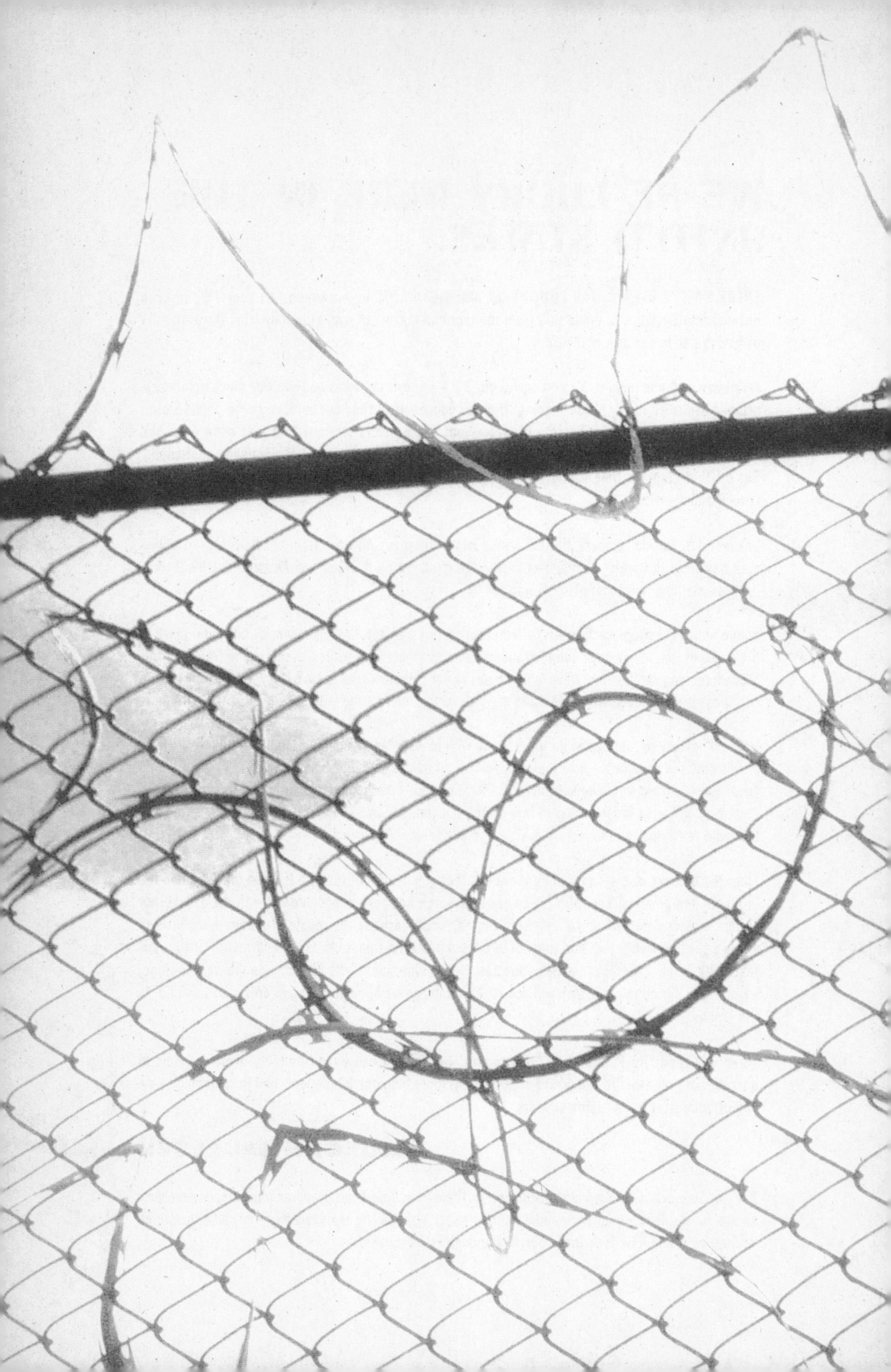

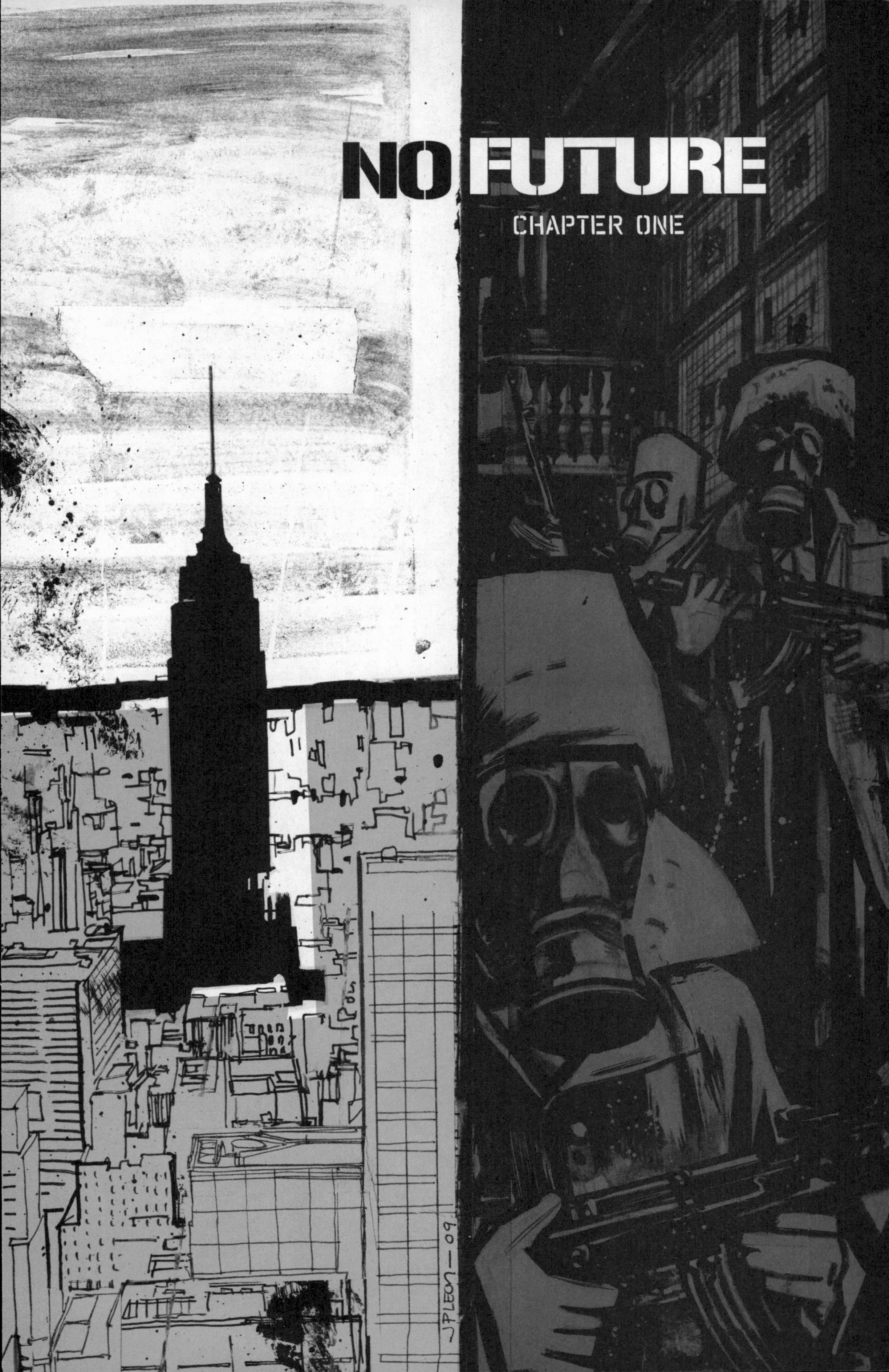
NO FUTURE
CHAPTER ONE
JPLEON—09

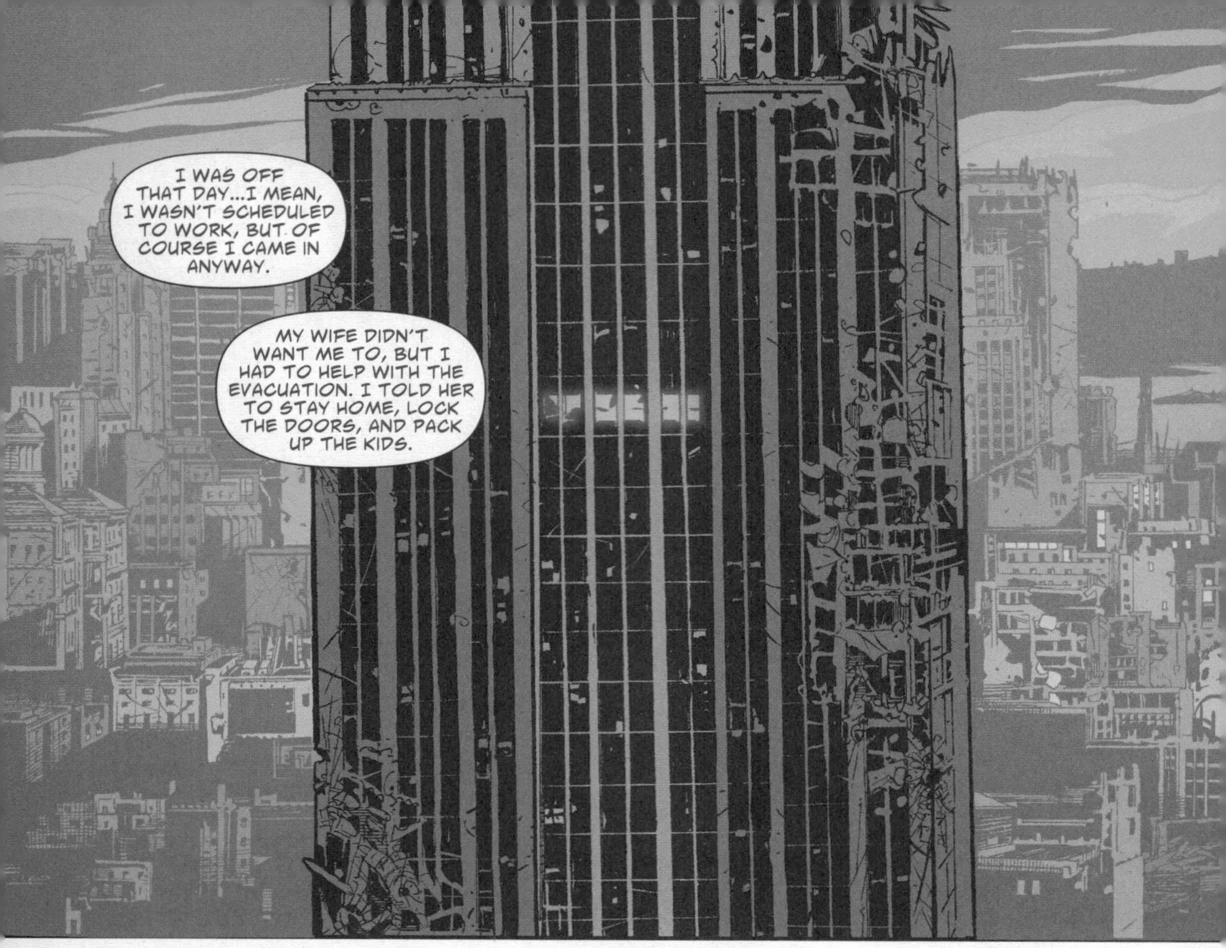
I WAS OFF THAT DAY...I MEAN, I WASN'T SCHEDULED TO WORK, BUT OF COURSE I CAME IN ANYWAY.
MY WIFE DIDN'T WANT ME TO, BUT I HAD TO HELP WITH THE EVACUATION. I TOLD HER TO STAY HOME, LOCK THE DOORS, AND PACK UP THE KIDS.

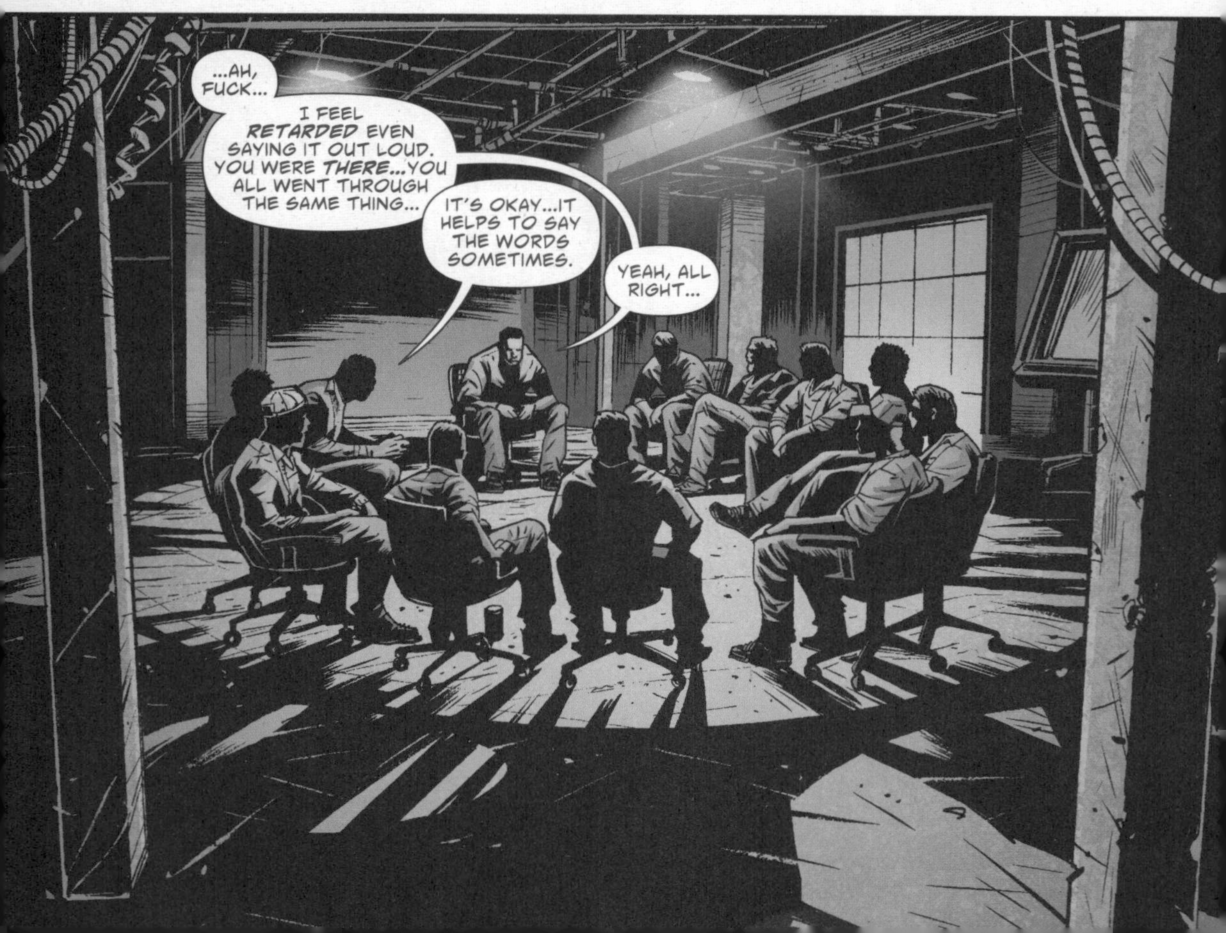
...AH, FUCK...
I FEEL *RETARDED* EVEN SAYING IT OUT LOUD. YOU WERE *THERE*...YOU ALL WENT THROUGH THE SAME THING...
IT'S OKAY...IT HELPS TO SAY THE WORDS SOMETIMES.
YEAH, ALL RIGHT...

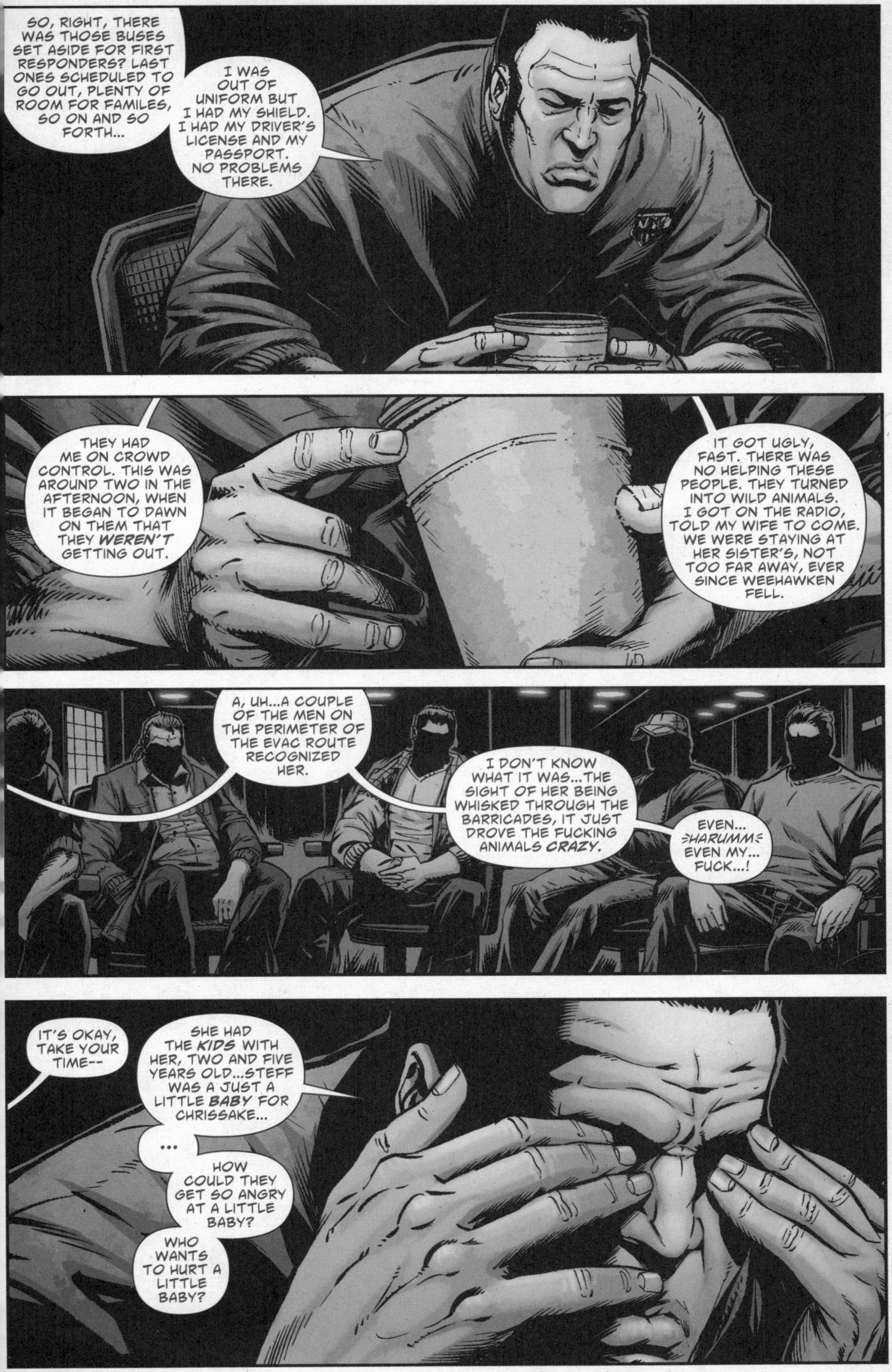
SO, RIGHT, THERE WAS THOSE BUSES SET ASIDE FOR FIRST RESPONDERS? LAST ONES SCHEDULED TO GO OUT, PLENTY OF ROOM FOR FAMILES, SO ON AND SO FORTH...
I WAS OUT OF UNIFORM BUT I HAD MY SHIELD. I HAD MY DRIVER'S LICENSE AND MY PASSPORT. NO PROBLEMS THERE.
THEY HAD ME ON CROWD CONTROL. THIS WAS AROUND TWO IN THE AFTERNOON, WHEN IT BEGAN TO DAWN ON THEM THAT THEY *WEREN'T* GETTING OUT.
IT GOT UGLY, FAST. THERE WAS NO HELPING THESE PEOPLE. THEY TURNED INTO WILD ANIMALS. I GOT ON THE RADIO, TOLD MY WIFE TO COME. WE WERE STAYING AT HER SISTER'S, NOT TOO FAR AWAY, EVER SINCE WEEHAWKEN FELL.
A, UH...A COUPLE OF THE MEN ON THE PERIMETER OF THE EVAC ROUTE RECOGNIZED HER.
I DON'T KNOW WHAT IT WAS...THE SIGHT OF HER BEING WHISKED THROUGH THE BARRICADES, IT JUST DROVE THE FUCKING ANIMALS *CRAZY.*
EVEN... *HARUMM* EVEN MY... FUCK...!
IT'S OKAY, TAKE YOUR TIME--
SHE HAD THE *KIDS* WITH HER, TWO AND FIVE YEARS OLD...STEFF WAS A JUST A LITTLE *BABY* FOR CHRISSAKE...
...
HOW COULD THEY GET SO ANGRY AT A LITTLE BABY?
WHO WANTS TO HURT A LITTLE BABY?

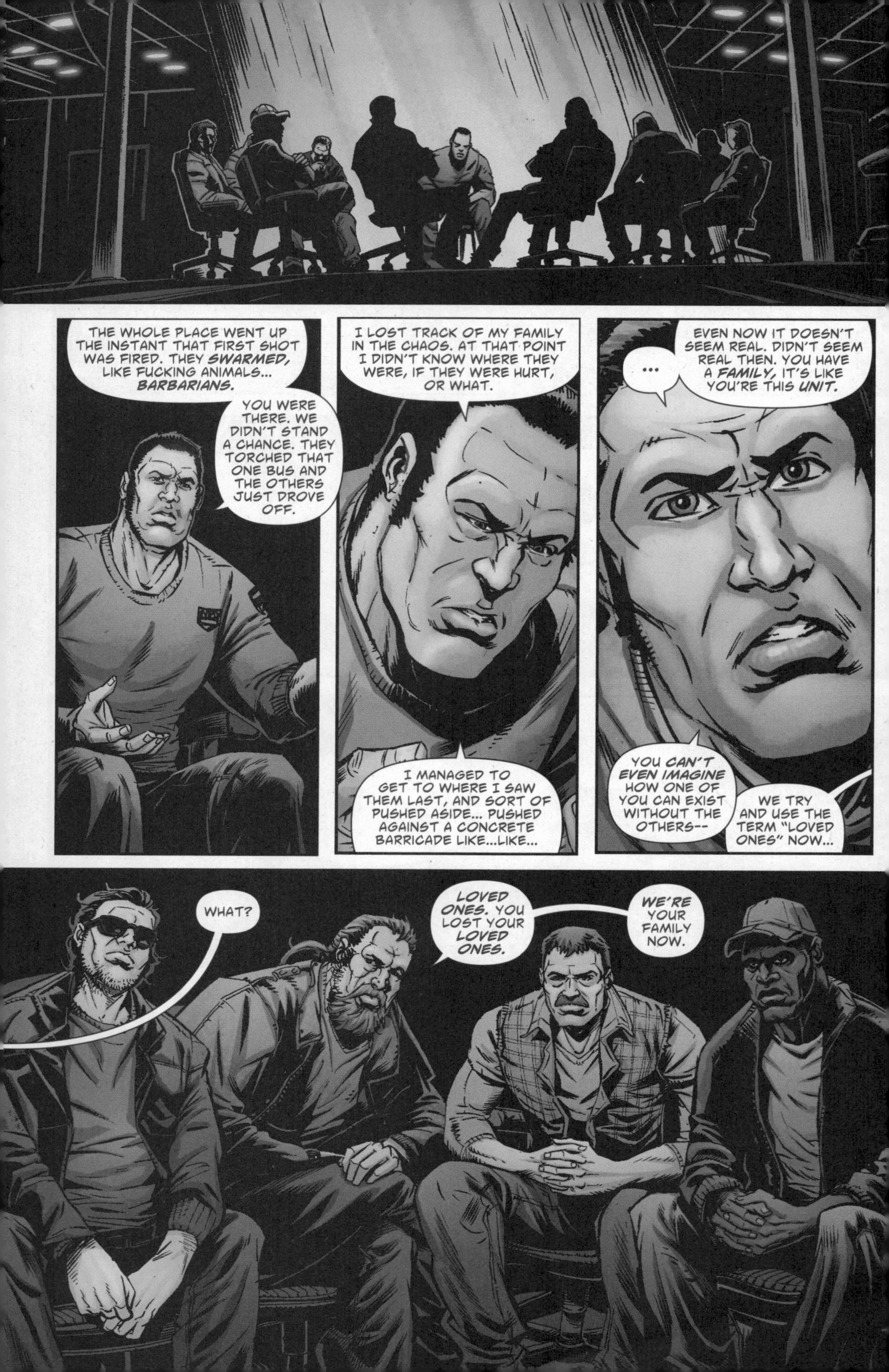
THE WHOLE PLACE WENT UP THE INSTANT THAT FIRST SHOT WAS FIRED. THEY SWARMED, LIKE FUCKING ANIMALS... BARBARIANS.
YOU WERE THERE. WE DIDN'T STAND A CHANCE. THEY TORCHED THAT ONE BUS AND THE OTHERS JUST DROVE OFF.
I LOST TRACK OF MY FAMILY IN THE CHAOS. AT THAT POINT I DIDN'T KNOW WHERE THEY WERE, IF THEY WERE HURT, OR WHAT.
I MANAGED TO GET TO WHERE I SAW THEM LAST, AND SORT OF PUSHED ASIDE... PUSHED AGAINST A CONCRETE BARRICADE LIKE...LIKE...
...
EVEN NOW IT DOESN'T SEEM REAL. DIDN'T SEEM REAL THEN. YOU HAVE A FAMILY, IT'S LIKE YOU'RE THIS UNIT.
YOU CAN'T EVEN IMAGINE HOW ONE OF YOU CAN EXIST WITHOUT THE OTHERS--
WE TRY AND USE THE TERM "LOVED ONES" NOW...
WHAT?
LOVED ONES. YOU LOST YOUR LOVED ONES.
WE'RE YOUR FAMILY NOW.

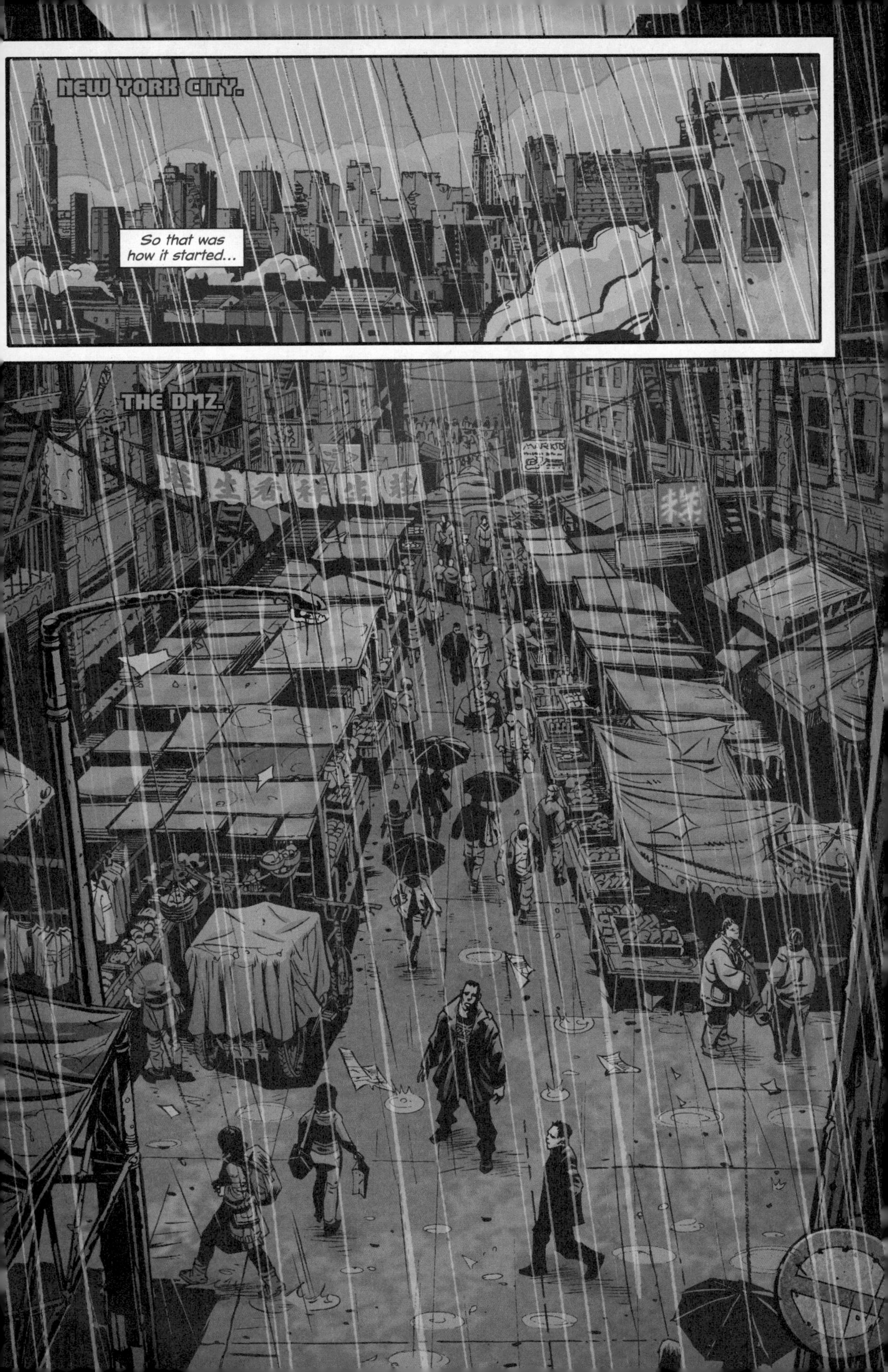
NEW YORK CITY.
So that was how it started...
THE DMZ.

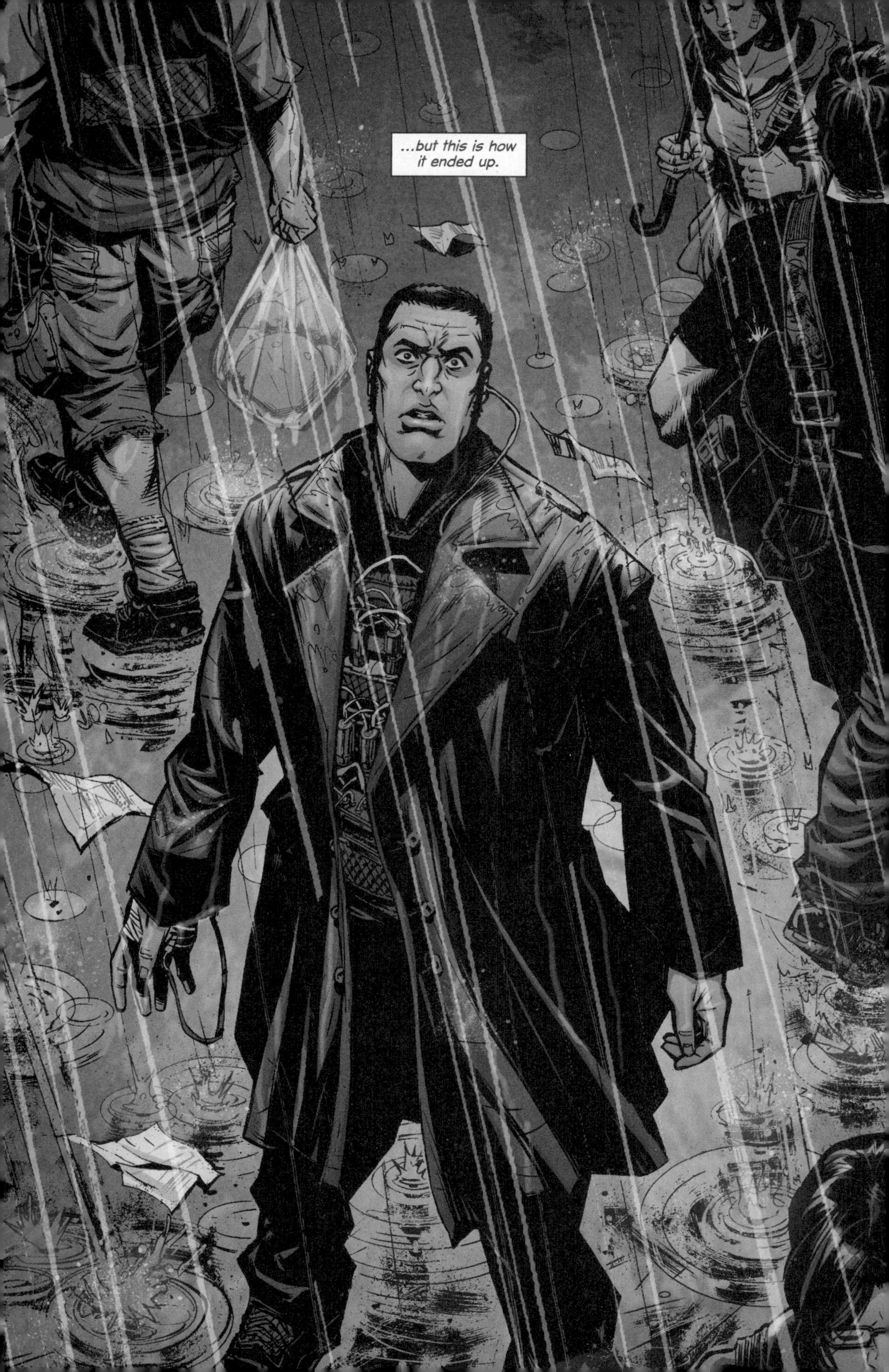
...but this is how it ended up.

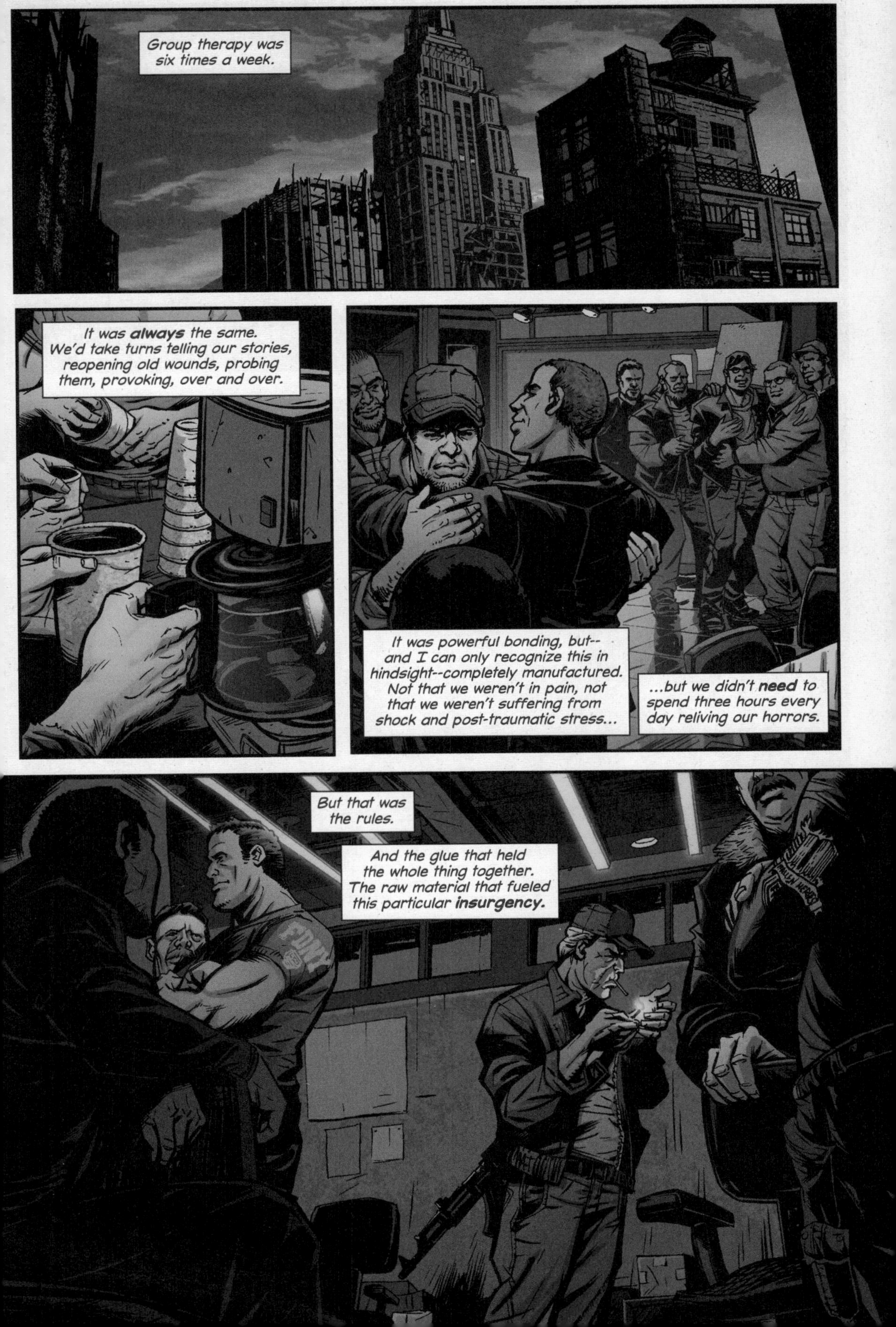
Group therapy was six times a week.
It was **always** the same. We'd take turns telling our stories, reopening old wounds, probing them, provoking, over and over.
It was powerful bonding, but-- and I can only recognize this in hindsight--completely manufactured. Not that we weren't in pain, not that we weren't suffering from shock and post-traumatic stress...
...but we didn't **need** to spend three hours every day reliving our horrors.
But that was the rules.
And the glue that held the whole thing together. The raw material that fueled this particular **insurgency.**
FDNY

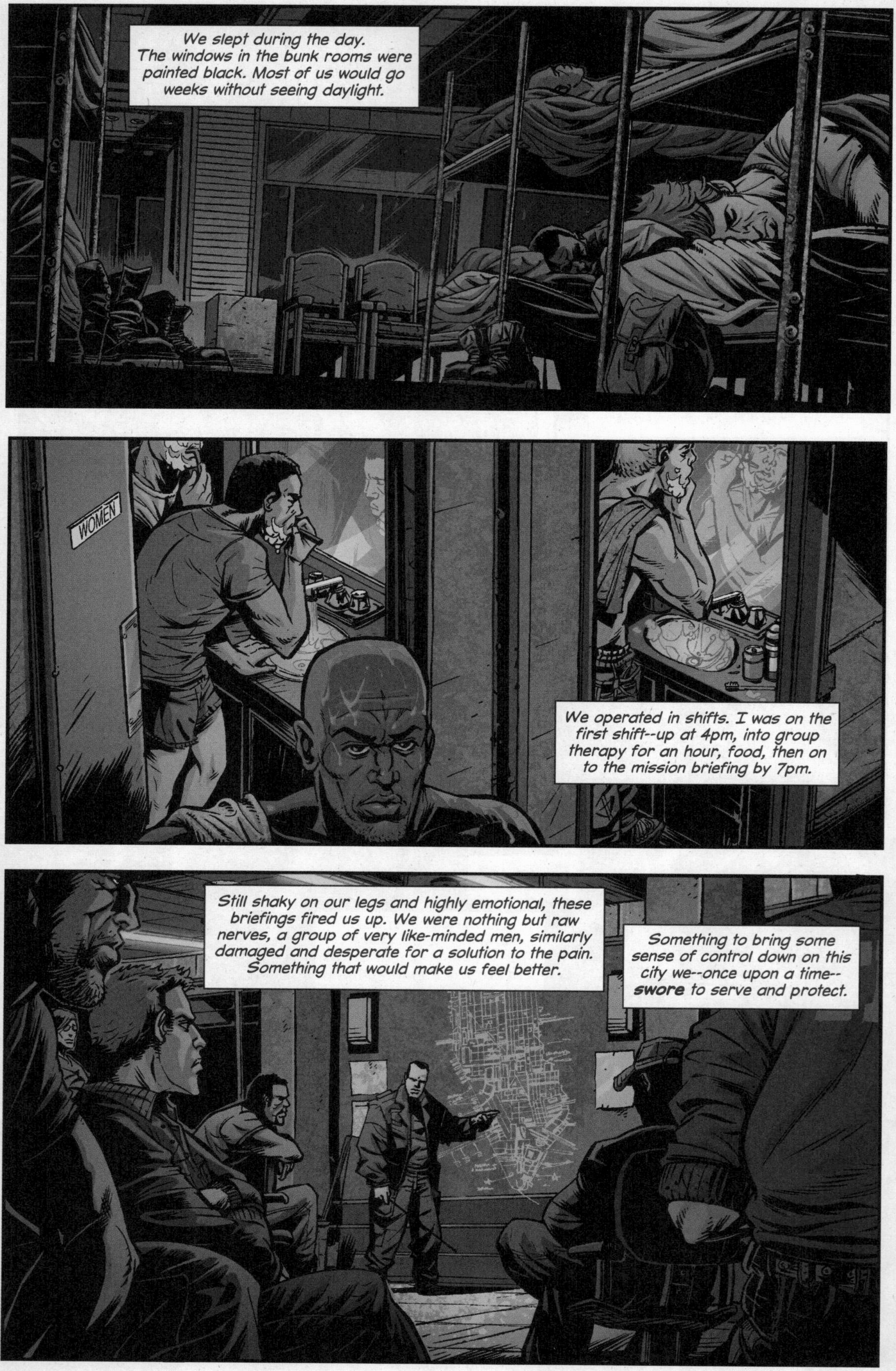
We slept during the day. The windows in the bunk rooms were painted black. Most of us would go weeks without seeing daylight.
WOMEN
We operated in shifts. I was on the first shift--up at 4pm, into group therapy for an hour, food, then on to the mission briefing by 7pm.
Still shaky on our legs and highly emotional, these briefings fired us up. We were nothing but raw nerves, a group of very like-minded men, similarly damaged and desperate for a solution to the pain. Something that would make us feel better.
Something to bring some sense of control down on this city we--once upon a time--**swore** to serve and protect.

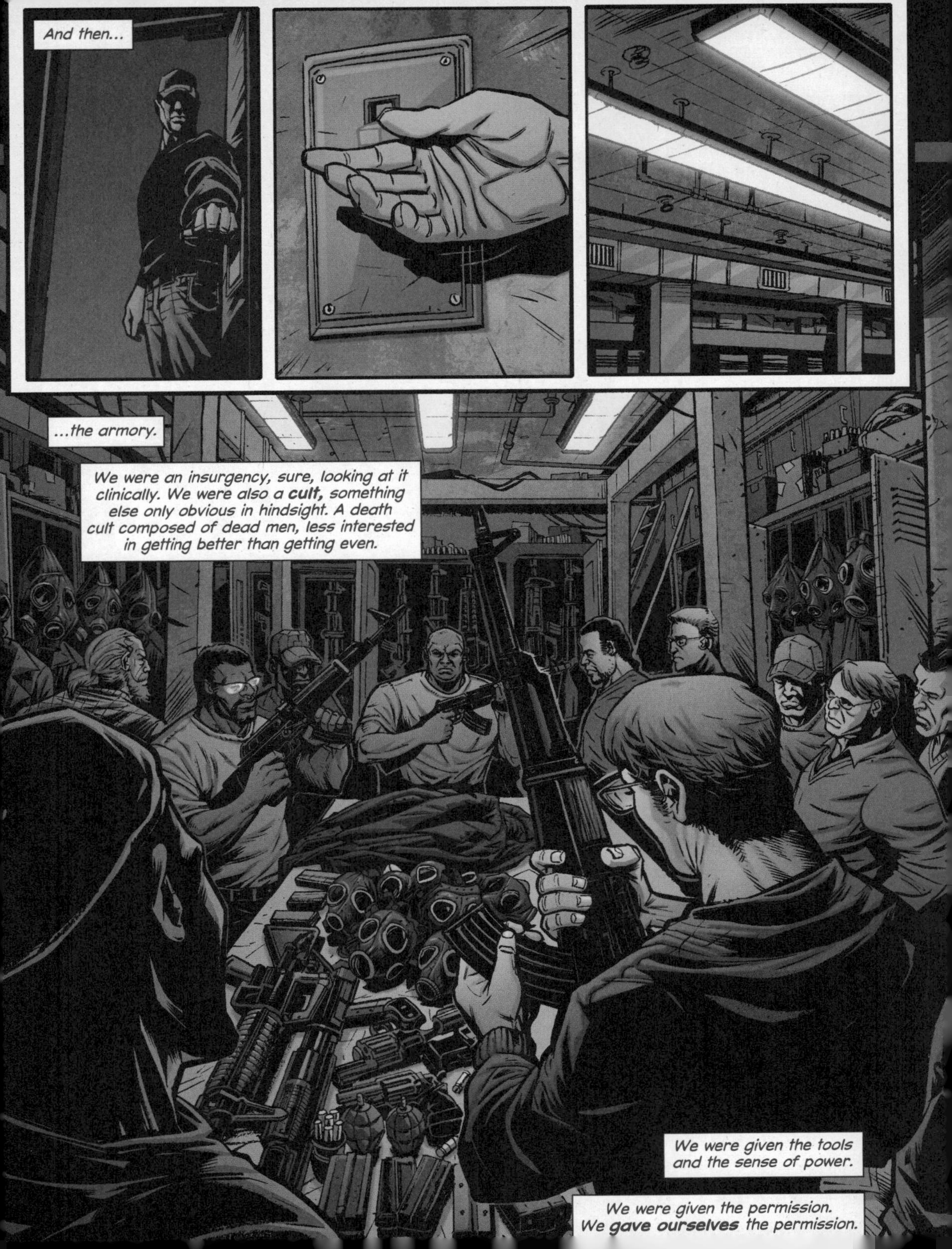
And then...
...the armory.
We were an insurgency, sure, looking at it clinically. We were also a **cult,** something else only obvious in hindsight. A death cult composed of dead men, less interested in getting better than getting even.
We were given the tools and the sense of power.
We were given the permission. We **gave ourselves** the permission.

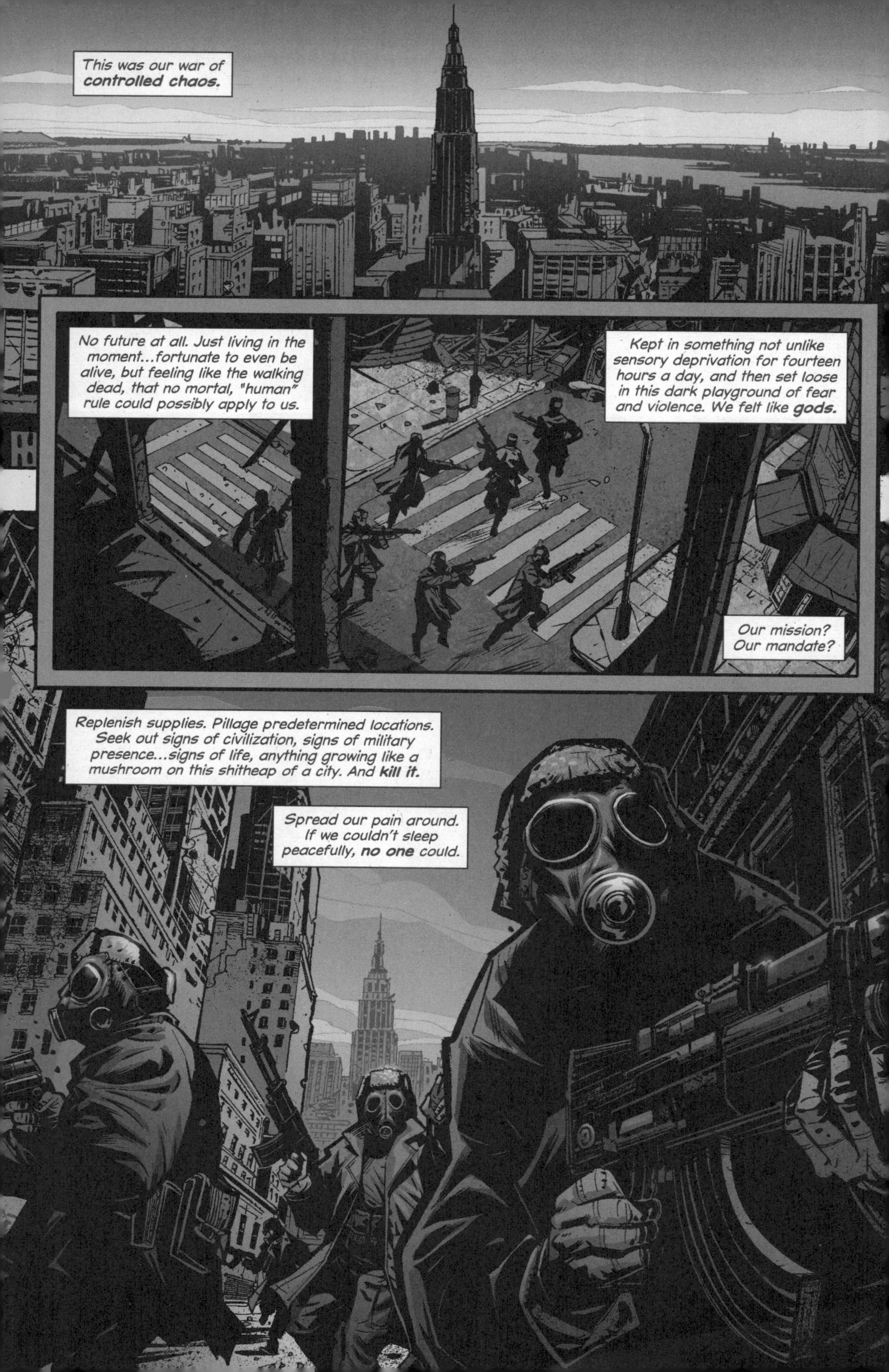
This was our war of **controlled chaos.**
No future at all. Just living in the moment...fortunate to even be alive, but feeling like the walking dead, that no mortal, "human" rule could possibly apply to us.
Kept in something not unlike sensory deprivation for fourteen hours a day, and then set loose in this dark playground of fear and violence. We felt like **gods.**
Our mission? Our mandate?
Replenish supplies. Pillage predetermined locations. Seek out signs of civilization, signs of military presence...signs of life, anything growing like a mushroom on this shitheap of a city. And **kill it.**
Spread our pain around. If we couldn't sleep peacefully, **no one** could.

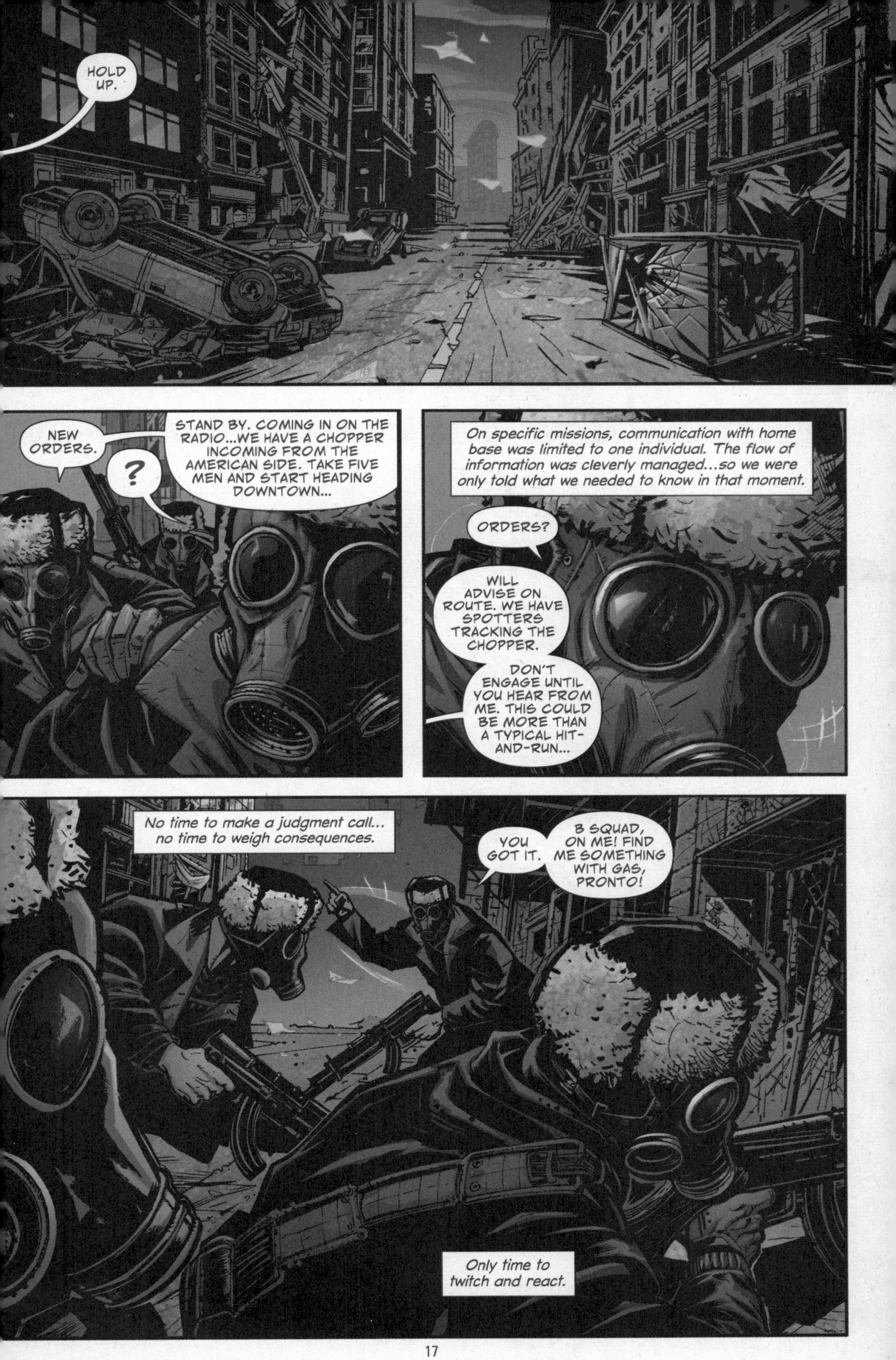
HOLD UP.
NEW ORDERS.
STAND BY. COMING IN ON THE RADIO...WE HAVE A CHOPPER INCOMING FROM THE AMERICAN SIDE. TAKE FIVE MEN AND START HEADING DOWNTOWN...
?
On specific missions, communication with home base was limited to one individual. The flow of information was cleverly managed...so we were only told what we needed to know in that moment.
ORDERS?
WILL ADVISE ON ROUTE. WE HAVE SPOTTERS TRACKING THE CHOPPER.
DON'T ENGAGE UNTIL YOU HEAR FROM ME. THIS COULD BE MORE THAN A TYPICAL HIT-AND-RUN...
No time to make a judgment call... no time to weigh consequences.
YOU GOT IT.
B SQUAD, ON ME! FIND ME SOMETHING WITH GAS, PRONTO!
Only time to twitch and react.

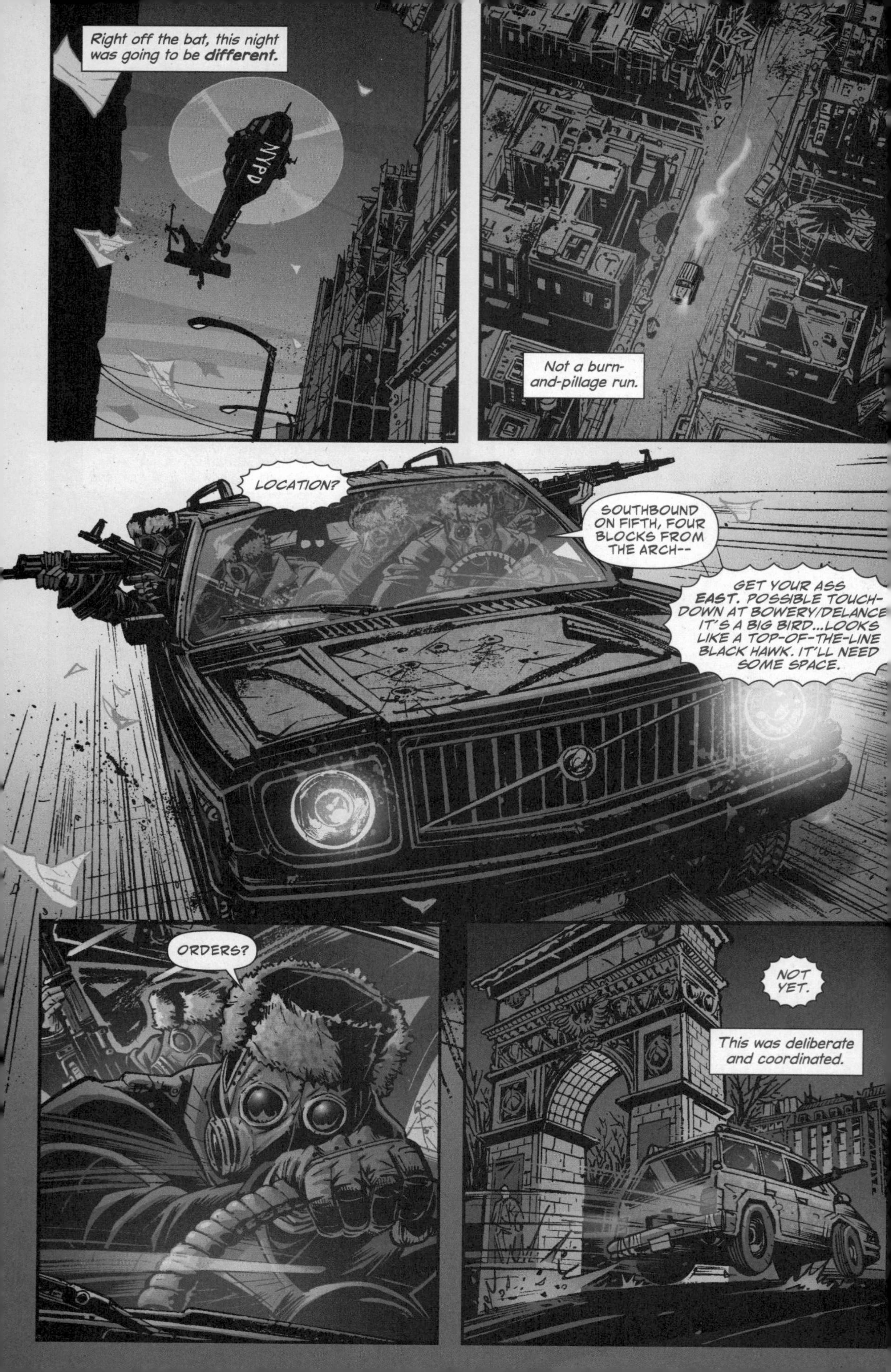
Right off the bat, this night was going to be **different.**
NYPD
Not a burn-and-pillage run.
LOCATION?
SOUTHBOUND ON FIFTH, FOUR BLOCKS FROM THE ARCH--
GET YOUR ASS EAST. POSSIBLE TOUCH-DOWN AT BOWERY/DELANCE IT'S A BIG BIRD...LOOKS LIKE A TOP-OF-THE-LINE BLACK HAWK. IT'LL NEED SOME SPACE.
ORDERS?
NOT YET.
This was deliberate and coordinated.

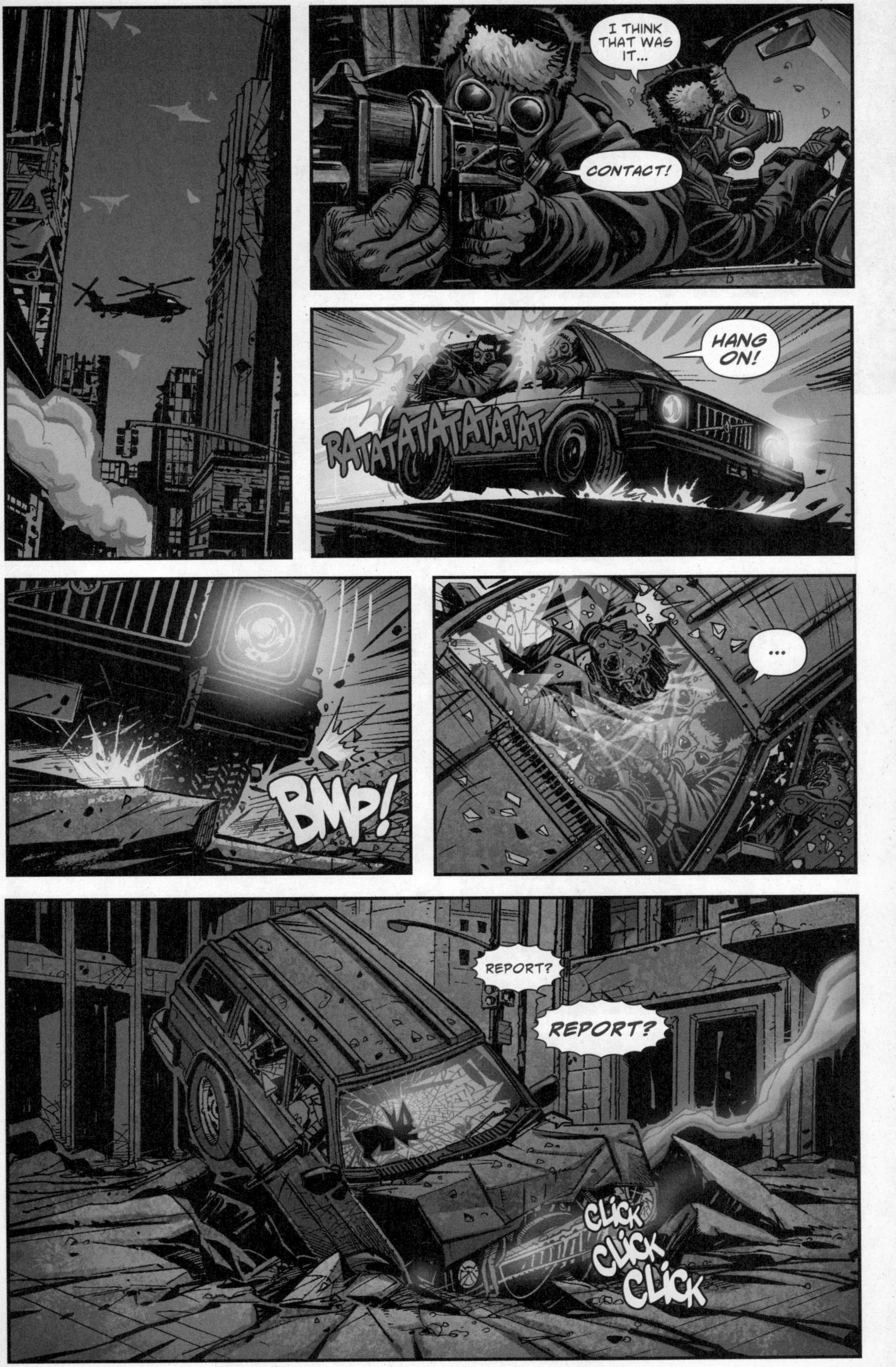
I THINK THAT WAS IT...
CONTACT!
HANG ON!
RATATATATATATAT
BMP!
...
REPORT?
REPORT?
CLICK
CLICK
CLICK

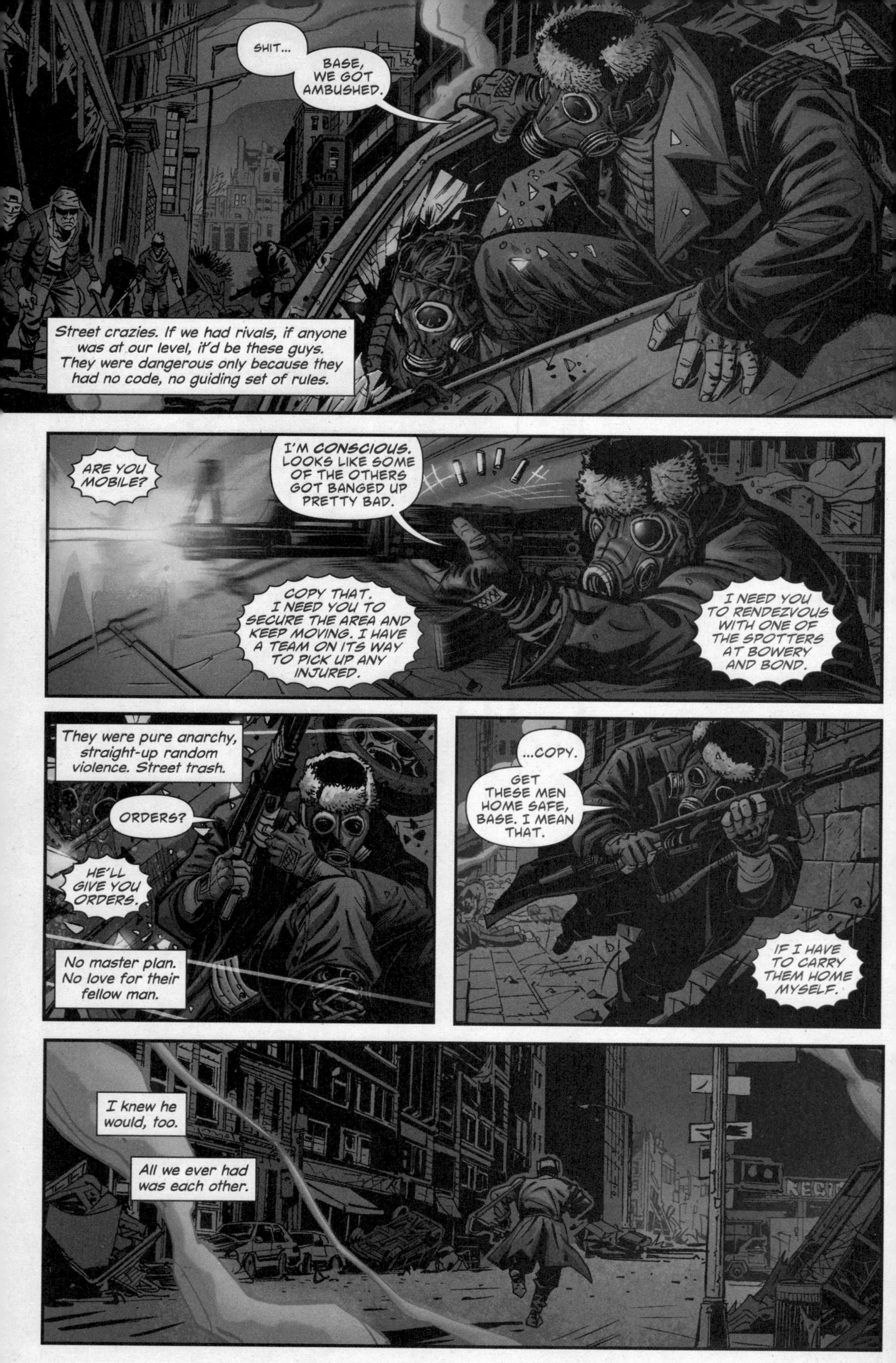
SHIT...
BASE, WE GOT AMBUSHED.
Street crazies. If we had rivals, if anyone was at our level, it'd be these guys. They were dangerous only because they had no code, no guiding set of rules.
ARE YOU MOBILE?
I'M CONSCIOUS. LOOKS LIKE SOME OF THE OTHERS GOT BANGED UP PRETTY BAD.
COPY THAT. I NEED YOU TO SECURE THE AREA AND KEEP MOVING. I HAVE A TEAM ON ITS WAY TO PICK UP ANY INJURED.
I NEED YOU TO RENDEZVOUS WITH ONE OF THE SPOTTERS AT BOWERY AND BOND.
They were pure anarchy, straight-up random violence. Street trash.
ORDERS?
HE'LL GIVE YOU ORDERS.
No master plan. No love for their fellow man.
...COPY.
GET THESE MEN HOME SAFE, BASE. I MEAN THAT.
IF I HAVE TO CARRY THEM HOME MYSELF.
I knew he would, too.
All we ever had was each other.

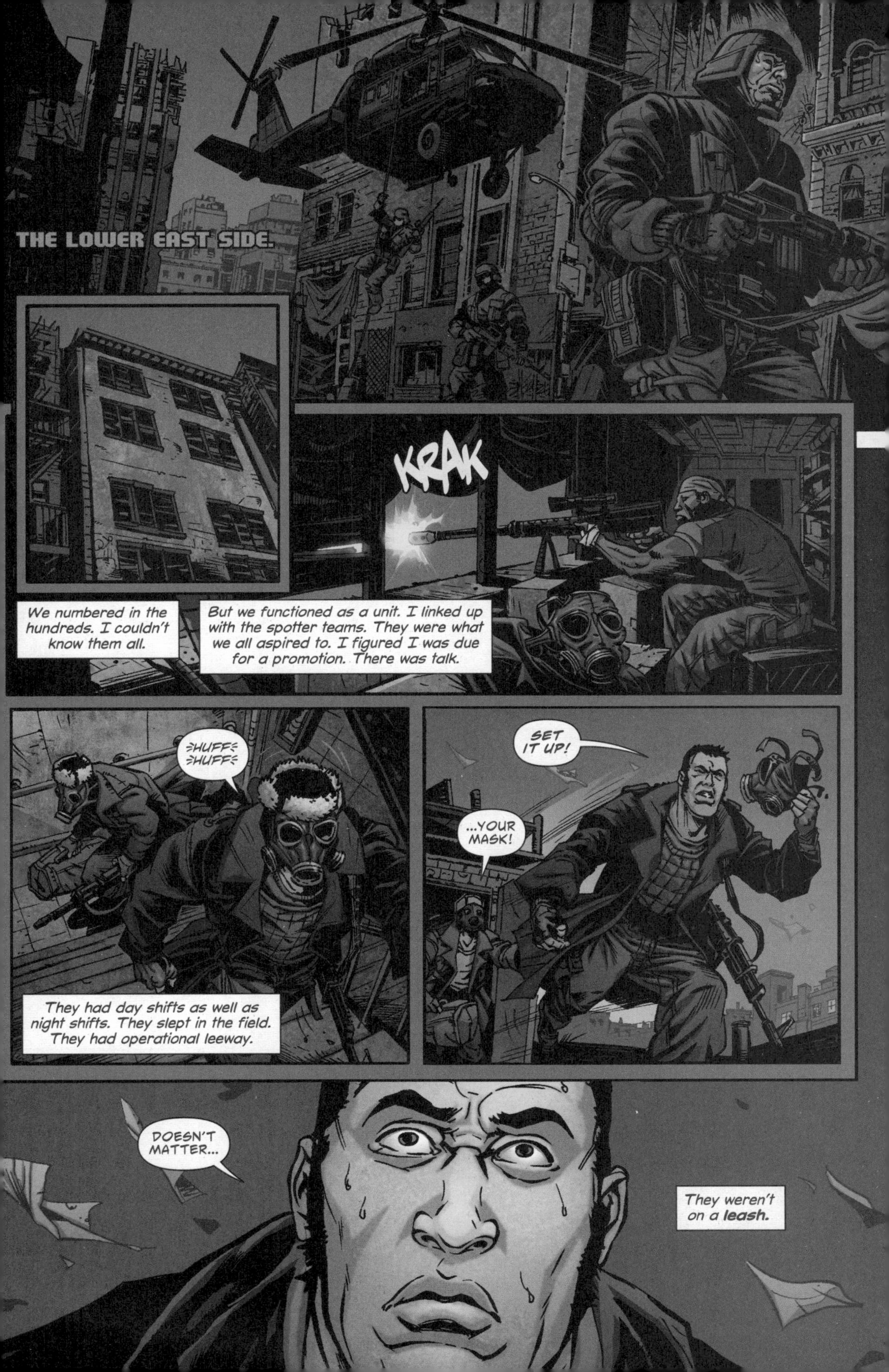

THE LOWER EAST SIDE.
We numbered in the hundreds. I couldn't know them all.
KRAK
But we functioned as a unit. I linked up with the spotter teams. They were what we all aspired to. I figured I was due for a promotion. There was talk.
HUFF HUFF
They had day shifts as well as night shifts. They slept in the field. They had operational leeway.
SET IT UP!
...YOUR MASK!
DOESN'T MATTER...
They weren't on a **leash.**

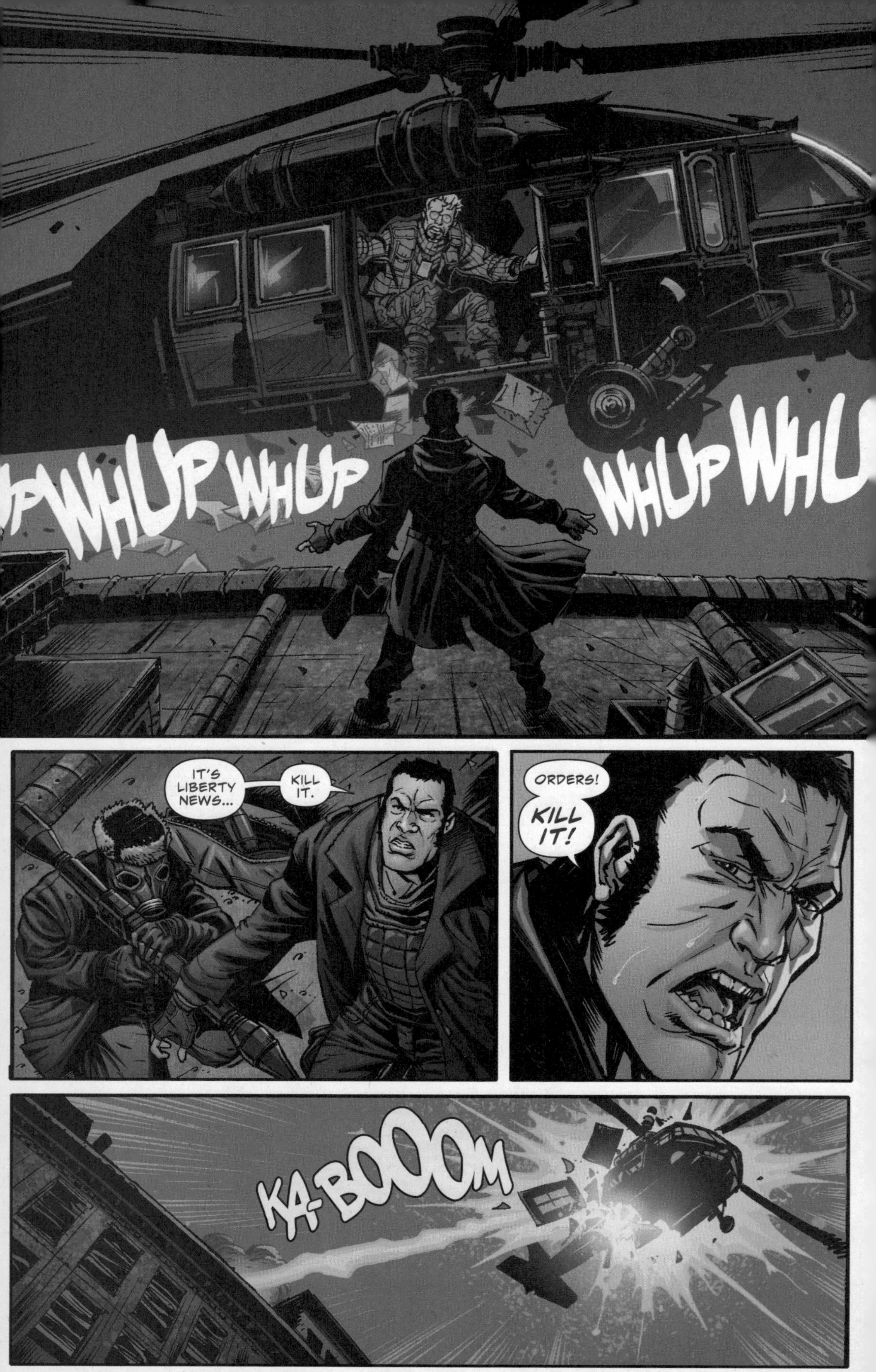
WHUP WHUP
WHUP
IT'S LIBERTY NEWS...
KILL IT.
ORDERS!
KILL IT!
KA-BOOOM

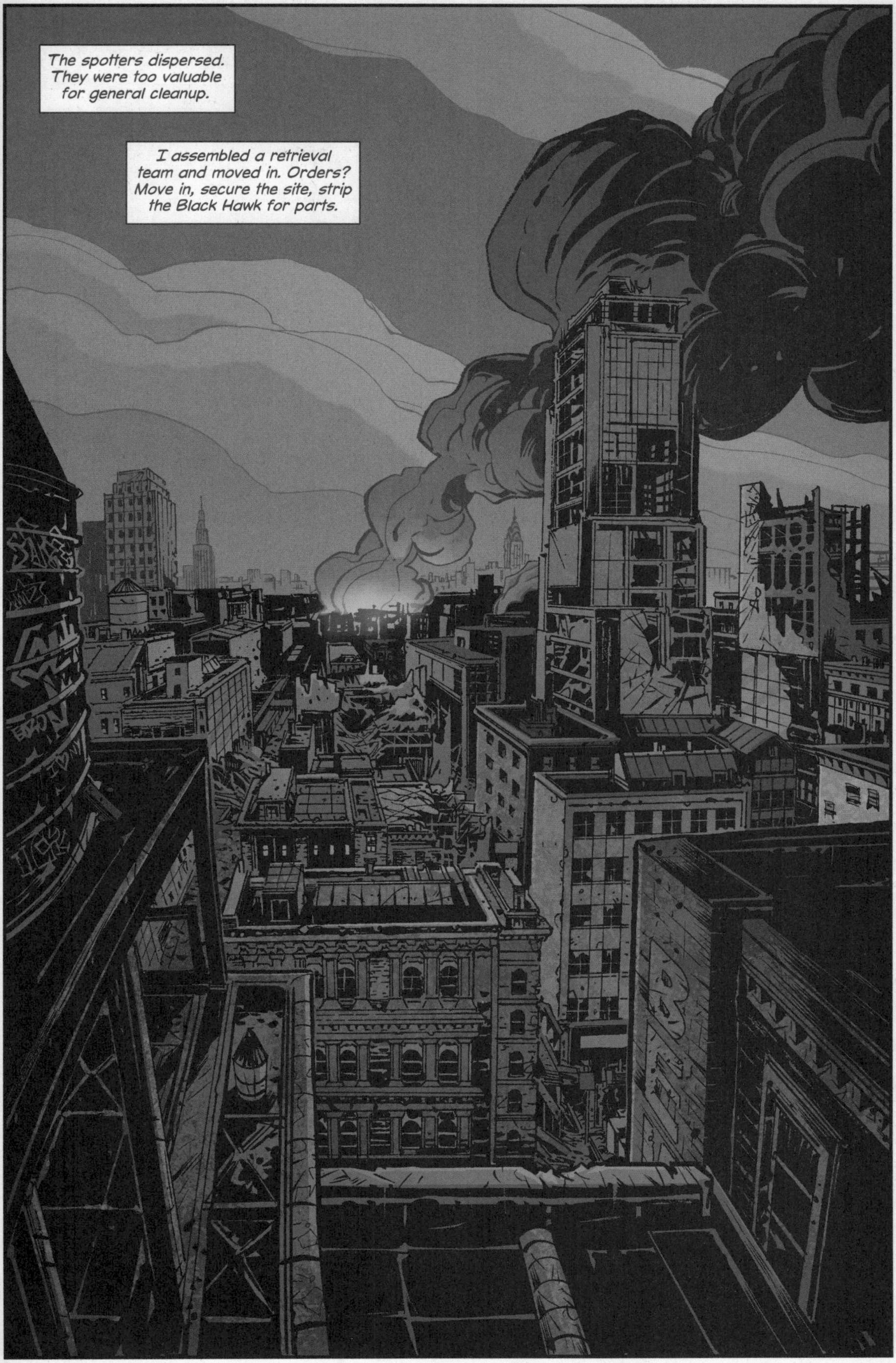
The spotters dispersed. They were too valuable for general cleanup.
I assembled a retrieval team and moved in. Orders? Move in, secure the site, strip the Black Hawk for parts.

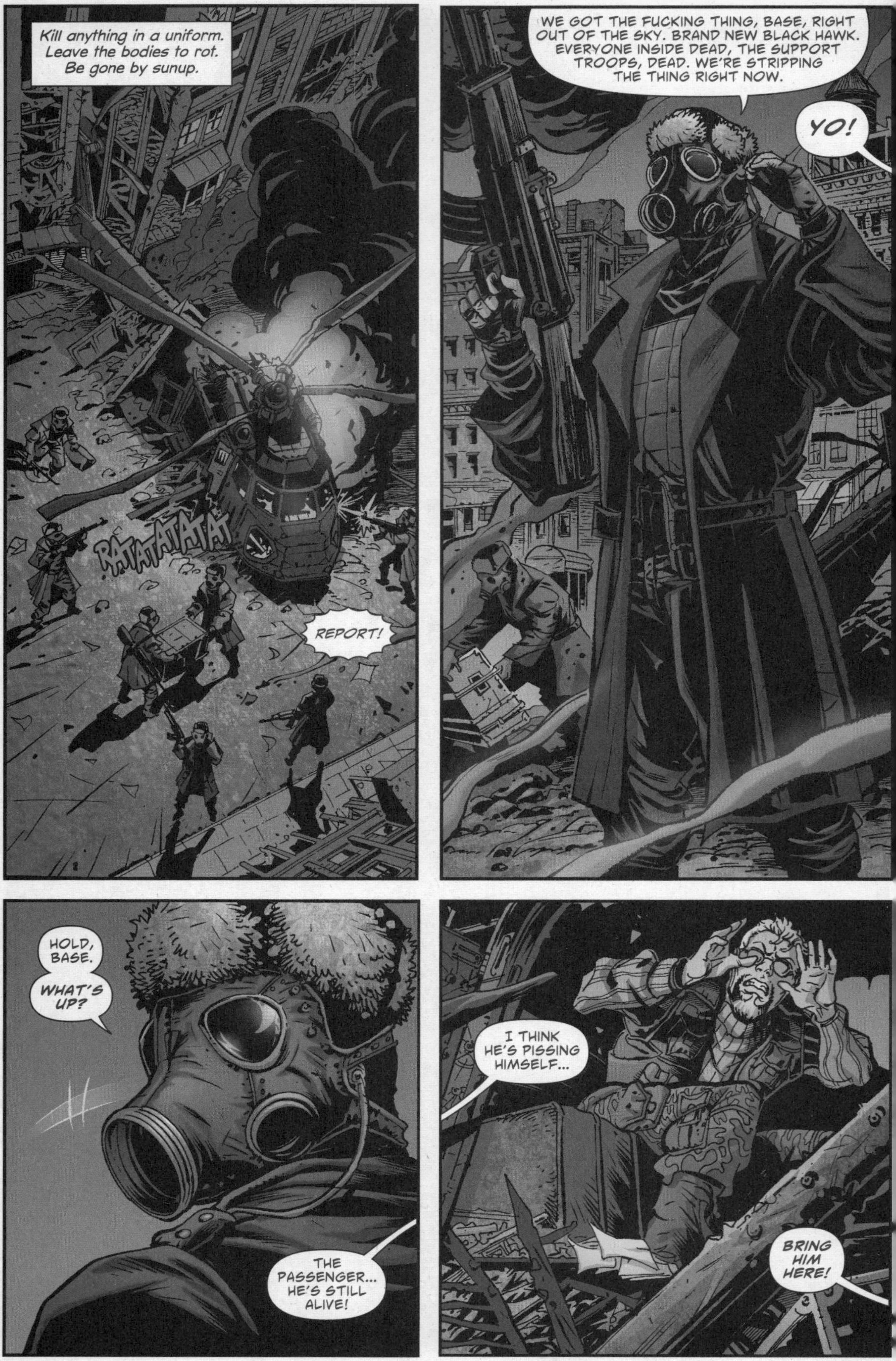
Kill anything in a uniform.
Leave the bodies to rot.
Be gone by sunup.
RATATATATAT
REPORT!
WE GOT THE FUCKING THING, BASE, RIGHT OUT OF THE SKY. BRAND NEW BLACK HAWK. EVERYONE INSIDE DEAD, THE SUPPORT TROOPS, DEAD. WE'RE STRIPPING THE THING RIGHT NOW.
YO!
HOLD, BASE.
WHAT'S UP?
THE PASSENGER... HE'S STILL ALIVE!
I THINK HE'S PISSING HIMSELF...
BRING HIM HERE!

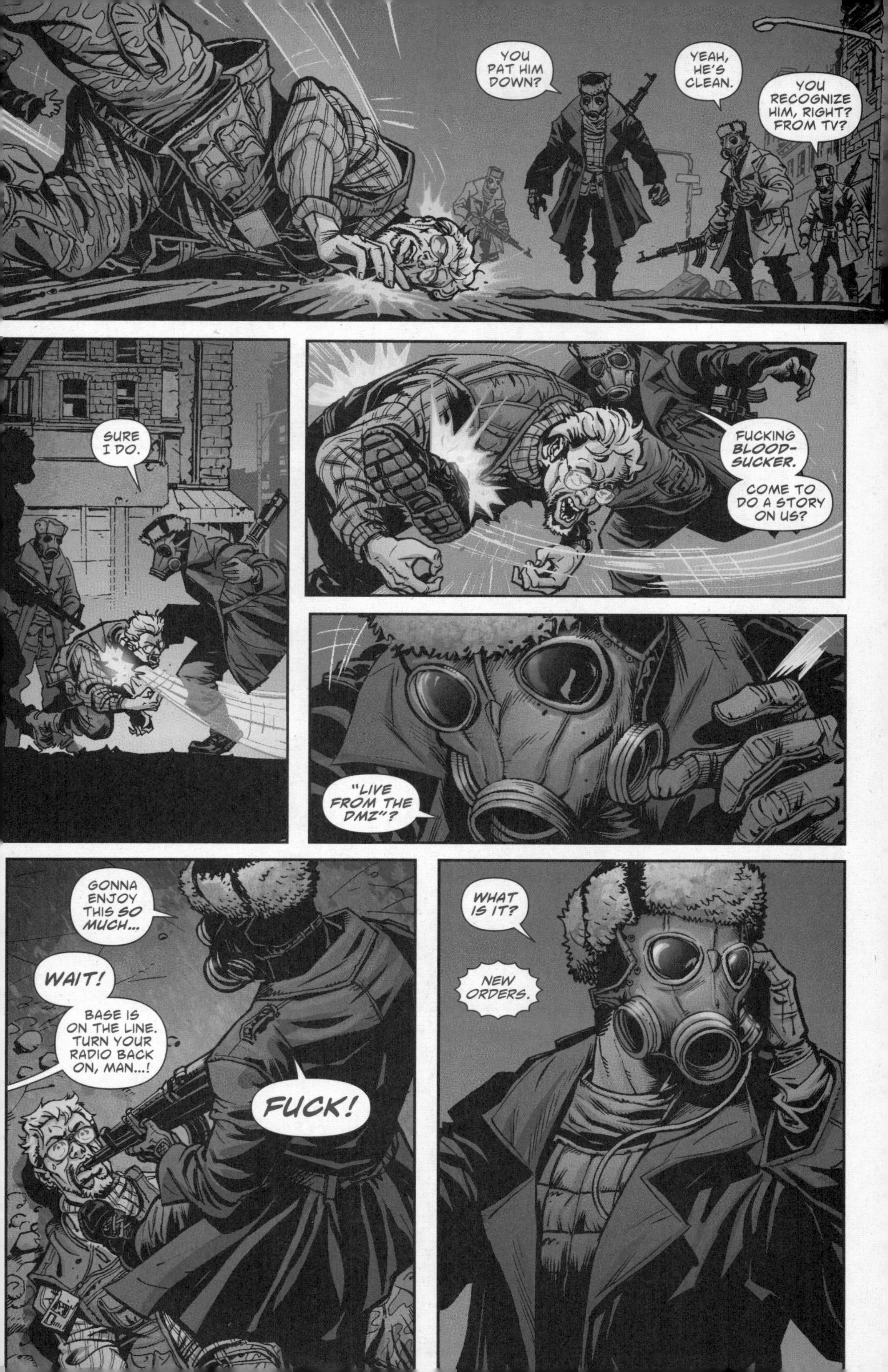
YOU PAT HIM DOWN?
YEAH, HE'S CLEAN.
YOU RECOGNIZE HIM, RIGHT? FROM TV?
SURE I DO.
FUCKING BLOOD-SUCKER.
COME TO DO A STORY ON US?
"LIVE FROM THE DMZ"?
GONNA ENJOY THIS SO MUCH...
WAIT!
BASE IS ON THE LINE. TURN YOUR RADIO BACK ON, MAN...!
FUCK!
WHAT IS IT?
NEW ORDERS.

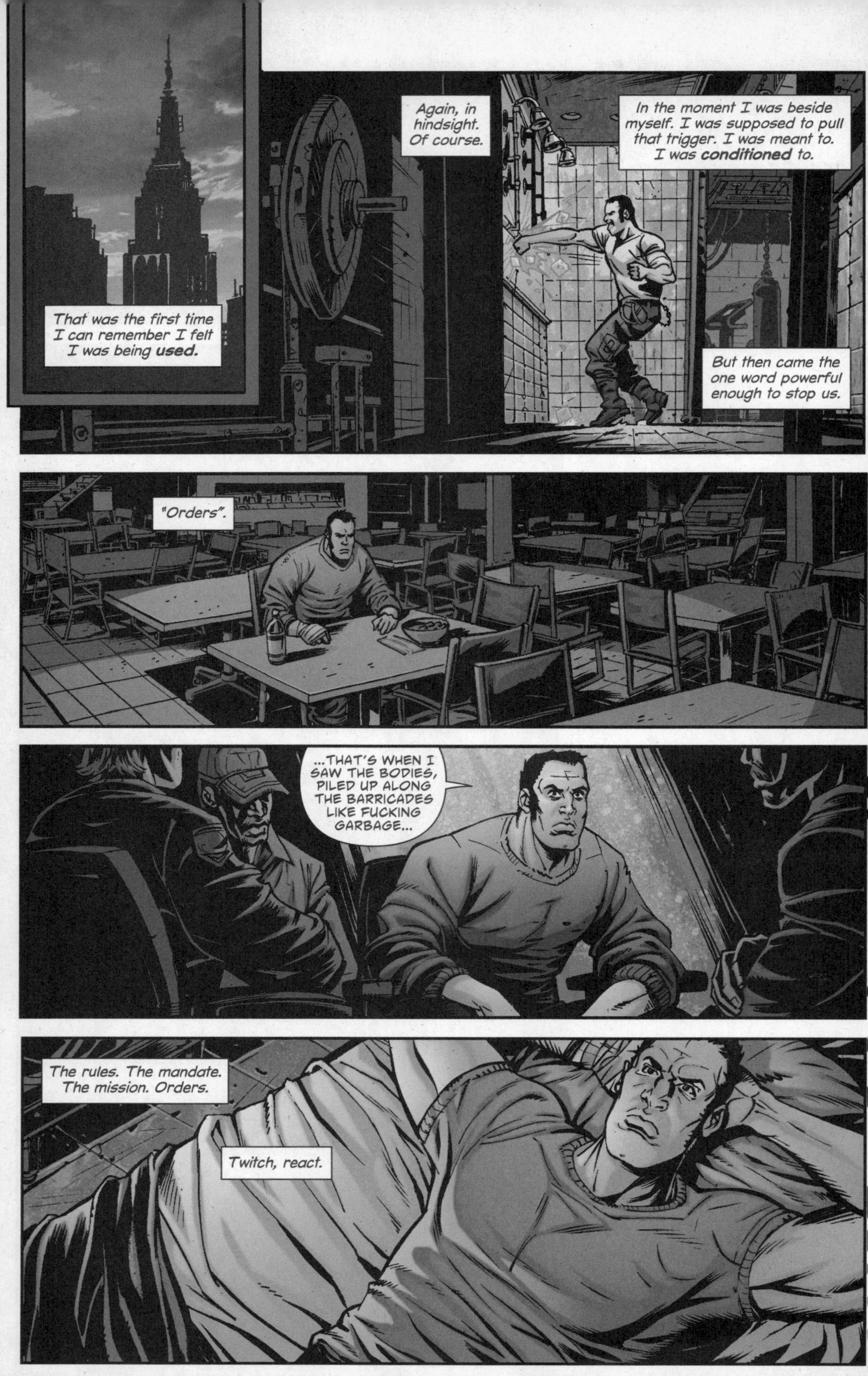
That was the first time I can remember I felt I was being **used.**
Again, in hindsight. Of course.
In the moment I was beside myself. I was supposed to pull that trigger. I was meant to. I was **conditioned** to.
But then came the one word powerful enough to stop us.
"Orders".
...THAT'S WHEN I SAW THE BODIES, PILED UP ALONG THE BARRICADES LIKE FUCKING GARBAGE...
The rules. The mandate. The mission. Orders.
Twitch, react.

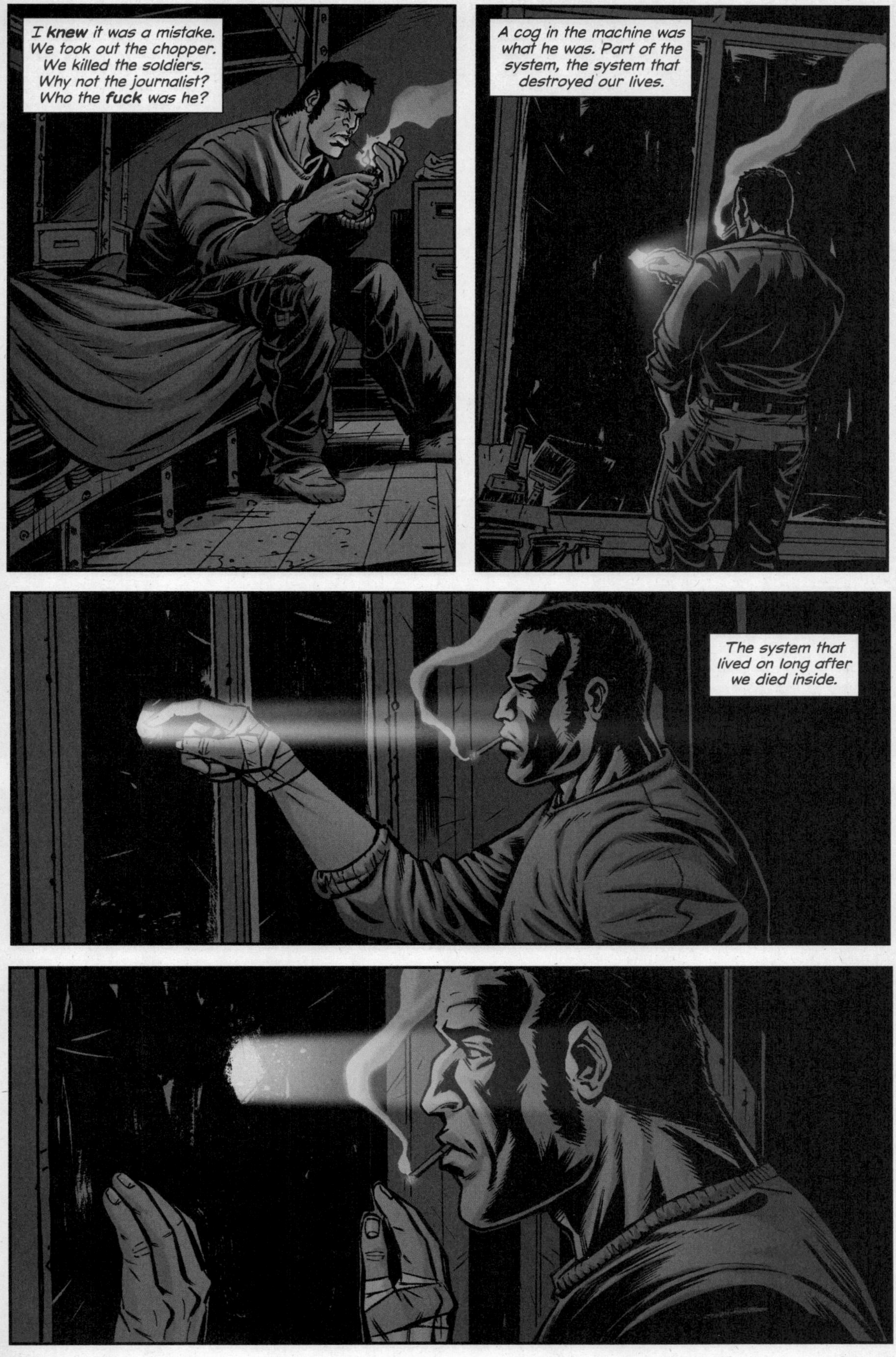
I **knew** it was a mistake. We took out the chopper. We killed the soldiers. Why not the journalist? Who the **fuck** was he?
A cog in the machine was what he was. Part of the system, the system that destroyed our lives.
The system that lived on long after we died inside.

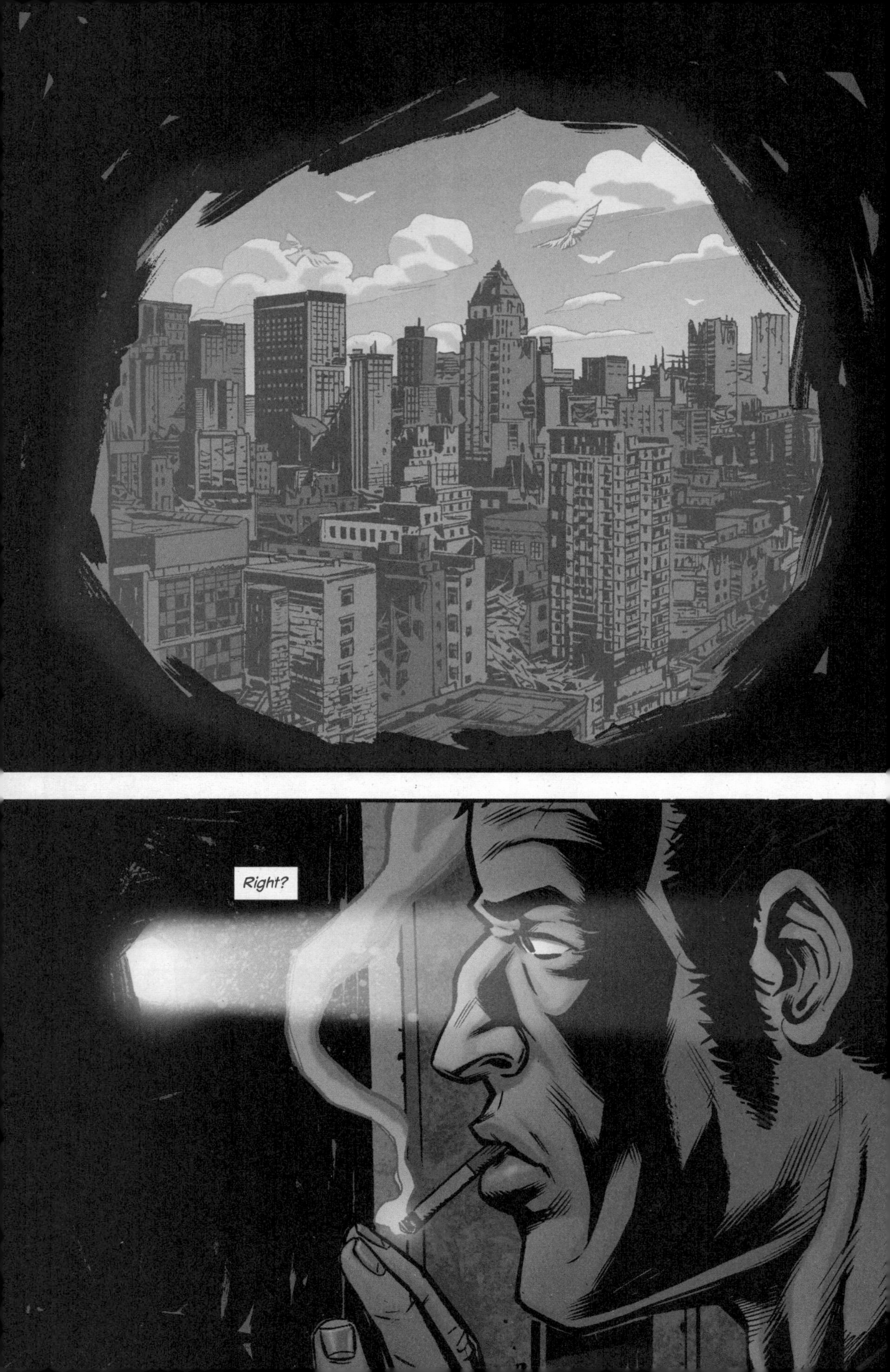
Right?

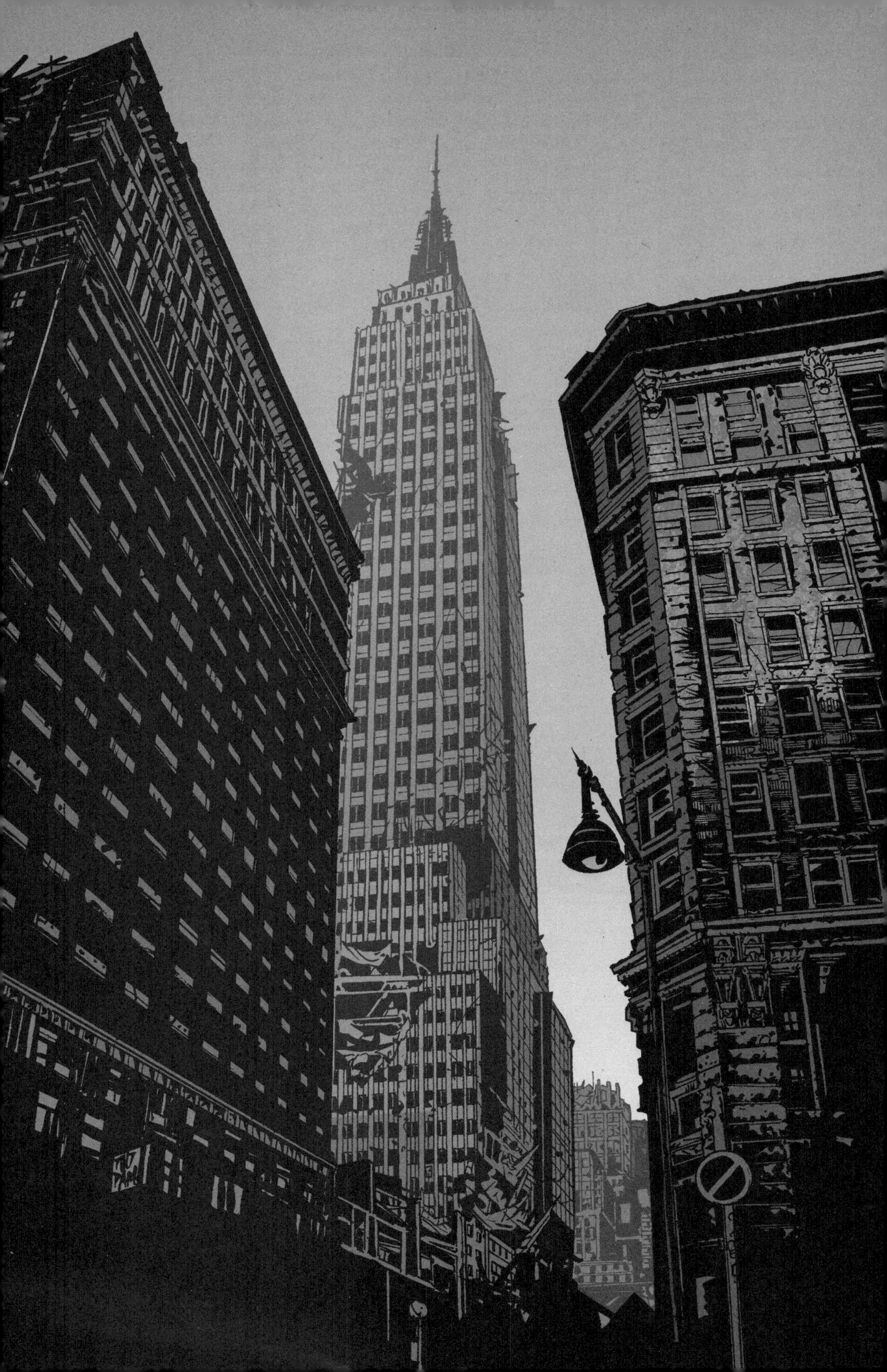

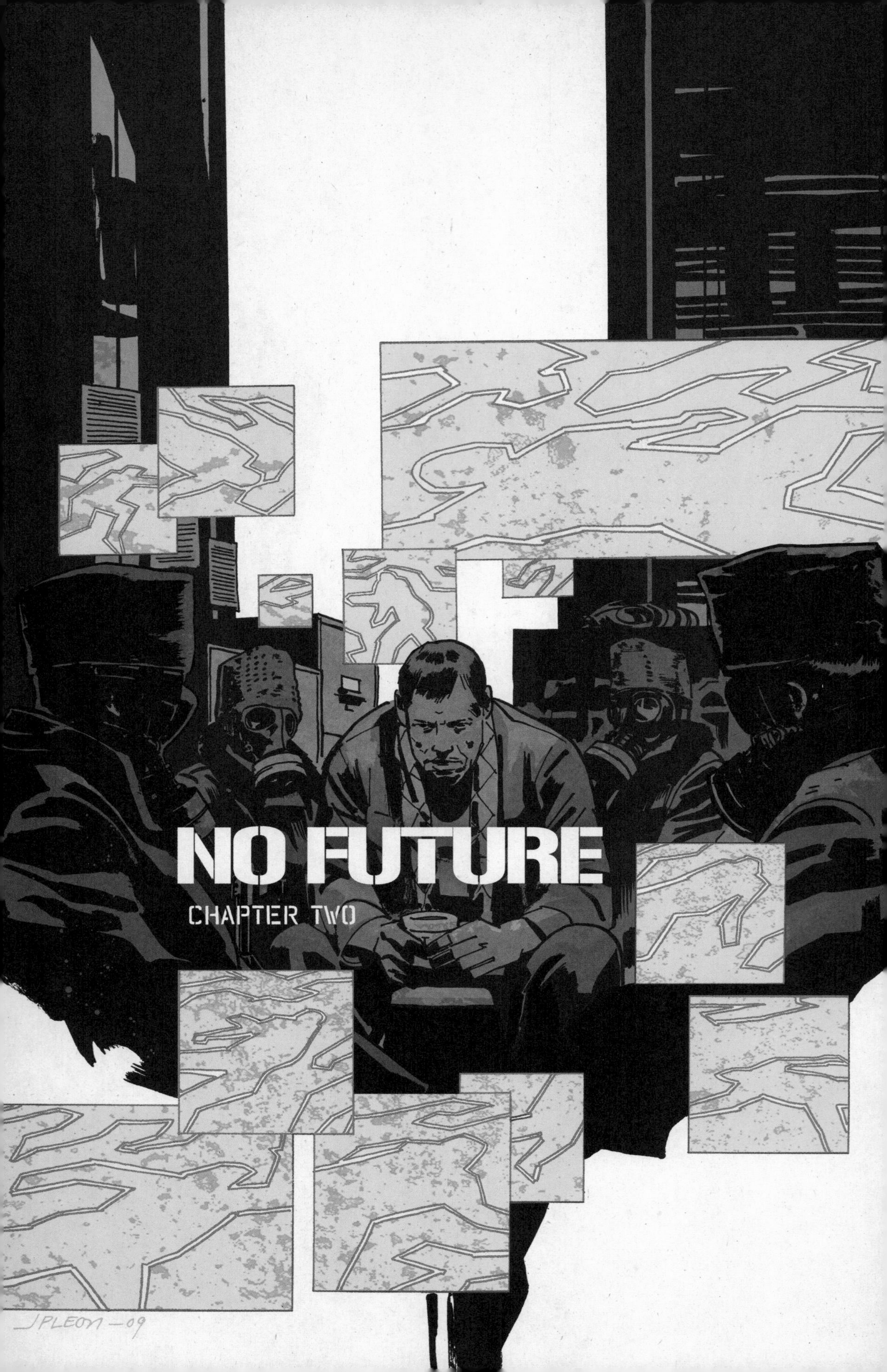
NO FUTURE
CHAPTER TWO
JPLEON -09

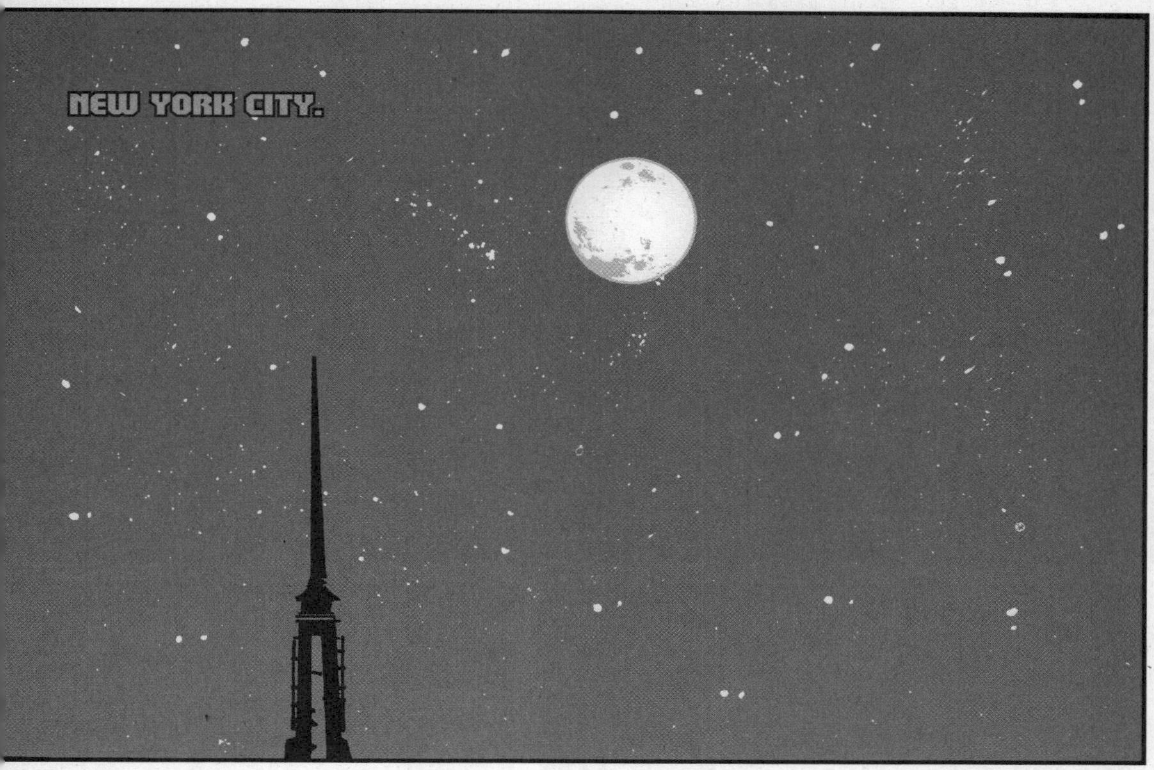
NEW YORK CITY.

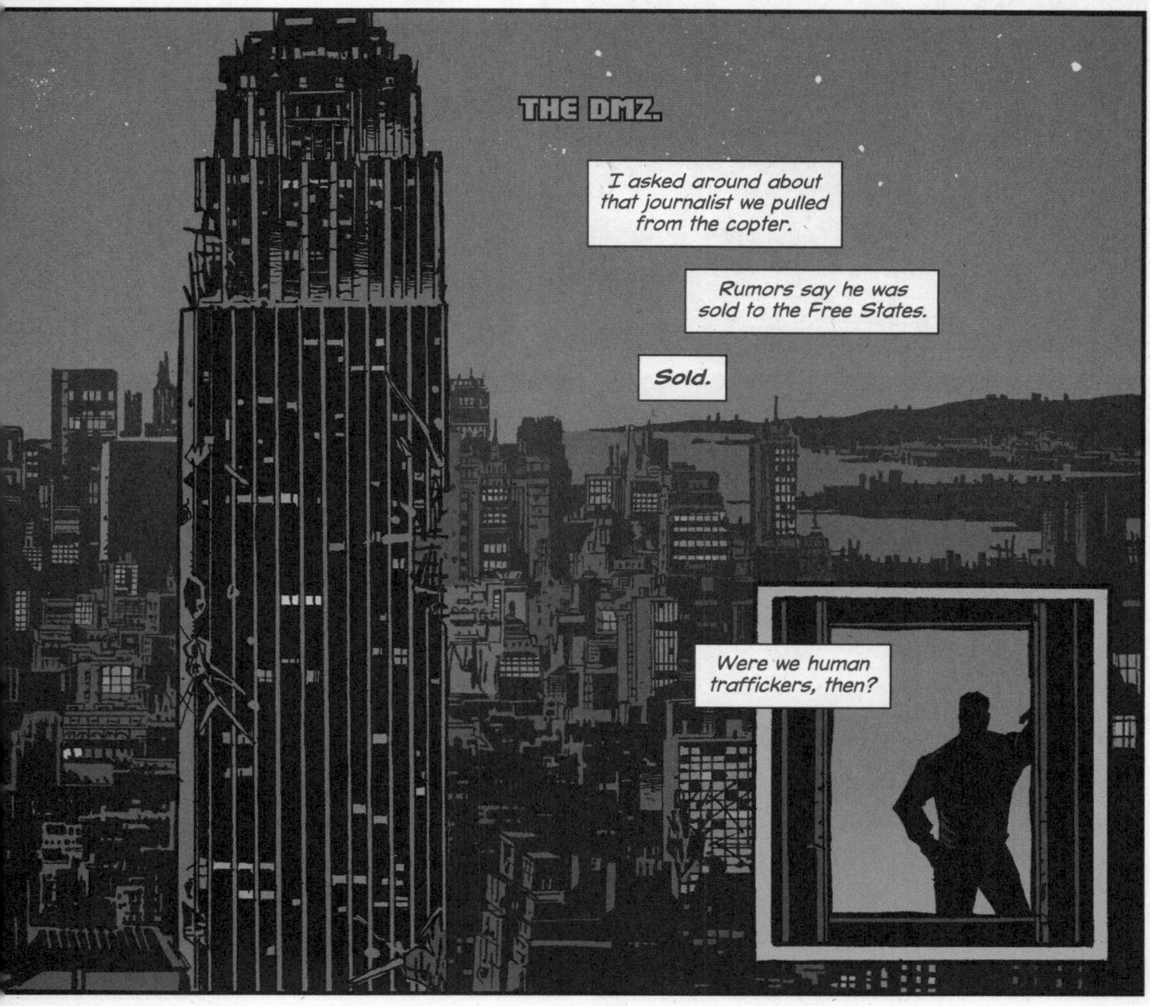
THE DMZ.
I asked around about that journalist we pulled from the copter.
Rumors say he was sold to the Free States.
Sold.
Were we human traffickers, then?

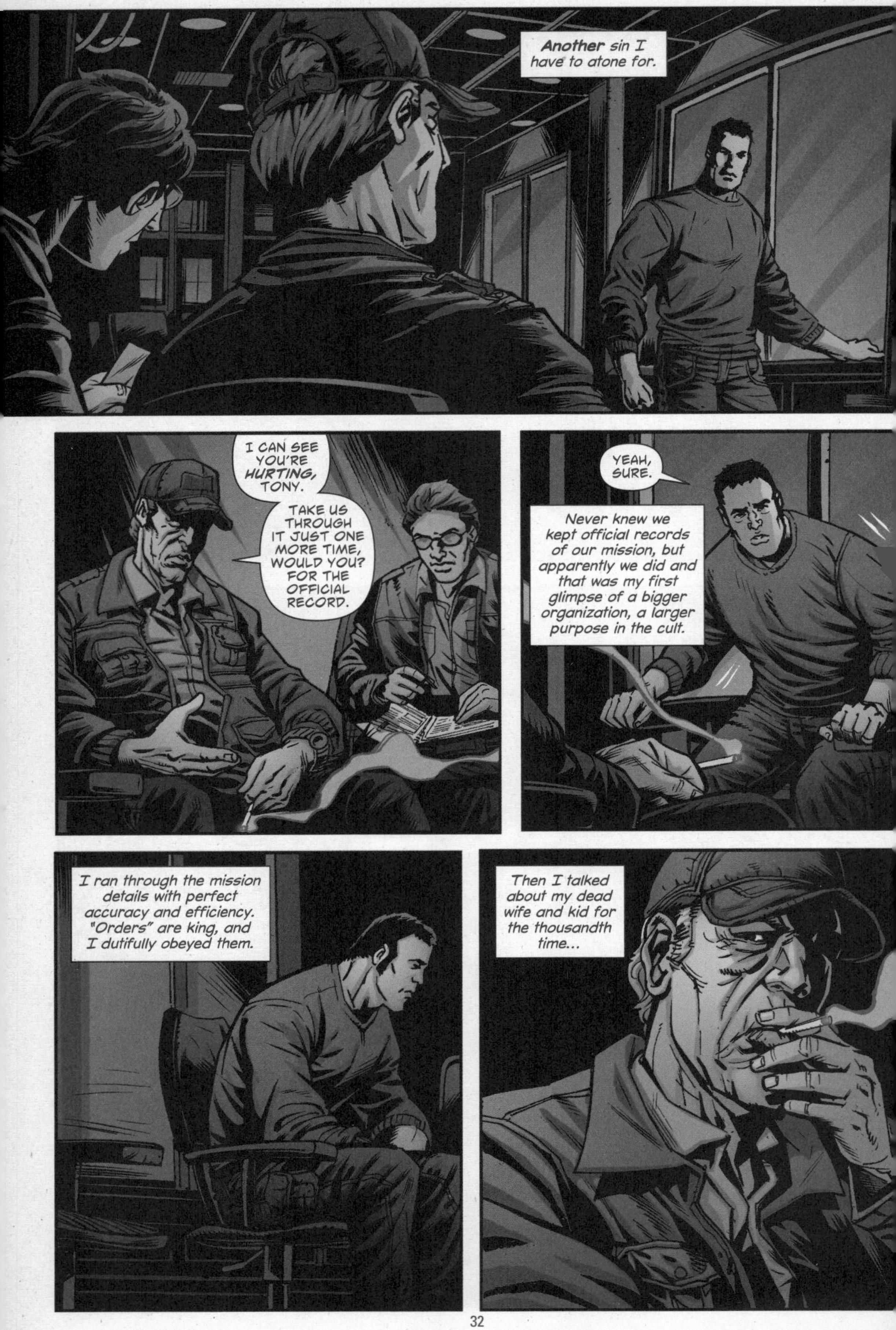
Another sin I have to atone for.
I CAN SEE YOU'RE HURTING, TONY.
TAKE US THROUGH IT JUST ONE MORE TIME, WOULD YOU? FOR THE OFFICIAL RECORD.
YEAH, SURE.
Never knew we kept official records of our mission, but apparently we did and that was my first glimpse of a bigger organization, a larger purpose in the cult.
I ran through the mission details with perfect accuracy and efficiency. "Orders" are king, and I dutifully obeyed them.
Then I talked about my dead wife and kid for the thousandth time...

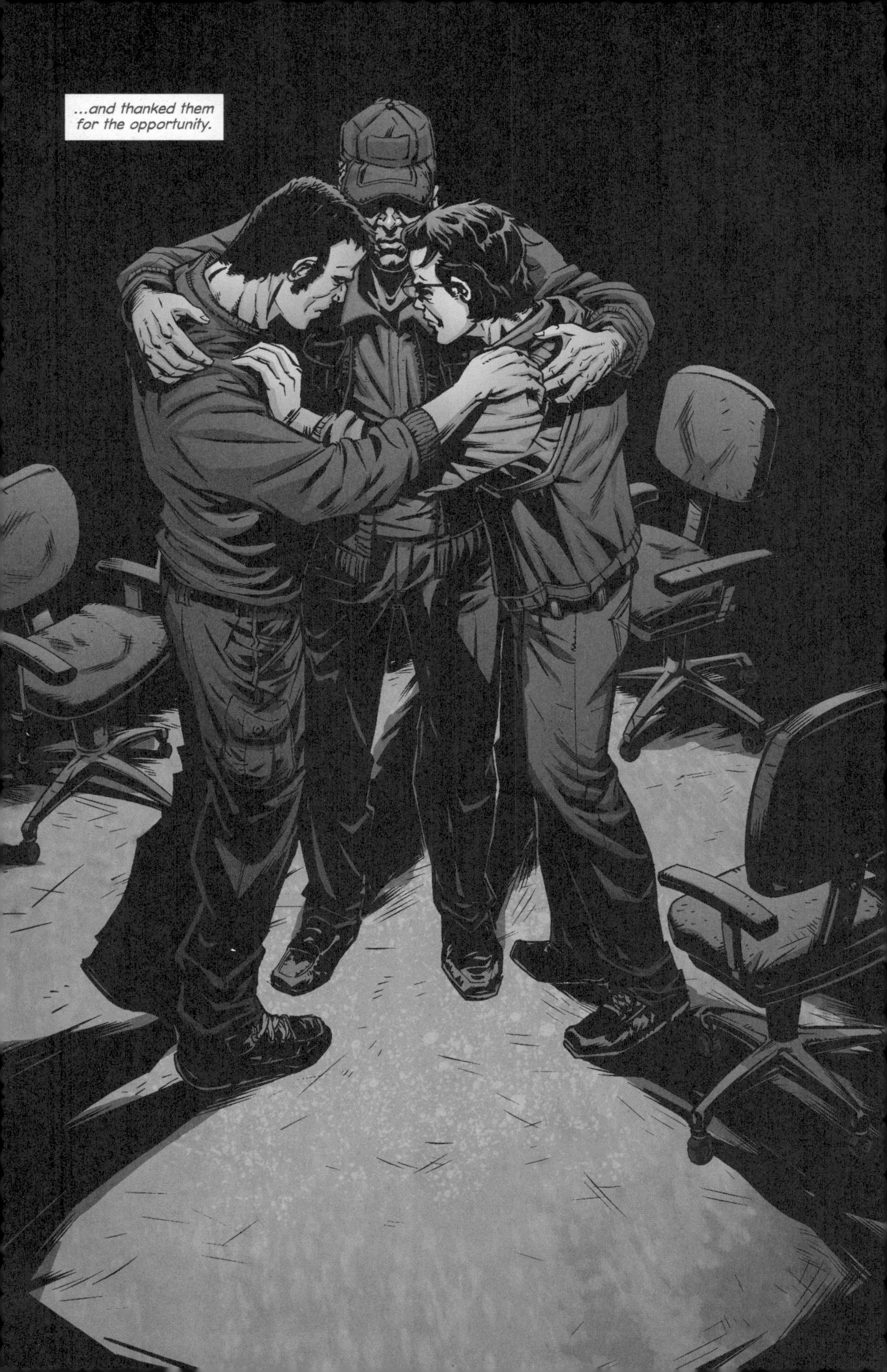
...and thanked them for the opportunity.

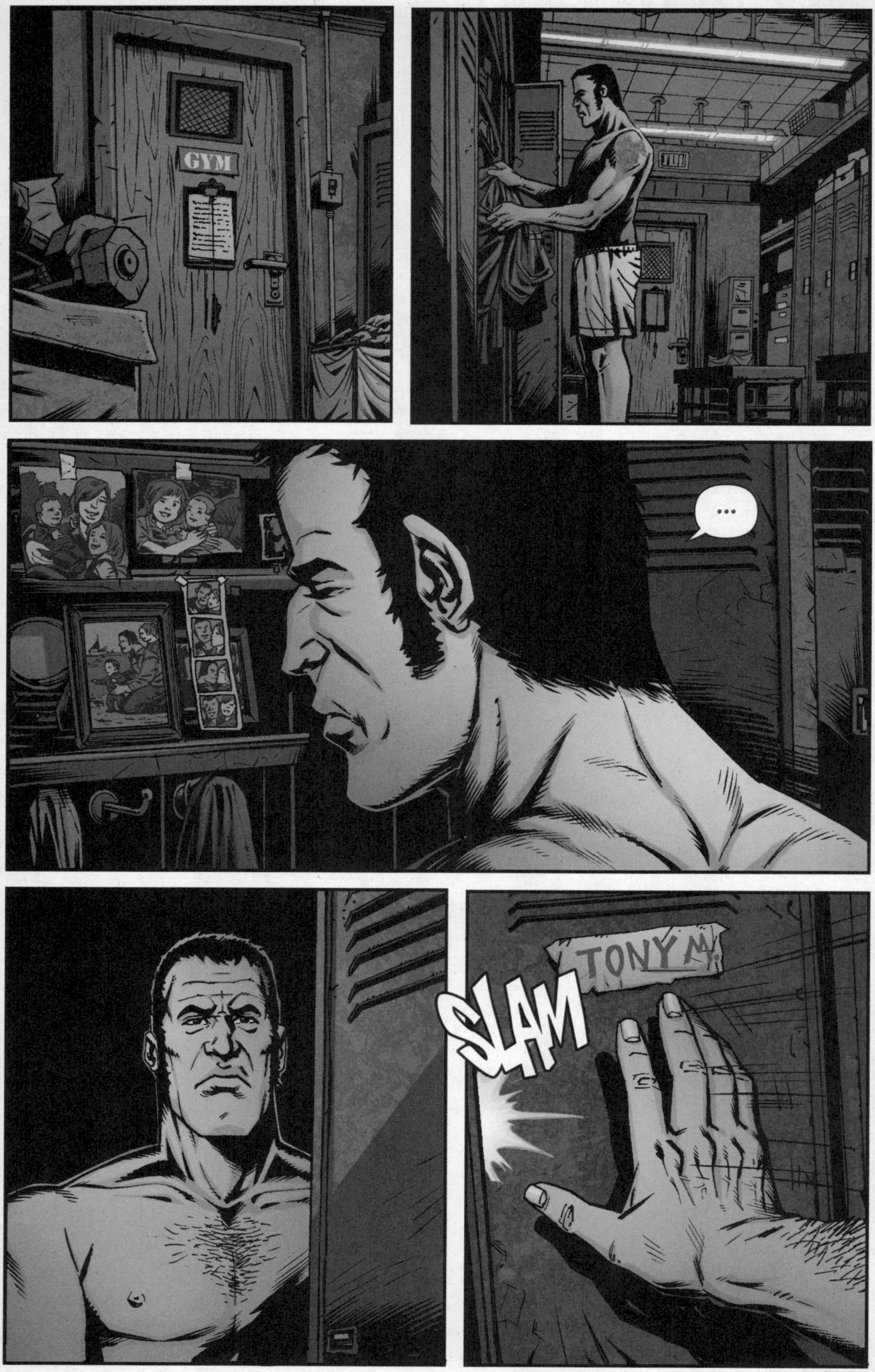
GYM
...
TONY M.
SLAM

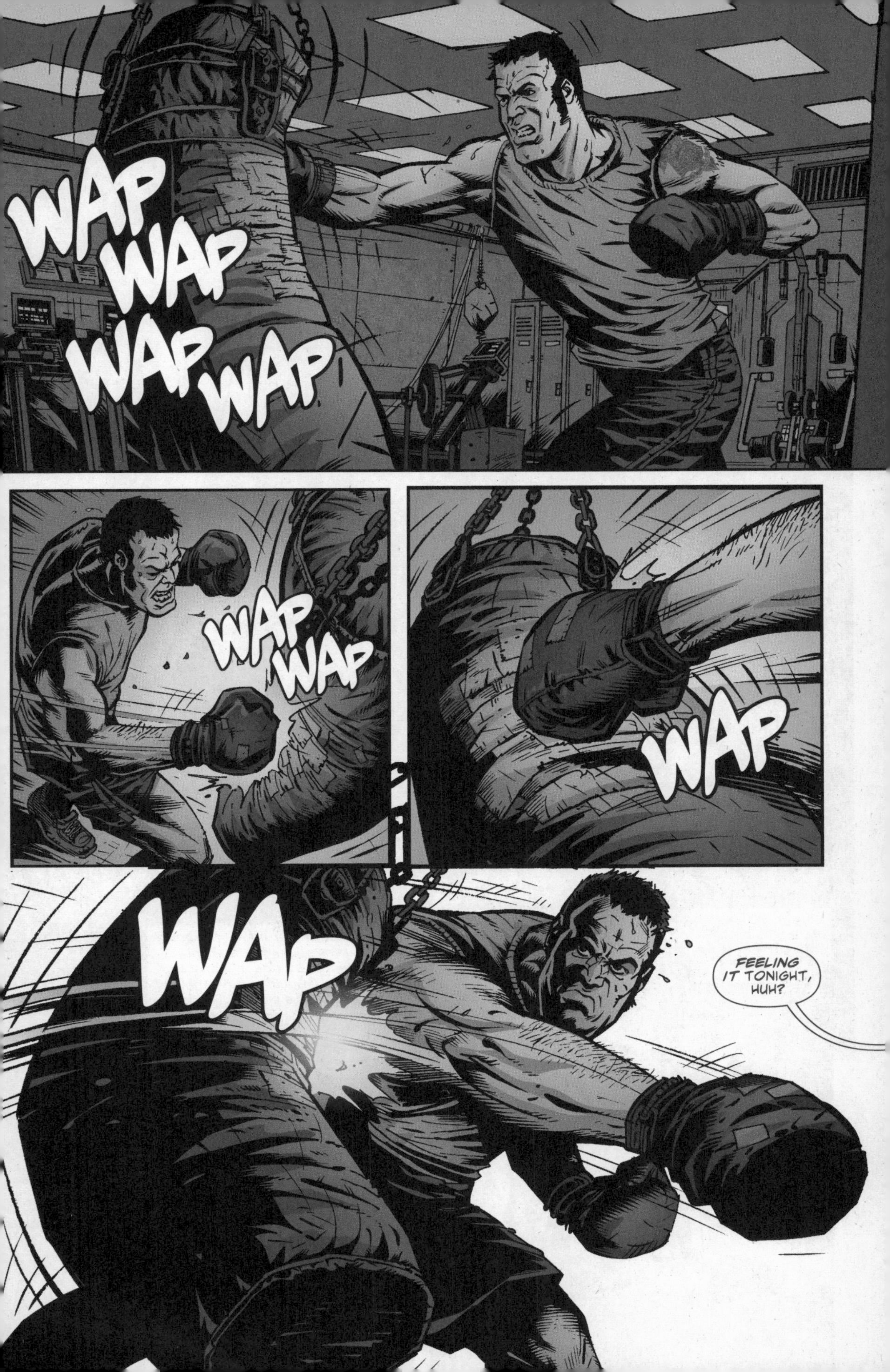
WAP
WAP
WAP
WAP
WAP
WAP
WAP
WAP
FEELING IT TONIGHT, HUH?

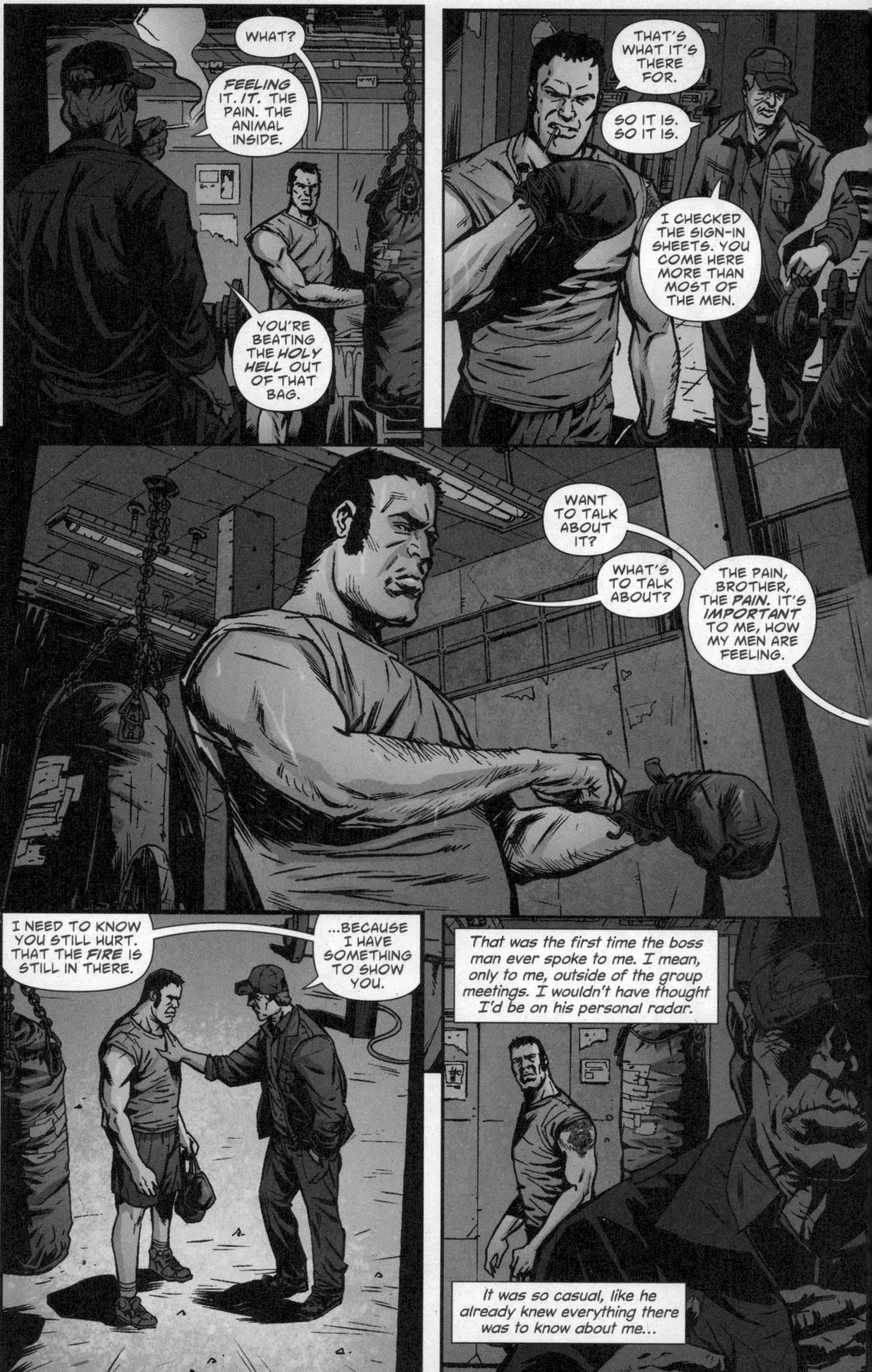
WHAT?
FEELING IT. IT. THE PAIN. THE ANIMAL INSIDE.
YOU'RE BEATING THE HOLY HELL OUT OF THAT BAG.
THAT'S WHAT IT'S THERE FOR.
SO IT IS. SO IT IS.
I CHECKED THE SIGN-IN SHEETS. YOU COME HERE MORE THAN MOST OF THE MEN.
WANT TO TALK ABOUT IT?
WHAT'S TO TALK ABOUT?
THE PAIN, BROTHER, THE PAIN. IT'S IMPORTANT TO ME, HOW MY MEN ARE FEELING.
I NEED TO KNOW YOU STILL HURT. THAT THE FIRE IS STILL IN THERE.
...BECAUSE I HAVE SOMETHING TO SHOW YOU.
That was the first time the boss man ever spoke to me. I mean, only to me, outside of the group meetings. I wouldn't have thought I'd be on his personal radar.
It was so casual, like he already knew everything there was to know about me...

...he went straight for the heart.

...

WHAT'S THIS?

YOU KNOW WHAT THIS IS.

KLIK

I did.

Evacuation day.

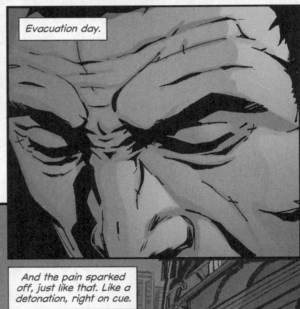

And the pain sparked off, just like that. Like a detonation, right on cue.

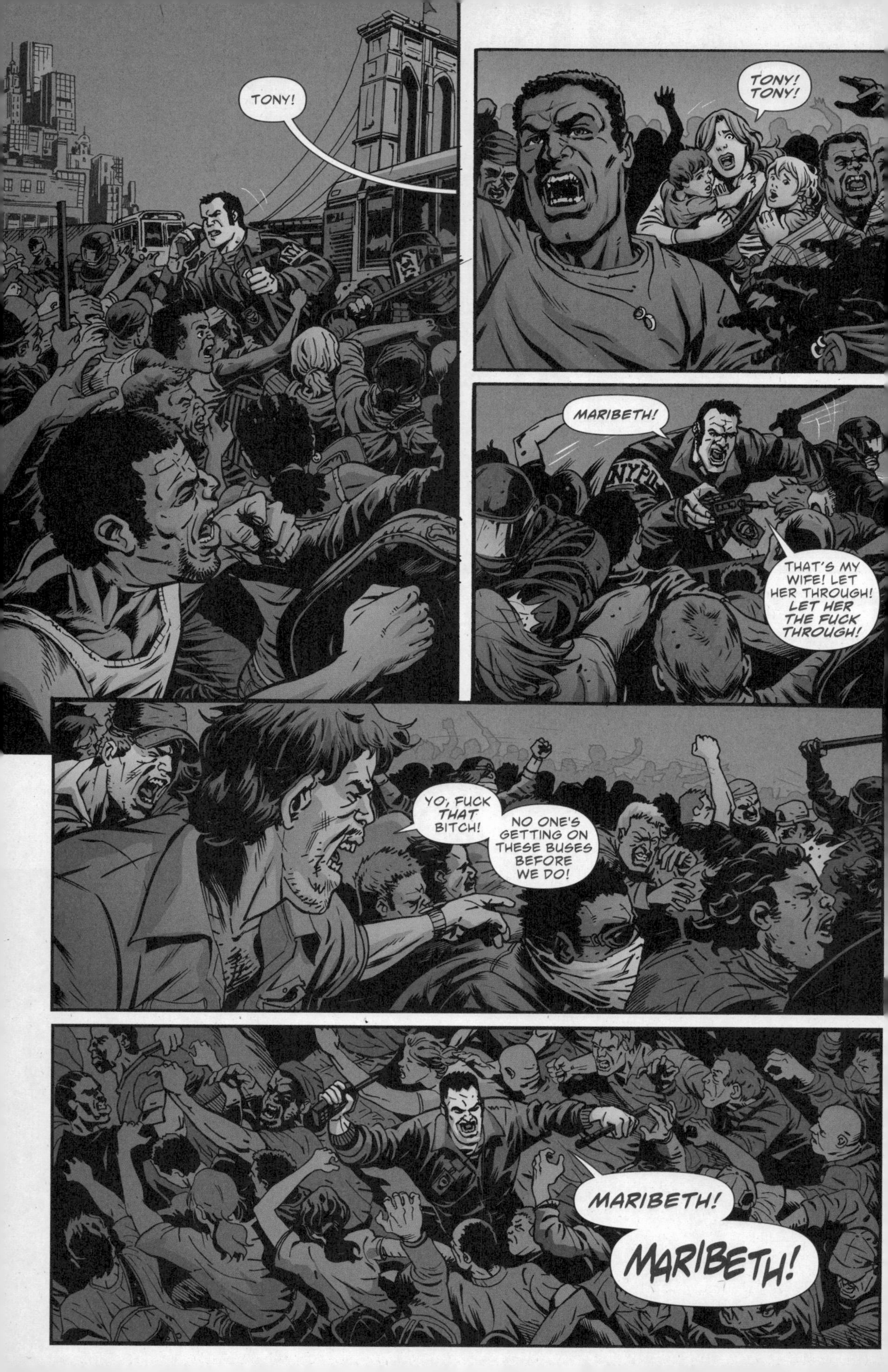
TONY!
TONY! TONY!
MARIBETH!
THAT'S MY WIFE! LET HER THROUGH! LET HER THE FUCK THROUGH!
YO, FUCK THAT BITCH!
NO ONE'S GETTING ON THESE BUSES BEFORE WE DO!
MARIBETH!
MARIBETH!

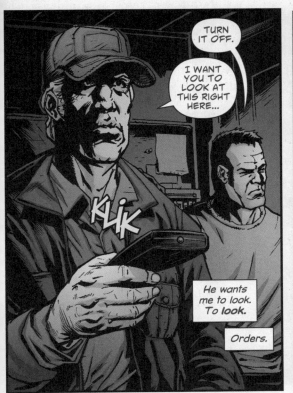

TURN IT OFF.

I WANT YOU TO LOOK AT THIS RIGHT HERE...

KLIK

He wants me to look. To *look*.

Orders.

SEE HIM?

...WHO IS THAT?

A GUY BY THE NAME OF MIKE COSTA. HE WAS THERE, OBVIOUSLY, WHEN YOUR WIFE AND CHILDREN WERE KILLED. HE WAS *RIGHT THERE*.

AND TONY?

HE'S STILL HERE. IN THE CITY.

THIS IS HIS CURRENT ADDRESS. GO. GO ALONE. TAKE YOUR TIME, AS MUCH AS YOU WANT. I TOOK YOU OFF THE DUTY ROSTER.

CONSIDER IT A *GIFT*, FROM ME TO YOU.

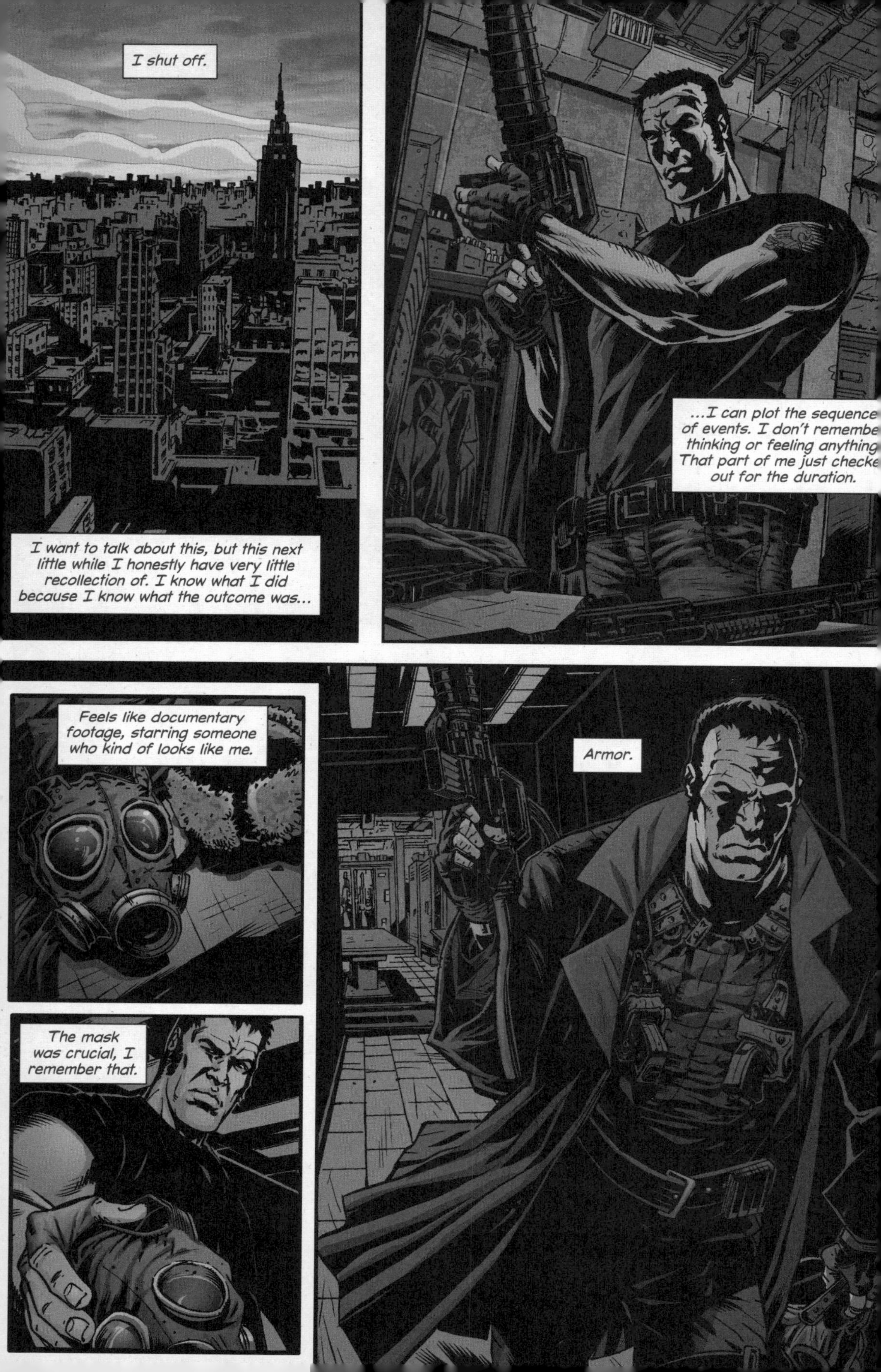

I shut off.
I want to talk about this, but this next little while I honestly have very little recollection of. I know what I did because I know what the outcome was...
...I can plot the sequence of events. I don't remembe thinking or feeling anything That part of me just checke out for the duration.
Feels like documentary footage, starring someone who kind of looks like me.
The mask was crucial, I remember that.
Armor.

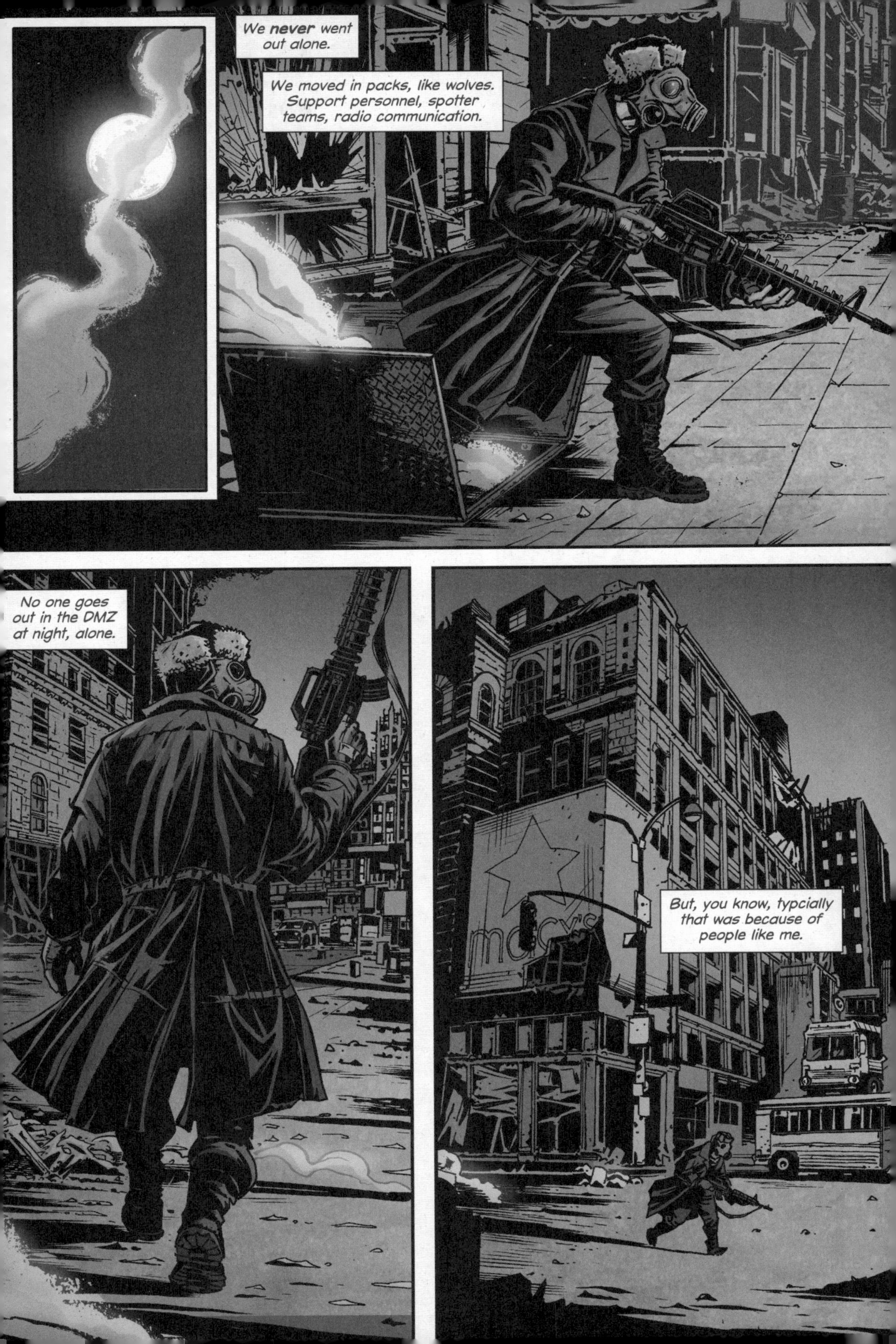
We **never** went out alone.
We moved in packs, like wolves. Support personnel, spotter teams, radio communication.
No one goes out in the DMZ at night, alone.
But, you know, typcially that was because of people like me.

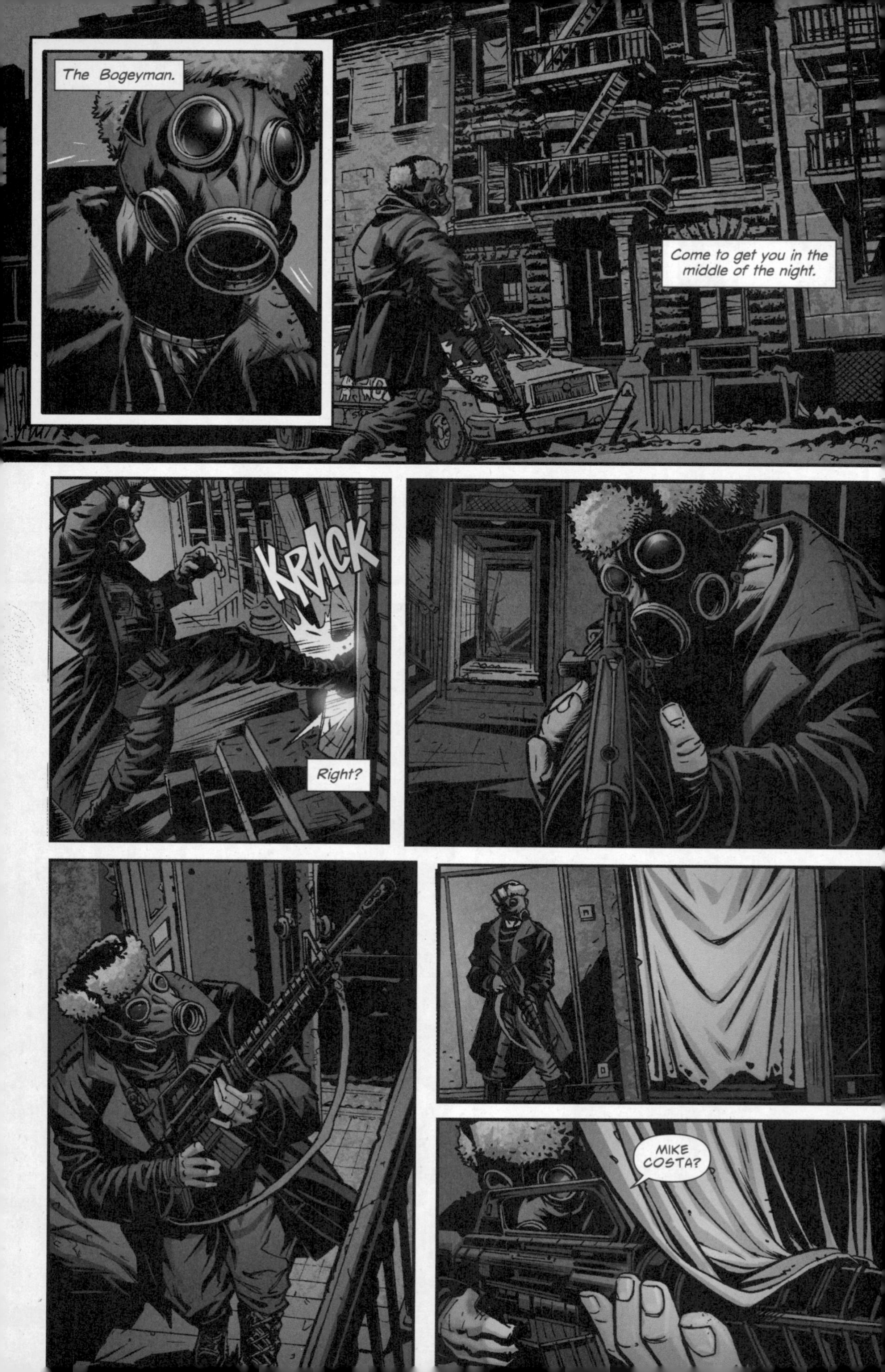
The Bogeyman.
Come to get you in the middle of the night.
KRACK
Right?
MIKE COSTA?

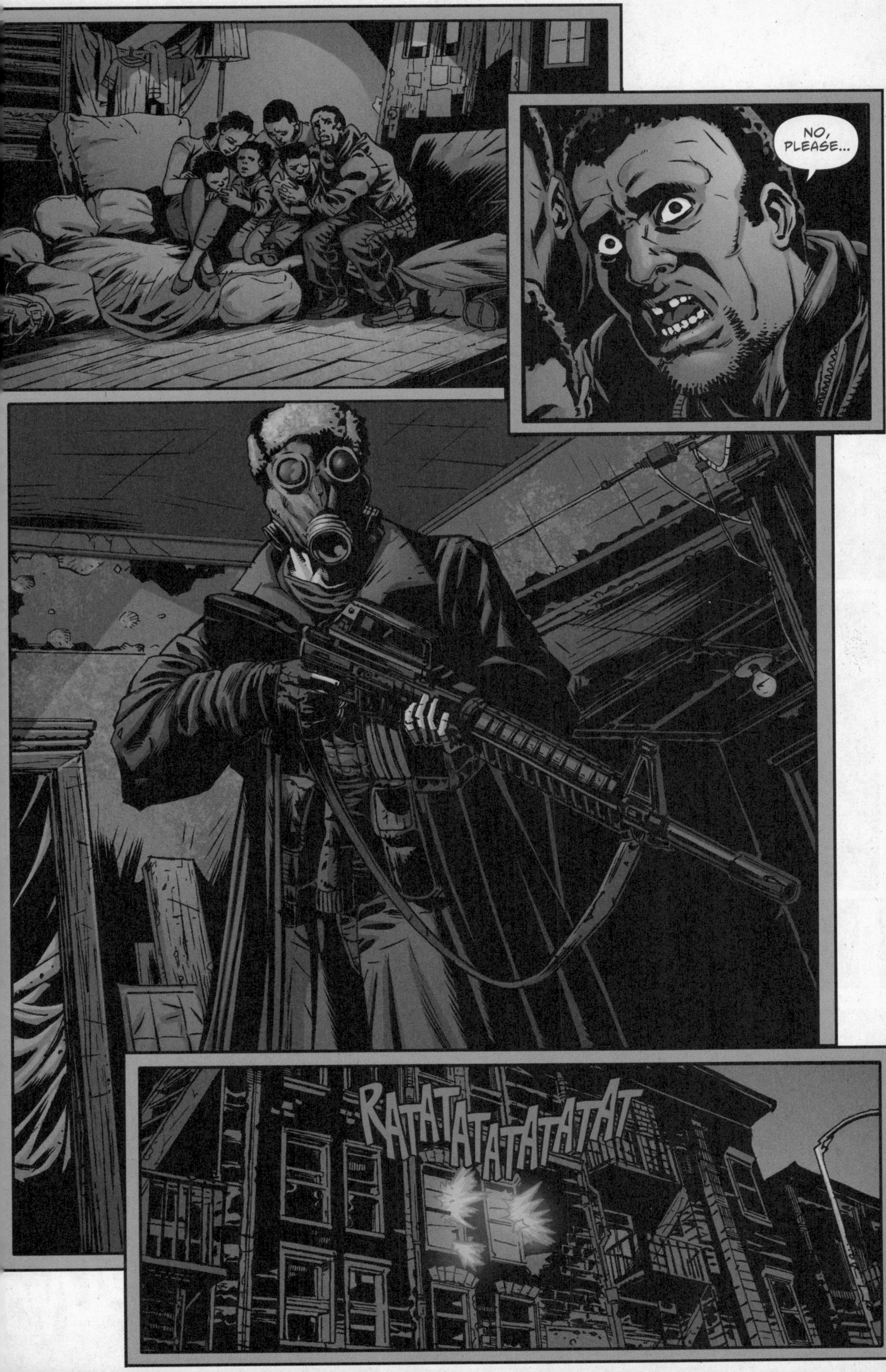
NO, PLEASE...
RATATATATATATAT

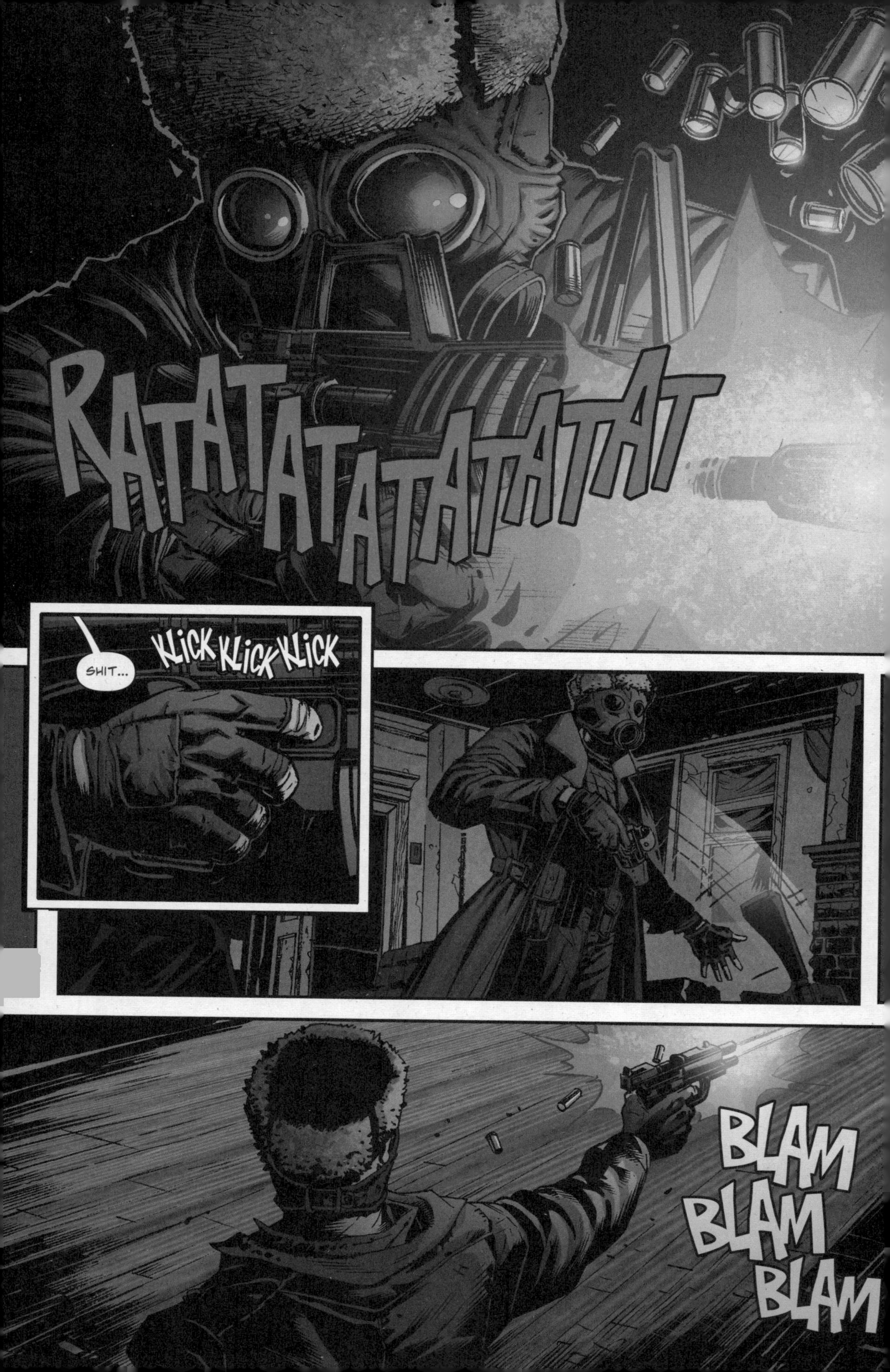
RATATATATATATAT
SHIT...
KLICK KLICK KLICK
BLAM
BLAM
BLAM

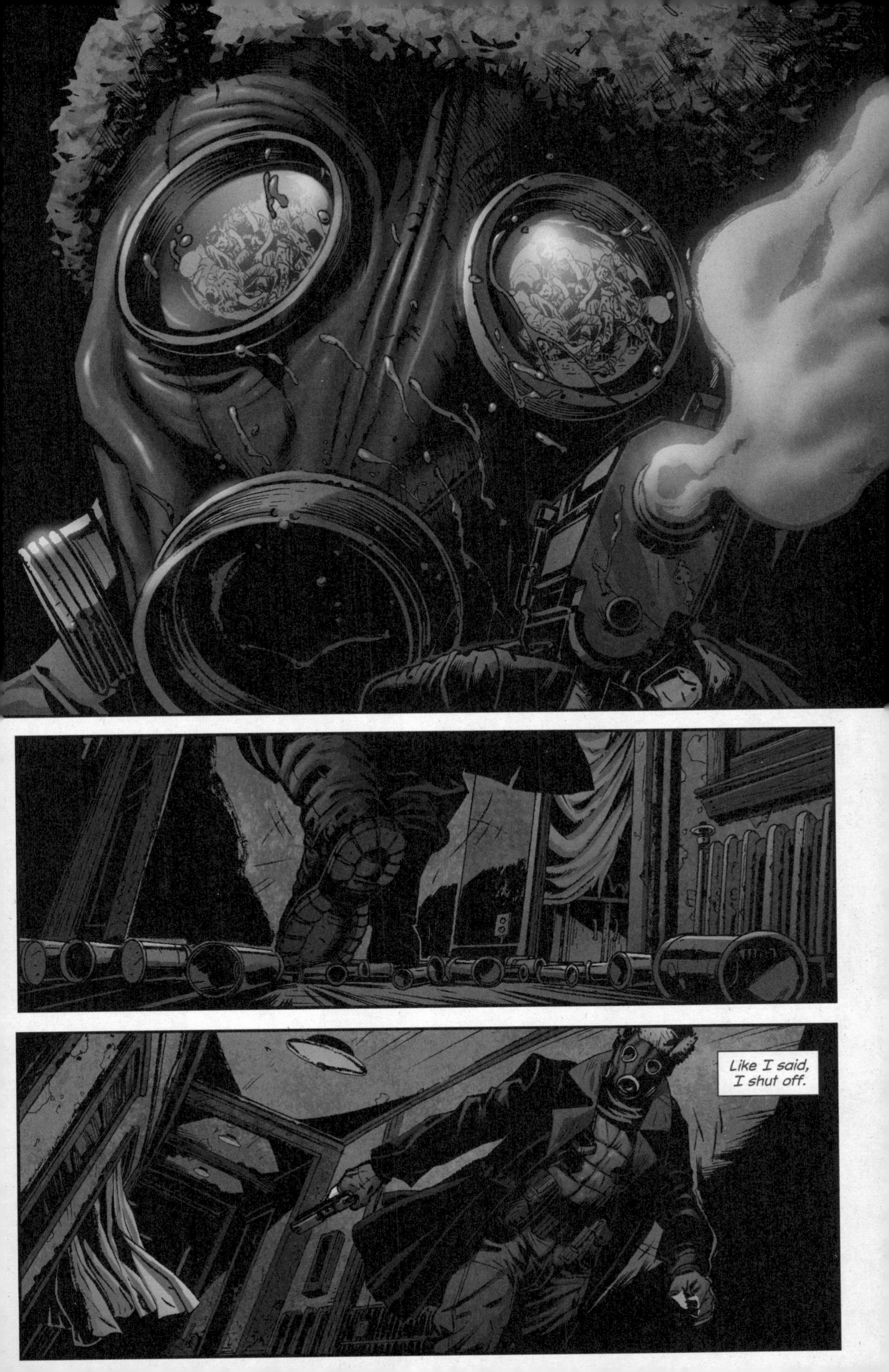
Like I said,
I shut off.

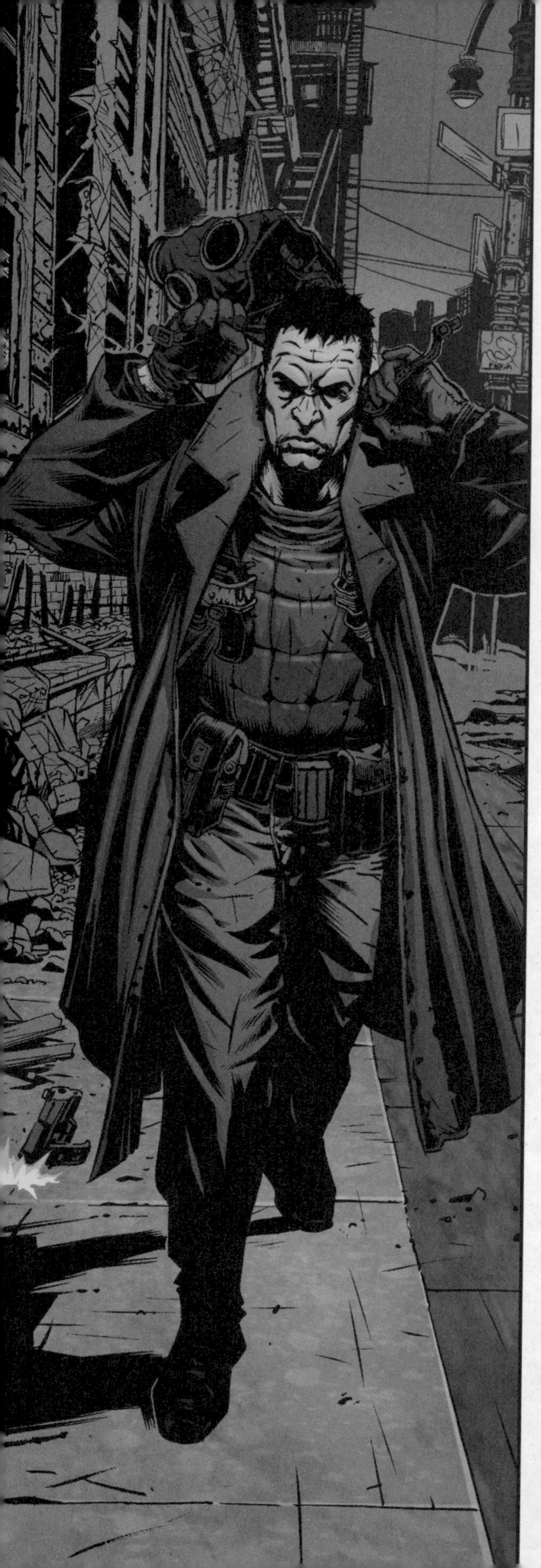

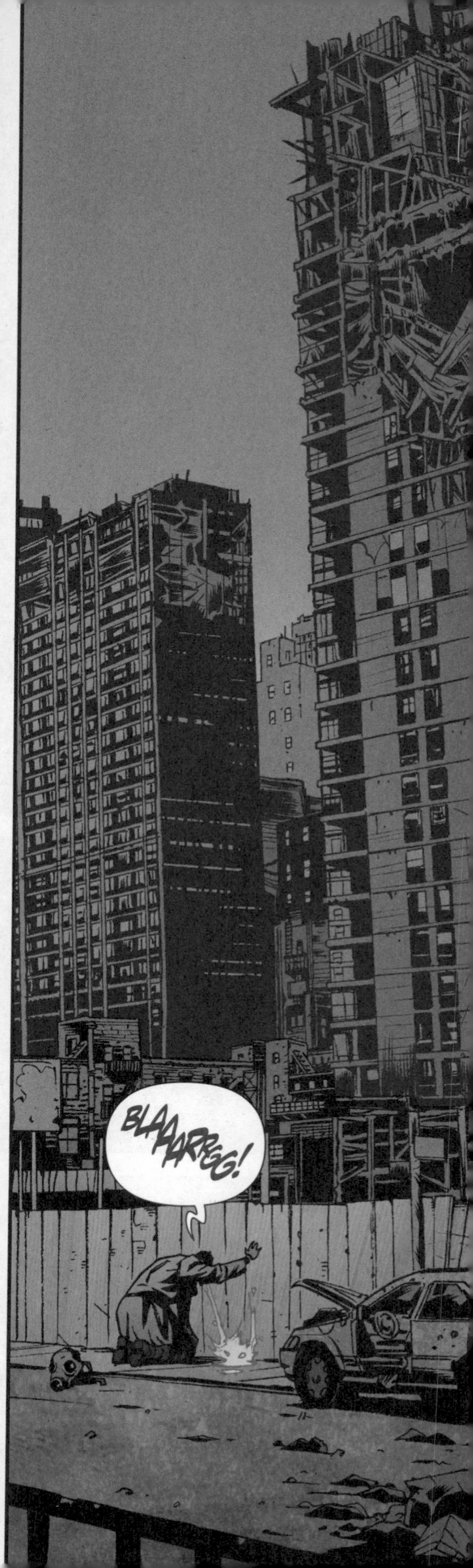
BLAAARRGG!

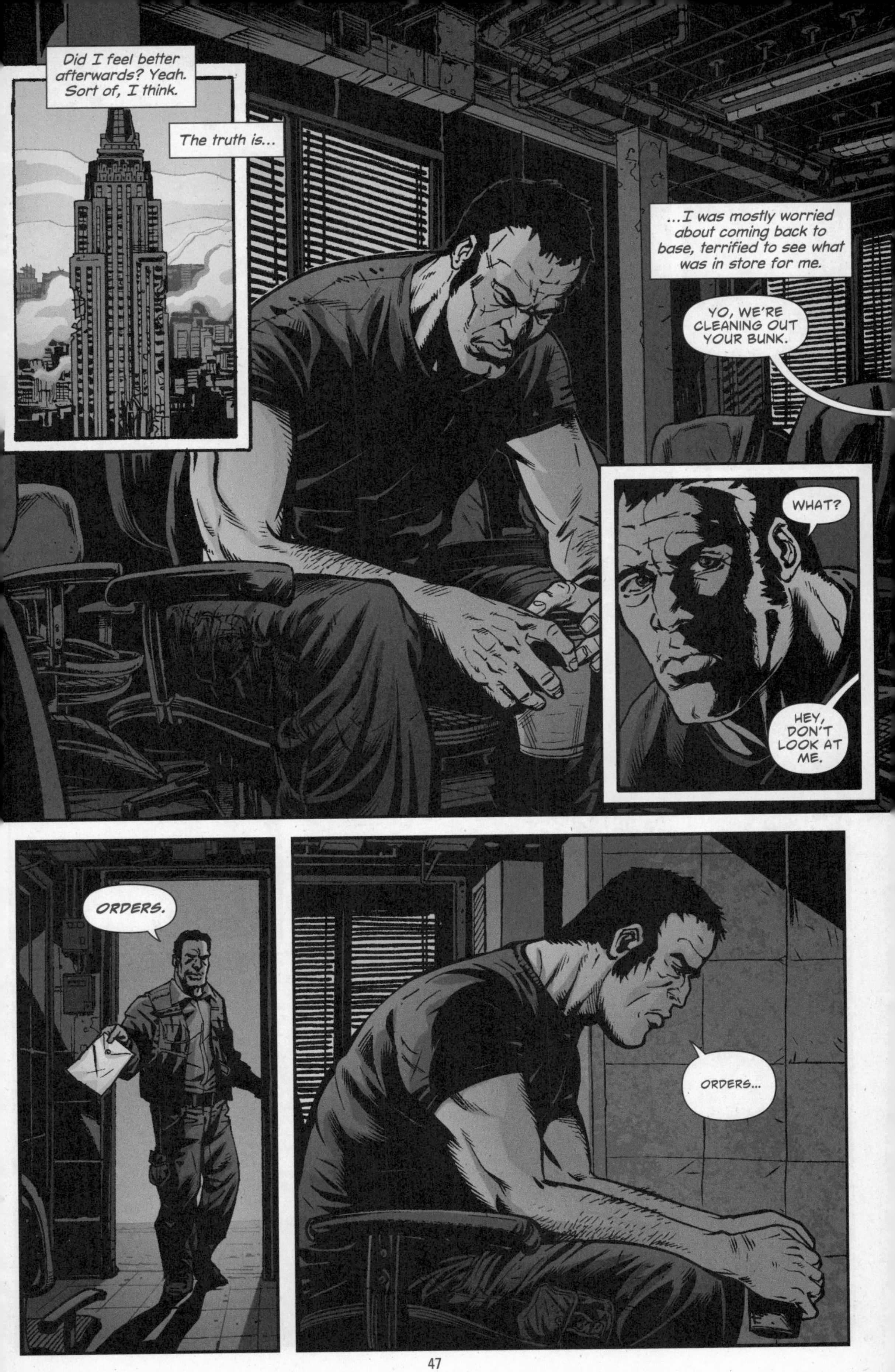
Did I feel better afterwards? Yeah. Sort of, I think.
The truth is...
...I was mostly worried about coming back to base, terrified to see what was in store for me.
YO, WE'RE CLEANING OUT YOUR BUNK.
WHAT?
HEY, DON'T LOOK AT ME.
ORDERS.
ORDERS...

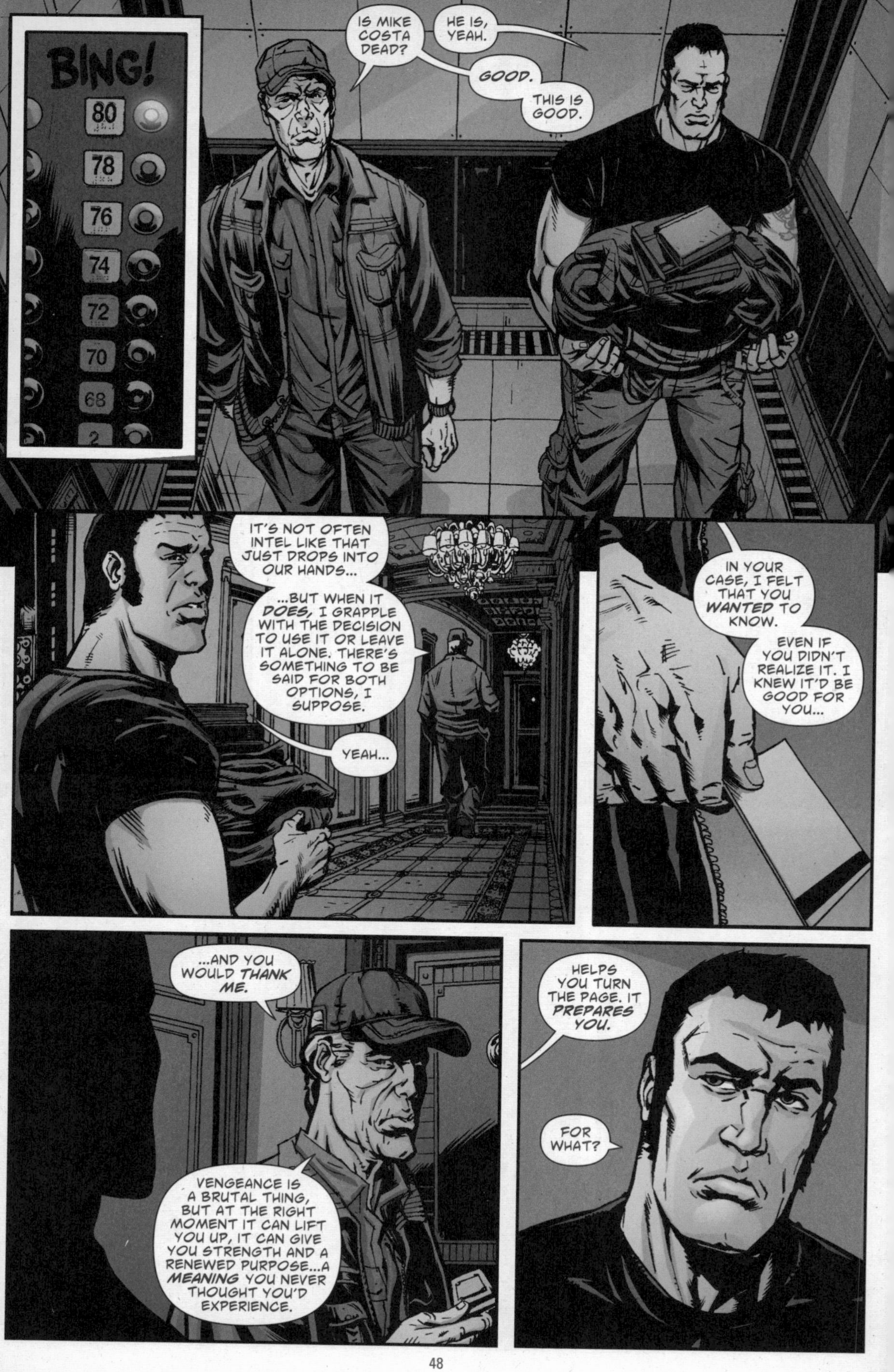
BING!
80
78
76
74
72
70
68
2
IS MIKE COSTA DEAD?
HE IS, YEAH.
GOOD.
THIS IS GOOD.
IT'S NOT OFTEN INTEL LIKE THAT JUST DROPS INTO OUR HANDS...
...BUT WHEN IT DOES, I GRAPPLE WITH THE DECISION TO USE IT OR LEAVE IT ALONE. THERE'S SOMETHING TO BE SAID FOR BOTH OPTIONS, I SUPPOSE.
YEAH...
IN YOUR CASE, I FELT THAT YOU WANTED TO KNOW.
EVEN IF YOU DIDN'T REALIZE IT. I KNEW IT'D BE GOOD FOR YOU...
...AND YOU WOULD THANK ME.
VENGEANCE IS A BRUTAL THING, BUT AT THE RIGHT MOMENT IT CAN LIFT YOU UP, IT CAN GIVE YOU STRENGTH AND A RENEWED PURPOSE...A MEANING YOU NEVER THOUGHT YOU'D EXPERIENCE.
HELPS YOU TURN THE PAGE. IT PREPARES YOU.
FOR WHAT?

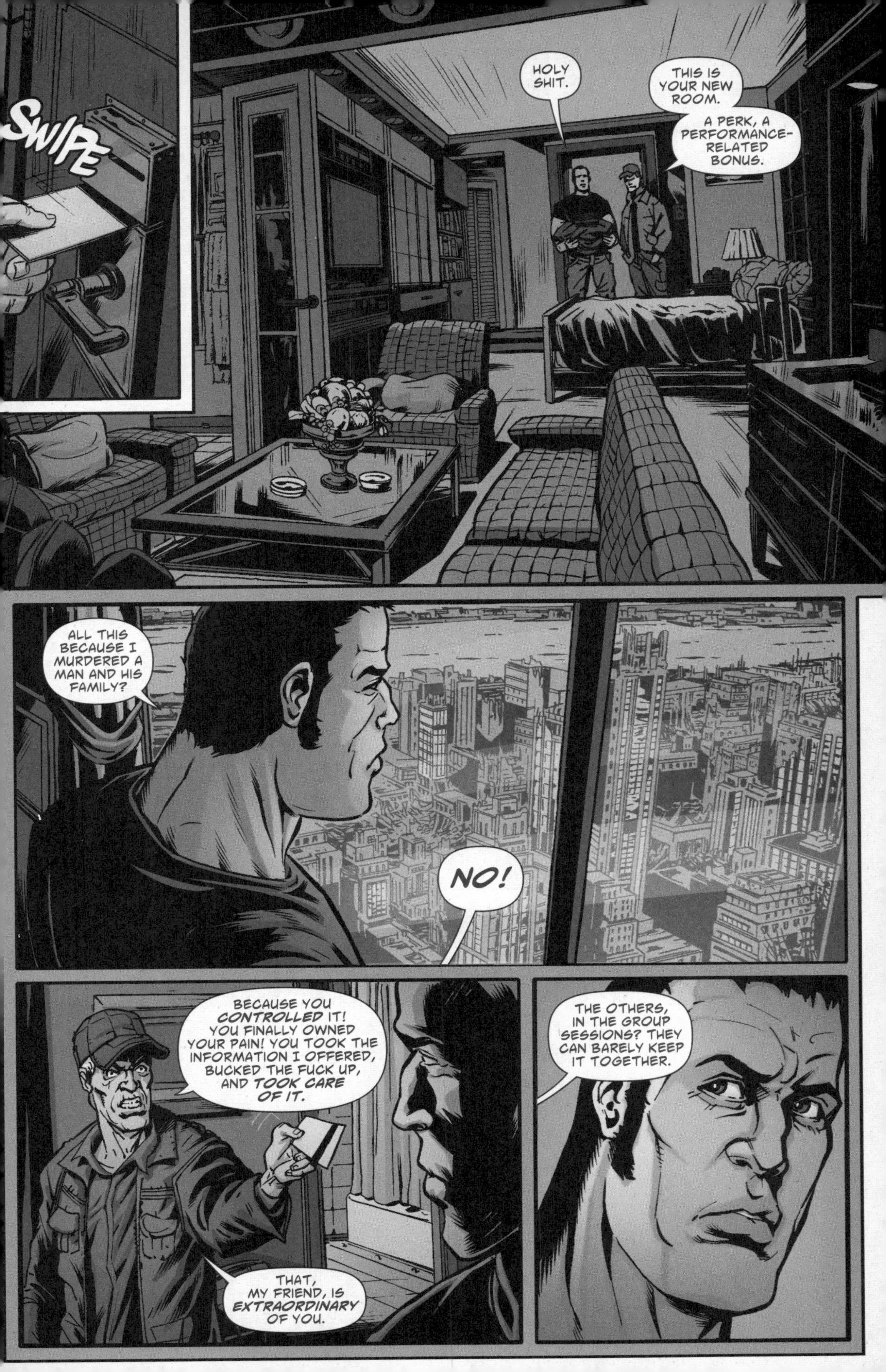
SWIPE
HOLY SHIT.
THIS IS YOUR NEW ROOM.
A PERK, A PERFORMANCE-RELATED BONUS.
ALL THIS BECAUSE I MURDERED A MAN AND HIS FAMILY?
NO!
BECAUSE YOU CONTROLLED IT! YOU FINALLY OWNED YOUR PAIN! YOU TOOK THE INFORMATION I OFFERED, BUCKED THE FUCK UP, AND TOOK CARE OF IT.
THAT, MY FRIEND, IS EXTRAORDINARY OF YOU.
THE OTHERS, IN THE GROUP SESSIONS? THEY CAN BARELY KEEP IT TOGETHER.

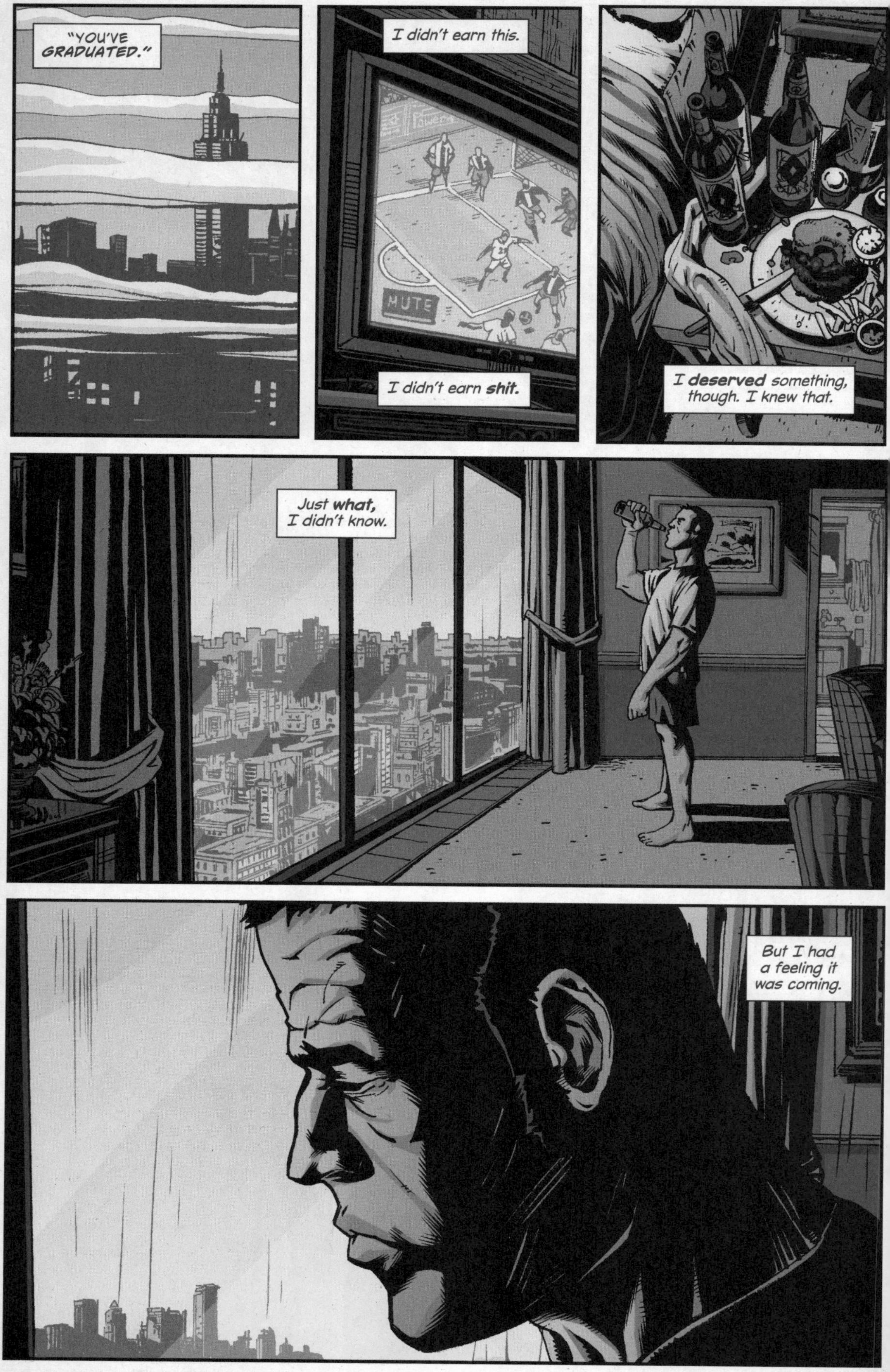
"YOU'VE GRADUATED."
I didn't earn this.
MUTE
I didn't earn **shit.**
I **deserved** something, though. I knew that.
Just **what,** I didn't know.
But I had a feeling it was coming.

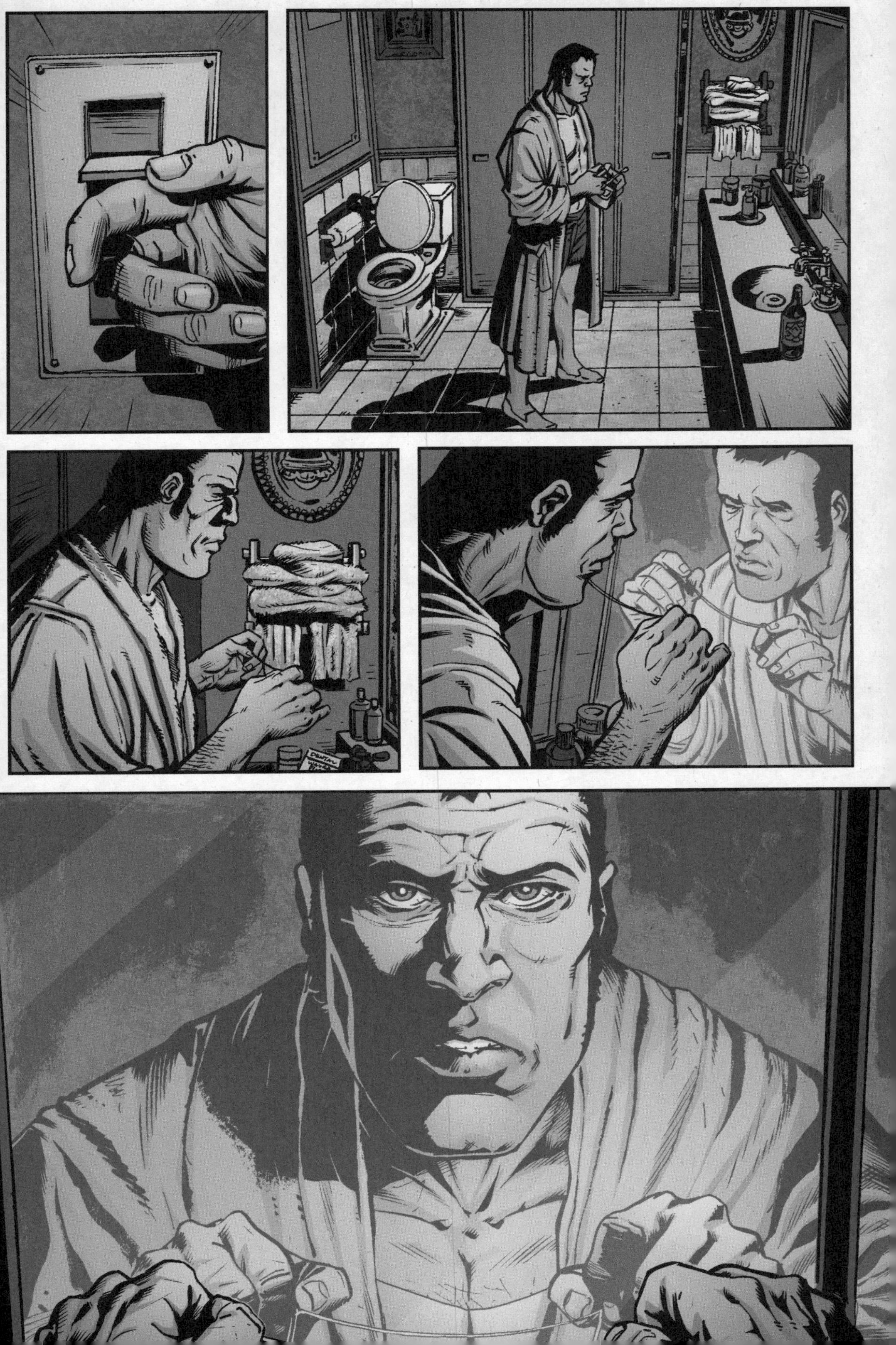
DENTAL

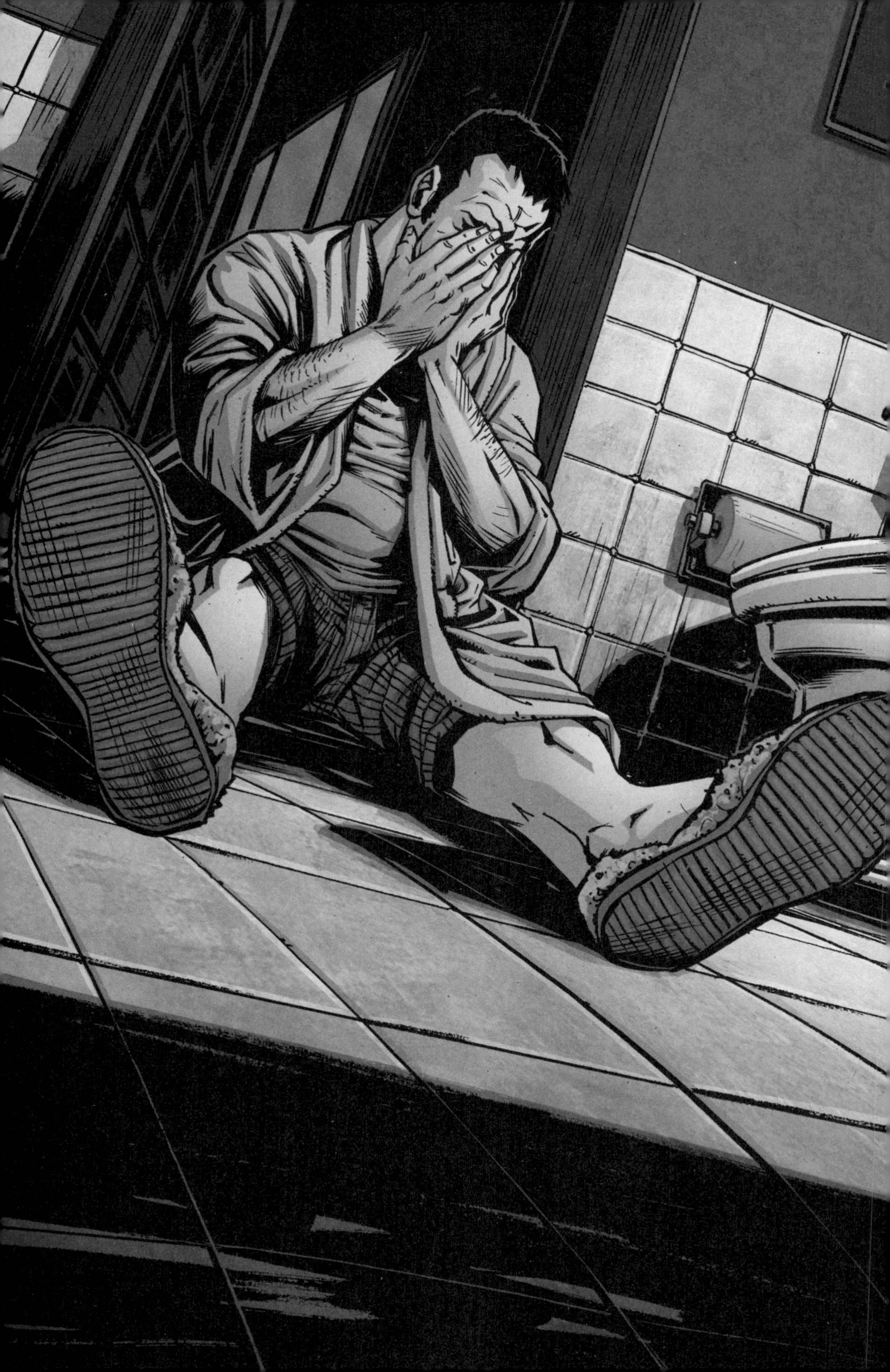

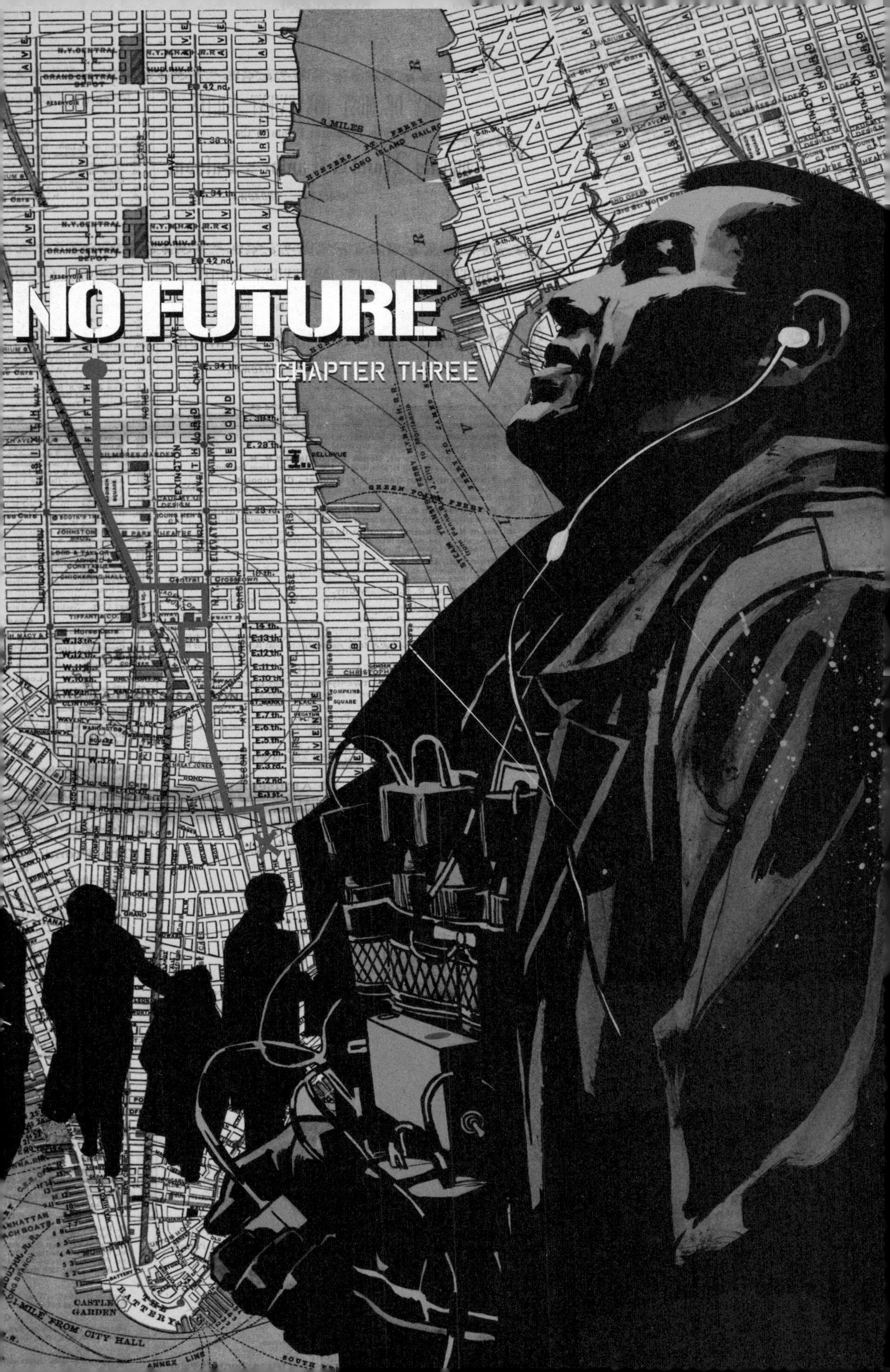
NO FUTURE
CHAPTER THREE
GRAND CENTRAL DEPOT
N.Y. CENTRAL
LONG ISLAND RAILROAD
BELLEVUE
TOMPKINS SQUARE
CASTLE GARDEN
THE BATTERY
1 MILE FROM CITY HALL

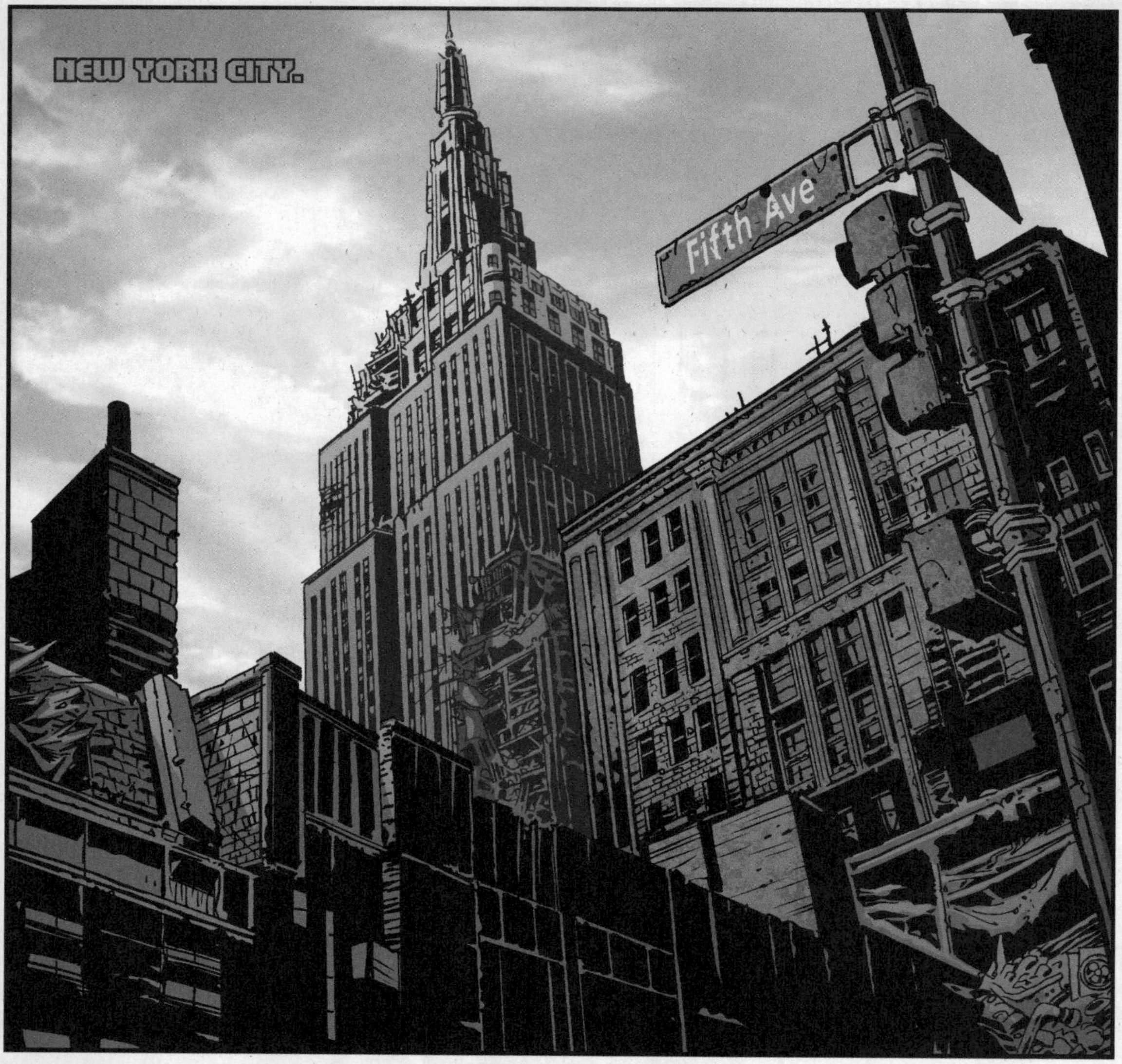
NEW YORK CITY.
Fifth Ave

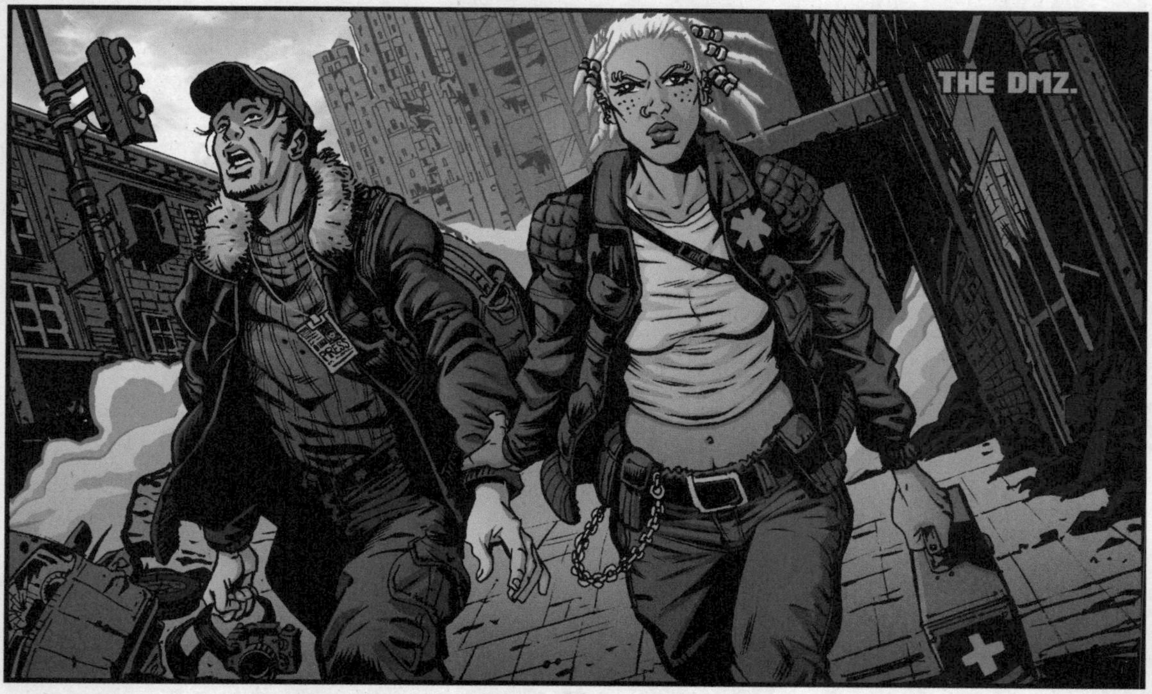
THE DMZ.

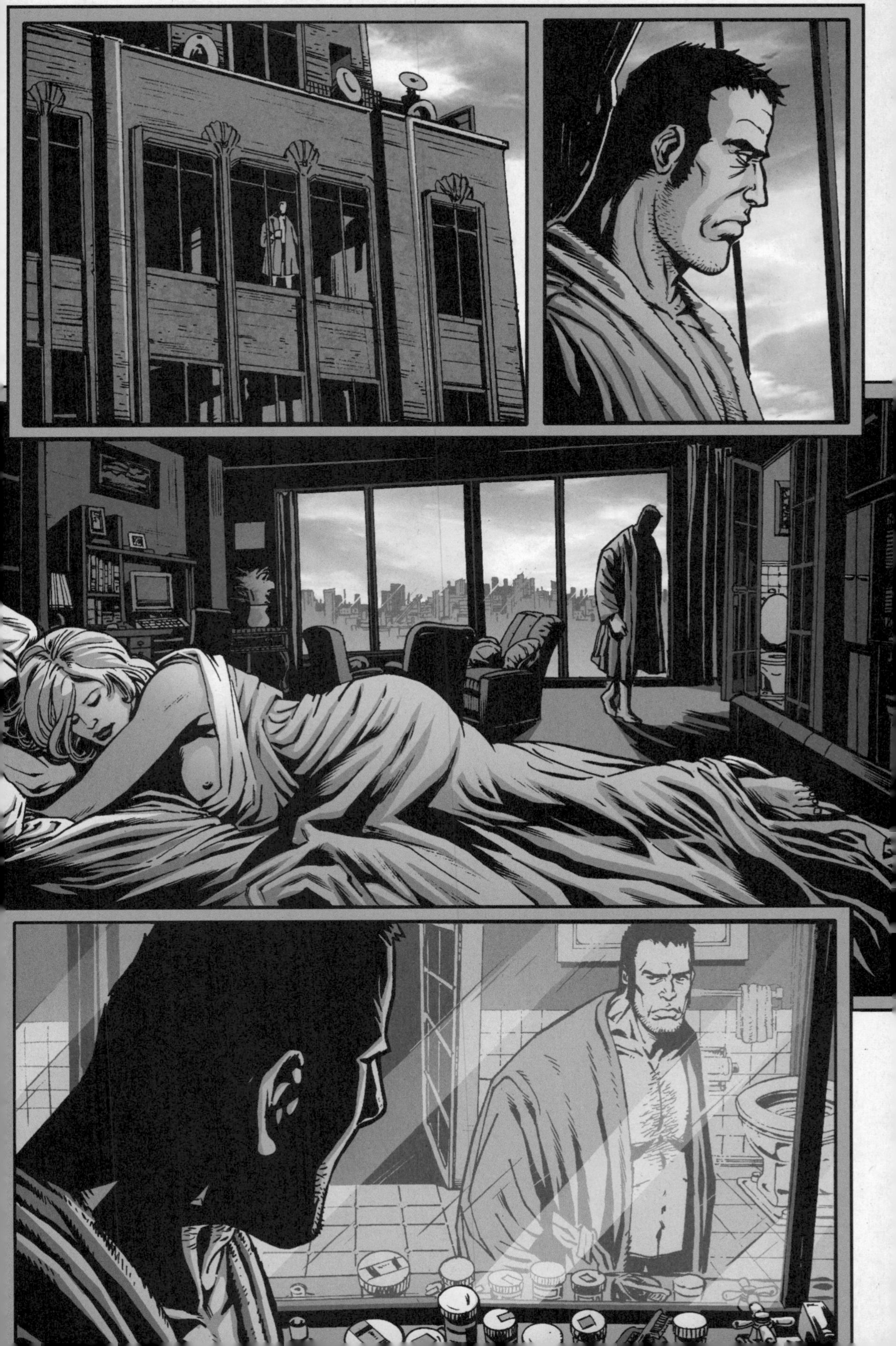

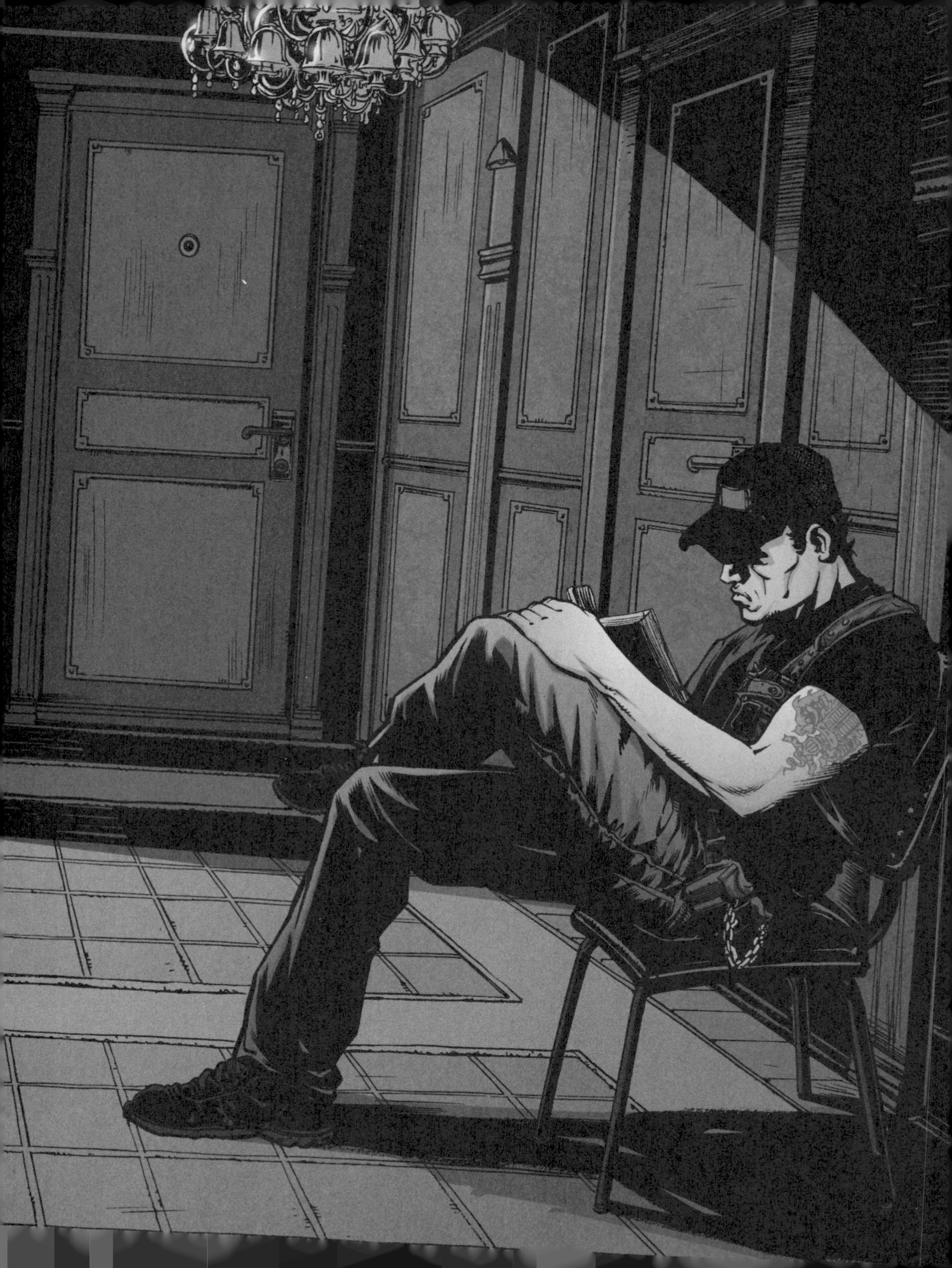

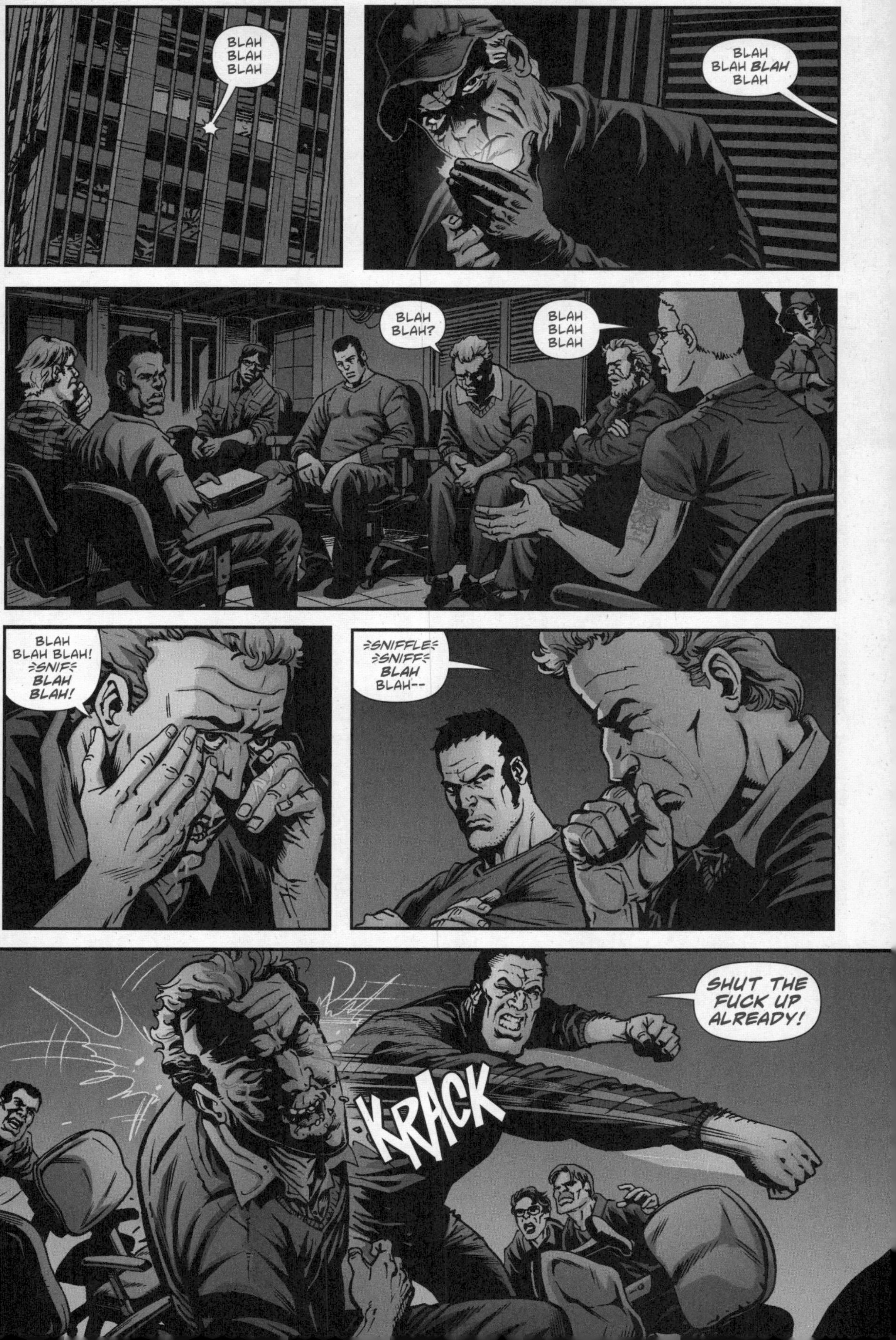
BLAH
BLAH
BLAH
BLAH
BLAH BLAH
BLAH
BLAH
BLAH?
BLAH
BLAH
BLAH
BLAH
BLAH BLAH!
SNIF
BLAH
BLAH!
SNIFFLE
SNIFF
BLAH
BLAH--
SHUT THE
FUCK UP
ALREADY!
KRACK

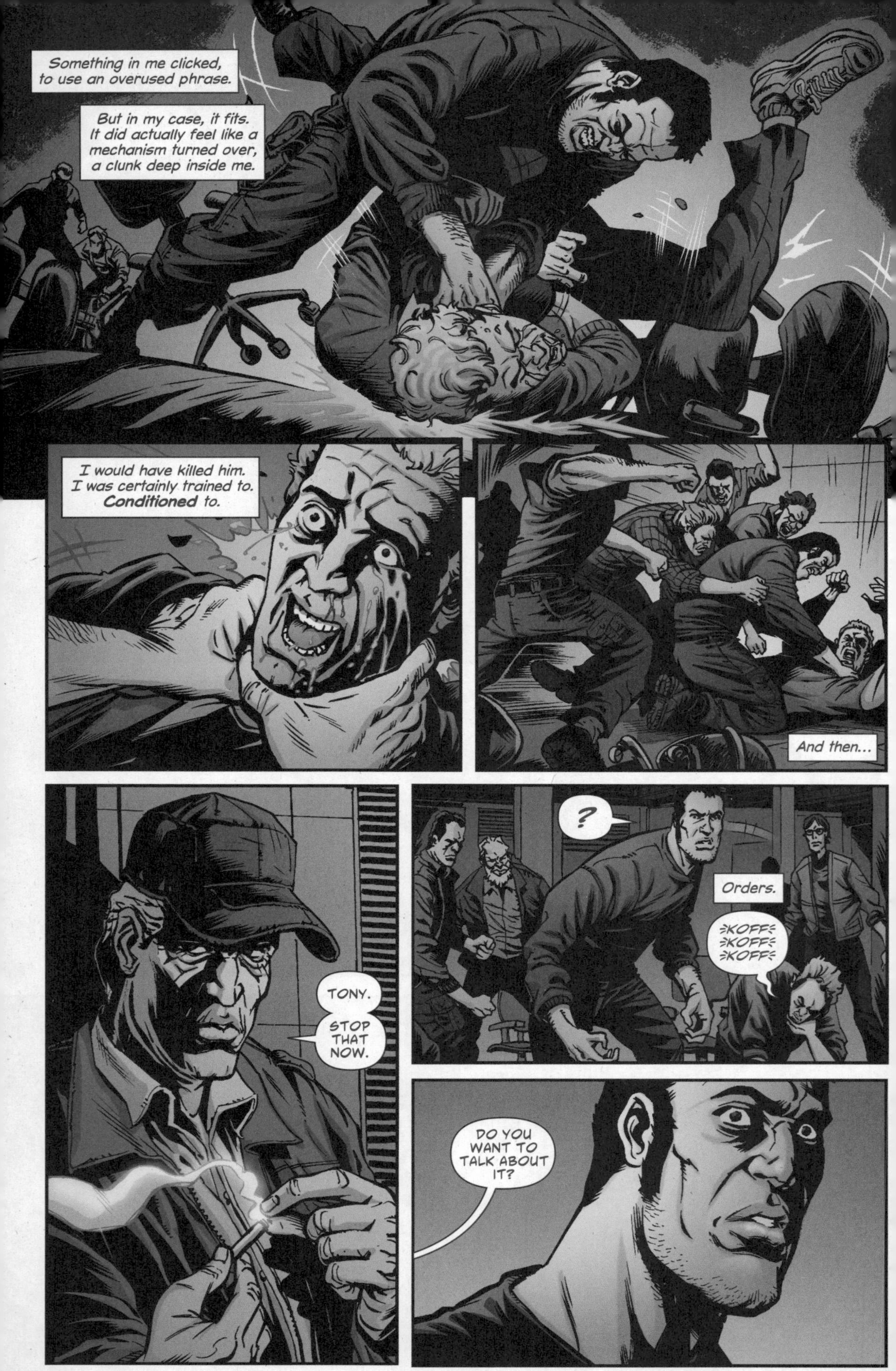
Something in me clicked, to use an overused phrase.
But in my case, it fits. It did actually feel like a mechanism turned over, a clunk deep inside me.
I would have killed him. I was certainly trained to. **Conditioned** to.
And then...
TONY.
STOP THAT NOW.
?
Orders.
KOFF KOFF KOFF
DO YOU WANT TO TALK ABOUT IT?

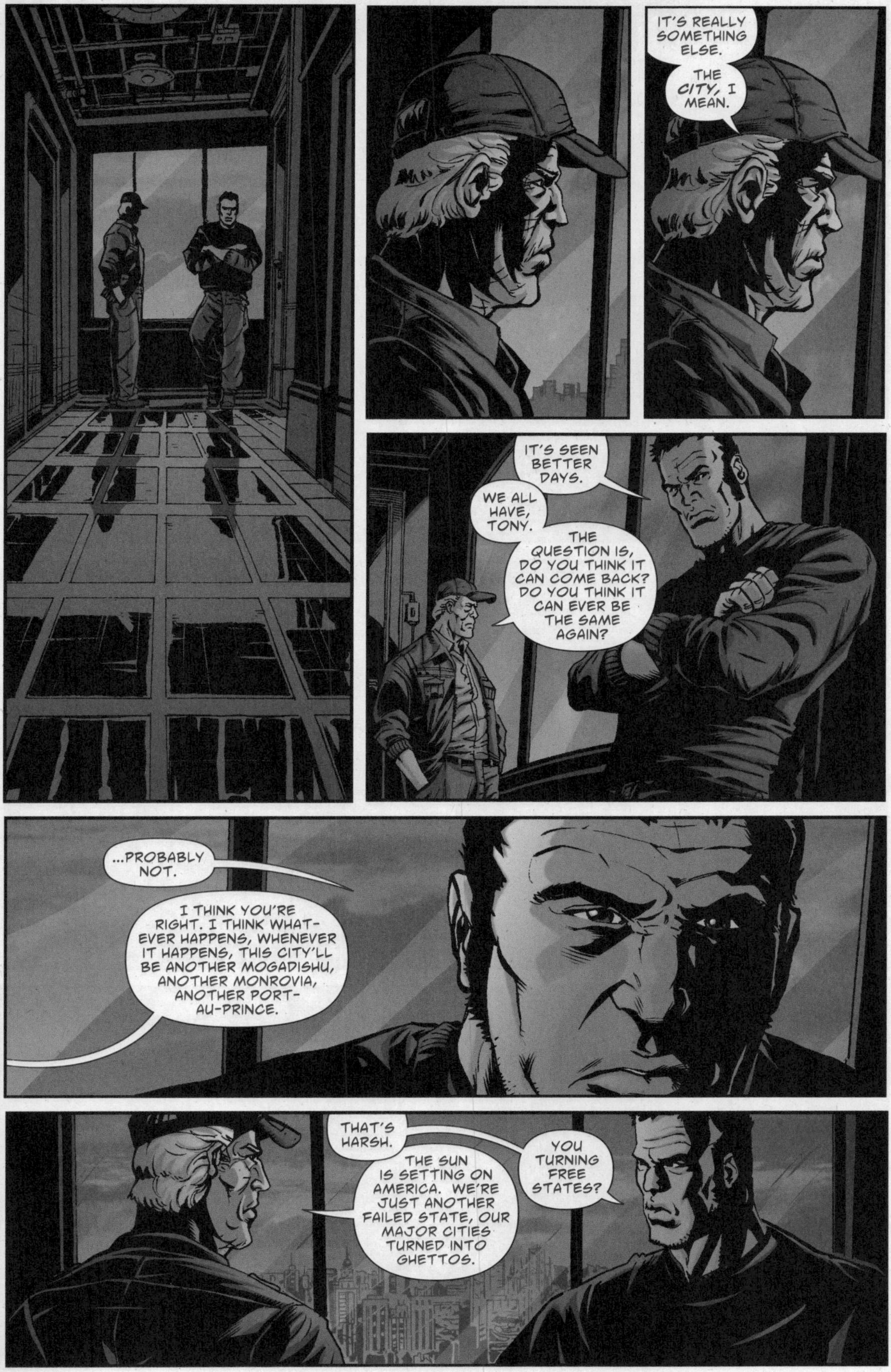
IT'S REALLY SOMETHING ELSE.
THE CITY, I MEAN.
IT'S SEEN BETTER DAYS.
WE ALL HAVE, TONY.
THE QUESTION IS, DO YOU THINK IT CAN COME BACK? DO YOU THINK IT CAN EVER BE THE SAME AGAIN?
...PROBABLY NOT.
I THINK YOU'RE RIGHT. I THINK WHAT-EVER HAPPENS, WHENEVER IT HAPPENS, THIS CITY'LL BE ANOTHER MOGADISHU, ANOTHER MONROVIA, ANOTHER PORT-AU-PRINCE.
THAT'S HARSH.
YOU TURNING FREE STATES?
THE SUN IS SETTING ON AMERICA. WE'RE JUST ANOTHER FAILED STATE, OUR MAJOR CITIES TURNED INTO GHETTOS.

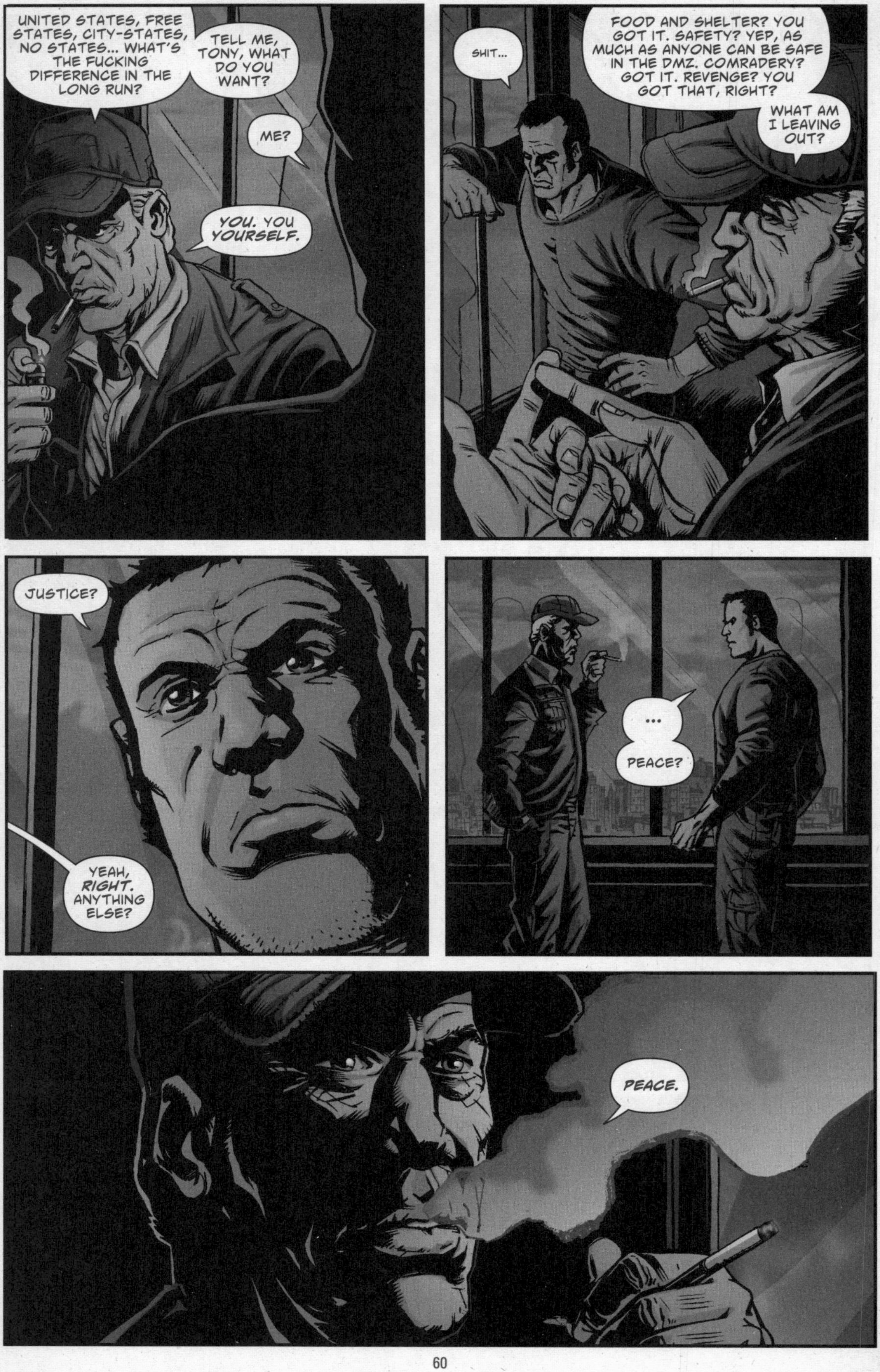
UNITED STATES, FREE STATES, CITY-STATES, NO STATES... WHAT'S THE FUCKING DIFFERENCE IN THE LONG RUN?
TELL ME, TONY, WHAT DO YOU WANT?
ME?
YOU. YOU YOURSELF.
SHIT...
FOOD AND SHELTER? YOU GOT IT. SAFETY? YEP, AS MUCH AS ANYONE CAN BE SAFE IN THE DMZ. COMRADERY? GOT IT. REVENGE? YOU GOT THAT, RIGHT?
WHAT AM I LEAVING OUT?
JUSTICE?
YEAH, RIGHT. ANYTHING ELSE?
...
PEACE?
PEACE.

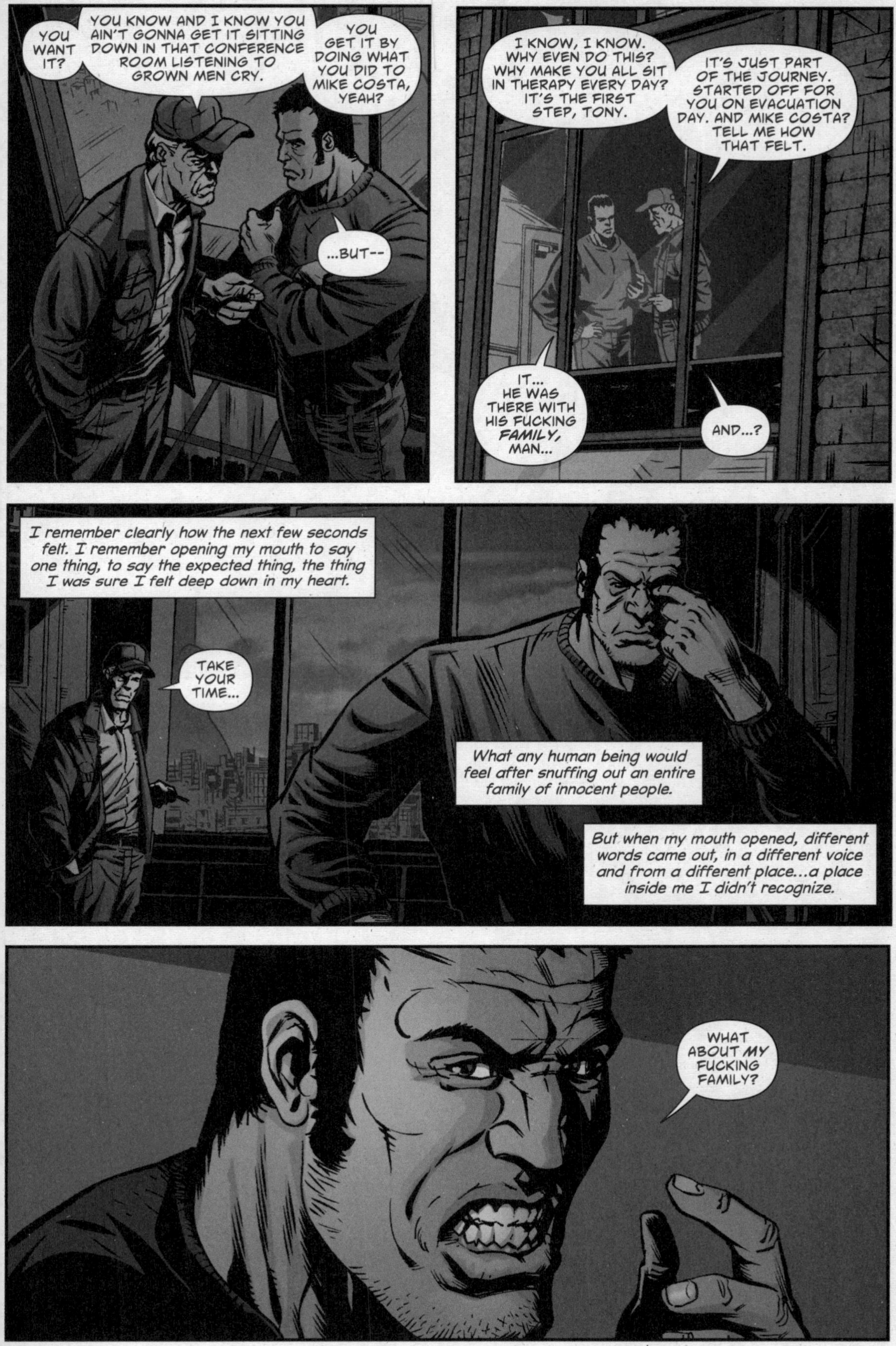
YOU WANT IT?
YOU KNOW AND I KNOW YOU AIN'T GONNA GET IT SITTING DOWN IN THAT CONFERENCE ROOM LISTENING TO GROWN MEN CRY.
YOU GET IT BY DOING WHAT YOU DID TO MIKE COSTA, YEAH?
...BUT--
I KNOW, I KNOW. WHY EVEN DO THIS? WHY MAKE YOU ALL SIT IN THERAPY EVERY DAY? IT'S THE FIRST STEP, TONY.
IT'S JUST PART OF THE JOURNEY. STARTED OFF FOR YOU ON EVACUATION DAY. AND MIKE COSTA? TELL ME HOW THAT FELT.
IT... HE WAS THERE WITH HIS FUCKING *FAMILY,* MAN...
AND...?
I remember clearly how the next few seconds felt. I remember opening my mouth to say one thing, to say the expected thing, the thing I was sure I felt deep down in my heart.
TAKE YOUR TIME...
What any human being would feel after snuffing out an entire family of innocent people.
But when my mouth opened, different words came out, in a different voice and from a different place...a place inside me I didn't recognize.
WHAT ABOUT *MY* FUCKING FAMILY?

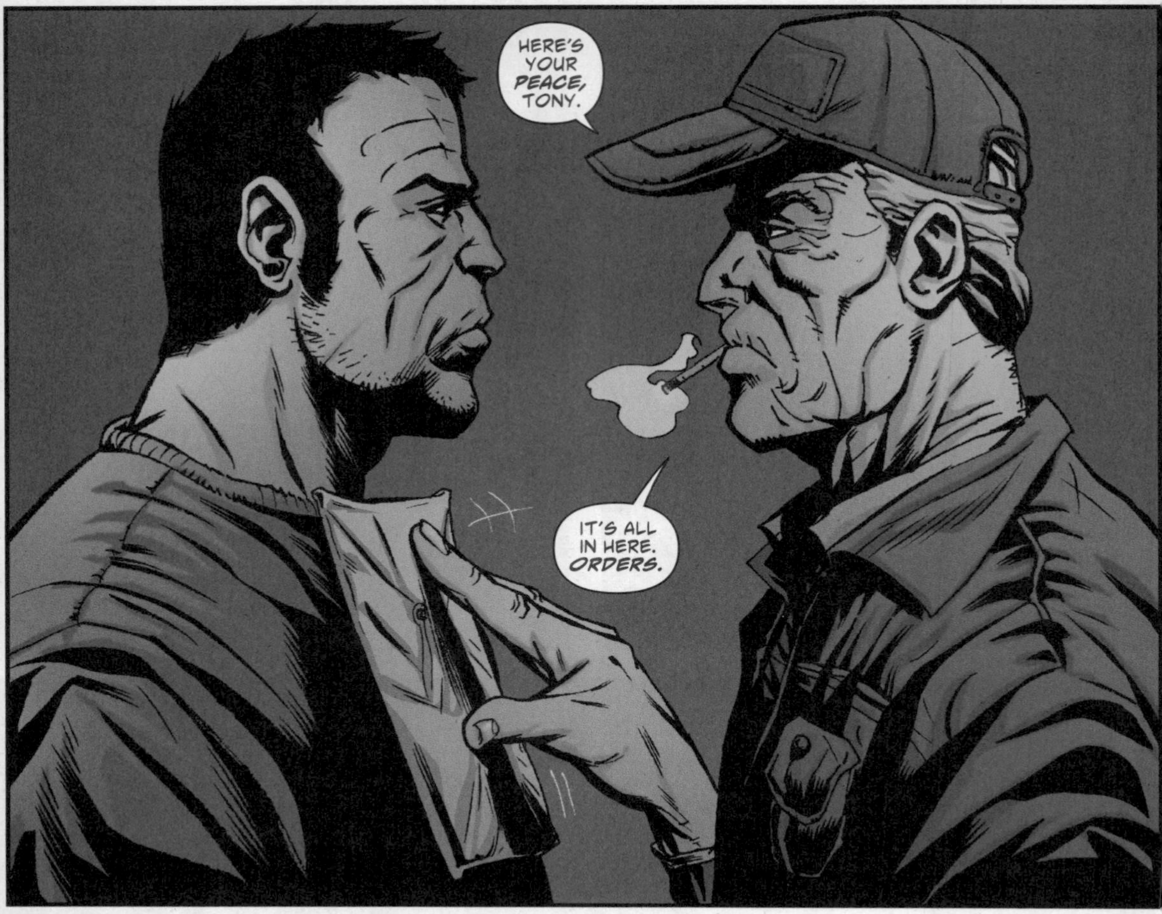
HERE'S YOUR *PEACE,* TONY.
IT'S ALL IN HERE. *ORDERS.*

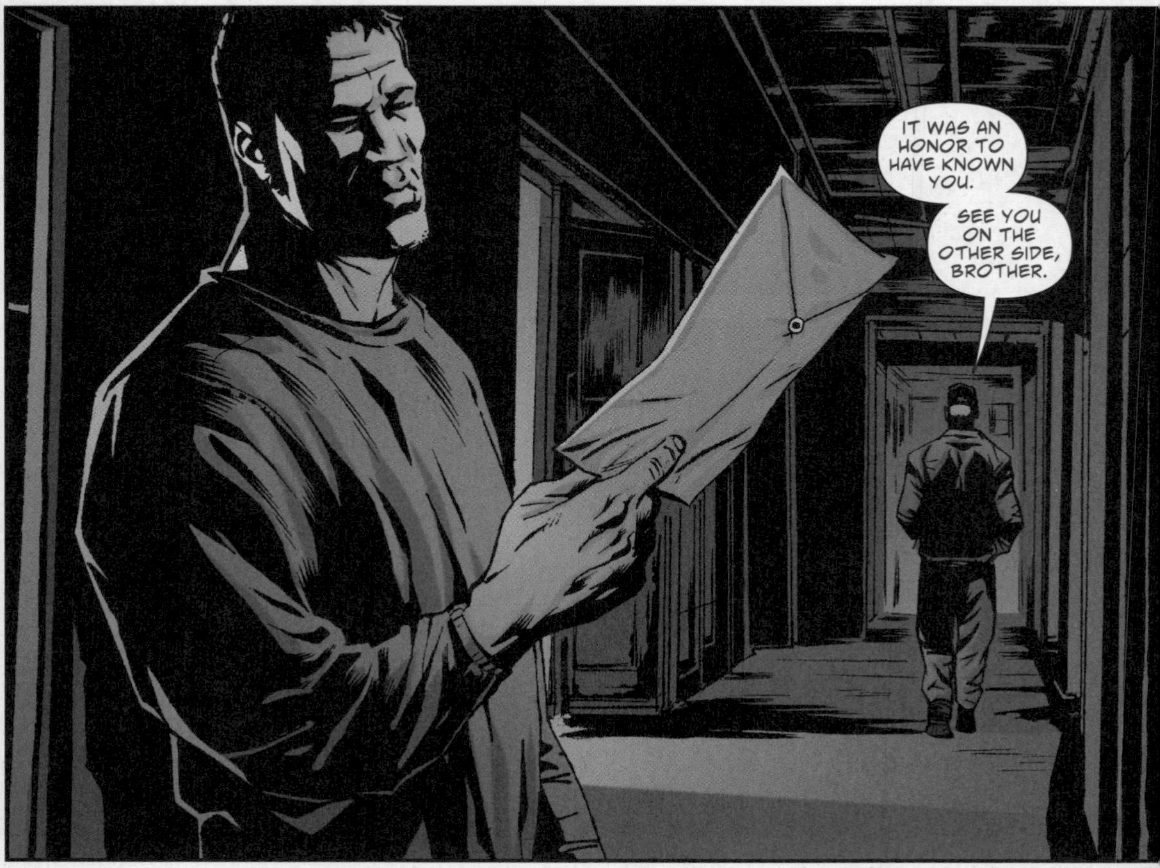
IT WAS AN HONOR TO HAVE KNOWN YOU.
SEE YOU ON THE OTHER SIDE, BROTHER.

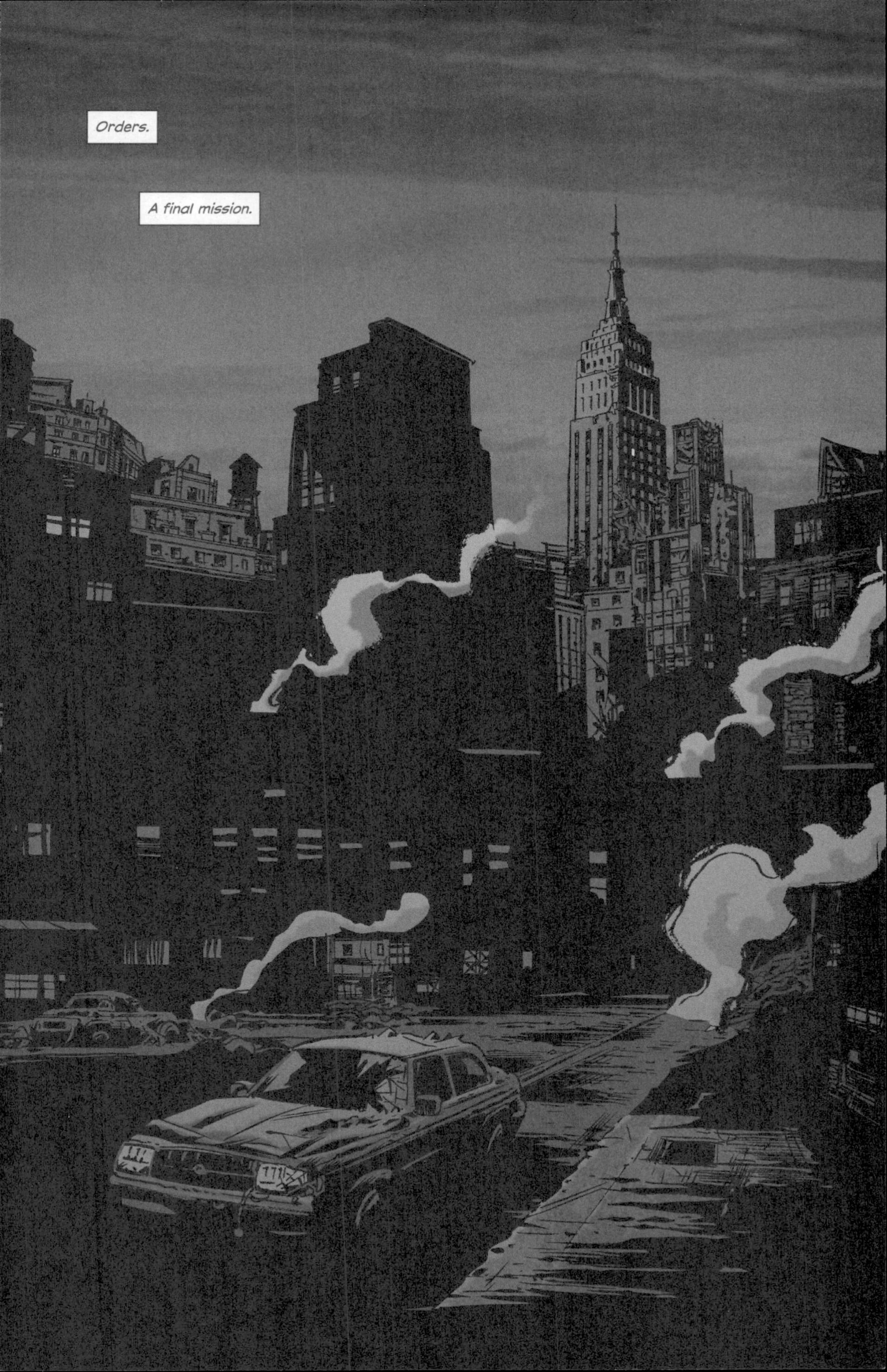
Orders.
A final mission.

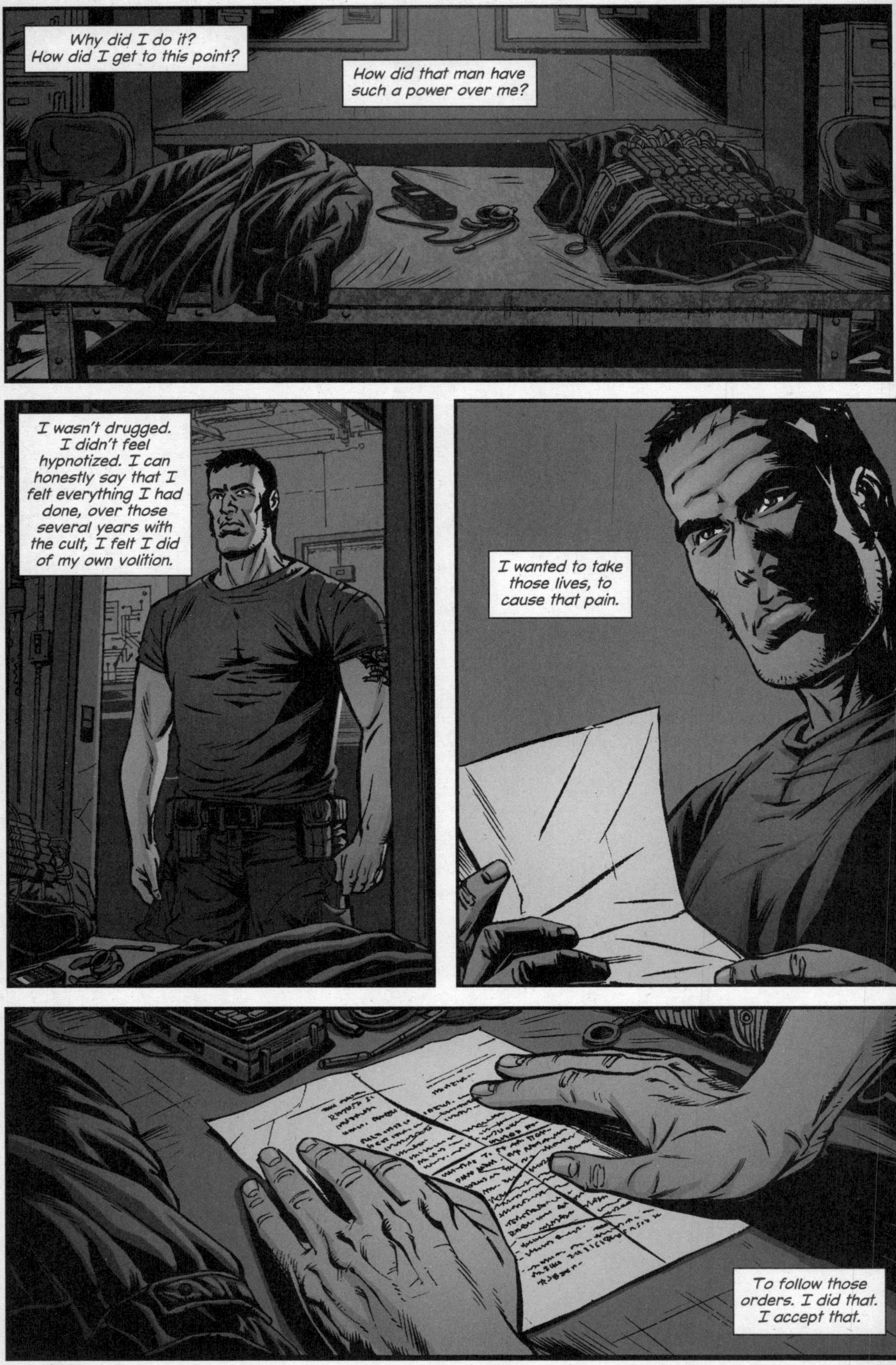
Why did I do it? How did I get to this point?
How did that man have such a power over me?
I wasn't drugged. I didn't feel hypnotized. I can honestly say that I felt everything I had done, over those several years with the cult, I felt I did of my own volition.
I wanted to take those lives, to cause that pain.
To follow those orders. I did that. I accept that.

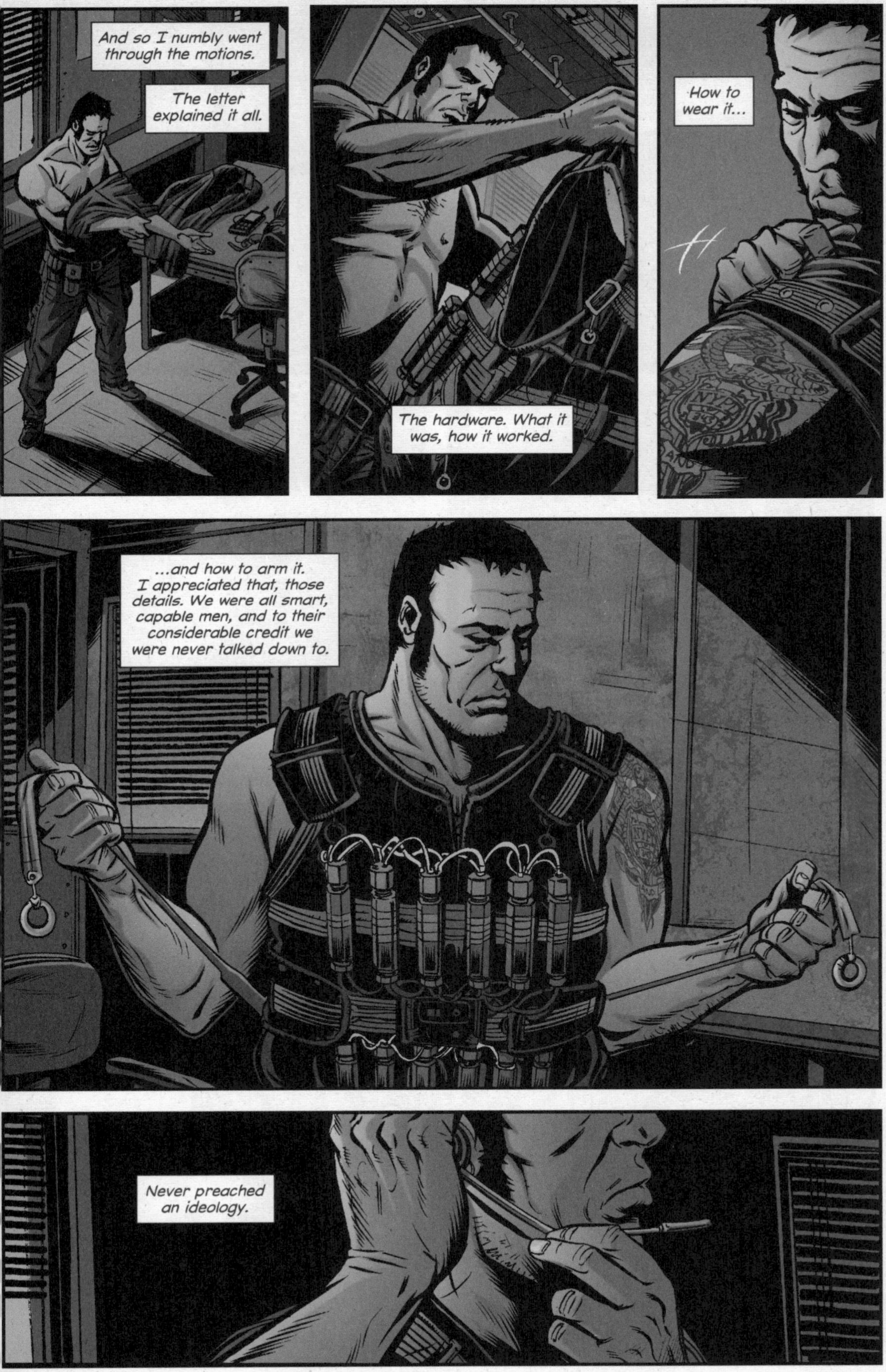
And so I numbly went through the motions.
The letter explained it all.
The hardware. What it was, how it worked.
How to wear it...
...and how to arm it. I appreciated that, those details. We were all smart, capable men, and to their considerable credit we were never talked down to.
Never preached an ideology.

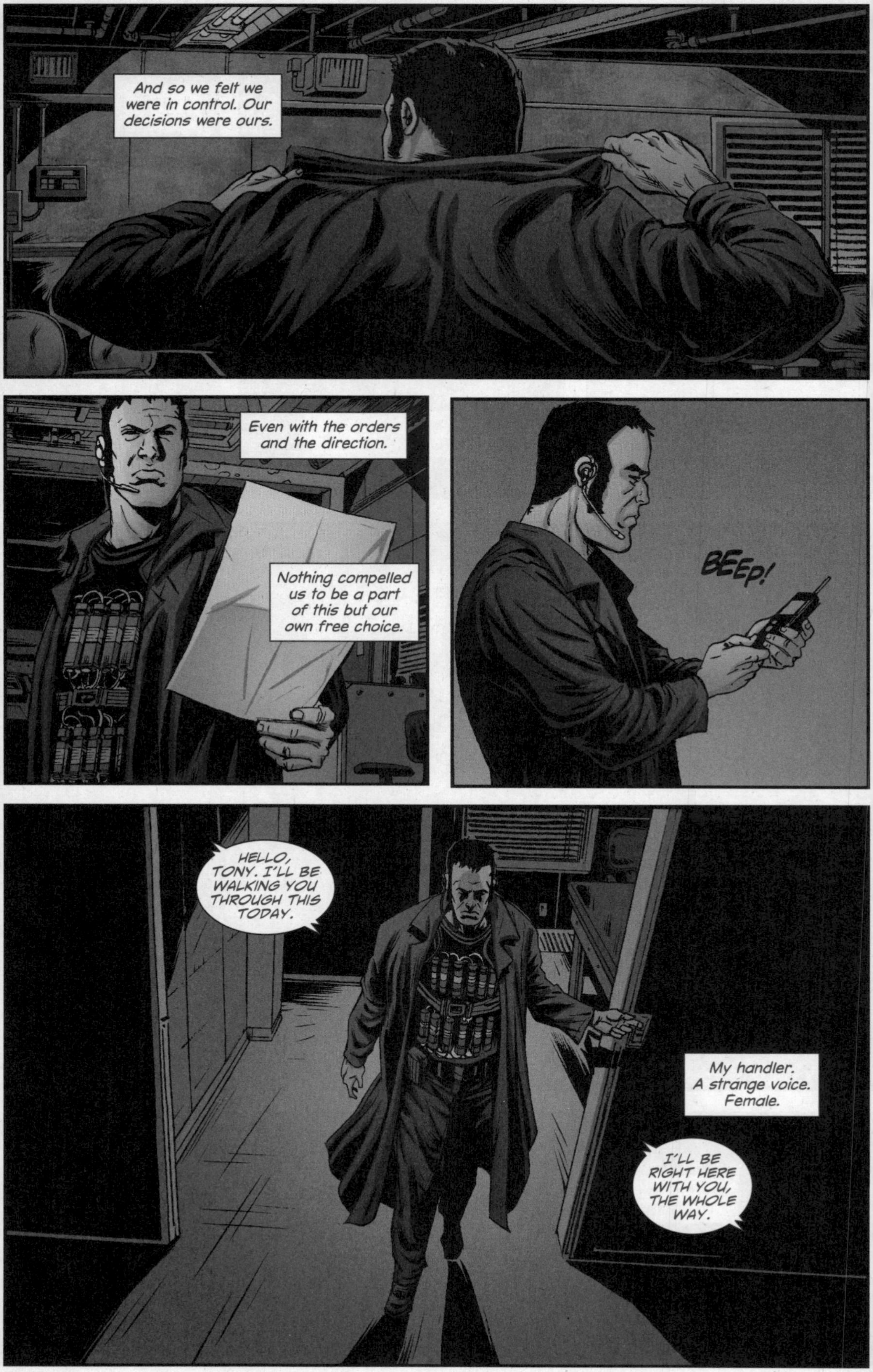
And so we felt we were in control. Our decisions were ours.
Even with the orders and the direction.
Nothing compelled us to be a part of this but our own free choice.
BEEP!
HELLO, TONY. I'LL BE WALKING YOU THROUGH THIS TODAY.
My handler. A strange voice. Female.
I'LL BE RIGHT HERE WITH YOU, THE WHOLE WAY.

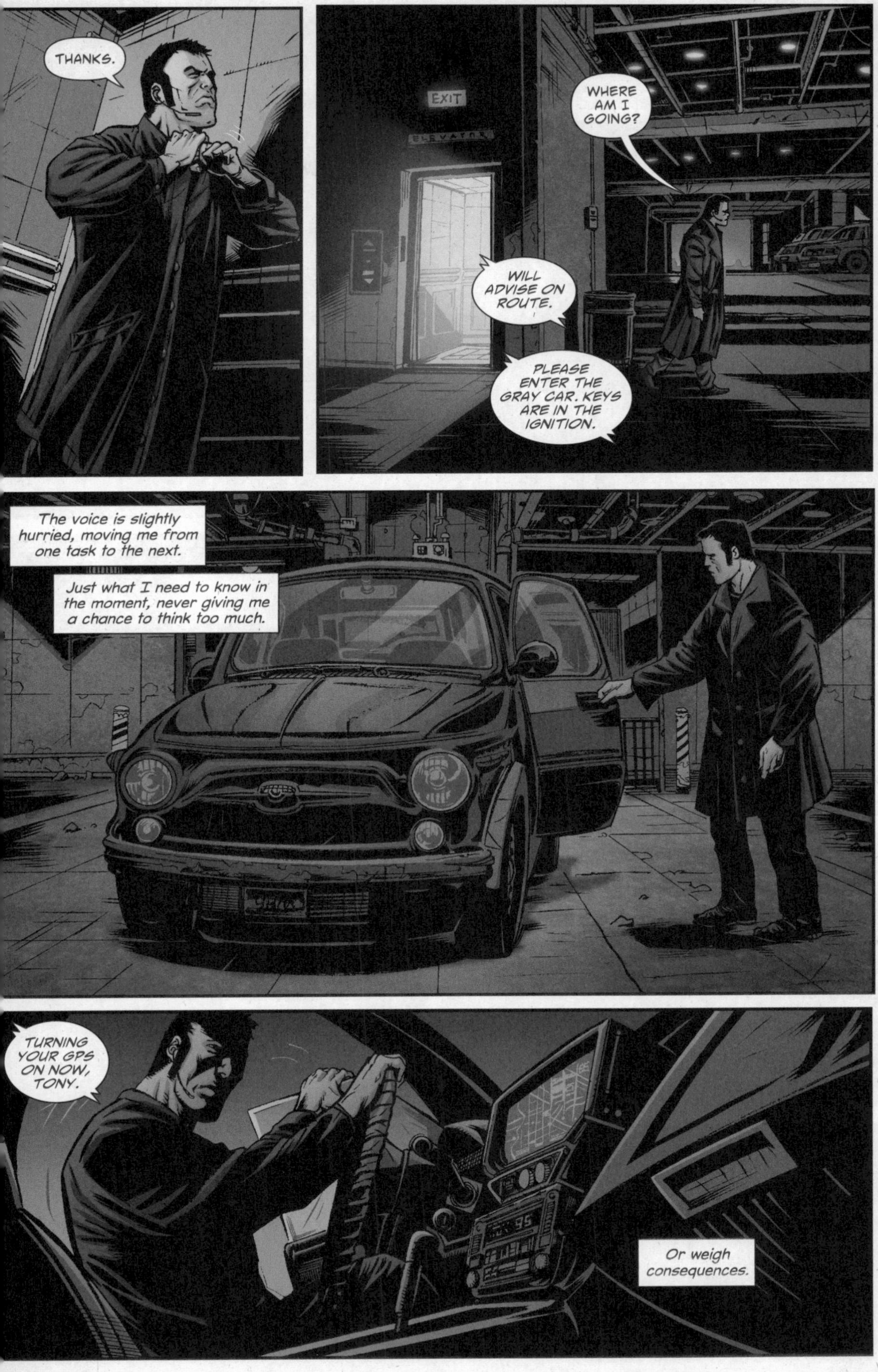
THANKS.
EXIT
WHERE AM I GOING?
WILL ADVISE ON ROUTE.
PLEASE ENTER THE GRAY CAR. KEYS ARE IN THE IGNITION.
The voice is slightly hurried, moving me from one task to the next.
Just what I need to know in the moment, never giving me a chance to think too much.
TURNING YOUR GPS ON NOW, TONY.
Or weigh consequences.

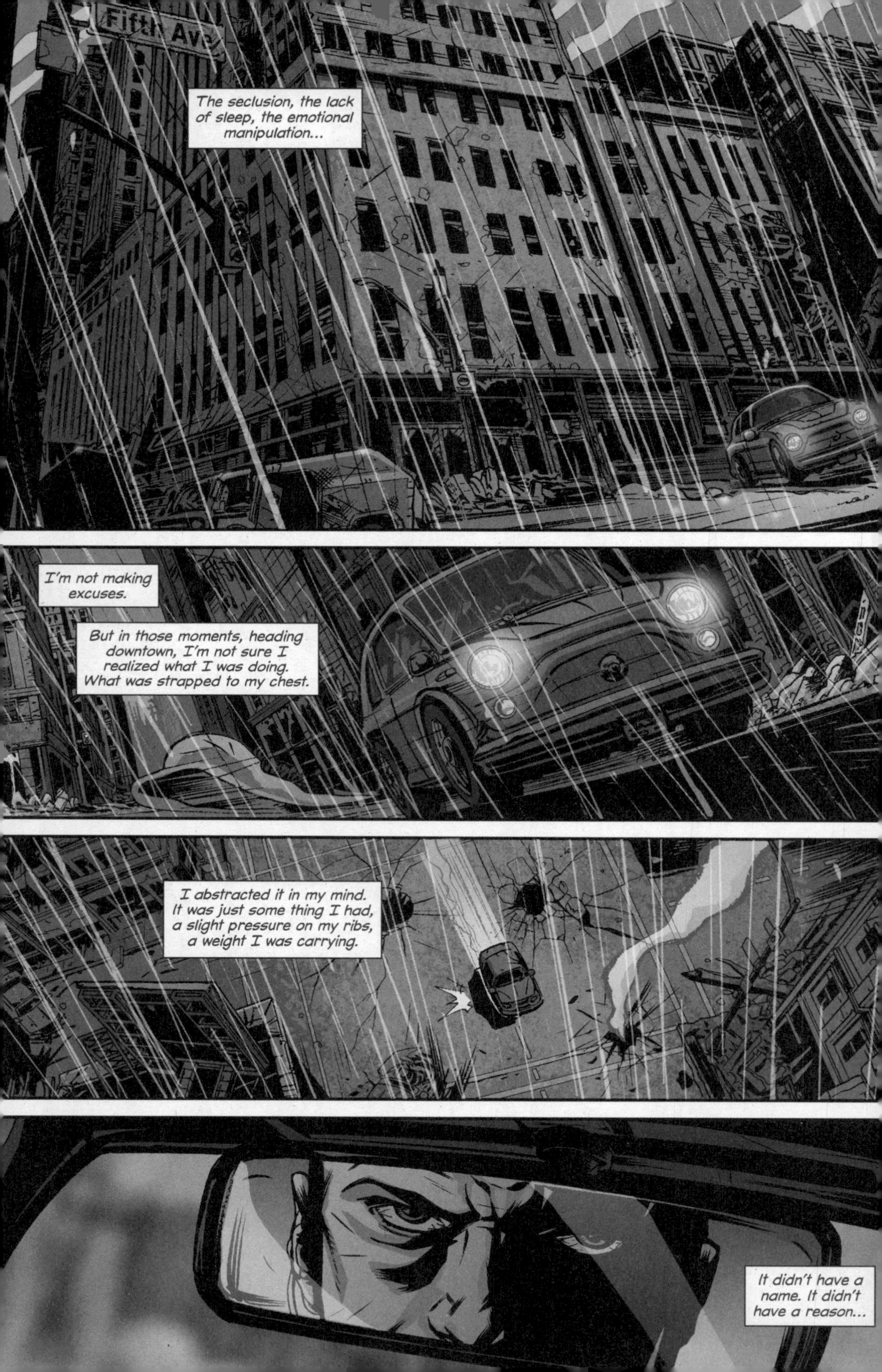
Fifth Ave
The seclusion, the lack of sleep, the emotional manipulation...
I'm not making excuses.
But in those moments, heading downtown, I'm not sure I realized what I was doing. What was strapped to my chest.
I abstracted it in my mind. It was just some thing I had, a slight pressure on my ribs, a weight I was carrying.
It didn't have a name. It didn't have a reason...

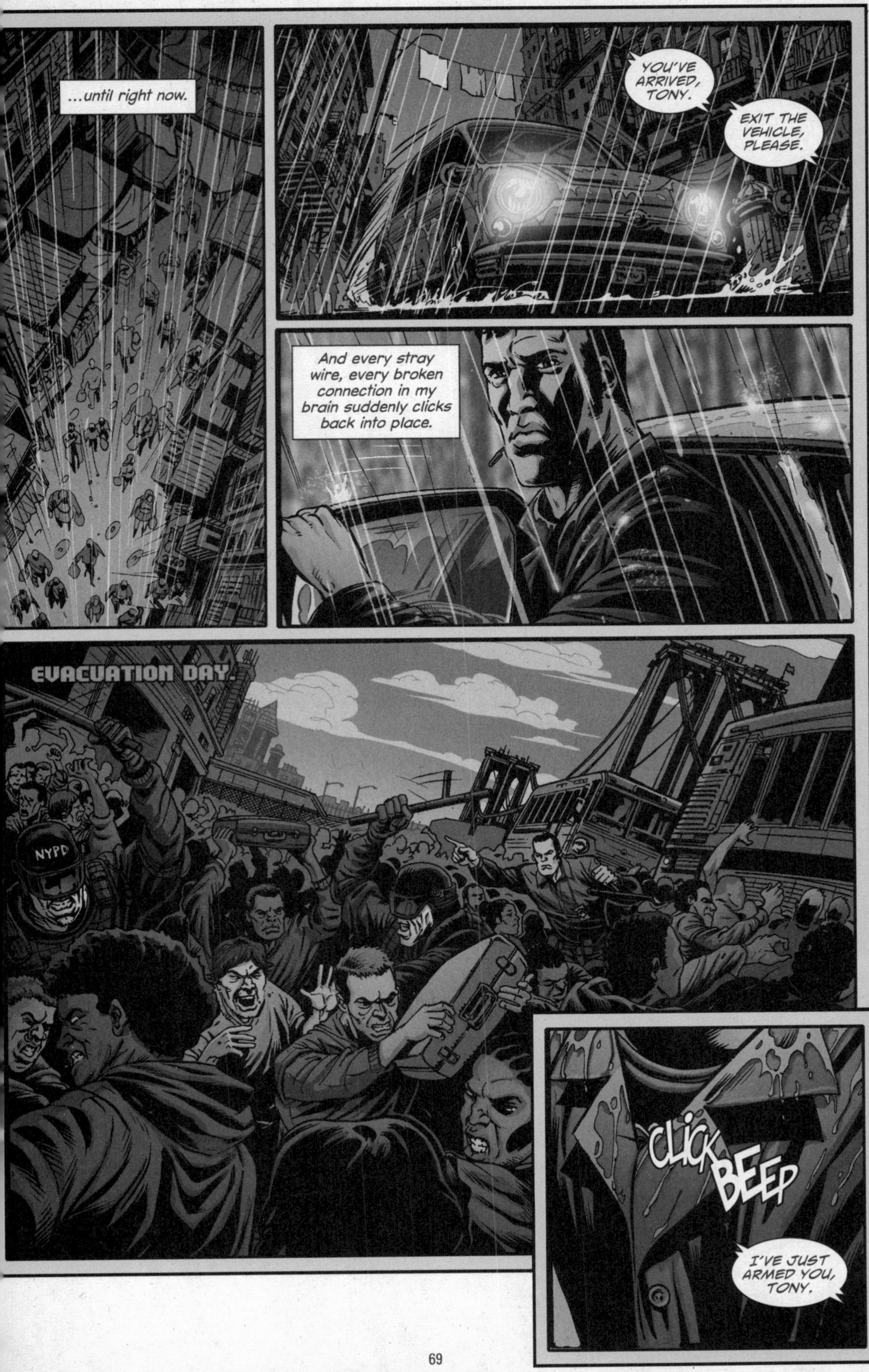

...until right now.
YOU'VE ARRIVED, TONY.
EXIT THE VEHICLE, PLEASE.
And every stray wire, every broken connection in my brain suddenly clicks back into place.
EVACUATION DAY.
NYPD
CLICK
BEEP
I'VE JUST ARMED YOU, TONY.

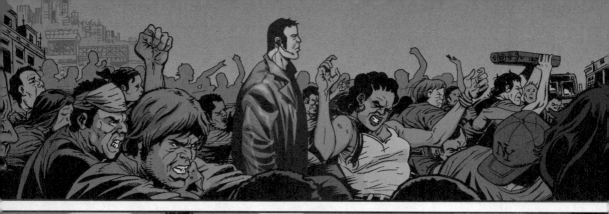

MARIBETH!

MARIBETH!

TONY...!

NO...

And now I remember.

I remember it all, every single moment, in excruciating detail.

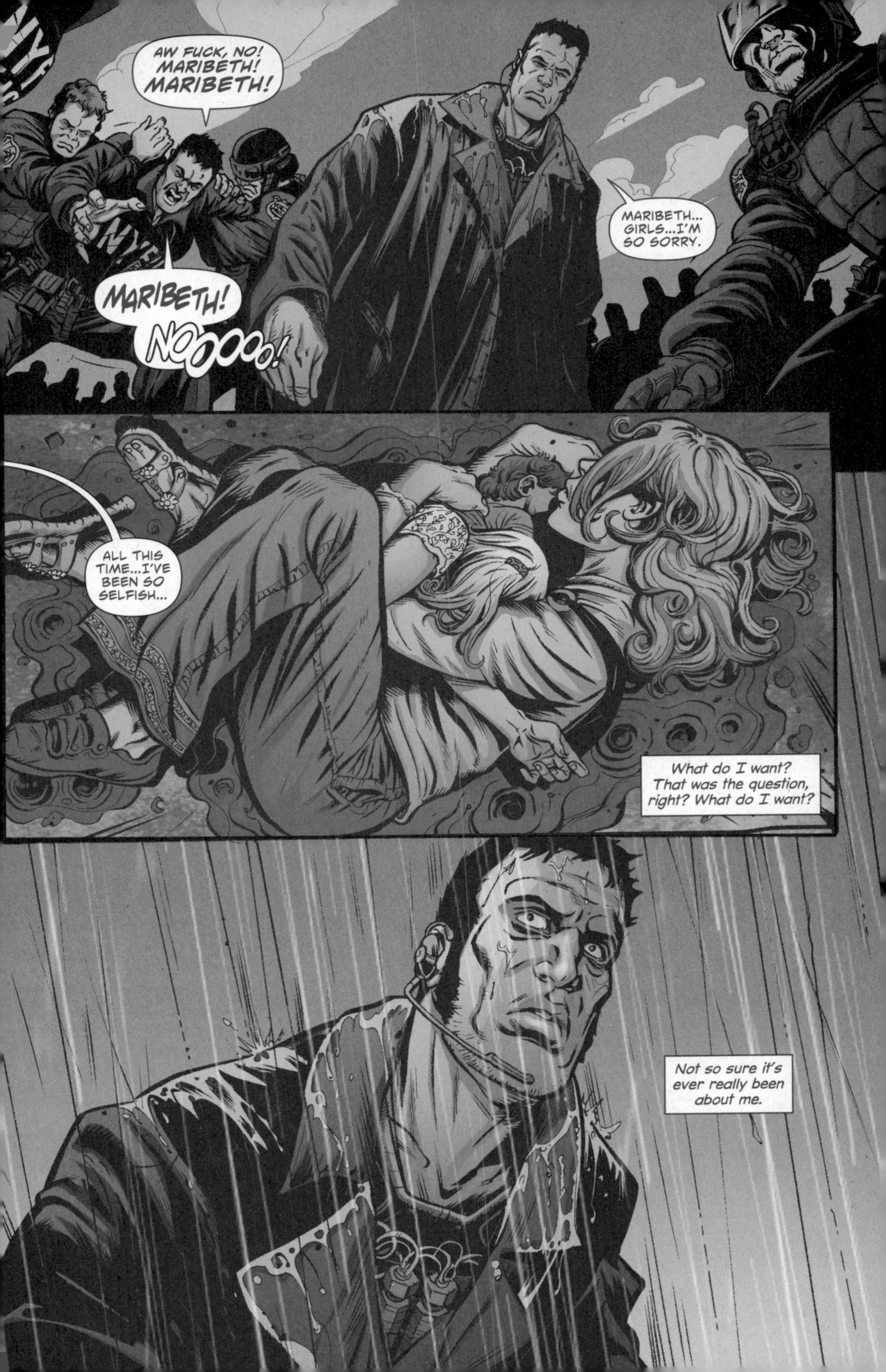

AW FUCK, NO! MARIBETH! MARIBETH!
MARIBETH! NOOOOO!
MARIBETH... GIRLS...I'M SO SORRY.
ALL THIS TIME...I'VE BEEN SO SELFISH...
What do I want? That was the question, right? What do I want?
Not so sure it's ever really been about me.

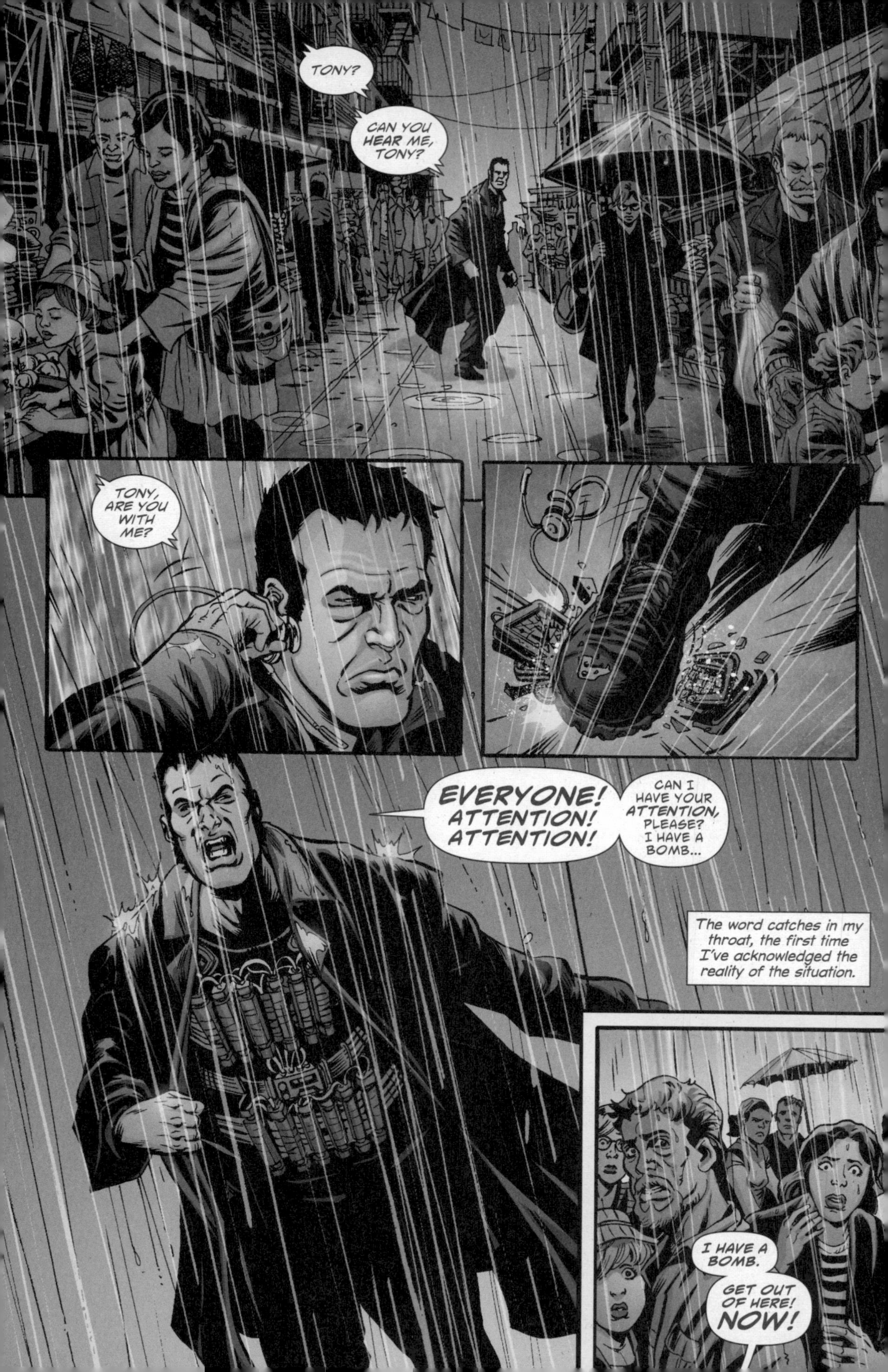
TONY?
CAN YOU HEAR ME, TONY?
TONY, ARE YOU WITH ME?
EVERYONE! ATTENTION! ATTENTION!
CAN I HAVE YOUR ATTENTION, PLEASE? I HAVE A BOMB...
The word catches in my throat, the first time I've acknowledged the reality of the situation.
I HAVE A BOMB.
GET OUT OF HERE! NOW!

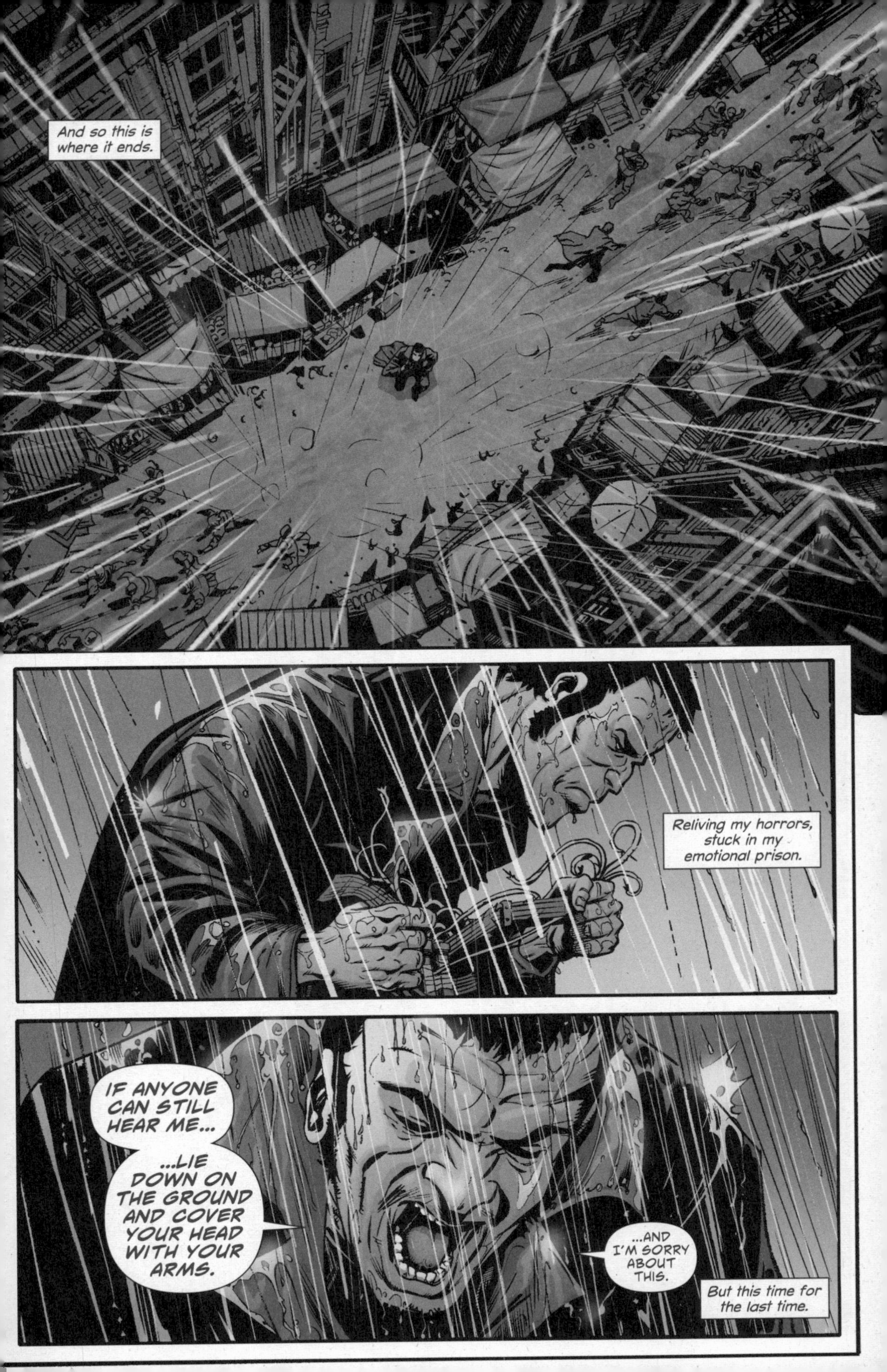
And so this is where it ends.
Reliving my horrors, stuck in my emotional prison.
IF ANYONE CAN STILL HEAR ME...
...LIE DOWN ON THE GROUND AND COVER YOUR HEAD WITH YOUR ARMS.
...AND I'M SORRY ABOUT THIS.
But this time for the last time.

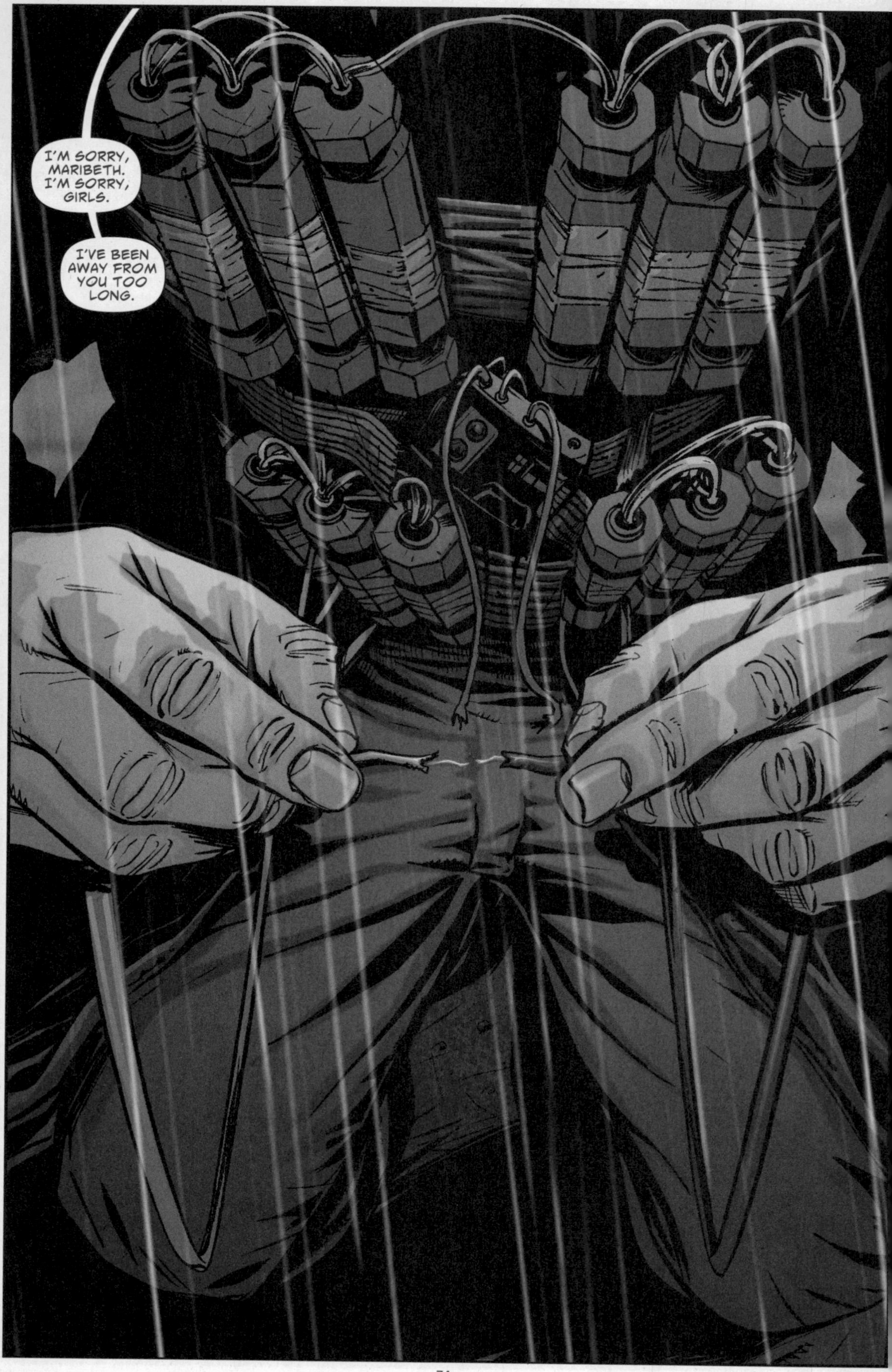
I'M SORRY, MARIBETH. I'M SORRY, GIRLS.
I'VE BEEN AWAY FROM YOU TOO LONG.

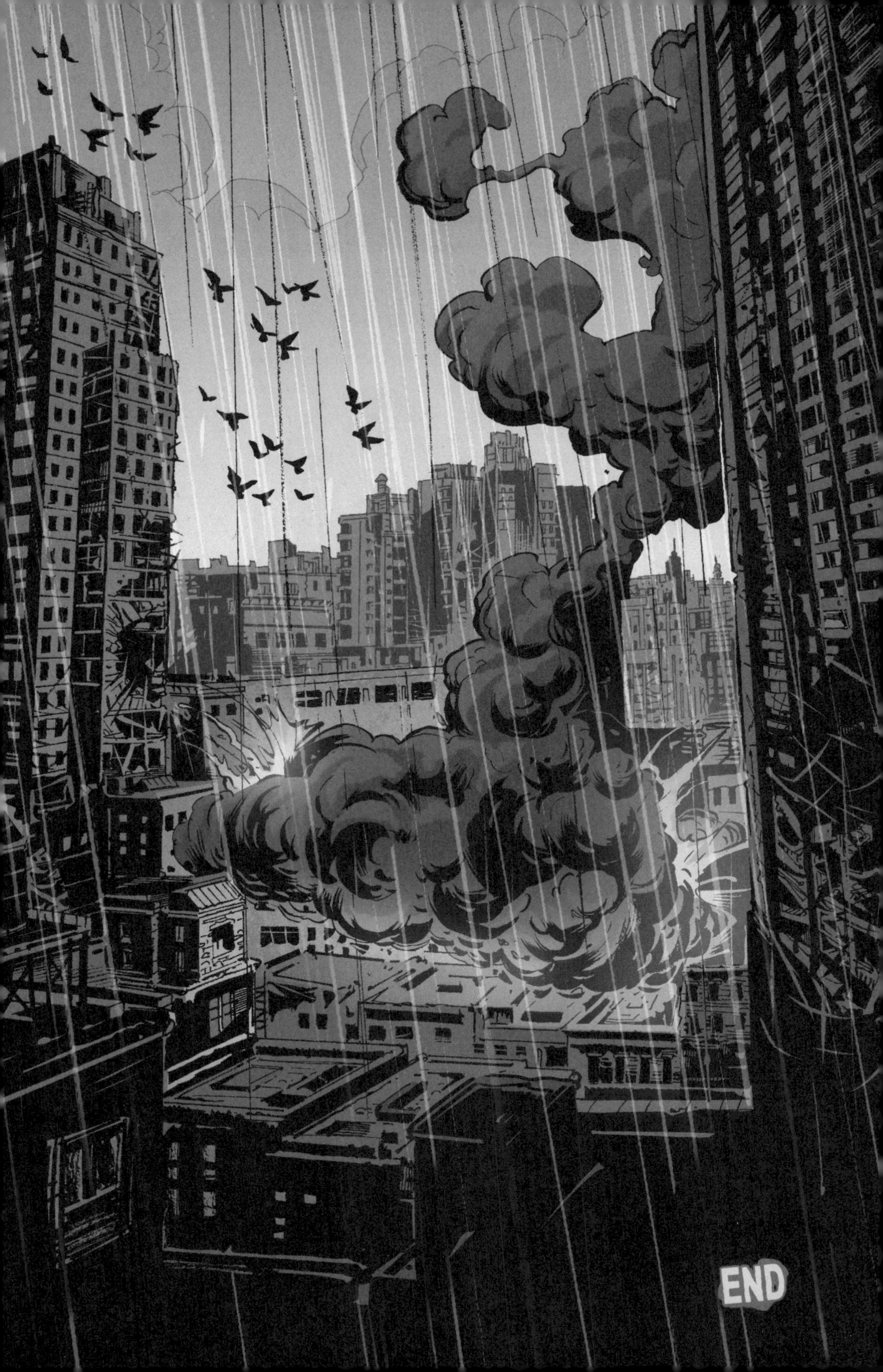
END

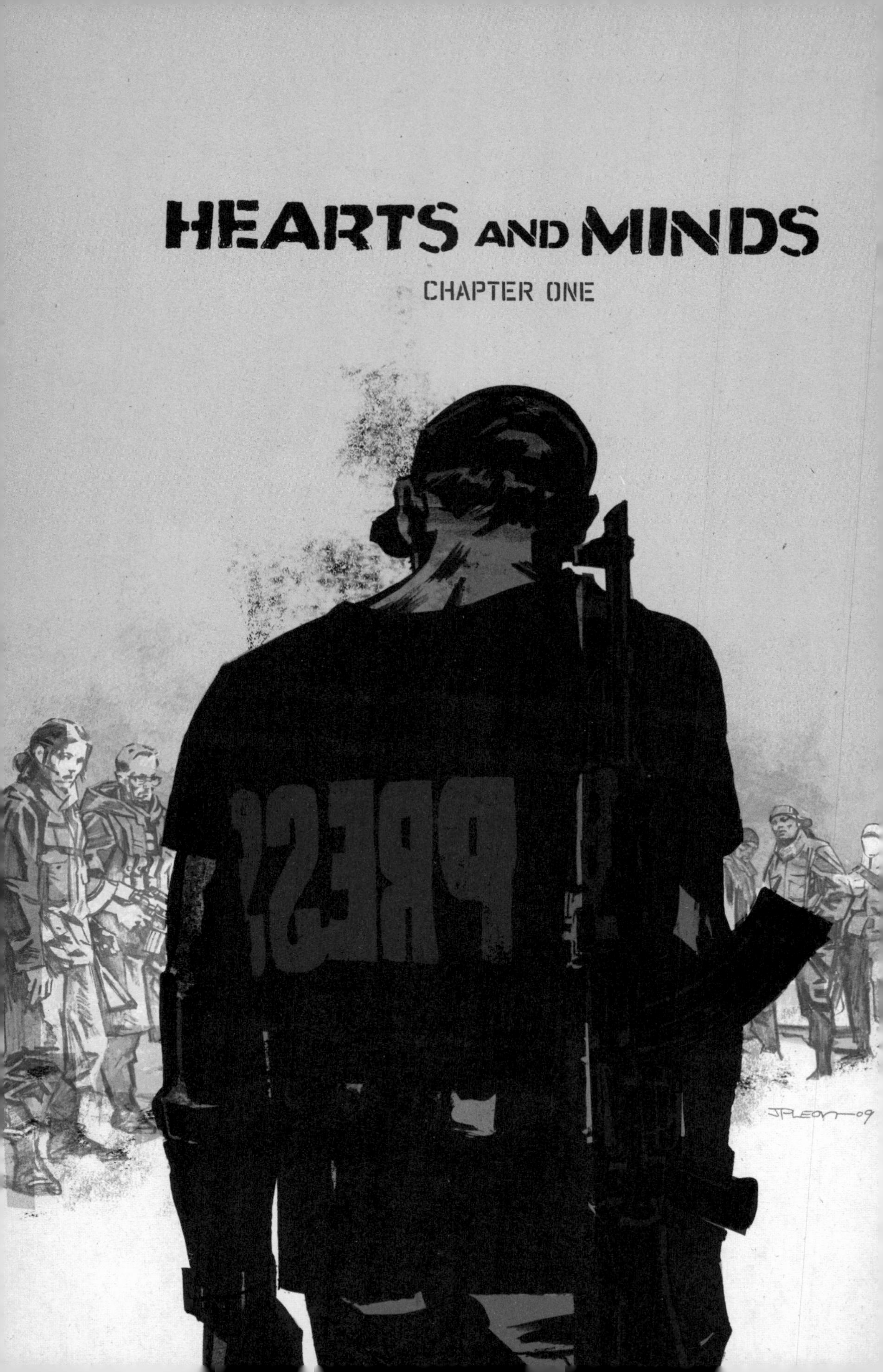
HEARTS AND MINDS
CHAPTER ONE

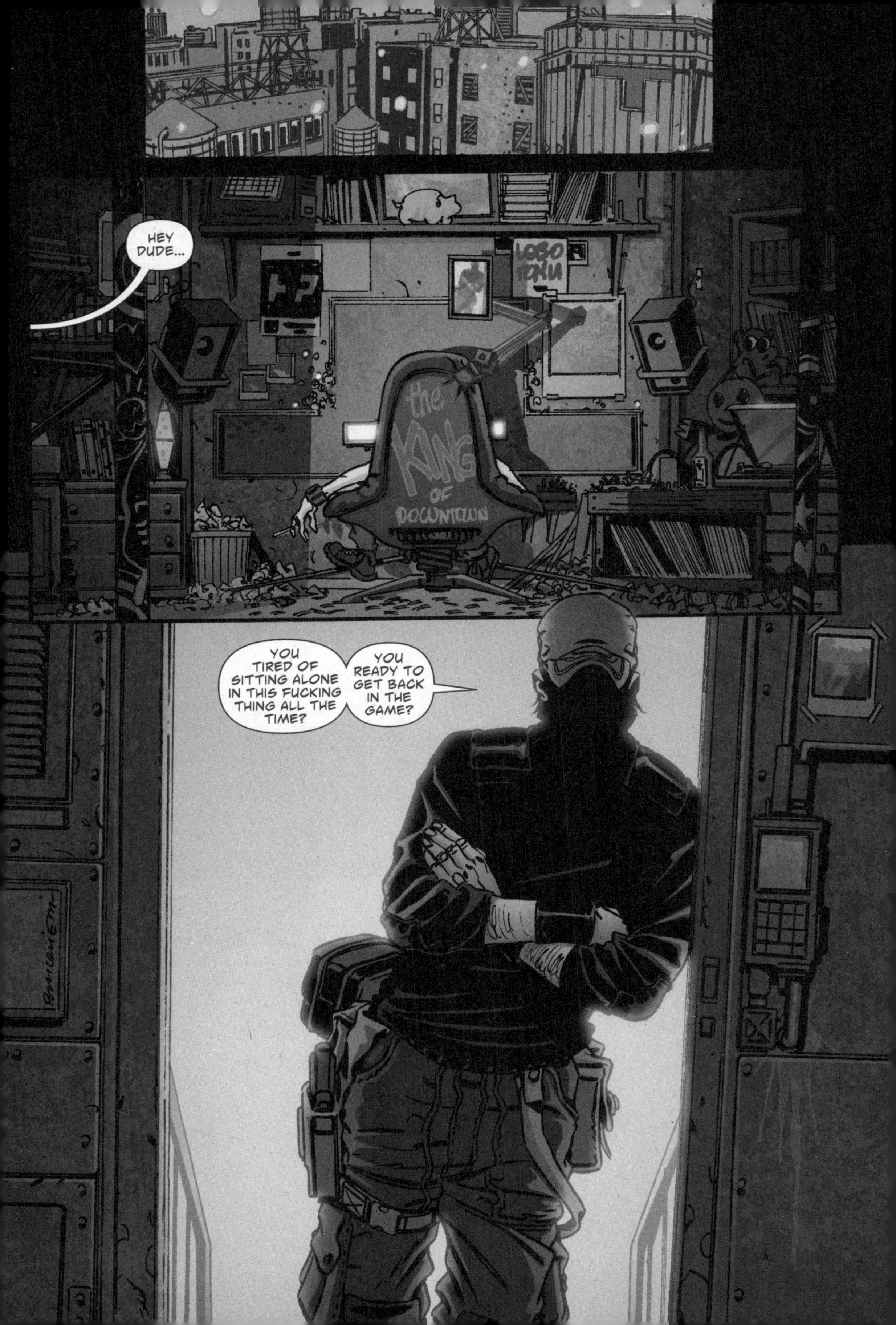
HEY DUDE...
LOBO TOKYO
the KING OF DOWNTOWN
YOU TIRED OF SITTING ALONE IN THIS FUCKING THING ALL THE TIME?
YOU READY TO GET BACK IN THE GAME?

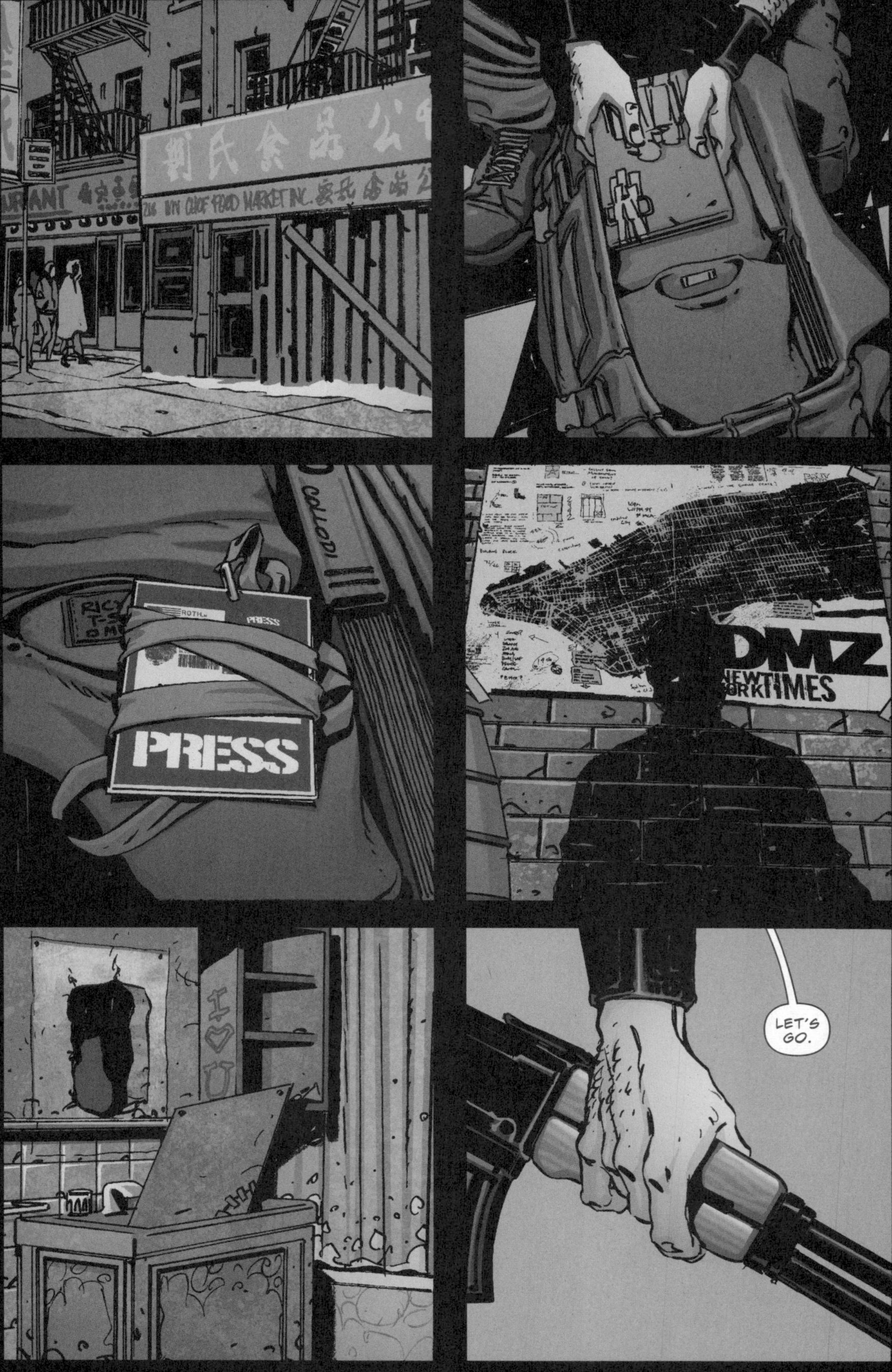

216 WN CHOF FOOD MARKET INC.
COLLODI
PRESS
PRESS
DMZ
NEWTIMES
LET'S GO.

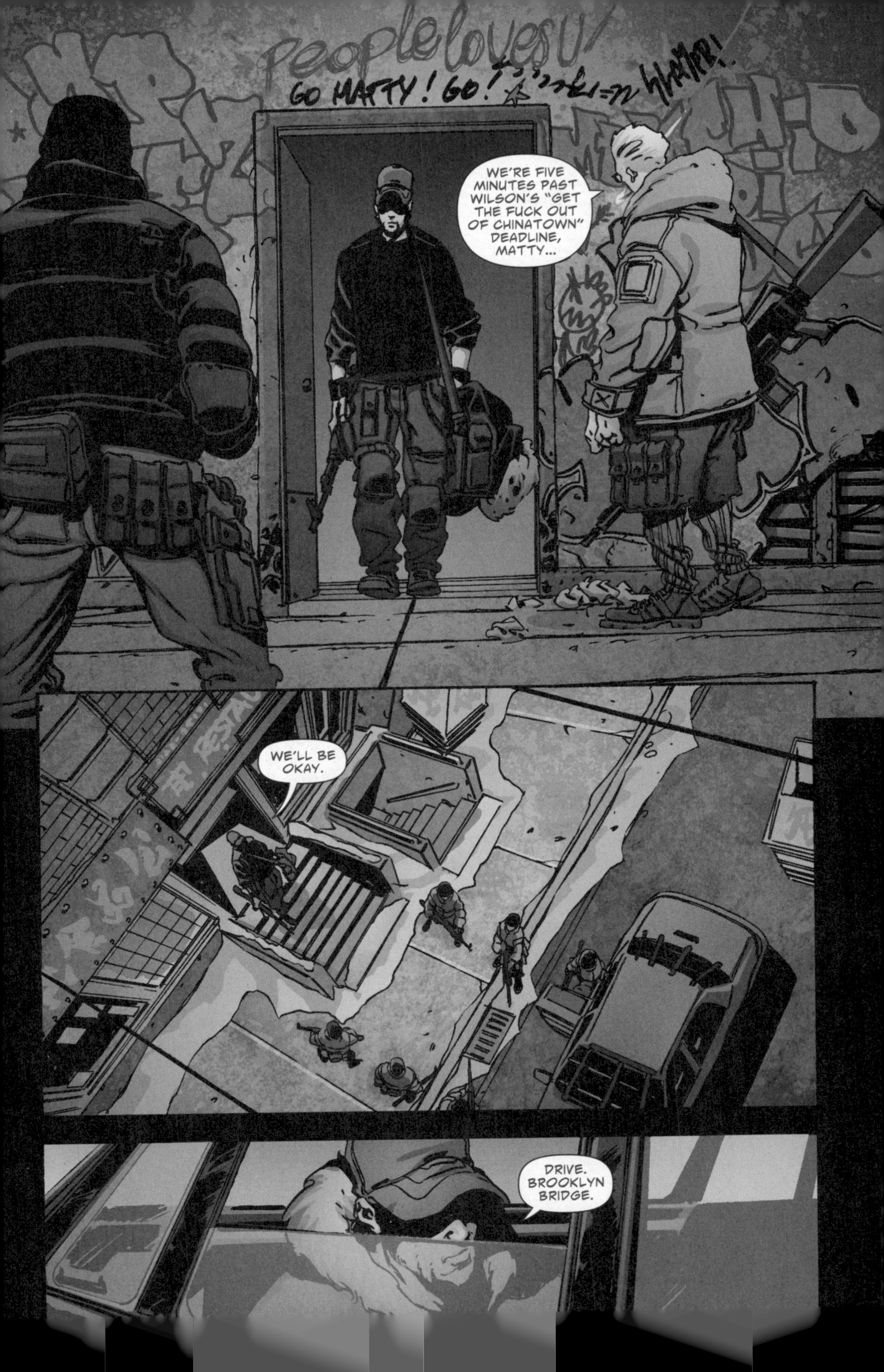
People loves U
GO MATTY! GO!
WE'RE FIVE MINUTES PAST WILSON'S "GET THE FUCK OUT OF CHINATOWN" DEADLINE, MATTY...
WE'LL BE OKAY.
DRIVE. BROOKLYN BRIDGE.

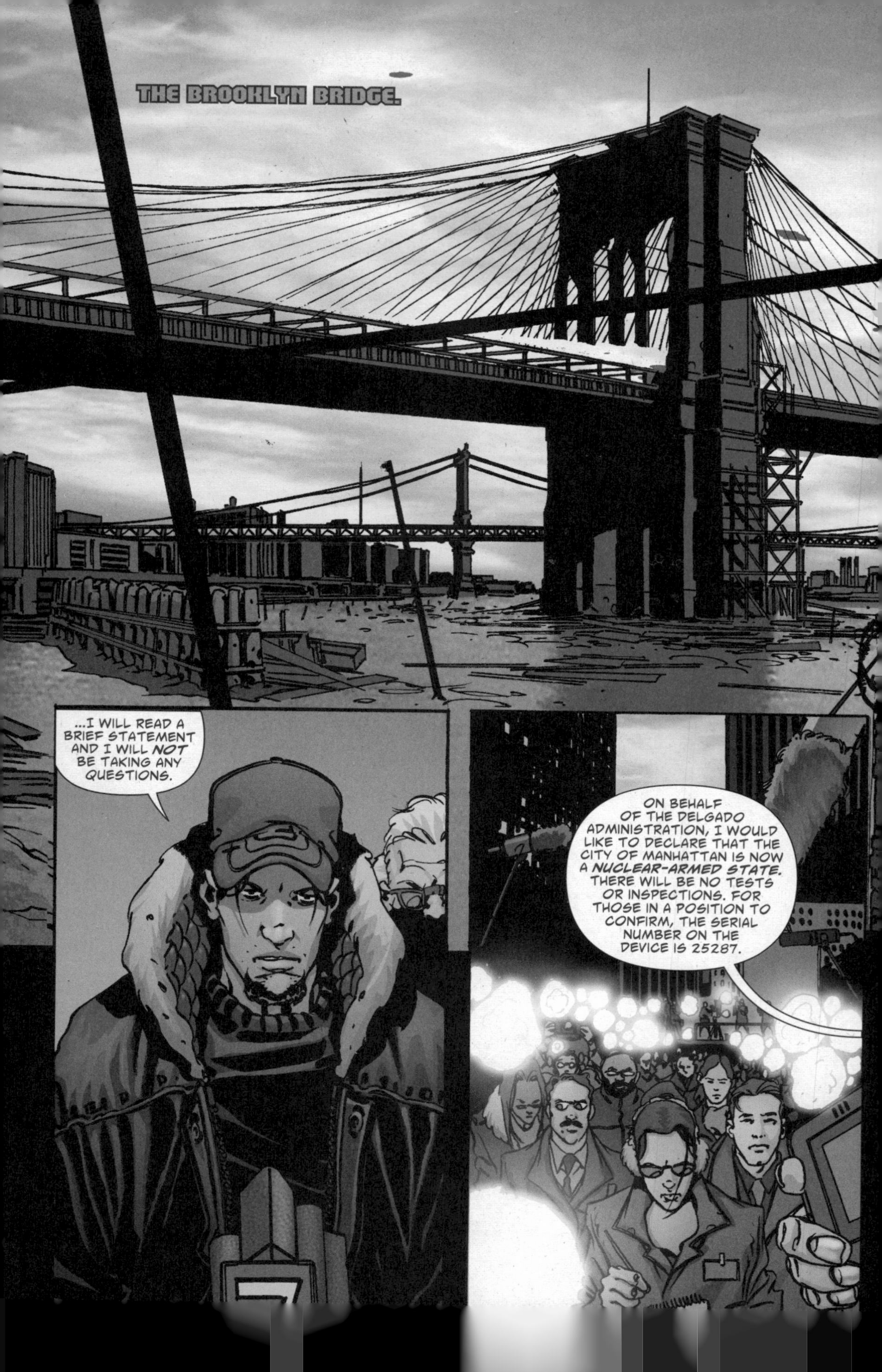
THE BROOKLYN BRIDGE.
...I WILL READ A BRIEF STATEMENT AND I WILL *NOT* BE TAKING ANY QUESTIONS.
ON BEHALF OF THE DELGADO ADMINISTRATION, I WOULD LIKE TO DECLARE THAT THE CITY OF MANHATTAN IS NOW A *NUCLEAR-ARMED STATE.* THERE WILL BE NO TESTS OR INSPECTIONS. FOR THOSE IN A POSITION TO CONFIRM, THE SERIAL NUMBER ON THE DEVICE IS 25287.

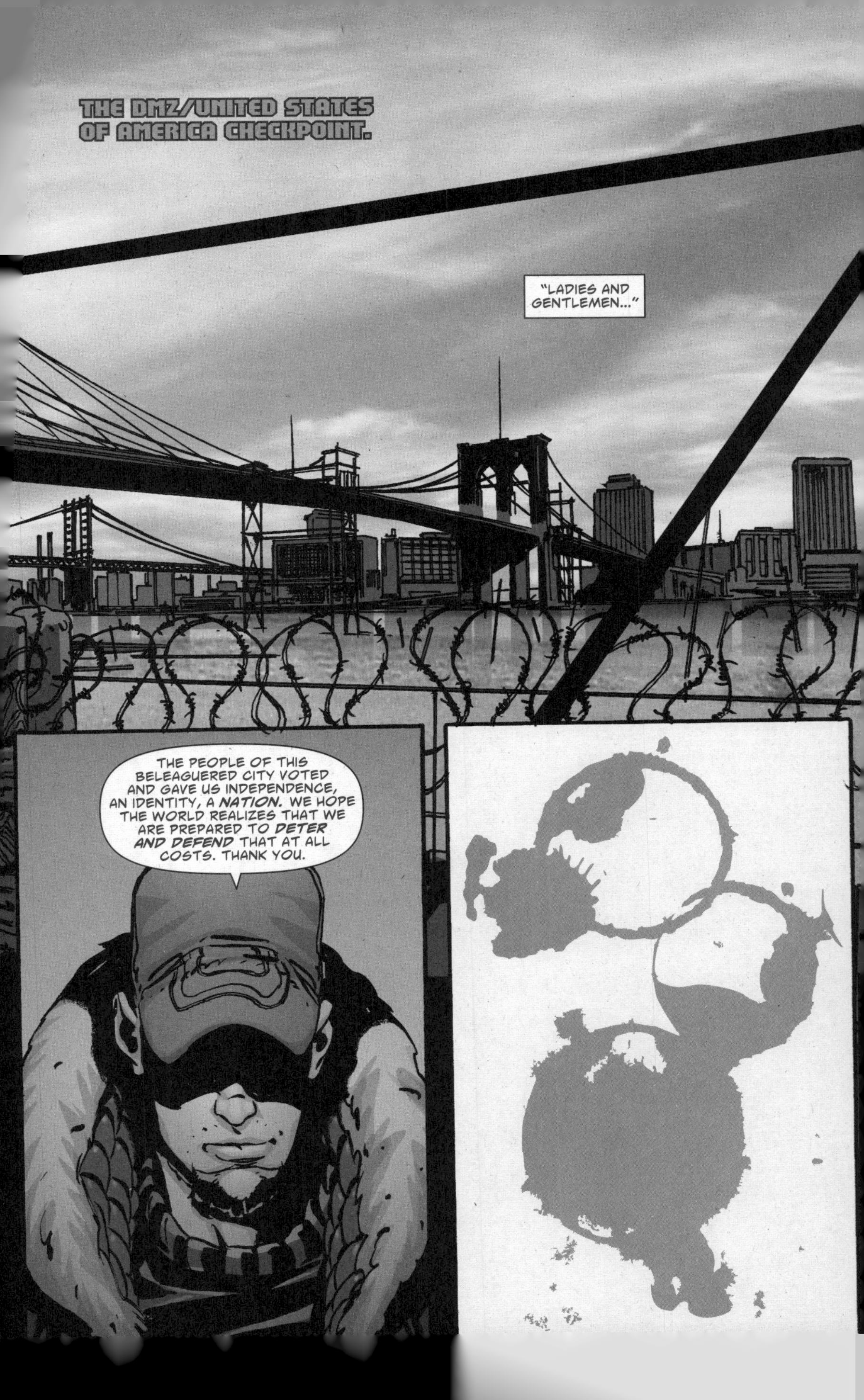
THE DMZ/UNITED STATES OF AMERICA CHECKPOINT.
"LADIES AND GENTLEMEN..."
THE PEOPLE OF THIS BELEAGUERED CITY VOTED AND GAVE US INDEPENDENCE, AN IDENTITY, A NATION. WE HOPE THE WORLD REALIZES THAT WE ARE PREPARED TO DETER AND DEFEND THAT AT ALL COSTS. THANK YOU.

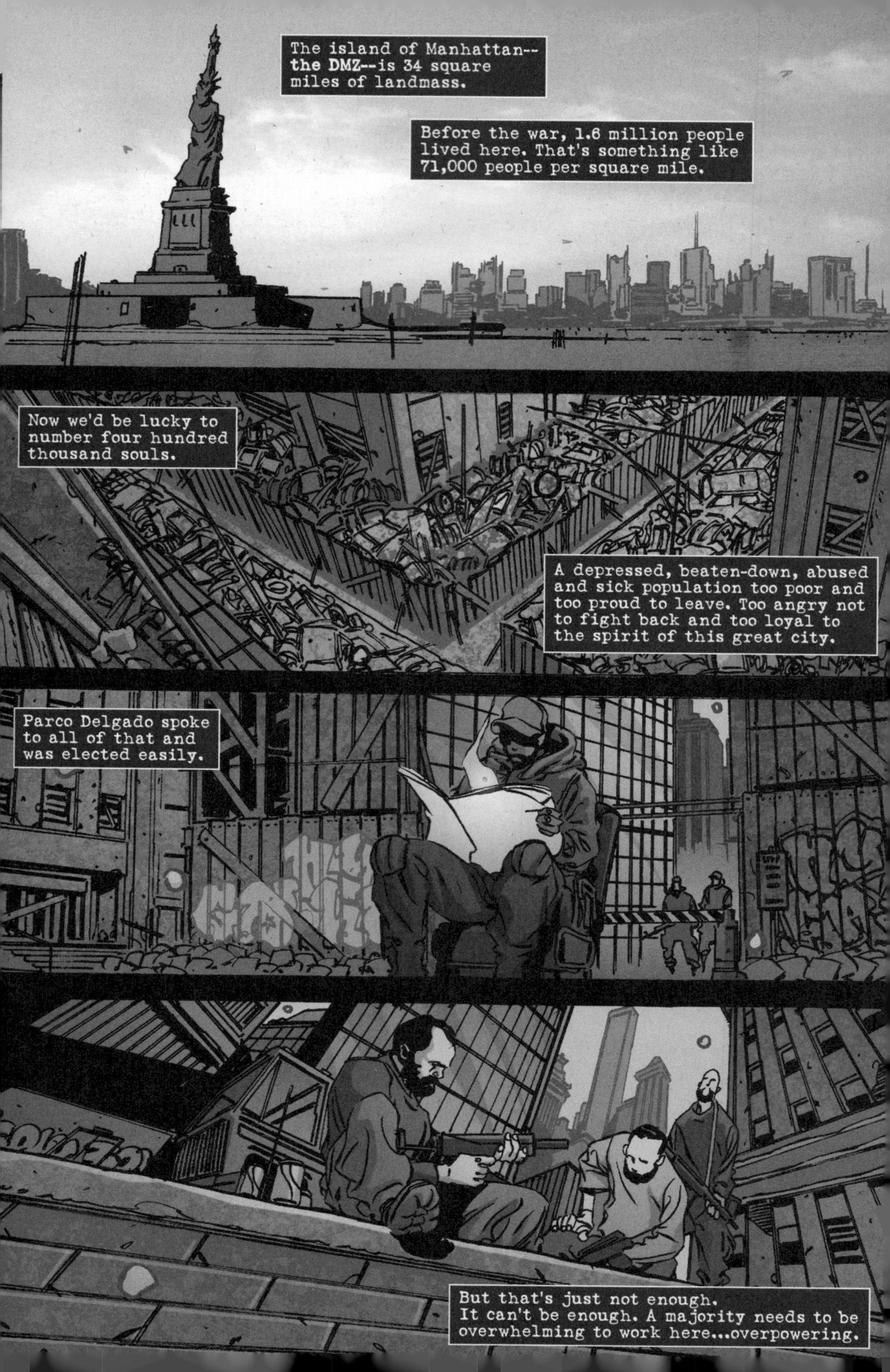
The island of Manhattan--the DMZ--is 34 square miles of landmass.
Before the war, 1.6 million people lived here. That's something like 71,000 people per square mile.
Now we'd be lucky to number four hundred thousand souls.
A depressed, beaten-down, abused and sick population too poor and too proud to leave. Too angry not to fight back and too loyal to the spirit of this great city.
Parco Delgado spoke to all of that and was elected easily.
But that's just not enough. It can't be enough. A majority needs to be overwhelming to work here...overpowering.

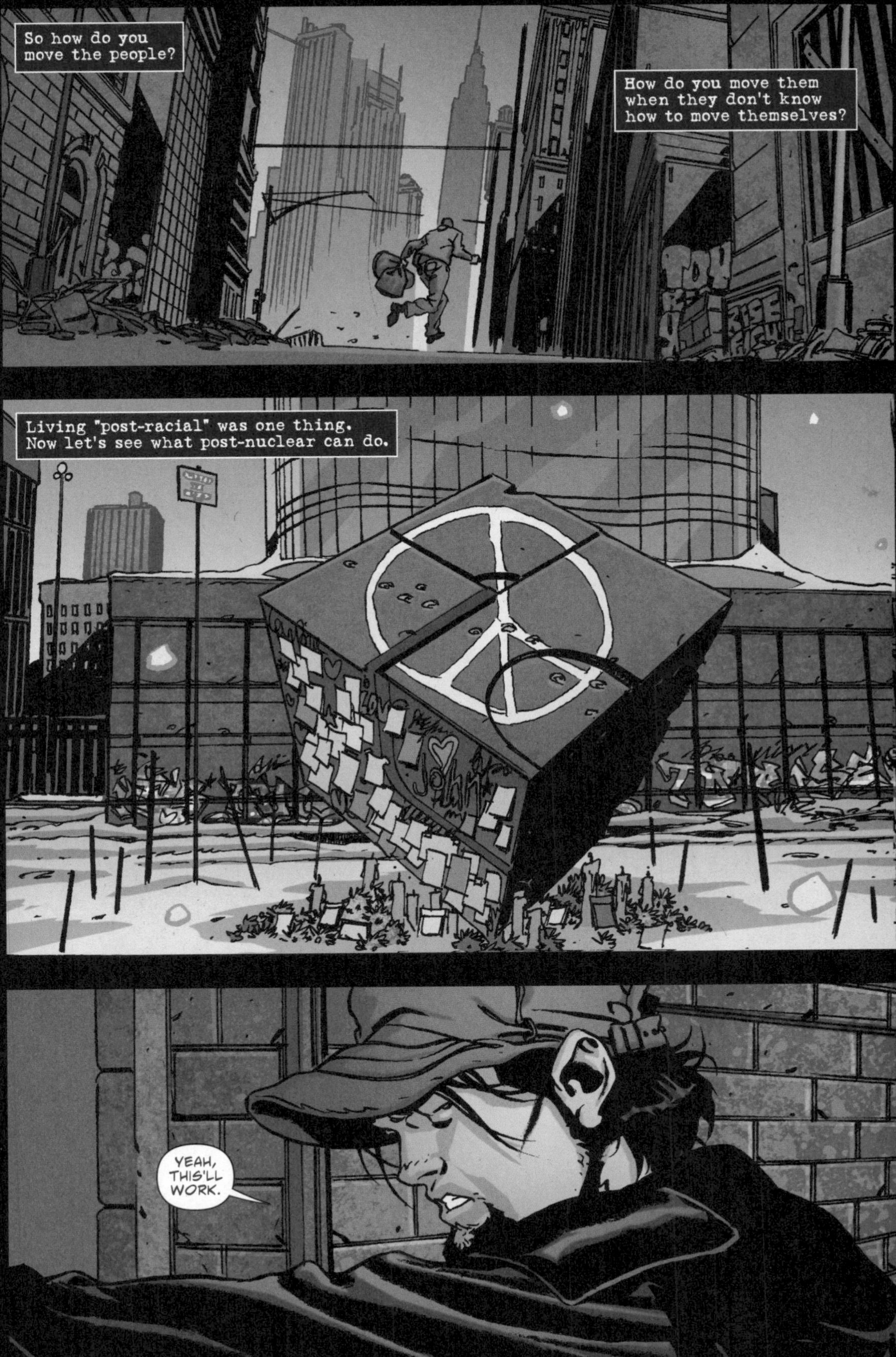
So how do you move the people?
How do you move them when they don't know how to move themselves?
Living "post-racial" was one thing. Now let's see what post-nuclear can do.
YEAH, THIS'LL WORK.

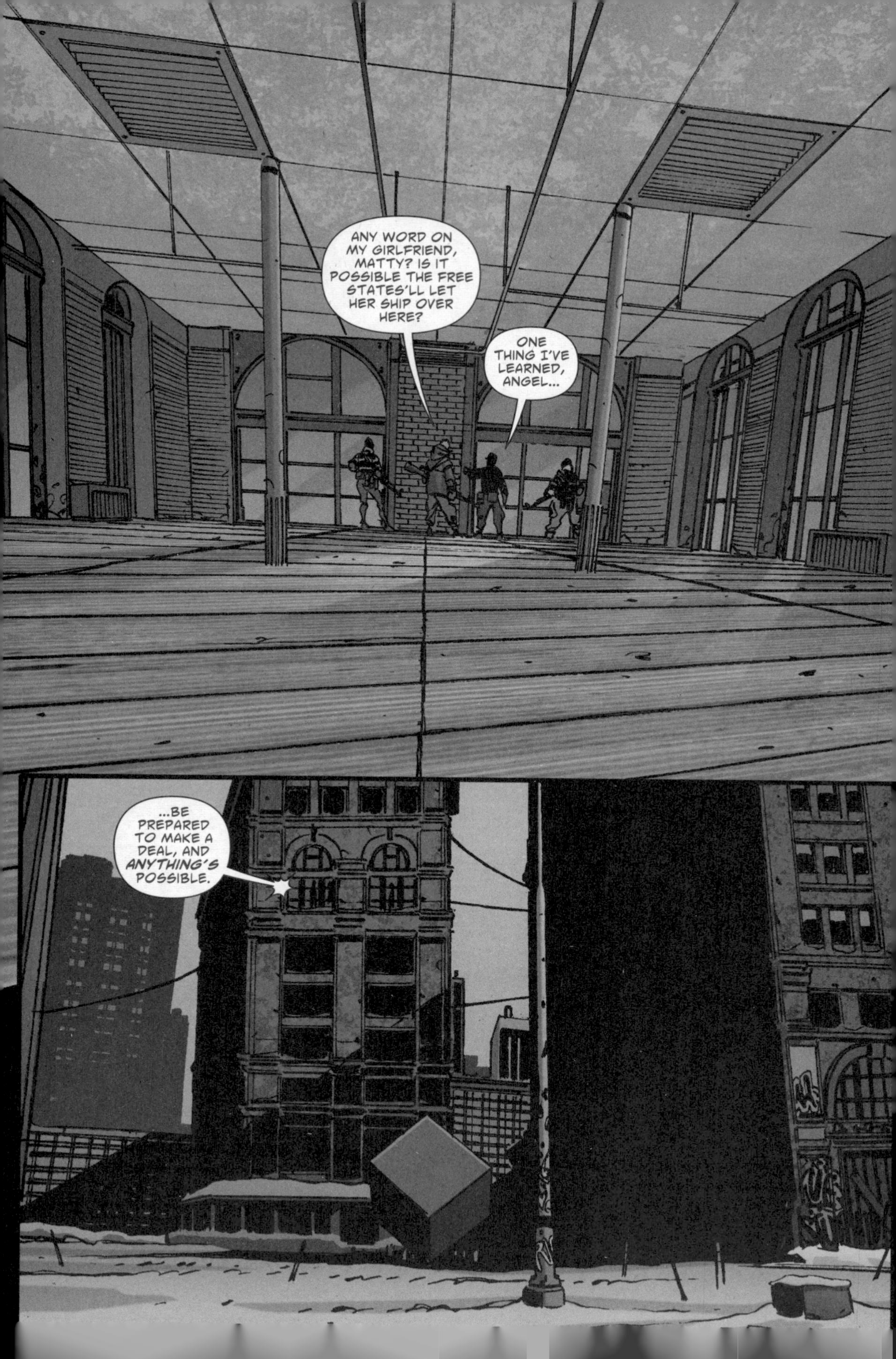
ANY WORD ON MY GIRLFRIEND, MATTY? IS IT POSSIBLE THE FREE STATES'LL LET HER SHIP OVER HERE?
ONE THING I'VE LEARNED, ANGEL...
...BE PREPARED TO MAKE A DEAL, AND *ANYTHING'S* POSSIBLE.

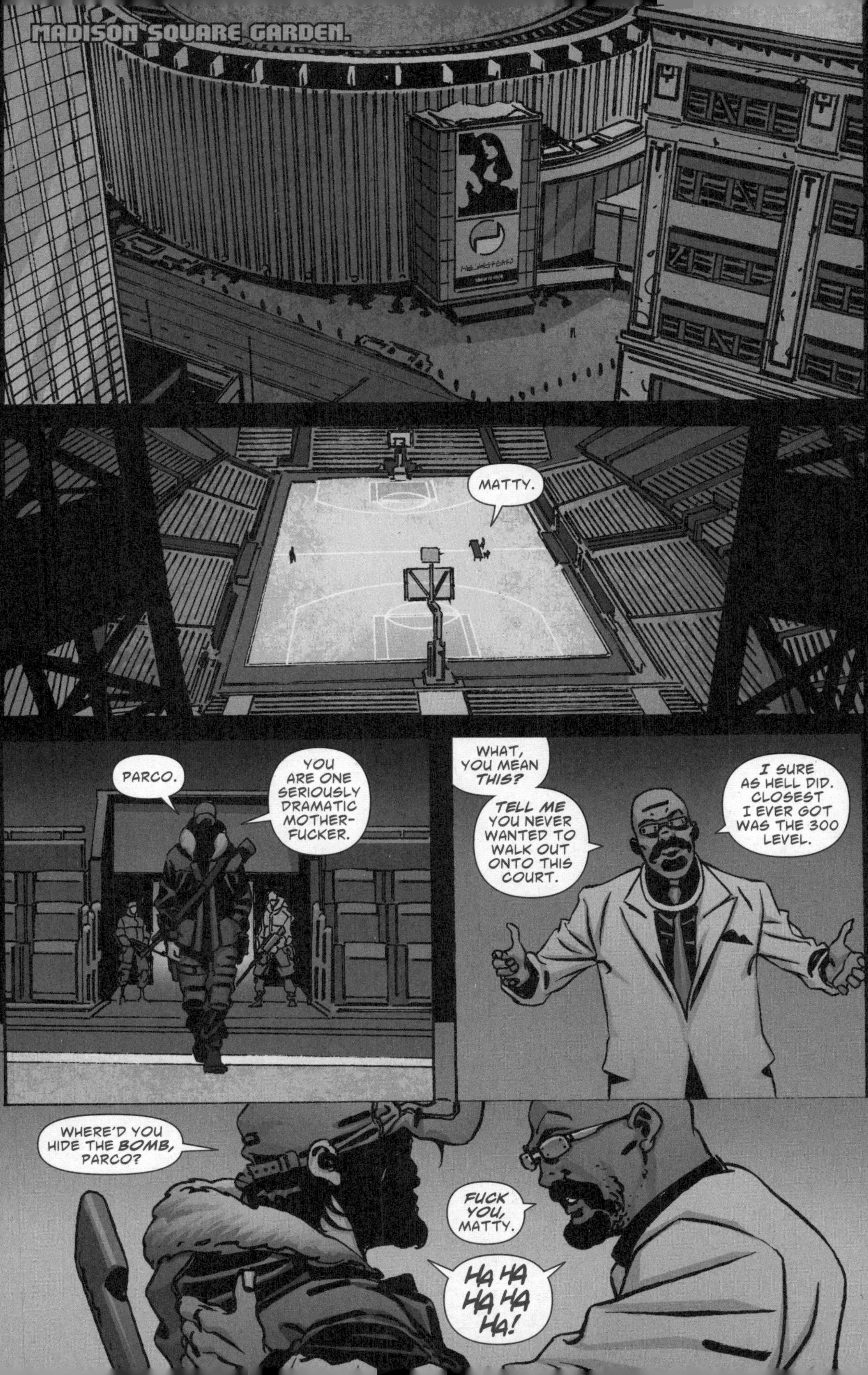
MADISON SQUARE GARDEN.
MATTY.
PARCO.
YOU ARE ONE SERIOUSLY DRAMATIC MOTHER-FUCKER.
WHAT, YOU MEAN THIS?
TELL ME YOU NEVER WANTED TO WALK OUT ONTO THIS COURT.
I SURE AS HELL DID. CLOSEST I EVER GOT WAS THE 300 LEVEL.
WHERE'D YOU HIDE THE BOMB, PARCO?
FUCK YOU, MATTY.
HA HA HA HA HA!

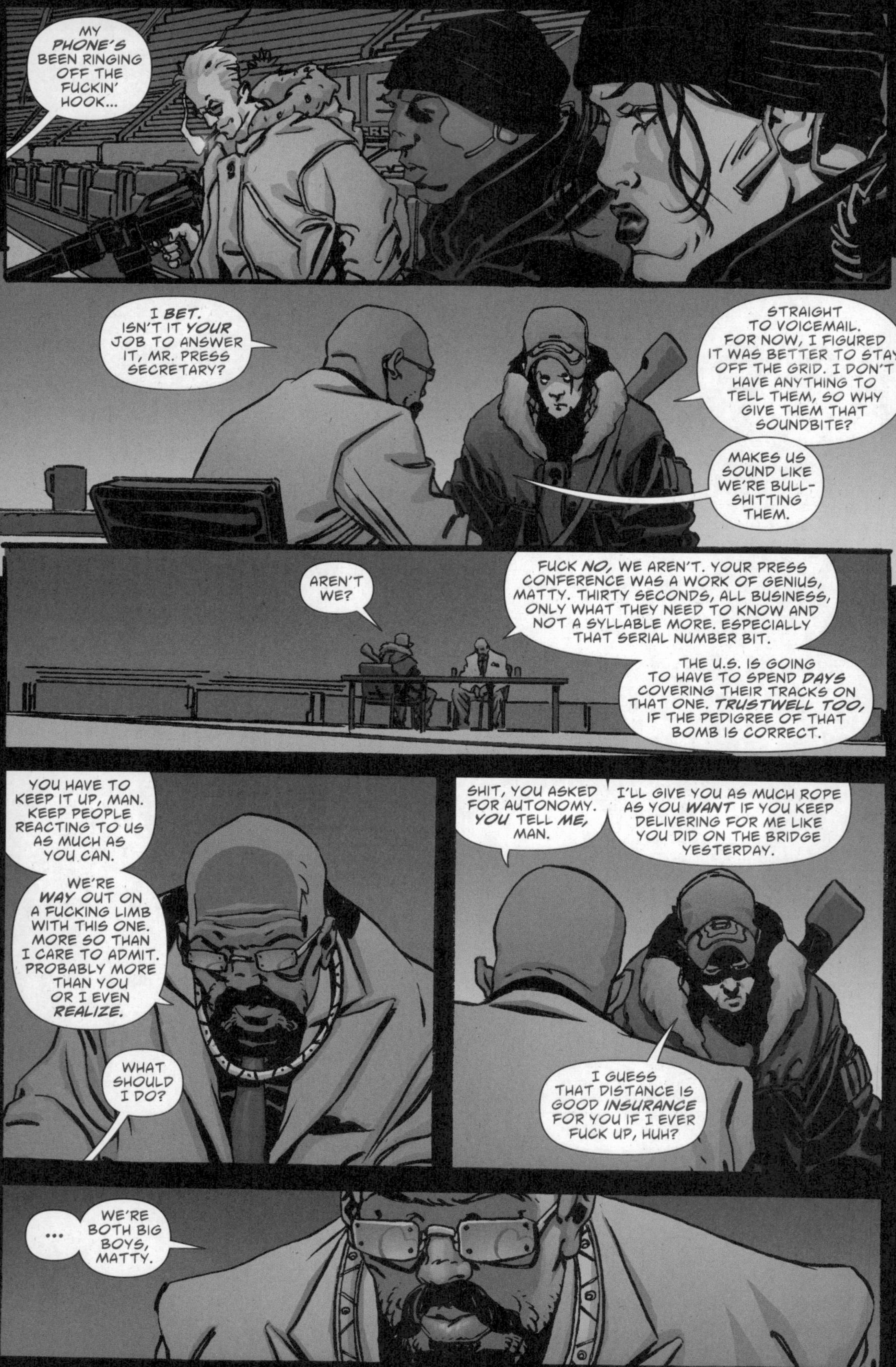
MY PHONE'S BEEN RINGING OFF THE FUCKIN' HOOK...
I BET. ISN'T IT YOUR JOB TO ANSWER IT, MR. PRESS SECRETARY?
STRAIGHT TO VOICEMAIL. FOR NOW, I FIGURED IT WAS BETTER TO STAY OFF THE GRID. I DON'T HAVE ANYTHING TO TELL THEM, SO WHY GIVE THEM THAT SOUNDBITE?
MAKES US SOUND LIKE WE'RE BULL-SHITTING THEM.
AREN'T WE?
FUCK NO, WE AREN'T. YOUR PRESS CONFERENCE WAS A WORK OF GENIUS, MATTY. THIRTY SECONDS, ALL BUSINESS, ONLY WHAT THEY NEED TO KNOW AND NOT A SYLLABLE MORE. ESPECIALLY THAT SERIAL NUMBER BIT.
THE U.S. IS GOING TO HAVE TO SPEND DAYS COVERING THEIR TRACKS ON THAT ONE. TRUSTWELL TOO, IF THE PEDIGREE OF THAT BOMB IS CORRECT.
YOU HAVE TO KEEP IT UP, MAN. KEEP PEOPLE REACTING TO US AS MUCH AS YOU CAN.
WE'RE WAY OUT ON A FUCKING LIMB WITH THIS ONE. MORE SO THAN I CARE TO ADMIT. PROBABLY MORE THAN YOU OR I EVEN REALIZE.
WHAT SHOULD I DO?
SHIT, YOU ASKED FOR AUTONOMY. YOU TELL ME, MAN.
I'LL GIVE YOU AS MUCH ROPE AS YOU WANT IF YOU KEEP DELIVERING FOR ME LIKE YOU DID ON THE BRIDGE YESTERDAY.
I GUESS THAT DISTANCE IS GOOD INSURANCE FOR YOU IF I EVER FUCK UP, HUH?
...
WE'RE BOTH BIG BOYS, MATTY.

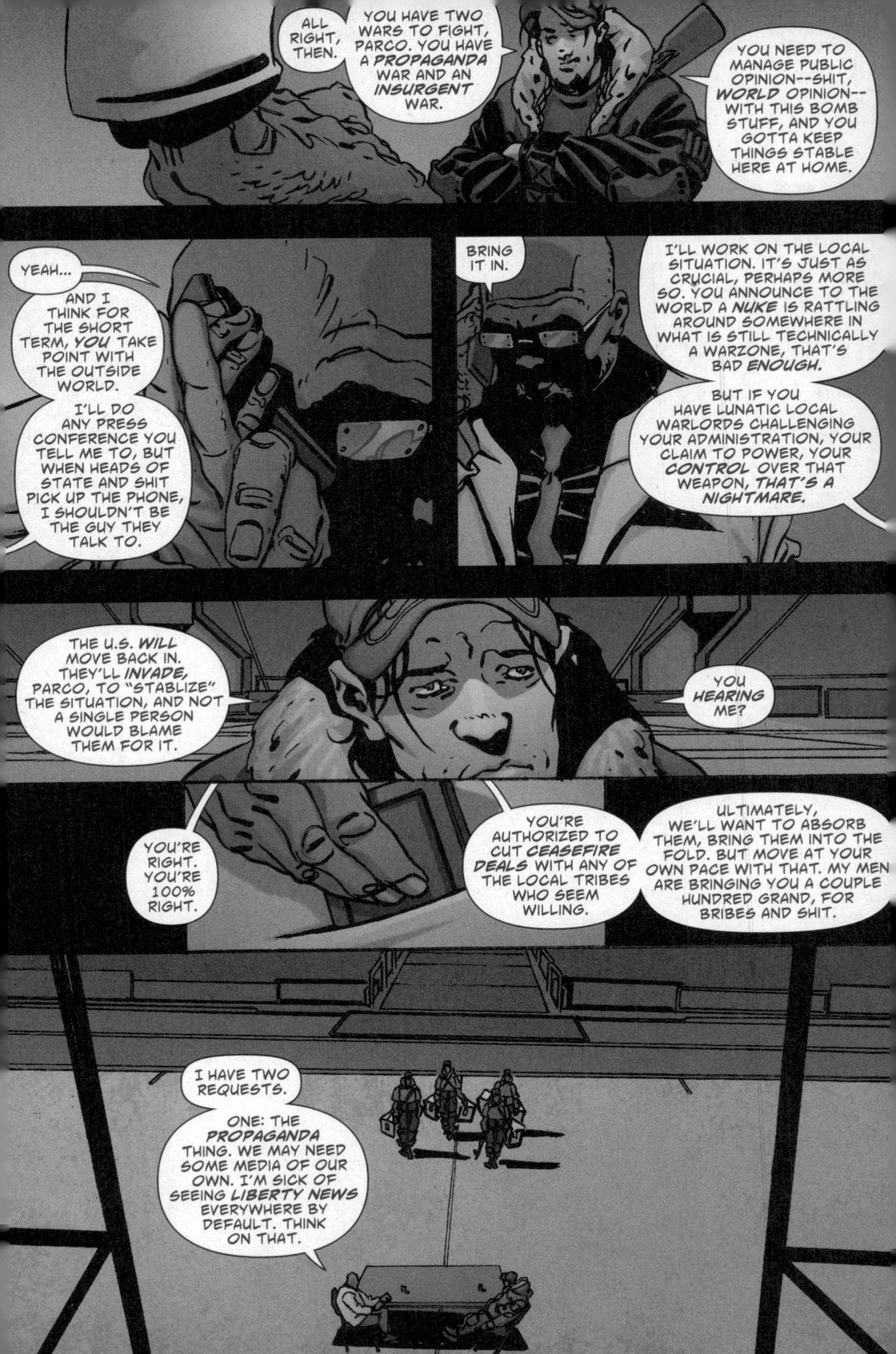
ALL RIGHT, THEN.
YOU HAVE TWO WARS TO FIGHT, PARCO. YOU HAVE A PROPAGANDA WAR AND AN INSURGENT WAR.
YOU NEED TO MANAGE PUBLIC OPINION--SHIT, WORLD OPINION--WITH THIS BOMB STUFF, AND YOU GOTTA KEEP THINGS STABLE HERE AT HOME.
YEAH...
AND I THINK FOR THE SHORT TERM, YOU TAKE POINT WITH THE OUTSIDE WORLD.
I'LL DO ANY PRESS CONFERENCE YOU TELL ME TO, BUT WHEN HEADS OF STATE AND SHIT PICK UP THE PHONE, I SHOULDN'T BE THE GUY THEY TALK TO.
BRING IT IN.
I'LL WORK ON THE LOCAL SITUATION. IT'S JUST AS CRUCIAL, PERHAPS MORE SO. YOU ANNOUNCE TO THE WORLD A NUKE IS RATTLING AROUND SOMEWHERE IN WHAT IS STILL TECHNICALLY A WARZONE, THAT'S BAD ENOUGH.
BUT IF YOU HAVE LUNATIC LOCAL WARLORDS CHALLENGING YOUR ADMINISTRATION, YOUR CLAIM TO POWER, YOUR CONTROL OVER THAT WEAPON, THAT'S A NIGHTMARE.
THE U.S. WILL MOVE BACK IN. THEY'LL INVADE, PARCO, TO "STABLIZE" THE SITUATION, AND NOT A SINGLE PERSON WOULD BLAME THEM FOR IT.
YOU HEARING ME?
YOU'RE RIGHT. YOU'RE 100% RIGHT.
YOU'RE AUTHORIZED TO CUT CEASEFIRE DEALS WITH ANY OF THE LOCAL TRIBES WHO SEEM WILLING.
ULTIMATELY, WE'LL WANT TO ABSORB THEM, BRING THEM INTO THE FOLD. BUT MOVE AT YOUR OWN PACE WITH THAT. MY MEN ARE BRINGING YOU A COUPLE HUNDRED GRAND, FOR BRIBES AND SHIT.
I HAVE TWO REQUESTS.
ONE: THE PROPAGANDA THING. WE MAY NEED SOME MEDIA OF OUR OWN. I'M SICK OF SEEING LIBERTY NEWS EVERYWHERE BY DEFAULT. THINK ON THAT.

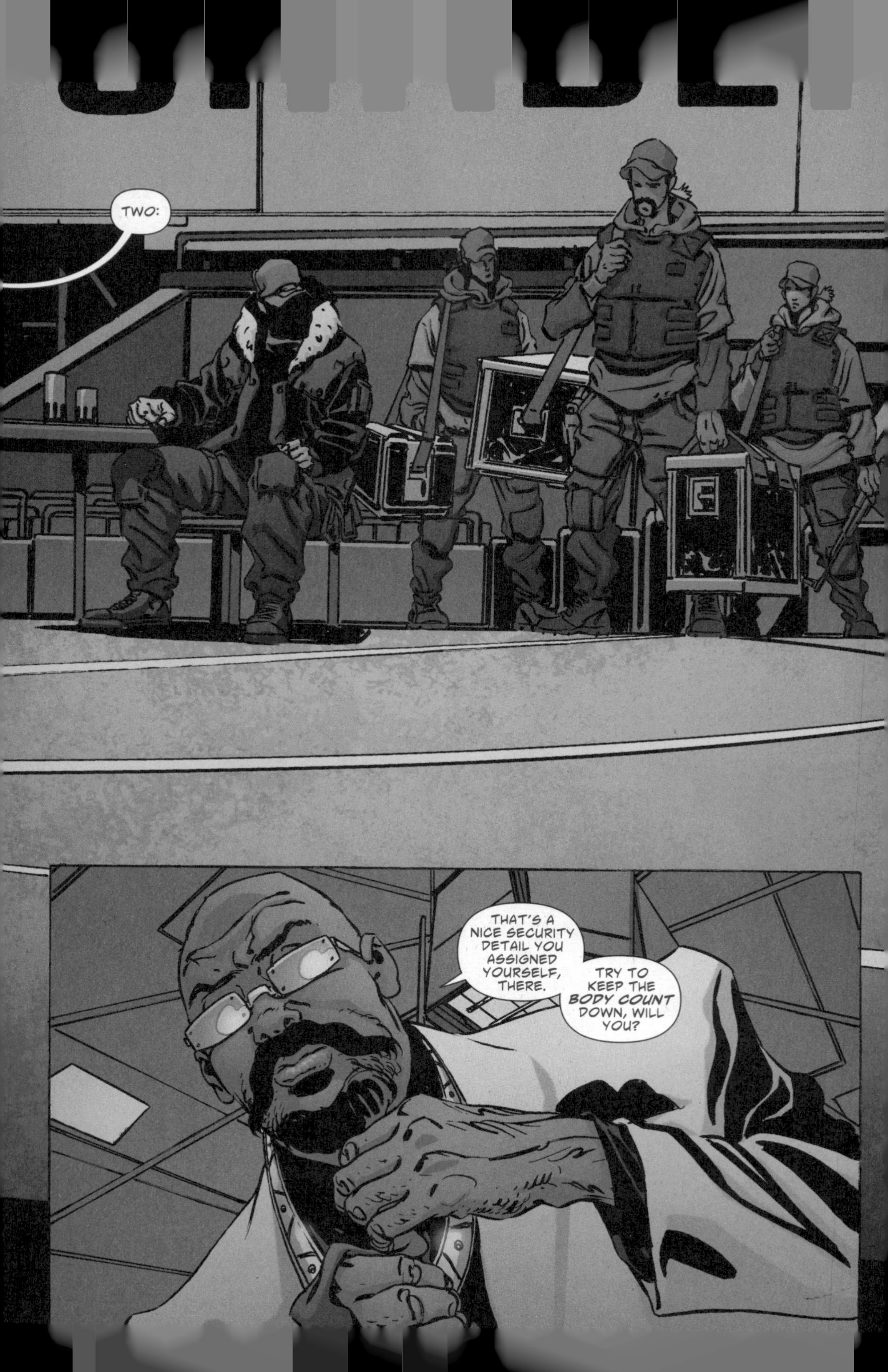
TWO:
THAT'S A NICE SECURITY DETAIL YOU ASSIGNED YOURSELF, THERE.
TRY TO KEEP THE BODY COUNT DOWN, WILL YOU?

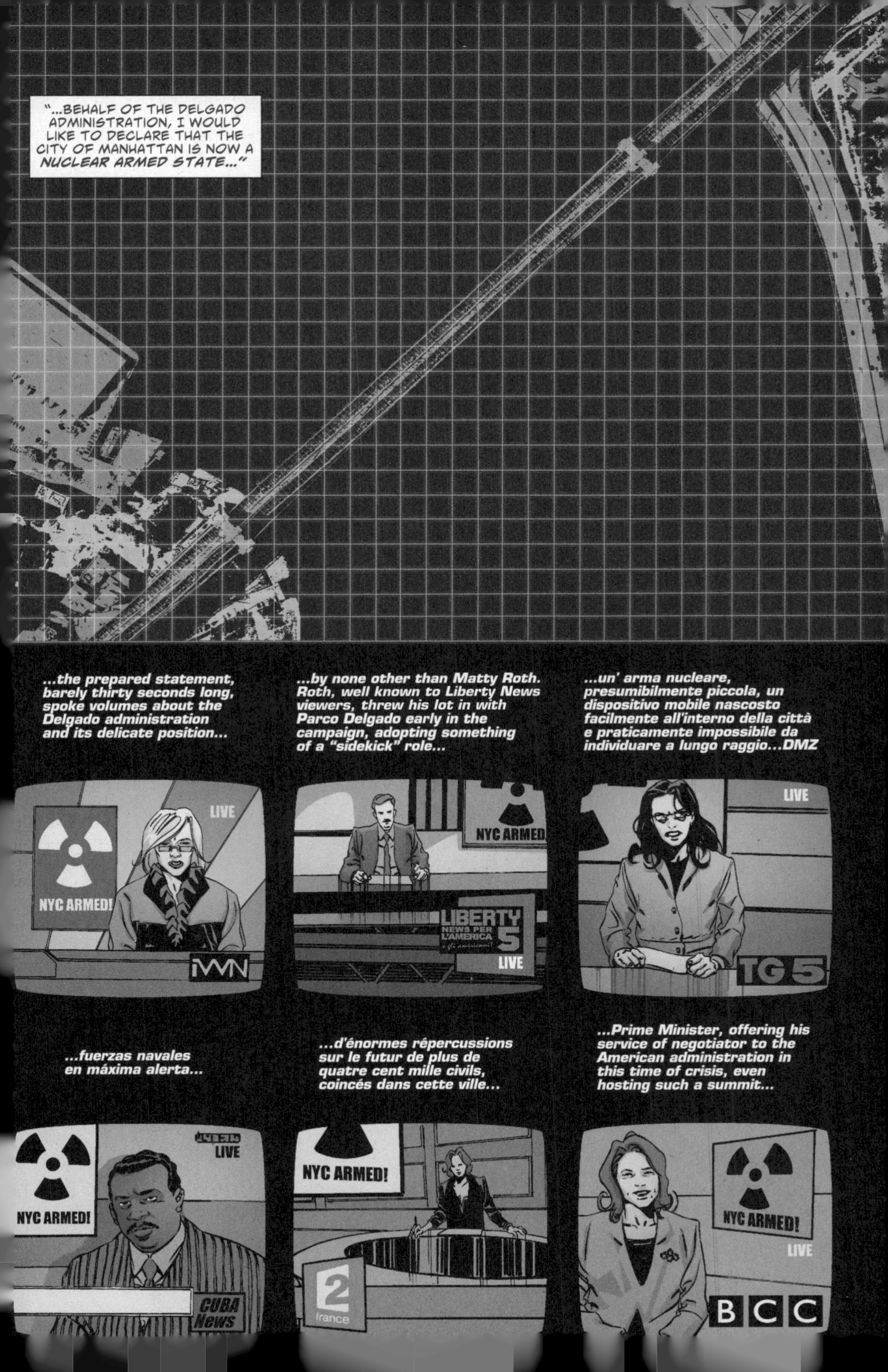

"...BEHALF OF THE DELGADO ADMINISTRATION, I WOULD LIKE TO DECLARE THAT THE CITY OF MANHATTAN IS NOW A *NUCLEAR ARMED STATE...*"
...the prepared statement, barely thirty seconds long, spoke volumes about the Delgado administration and its delicate position...
NYC ARMED!
LIVE
...by none other than Matty Roth. Roth, well known to Liberty News viewers, threw his lot in with Parco Delgado early in the campaign, adopting something of a "sidekick" role...
NYC ARMED
LIBERTY NEWS PER L'AMERICA 5
LIVE
...un' arma nucleare, presumibilmente piccola, un dispositivo mobile nascosto facilmente all'interno della città e praticamente impossibile da individuare a lungo raggio...DMZ
LIVE
TG 5
...fuerzas navales en máxima alerta...
LIVE
NYC ARMED!
CUBA News
...d'énormes répercussions sur le futur de plus de quatre cent mille civils, coincés dans cette ville...
NYC ARMED!
2 france
...Prime Minister, offering his service of negotiator to the American administration in this time of crisis, even hosting such a summit...
NYC ARMED!
LIVE
BCC

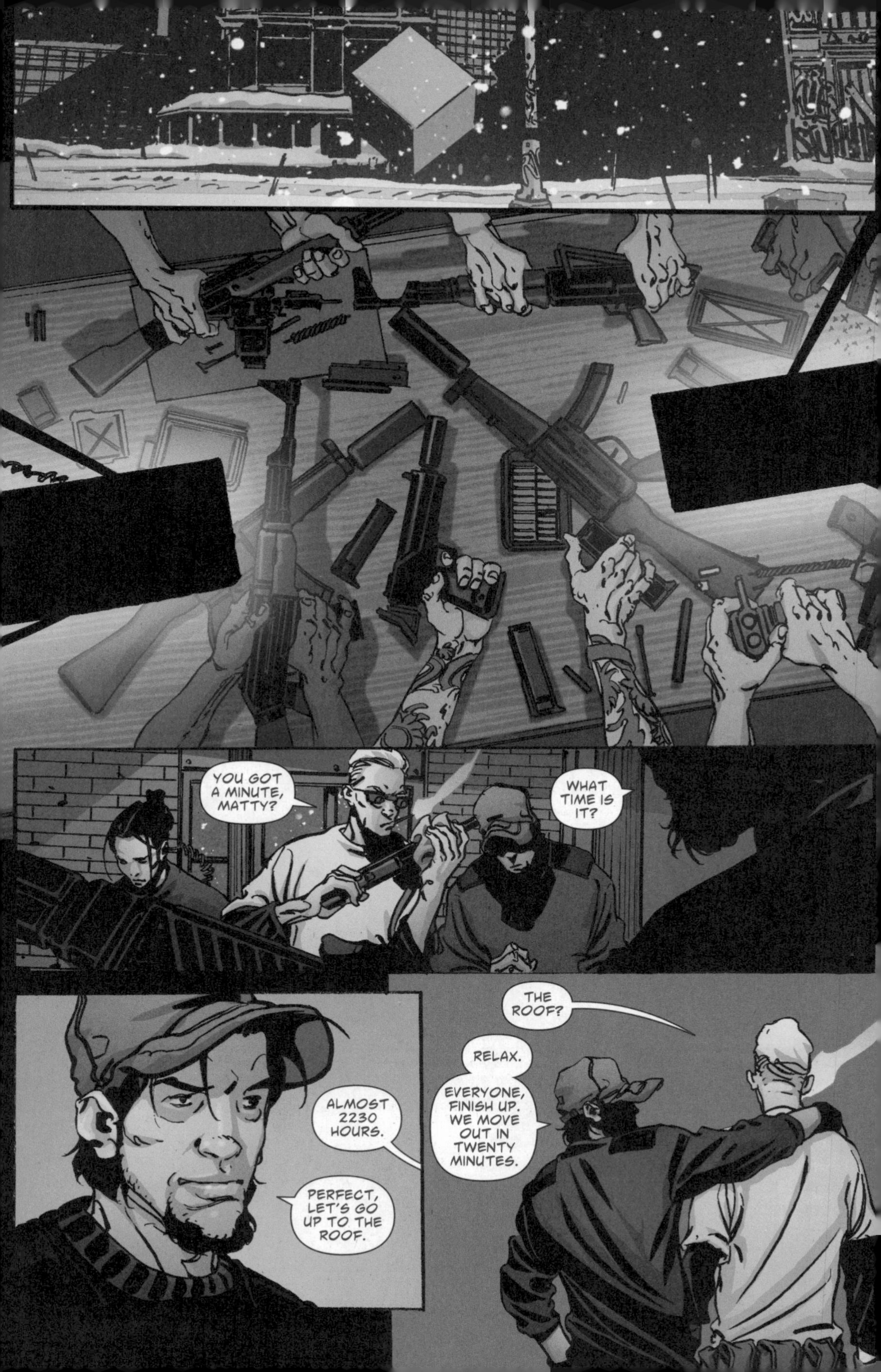
YOU GOT A MINUTE, MATTY?
WHAT TIME IS IT?
ALMOST 2230 HOURS.
PERFECT, LET'S GO UP TO THE ROOF.
THE ROOF?
RELAX.
EVERYONE, FINISH UP. WE MOVE OUT IN TWENTY MINUTES.

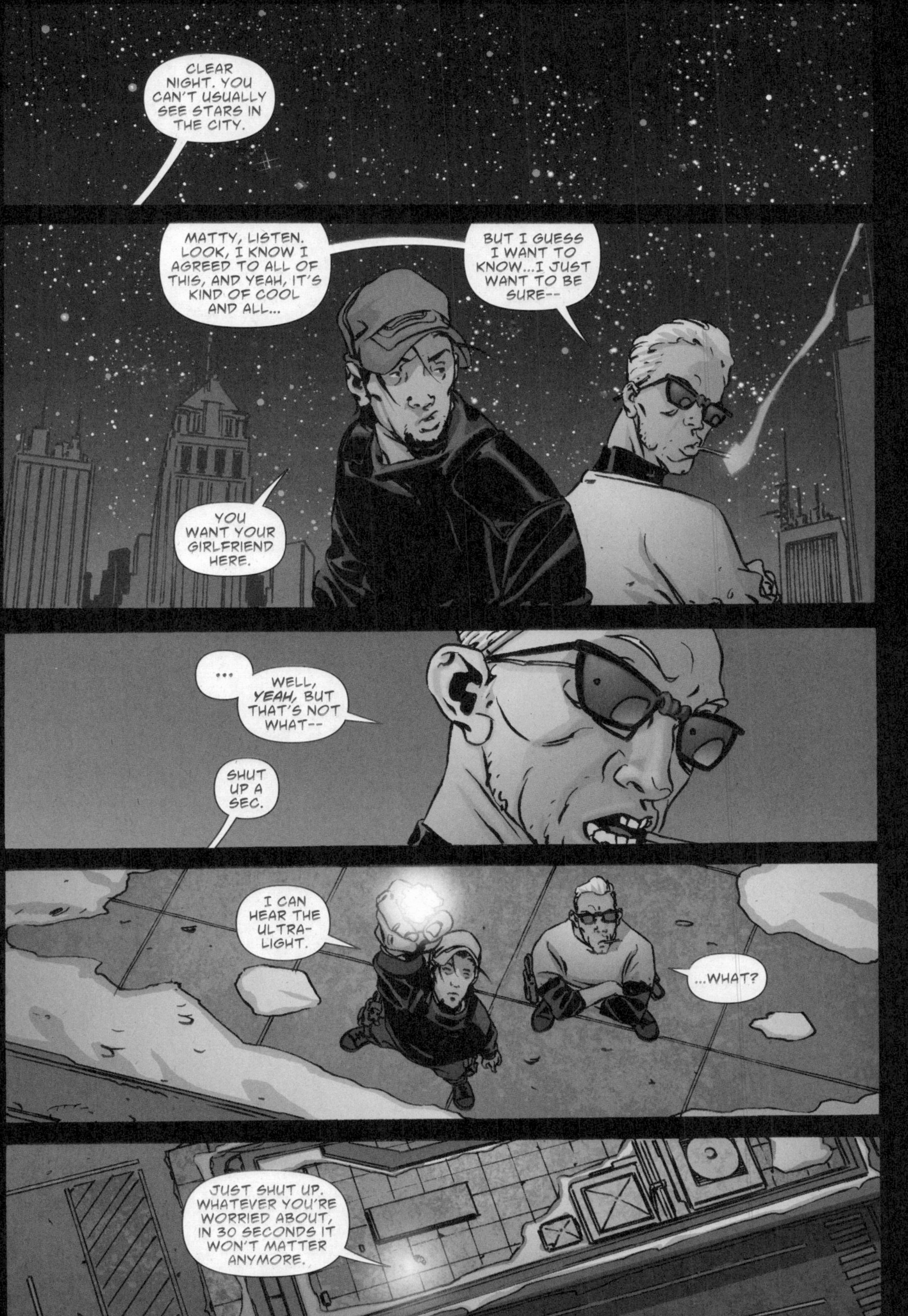
CLEAR NIGHT. YOU CAN'T USUALLY SEE STARS IN THE CITY.
MATTY, LISTEN. LOOK, I KNOW I AGREED TO ALL OF THIS, AND YEAH, IT'S KIND OF COOL AND ALL...
BUT I GUESS I WANT TO KNOW...I JUST WANT TO BE SURE--
YOU WANT YOUR GIRLFRIEND HERE.
...
WELL, *YEAH*, BUT THAT'S NOT WHAT--
SHUT UP A SEC.
I CAN HEAR THE ULTRA-LIGHT.
...WHAT?
JUST SHUT UP. WHATEVER YOU'RE WORRIED ABOUT, IN 30 SECONDS IT WON'T MATTER ANYMORE.

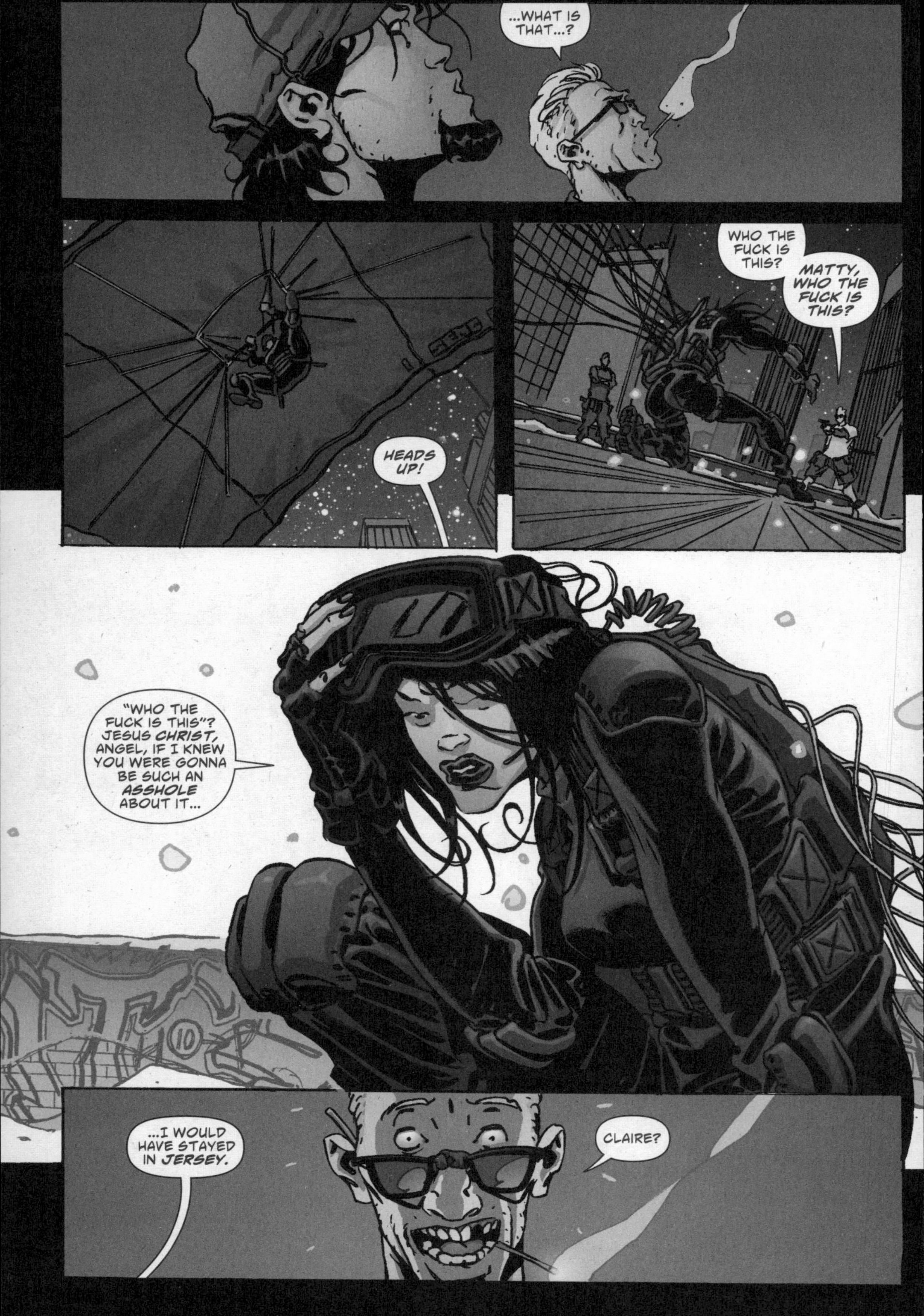
...WHAT IS THAT...?
HEADS UP!
WHO THE FUCK IS THIS?
MATTY, WHO THE FUCK IS THIS?
"WHO THE FUCK IS THIS"? JESUS CHRIST, ANGEL, IF I KNEW YOU WERE GONNA BE SUCH AN ASSHOLE ABOUT IT...
...I WOULD HAVE STAYED IN JERSEY.
CLAIRE?

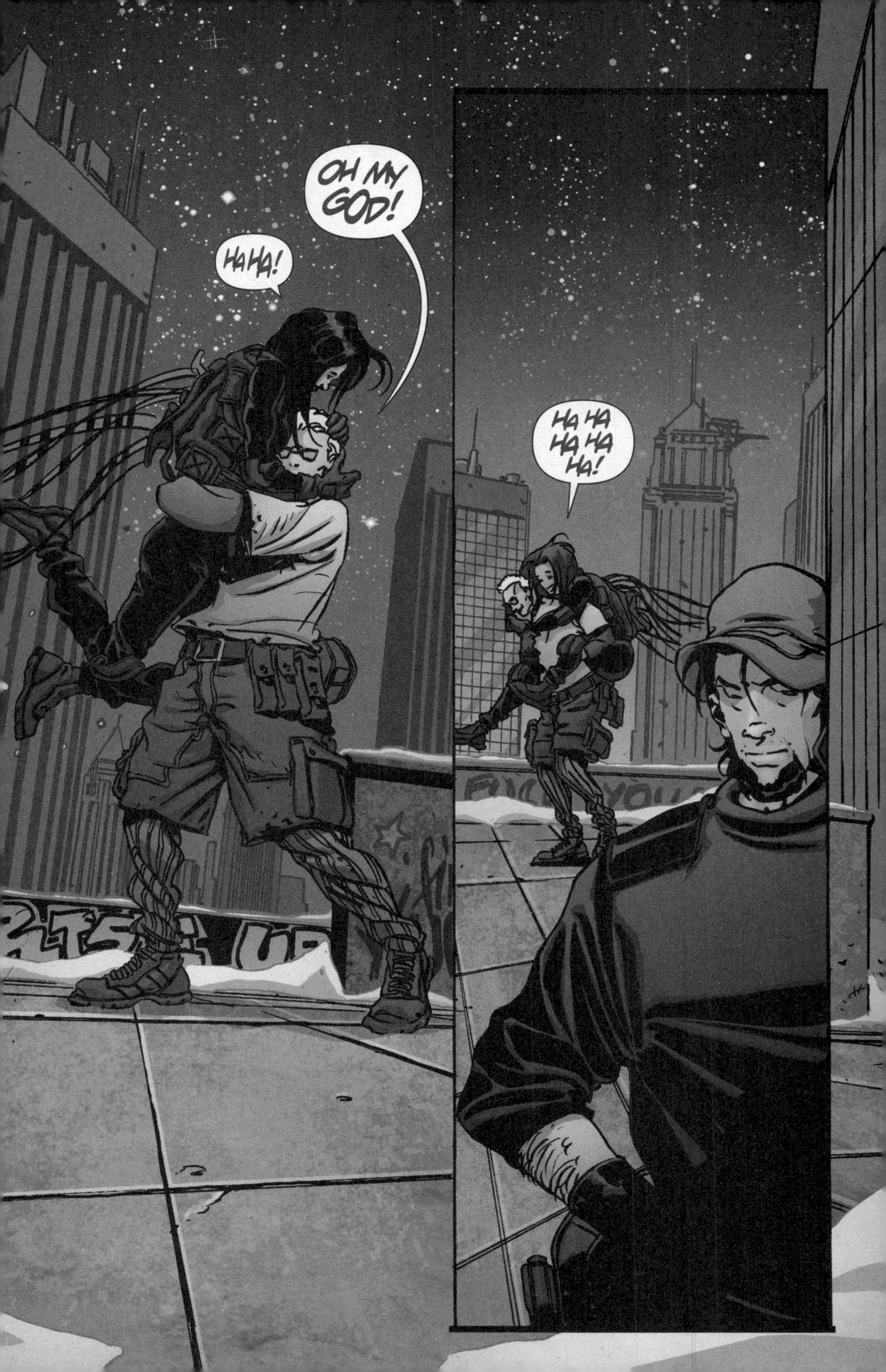
HA HA!
OH MY GOD!
HA HA HA HA HA!

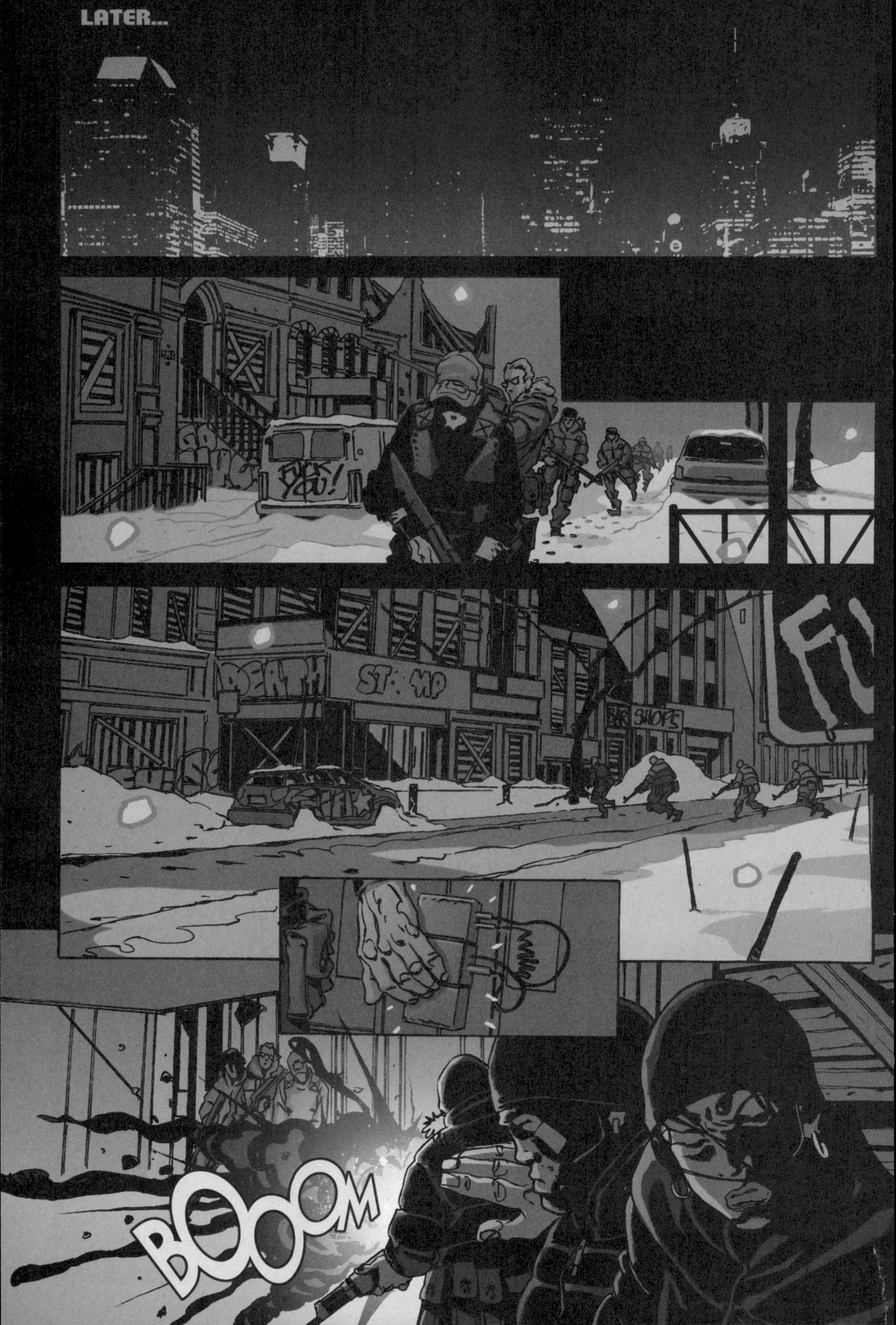
LATER...
FUCK YOU!
DEATH
BAR
SHOPS
BOOOM

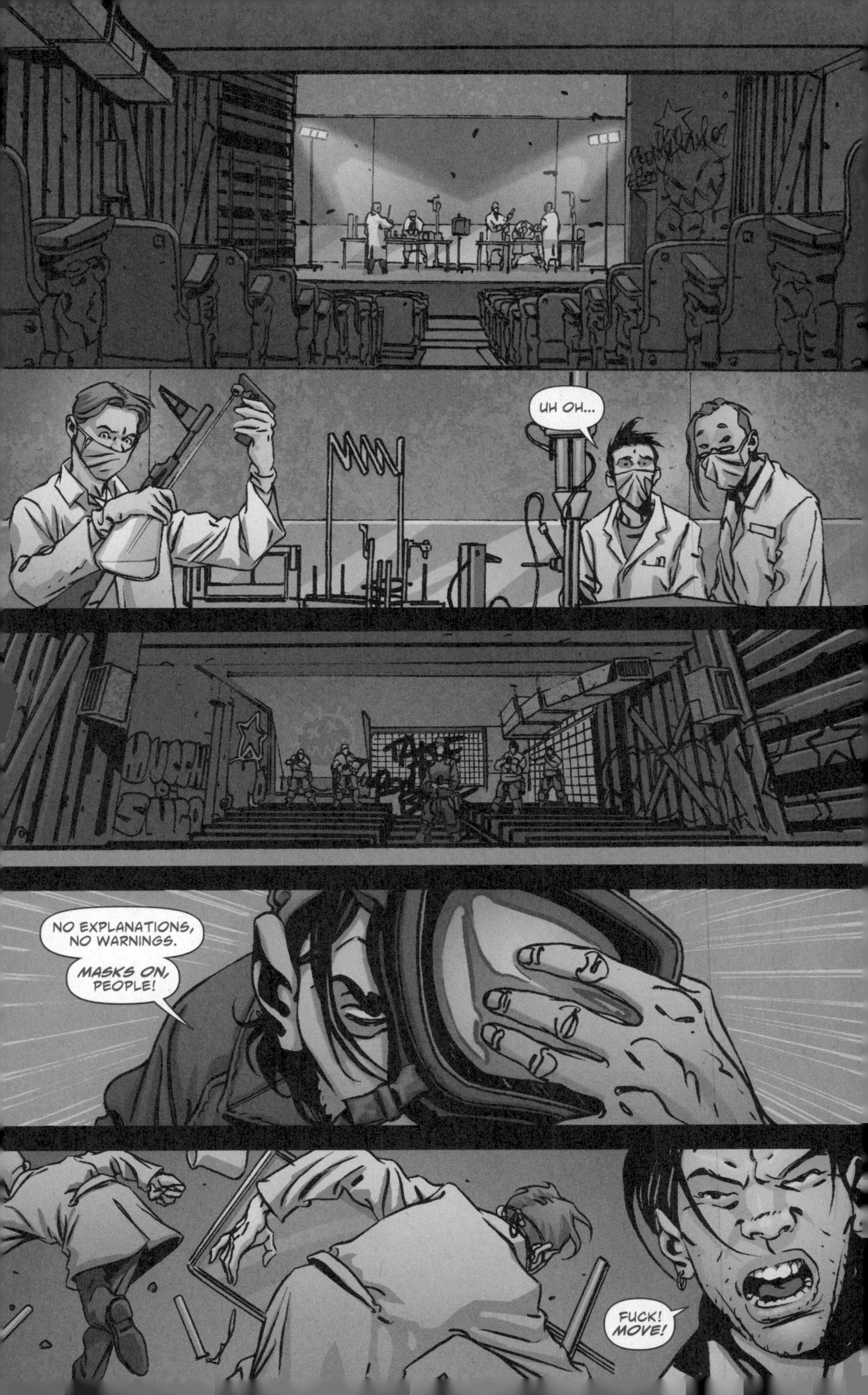
UH OH...
NO EXPLANATIONS, NO WARNINGS.
MASKS ON, PEOPLE!
FUCK! MOVE!

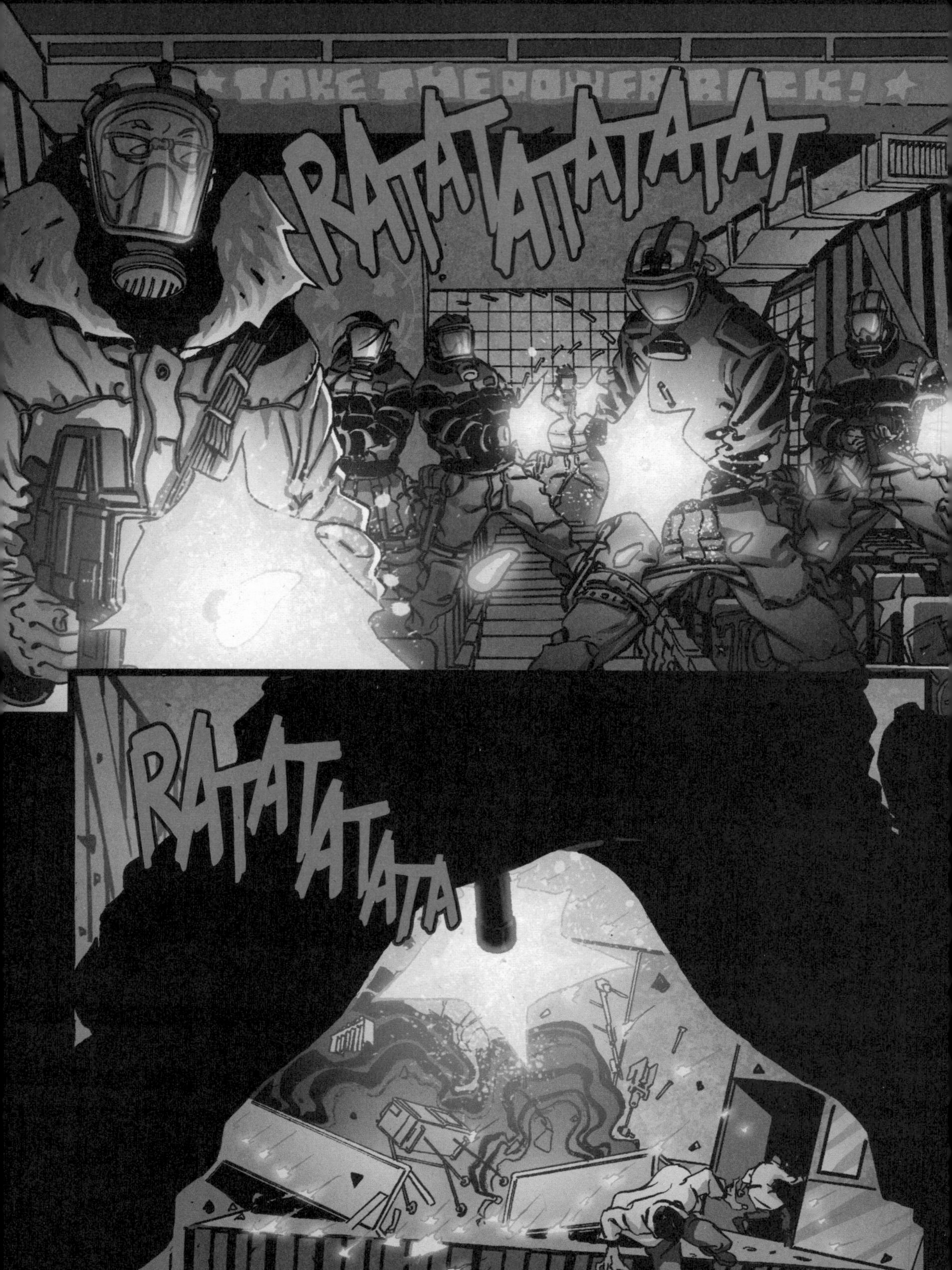
TAKE THE
RATATATATATAT
RATATATATATA

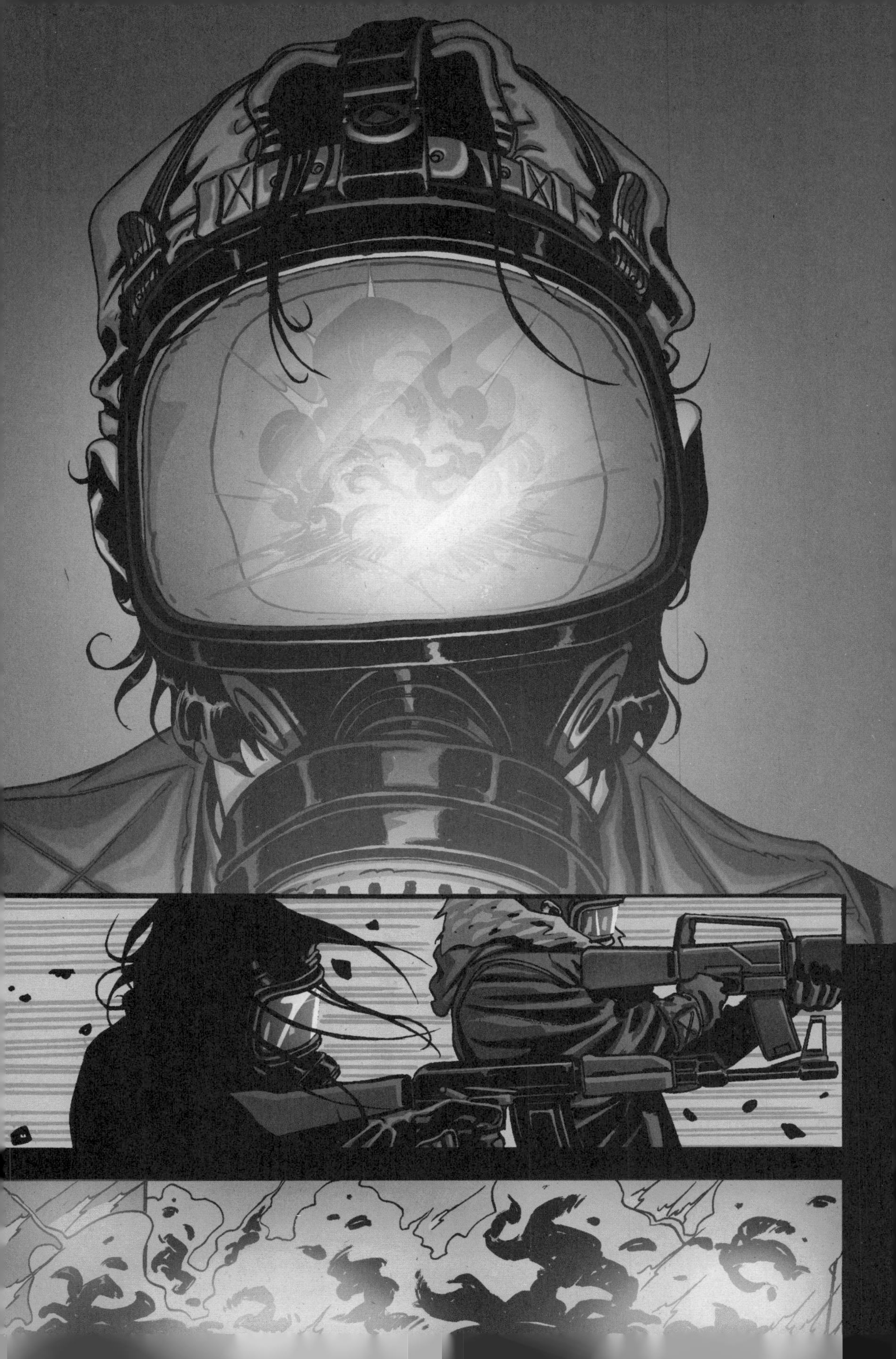

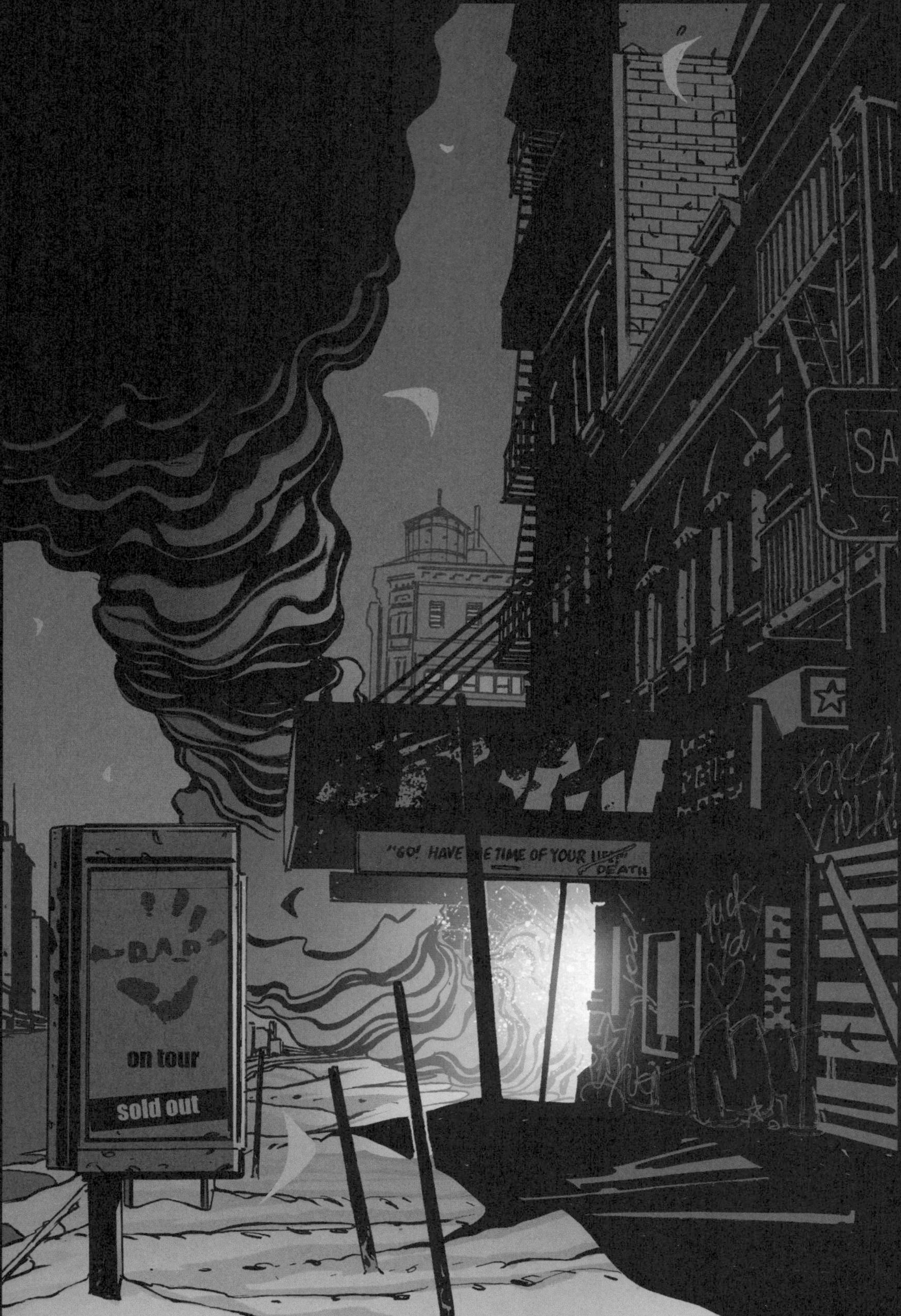

D.A.P.
on tour
sold out
"GO! HAVE
E TIME OF YOUR
DEATH
FORZA
VIOLA!
fuck ya

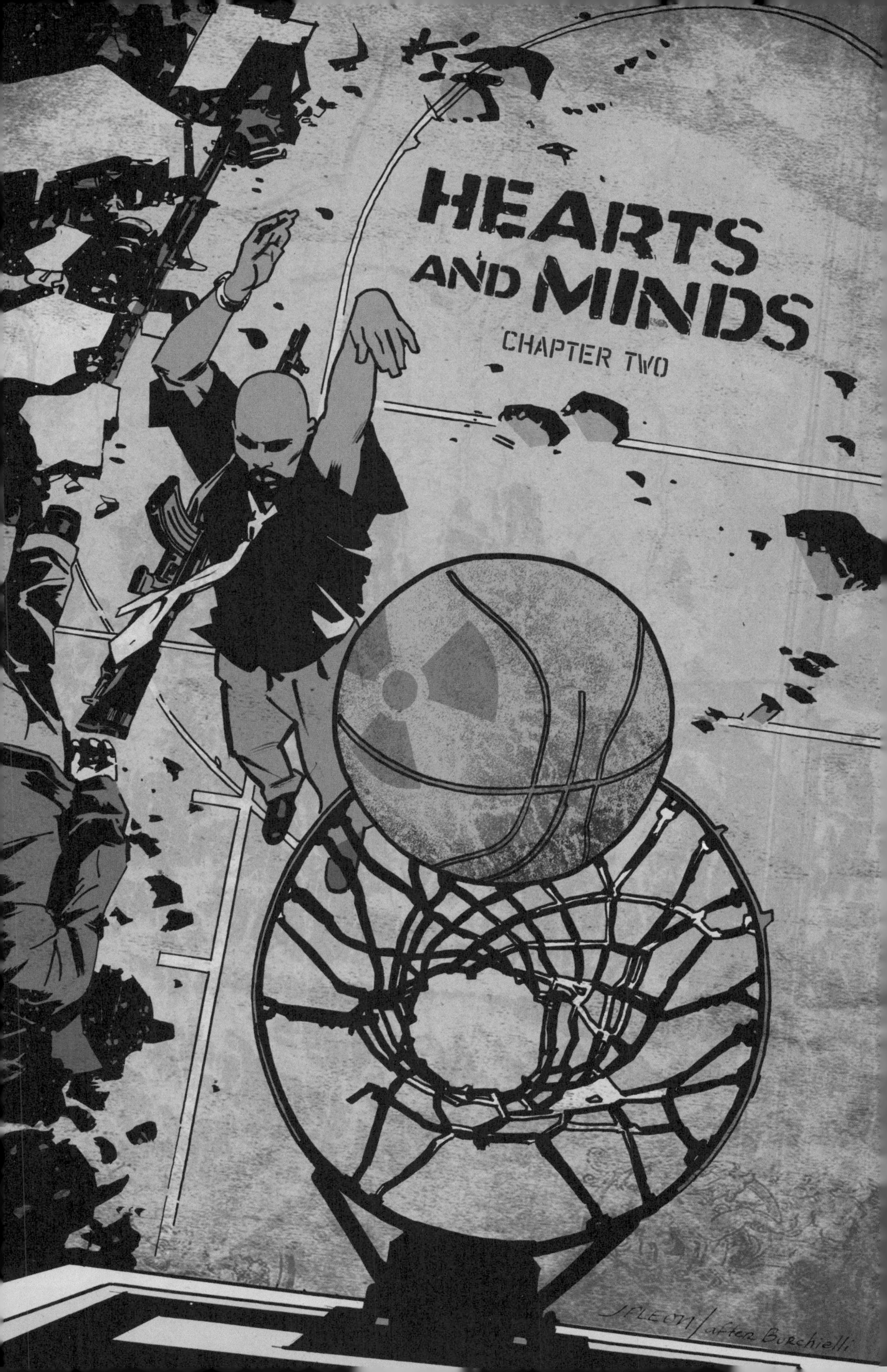
HEARTS AND MINDS
CHAPTER TWO
J.P.LEON/after Burchielli

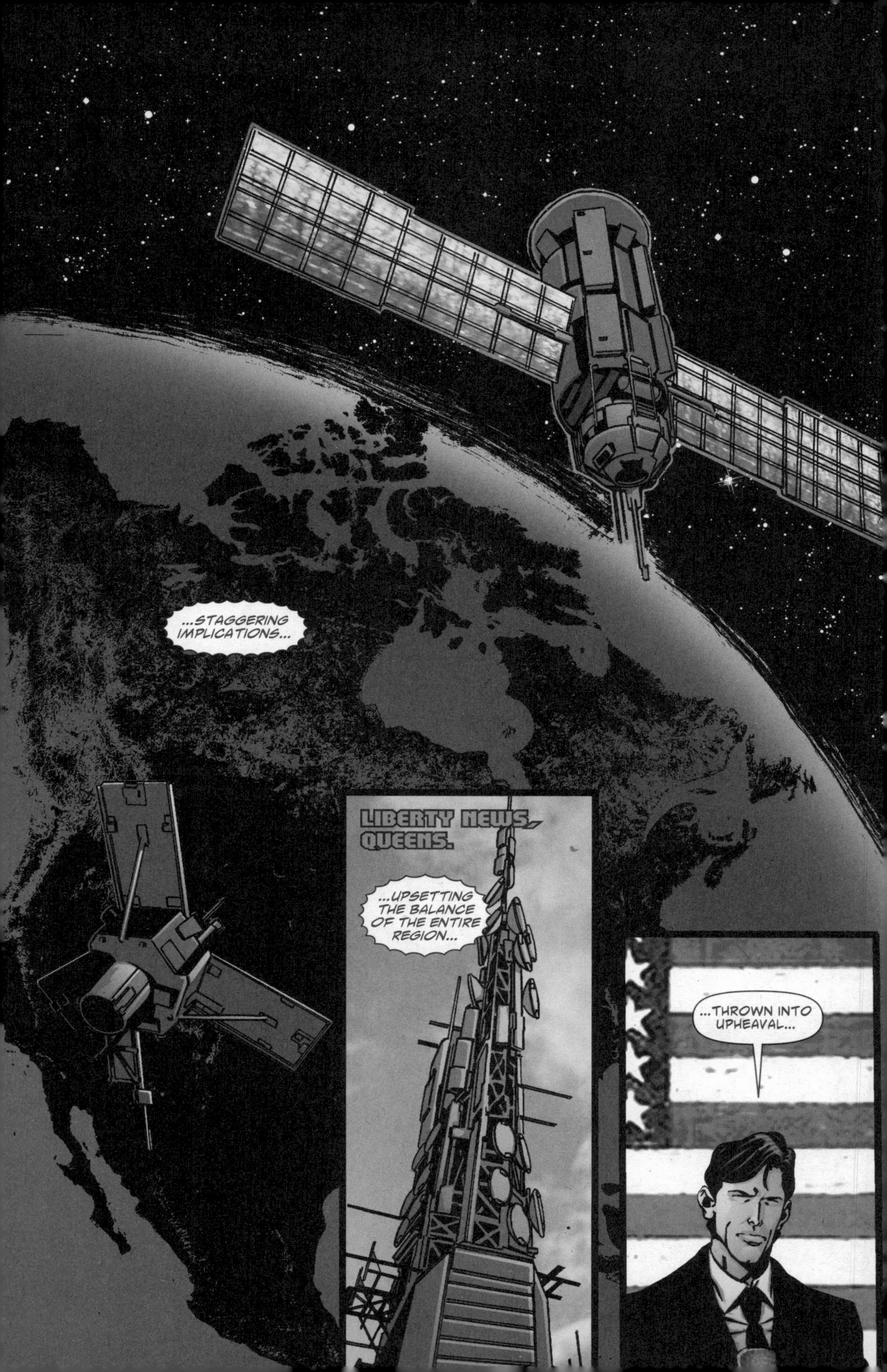
...STAGGERING IMPLICATIONS...
LIBERTY NEWS, QUEENS.
...UPSETTING THE BALANCE OF THE ENTIRE REGION...
...THROWN INTO UPHEAVAL...

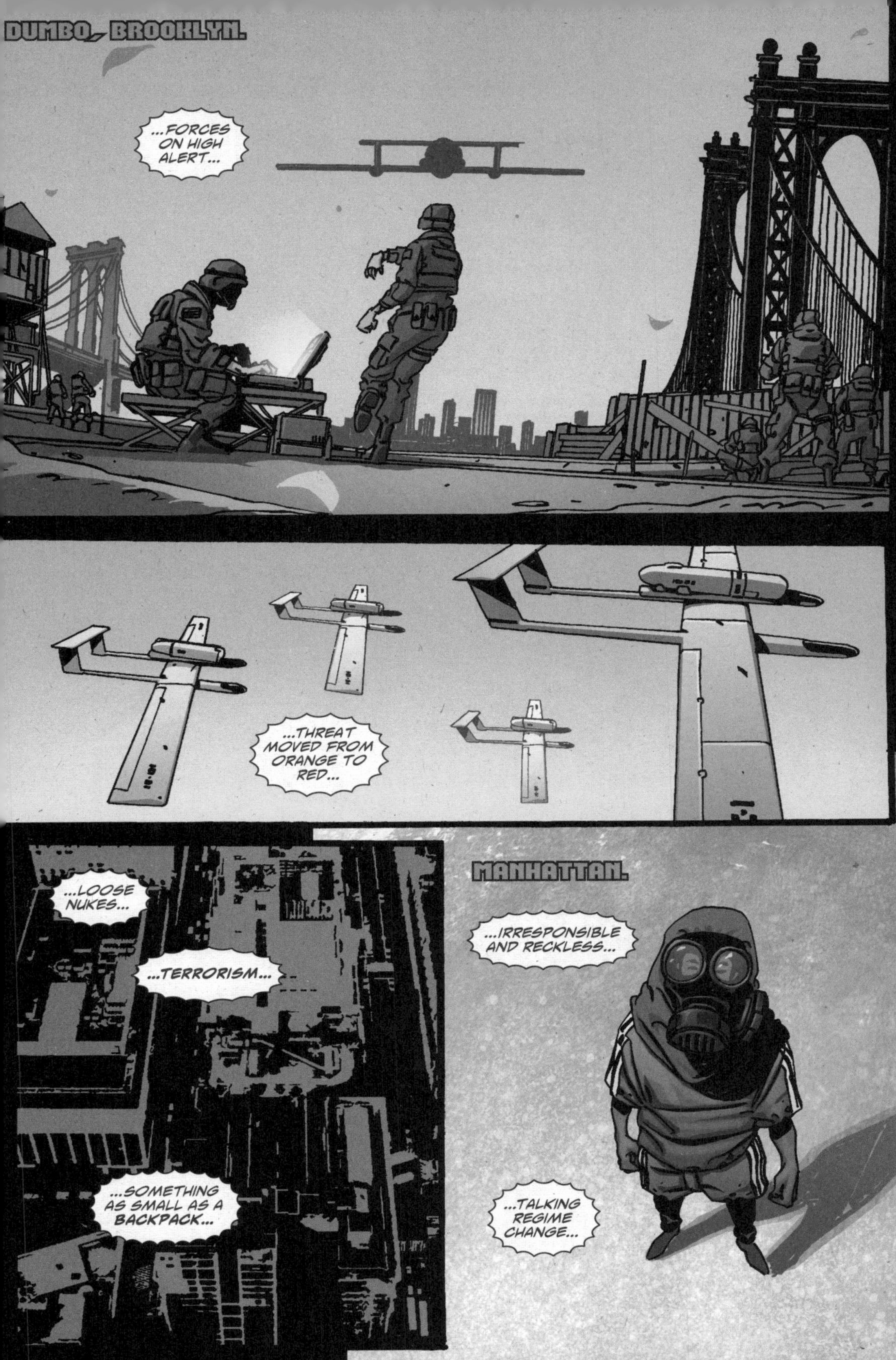
DUMBO, BROOKLYN.
...FORCES ON HIGH ALERT...
...THREAT MOVED FROM ORANGE TO RED...
...LOOSE NUKES...
...TERRORISM...
...SOMETHING AS SMALL AS A BACKPACK...
MANHATTAN.
...IRRESPONSIBLE AND RECKLESS...
...TALKING REGIME CHANGE...

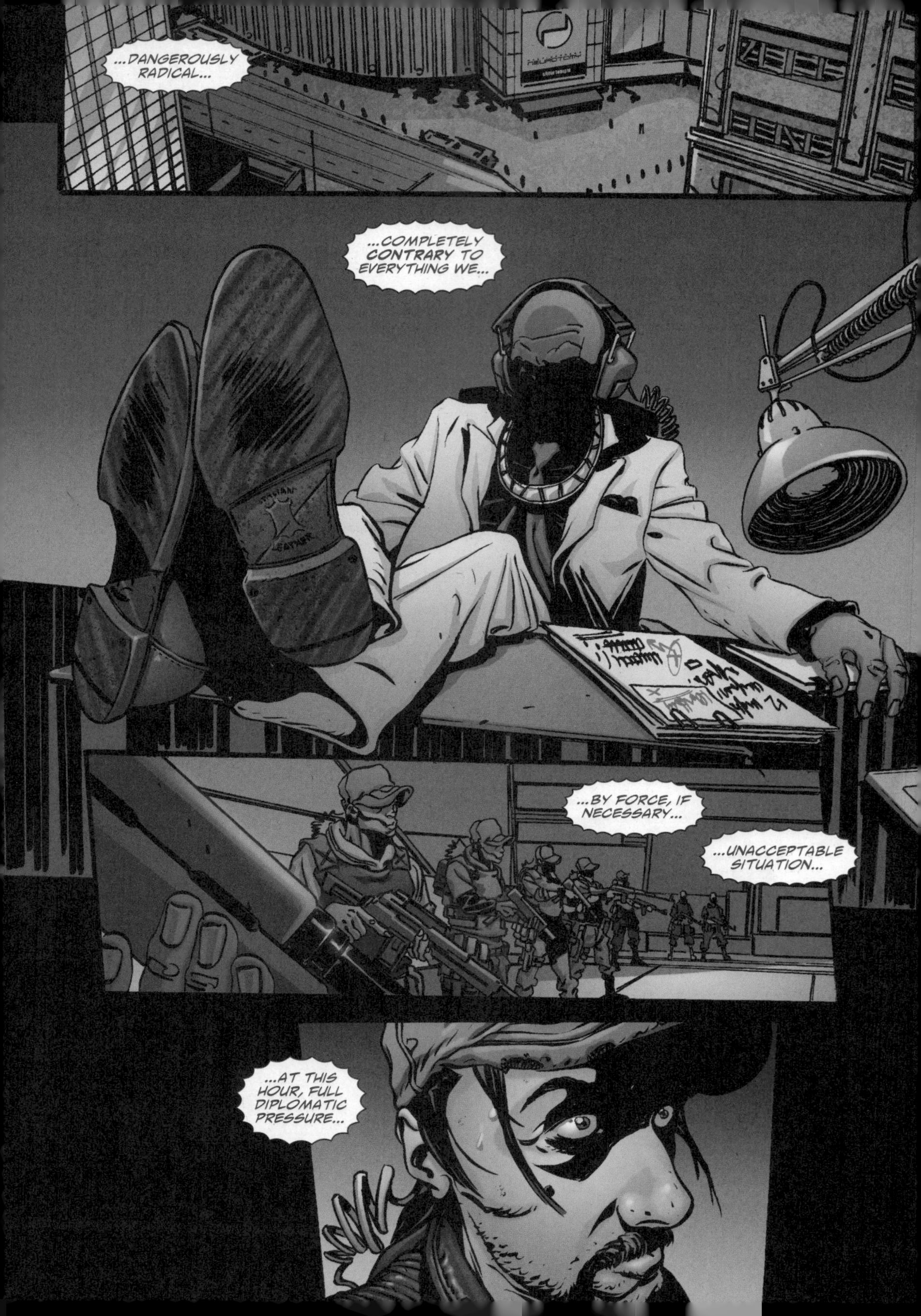
...DANGEROUSLY RADICAL...
...COMPLETELY CONTRARY TO EVERYTHING WE...
...BY FORCE, IF NECESSARY...
...UNACCEPTABLE SITUATION...
...AT THIS HOUR, FULL DIPLOMATIC PRESSURE...

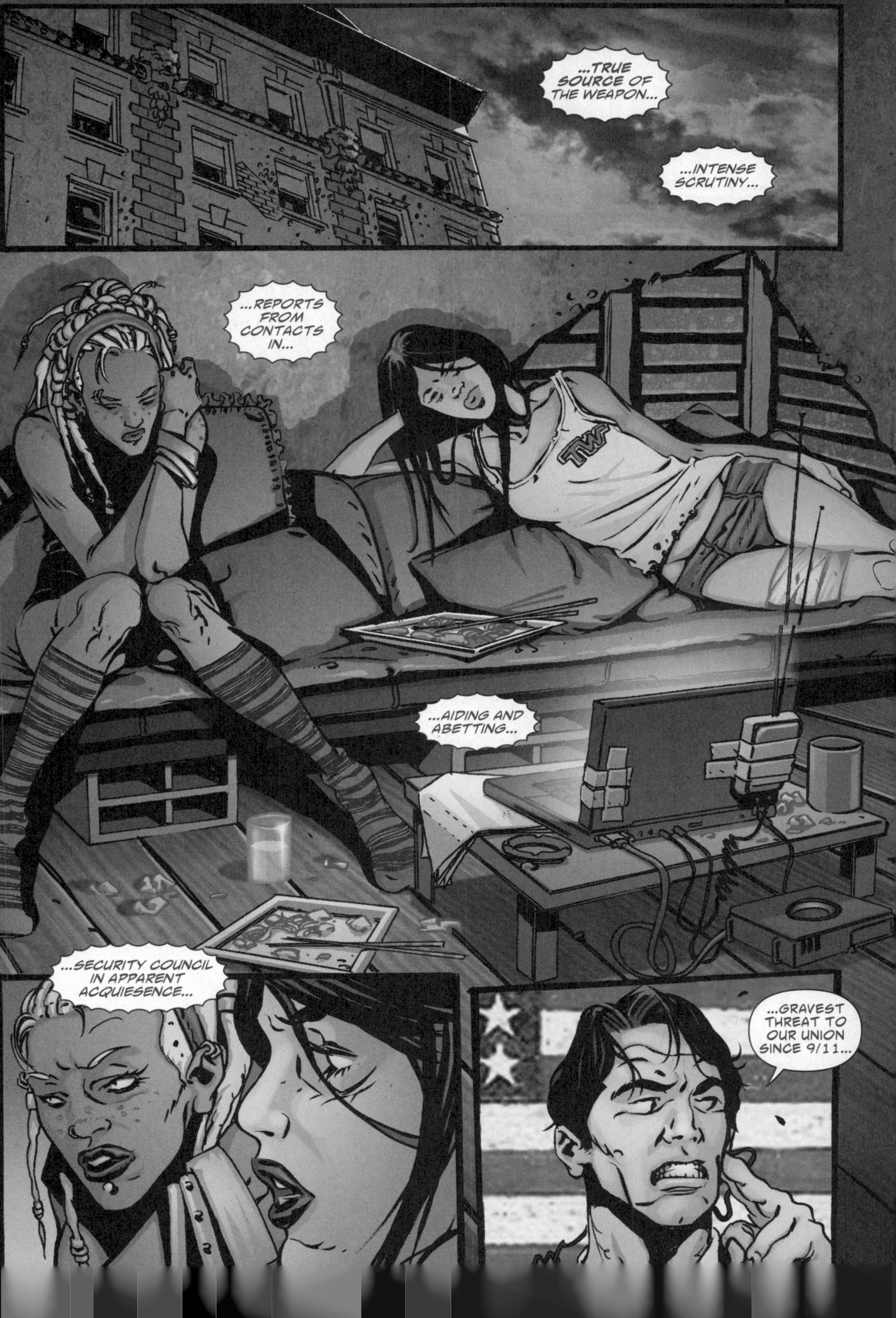
...TRUE SOURCE OF THE WEAPON...
...INTENSE SCRUTINY...
...REPORTS FROM CONTACTS IN...
...AIDING AND ABETTING...
...SECURITY COUNCIL IN APPARENT ACQUIESENCE...
...GRAVEST THREAT TO OUR UNION SINCE 9/11...

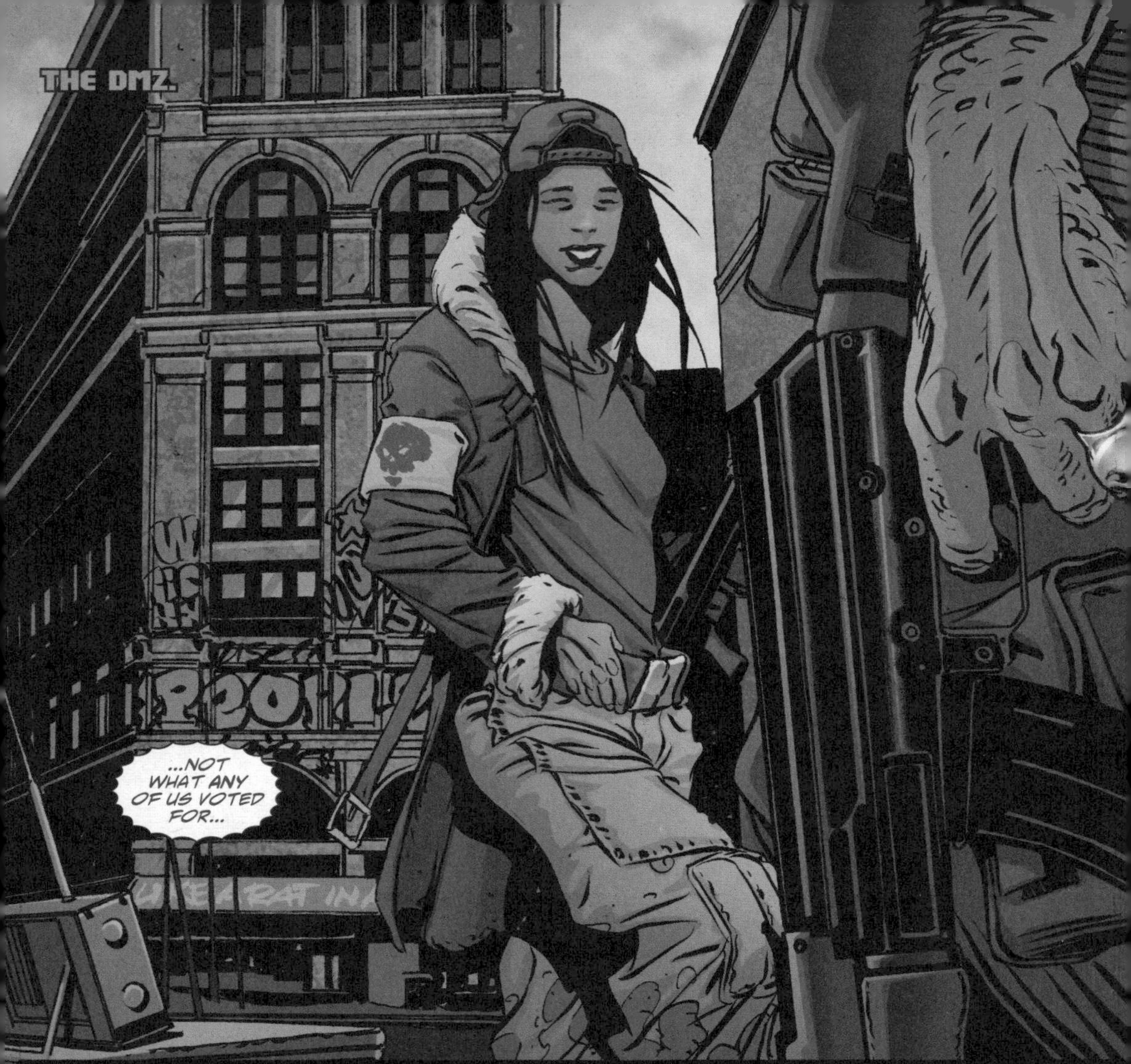
THE DMZ.
...NOT WHAT ANY OF US VOTED FOR...

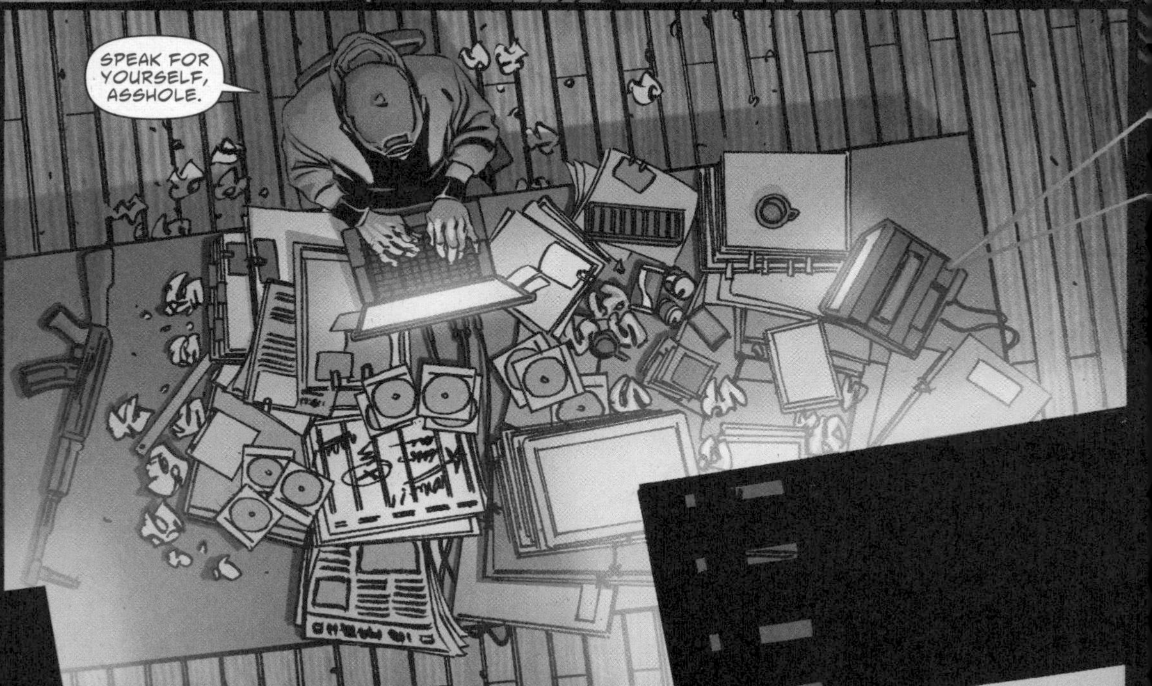
SPEAK FOR YOURSELF, ASSHOLE.

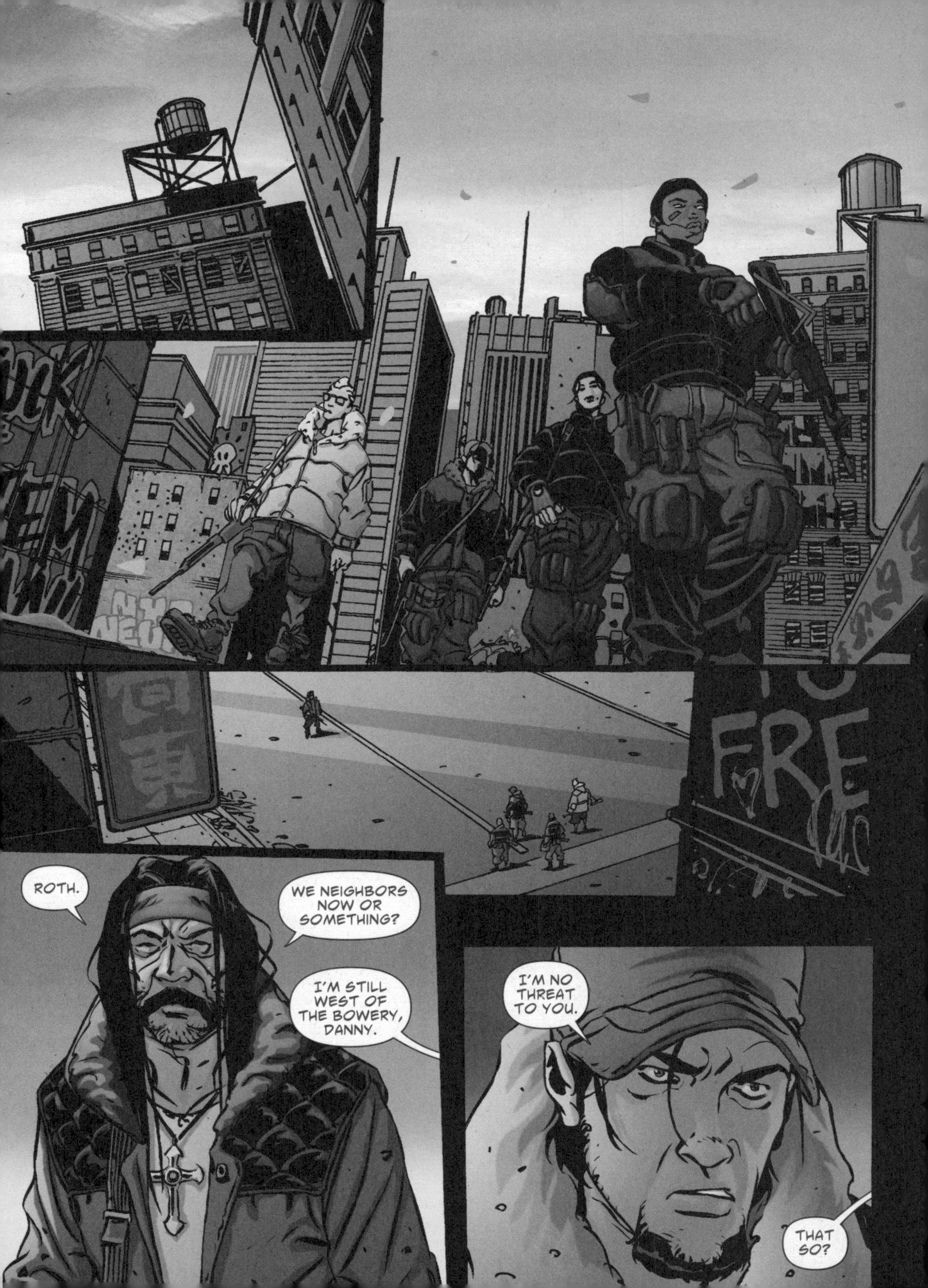
ROTH.
WE NEIGHBORS NOW OR SOMETHING?
I'M STILL WEST OF THE BOWERY, DANNY.
I'M NO THREAT TO YOU.
THAT SO?

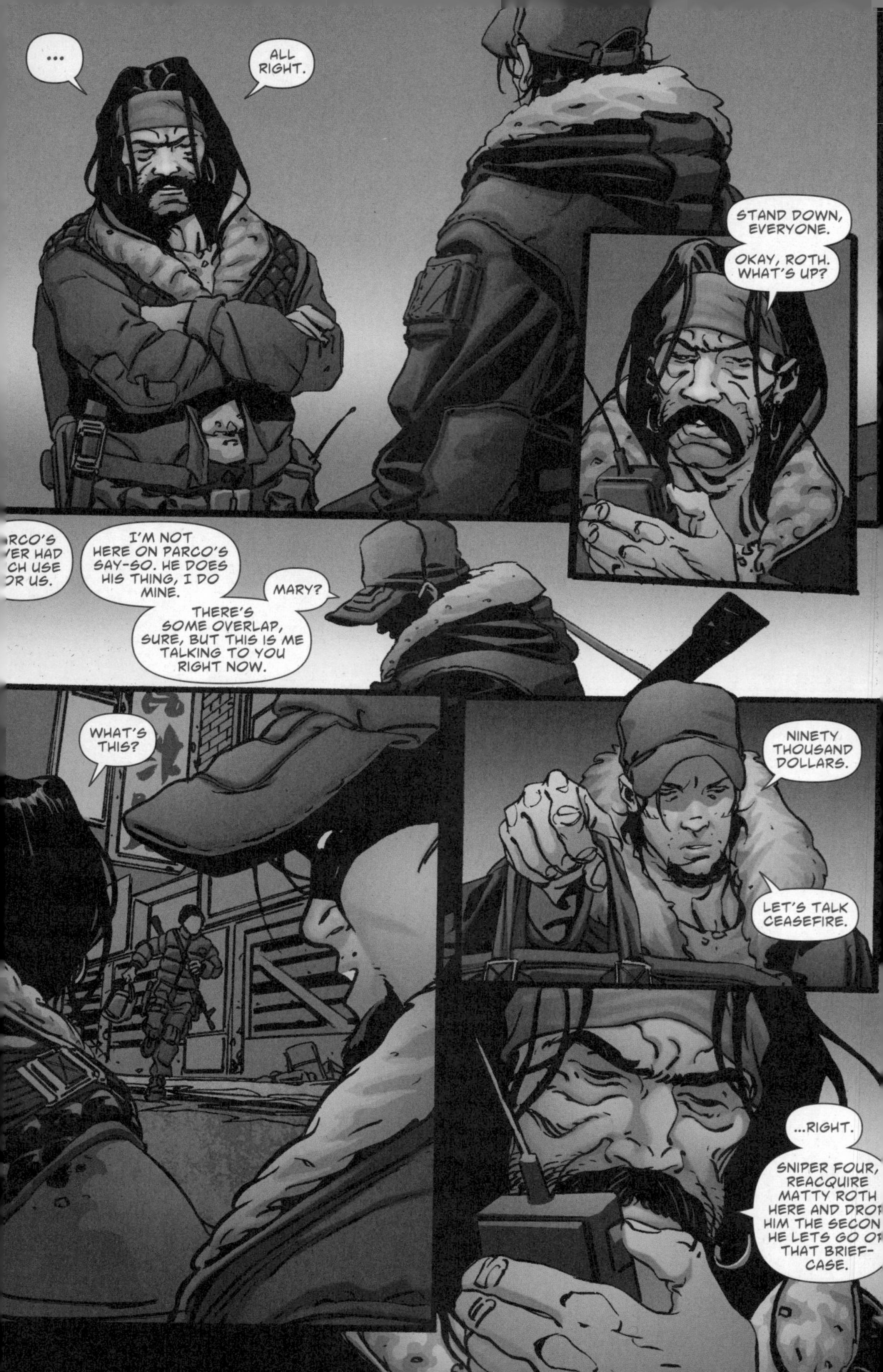
...
ALL RIGHT.
STAND DOWN, EVERYONE.
OKAY, ROTH. WHAT'S UP?
RCO'S VER HAD CH USE OR US.
I'M NOT HERE ON PARCO'S SAY-SO. HE DOES HIS THING, I DO MINE.
THERE'S SOME OVERLAP, SURE, BUT THIS IS ME TALKING TO YOU RIGHT NOW.
MARY?
WHAT'S THIS?
NINETY THOUSAND DOLLARS.
LET'S TALK CEASEFIRE.
...RIGHT.
SNIPER FOUR, REACQUIRE MATTY ROTH HERE AND DROP HIM THE SECON HE LETS GO OF THAT BRIEF-CASE.

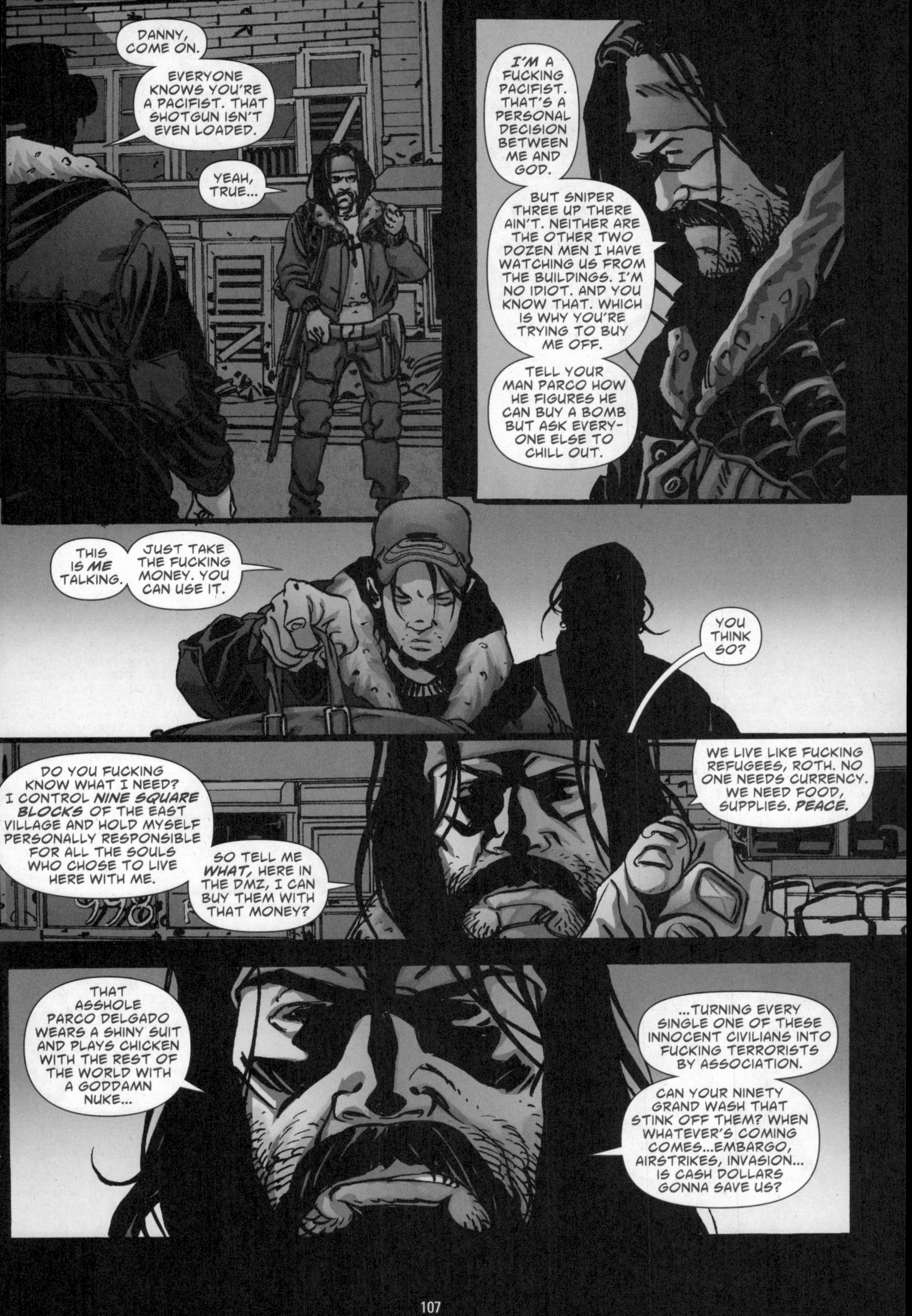
DANNY, COME ON.
EVERYONE KNOWS YOU'RE A PACIFIST. THAT SHOTGUN ISN'T EVEN LOADED.
YEAH, TRUE...
I'M A FUCKING PACIFIST. THAT'S A PERSONAL DECISION BETWEEN ME AND GOD.
BUT SNIPER THREE UP THERE AIN'T. NEITHER ARE THE OTHER TWO DOZEN MEN I HAVE WATCHING US FROM THE BUILDINGS. I'M NO IDIOT. AND YOU KNOW THAT. WHICH IS WHY YOU'RE TRYING TO BUY ME OFF.
TELL YOUR MAN PARCO HOW HE FIGURES HE CAN BUY A BOMB BUT ASK EVERY-ONE ELSE TO CHILL OUT.
THIS IS ME TALKING.
JUST TAKE THE FUCKING MONEY. YOU CAN USE IT.
YOU THINK SO?
DO YOU FUCKING KNOW WHAT I NEED? I CONTROL NINE SQUARE BLOCKS OF THE EAST VILLAGE AND HOLD MYSELF PERSONALLY RESPONSIBLE FOR ALL THE SOULS WHO CHOSE TO LIVE HERE WITH ME.
SO TELL ME WHAT, HERE IN THE DMZ, I CAN BUY THEM WITH THAT MONEY?
WE LIVE LIKE FUCKING REFUGEES, ROTH. NO ONE NEEDS CURRENCY. WE NEED FOOD, SUPPLIES. PEACE.
THAT ASSHOLE PARCO DELGADO WEARS A SHINY SUIT AND PLAYS CHICKEN WITH THE REST OF THE WORLD WITH A GODDAMN NUKE...
...TURNING EVERY SINGLE ONE OF THESE INNOCENT CIVILIANS INTO FUCKING TERRORISTS BY ASSOCIATION.
CAN YOUR NINETY GRAND WASH THAT STINK OFF THEM? WHEN WHATEVER'S COMING COMES...EMBARGO, AIRSTRIKES, INVASION... IS CASH DOLLARS GONNA SAVE US?

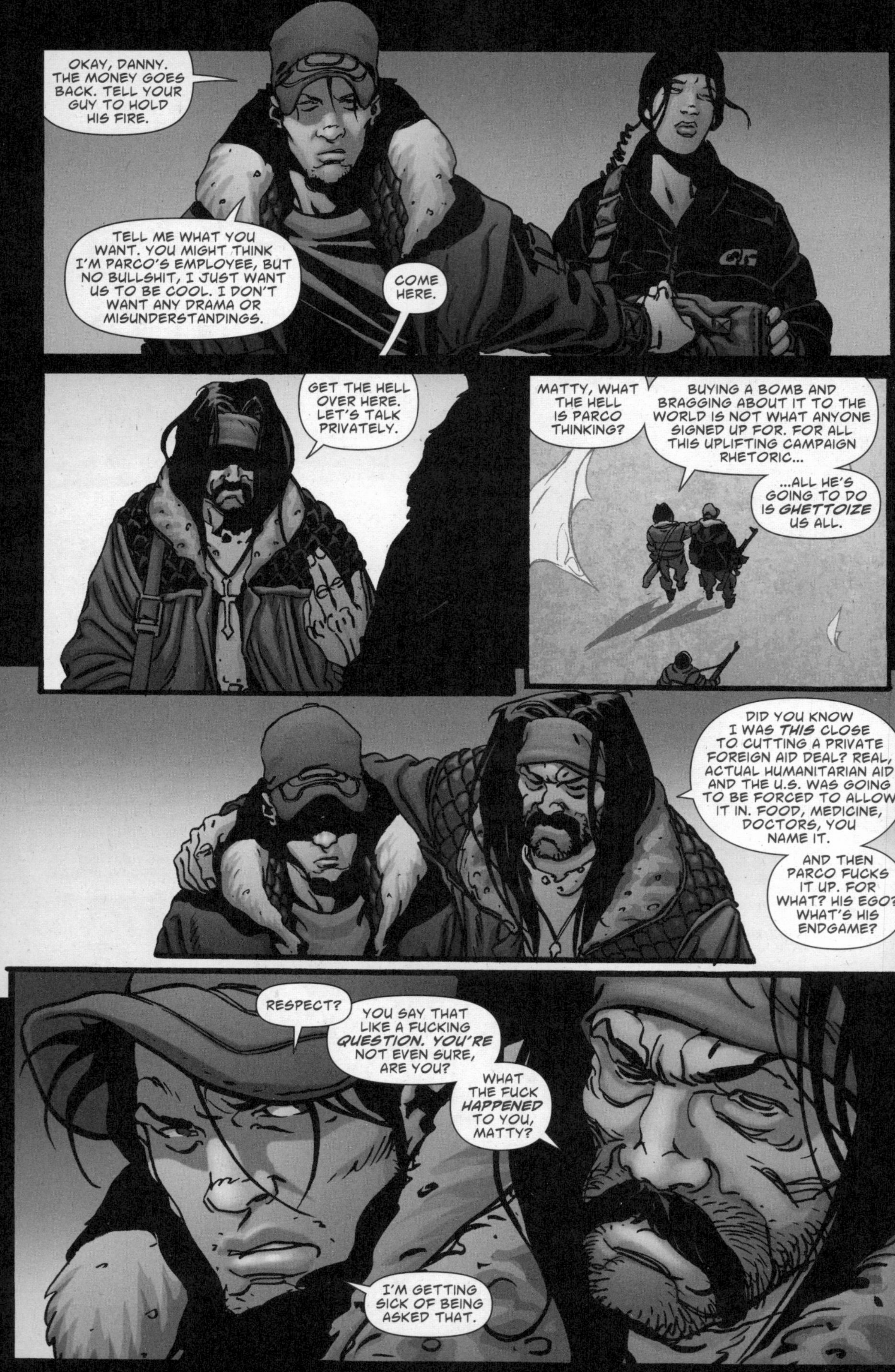

OKAY, DANNY. THE MONEY GOES BACK. TELL YOUR GUY TO HOLD HIS FIRE.
TELL ME WHAT YOU WANT. YOU MIGHT THINK I'M PARCO'S EMPLOYEE, BUT NO BULLSHIT, I JUST WANT US TO BE COOL. I DON'T WANT ANY DRAMA OR MISUNDERSTANDINGS.
COME HERE.
GET THE HELL OVER HERE. LET'S TALK PRIVATELY.
MATTY, WHAT THE HELL IS PARCO THINKING?
BUYING A BOMB AND BRAGGING ABOUT IT TO THE WORLD IS NOT WHAT ANYONE SIGNED UP FOR. FOR ALL THIS UPLIFTING CAMPAIGN RHETORIC...
...ALL HE'S GOING TO DO IS *GHETTOIZE* US ALL.
DID YOU KNOW I WAS *THIS* CLOSE TO CUTTING A PRIVATE FOREIGN AID DEAL? REAL, ACTUAL HUMANITARIAN AID AND THE U.S. WAS GOING TO BE FORCED TO ALLOW IT IN. FOOD, MEDICINE, DOCTORS, YOU NAME IT.
AND THEN PARCO FUCKS IT UP. FOR WHAT? HIS EGO? WHAT'S HIS ENDGAME?
RESPECT?
YOU SAY THAT LIKE A FUCKING *QUESTION. YOU'RE* NOT EVEN SURE, ARE YOU?
WHAT THE FUCK *HAPPENED* TO YOU, MATTY?
I'M GETTING SICK OF BEING ASKED THAT.

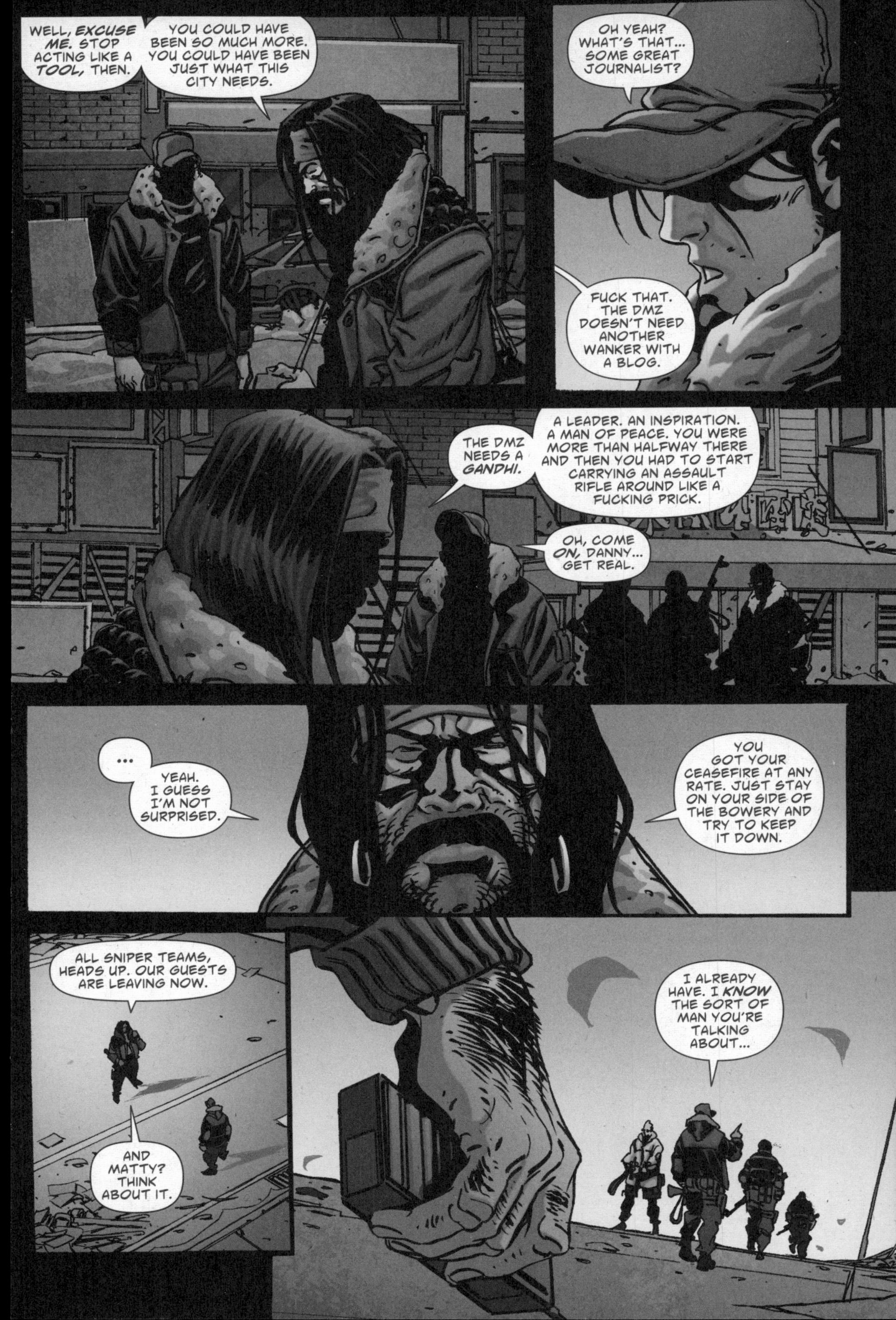

WELL, *EXCUSE ME.* STOP ACTING LIKE A *TOOL*, THEN.
YOU COULD HAVE BEEN SO MUCH MORE. YOU COULD HAVE BEEN JUST WHAT THIS CITY NEEDS.
OH YEAH? WHAT'S THAT... SOME GREAT JOURNALIST?
FUCK THAT. THE DMZ DOESN'T NEED ANOTHER WANKER WITH A BLOG.
THE DMZ NEEDS A *GANDHI.*
A LEADER. AN INSPIRATION. A MAN OF PEACE. YOU WERE MORE THAN HALFWAY THERE AND THEN YOU HAD TO START CARRYING AN ASSAULT RIFLE AROUND LIKE A FUCKING PRICK.
OH, COME *ON,* DANNY... GET REAL.
... YEAH. I GUESS I'M NOT SURPRISED.
YOU GOT YOUR CEASEFIRE AT ANY RATE. JUST STAY ON YOUR SIDE OF THE BOWERY AND TRY TO KEEP IT DOWN.
ALL SNIPER TEAMS, HEADS UP. OUR GUESTS ARE LEAVING NOW.
AND MATTY? THINK ABOUT IT.
I ALREADY HAVE. I *KNOW* THE SORT OF MAN YOU'RE TALKING ABOUT...

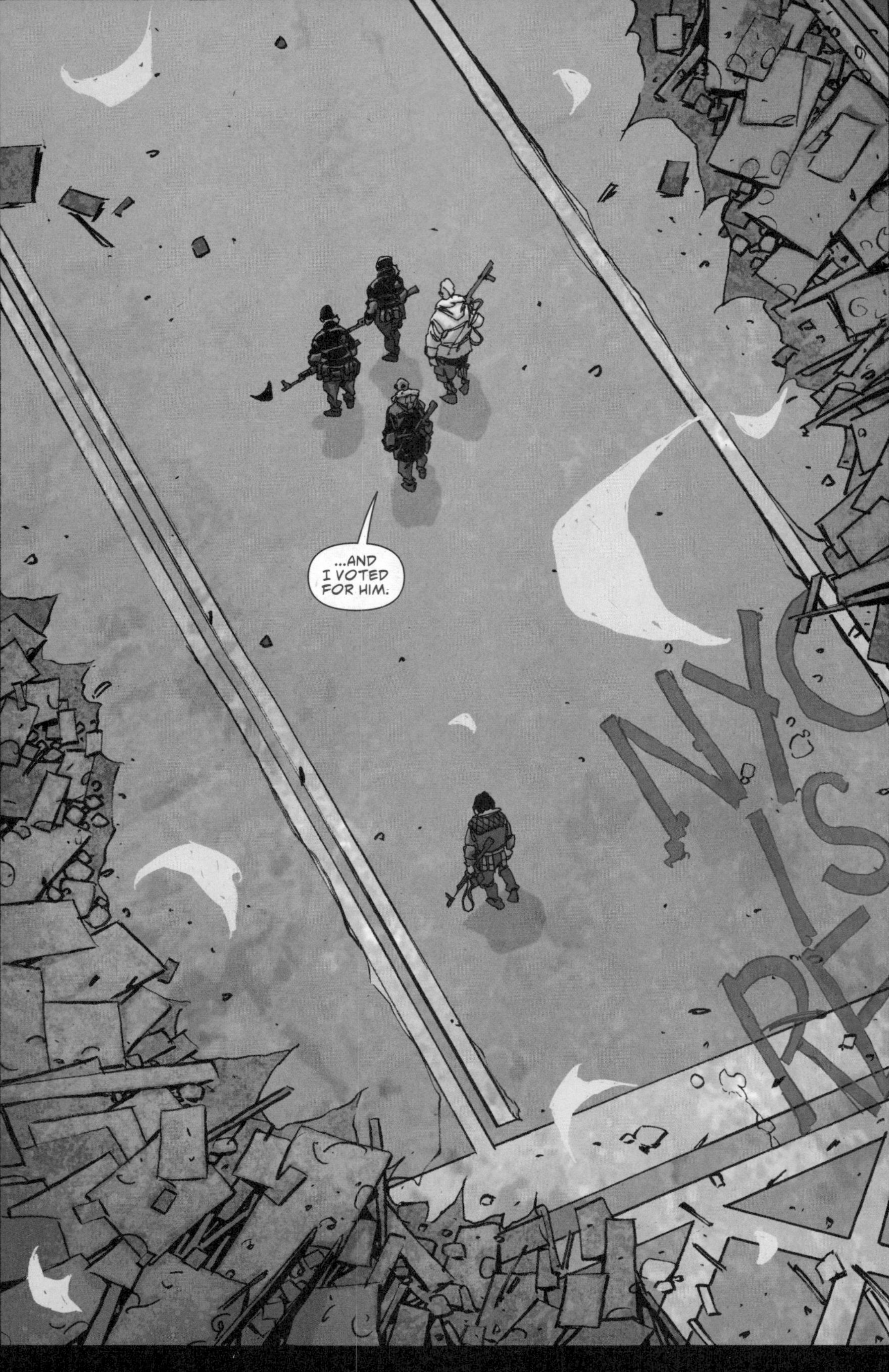
...AND I VOTED FOR HIM.

70,000 FEET.

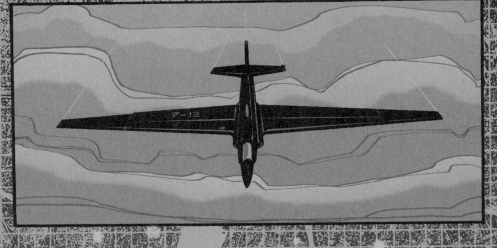

WHAT IS ALL THAT SHIT?

RADIATION SIGNATURES, SIR.

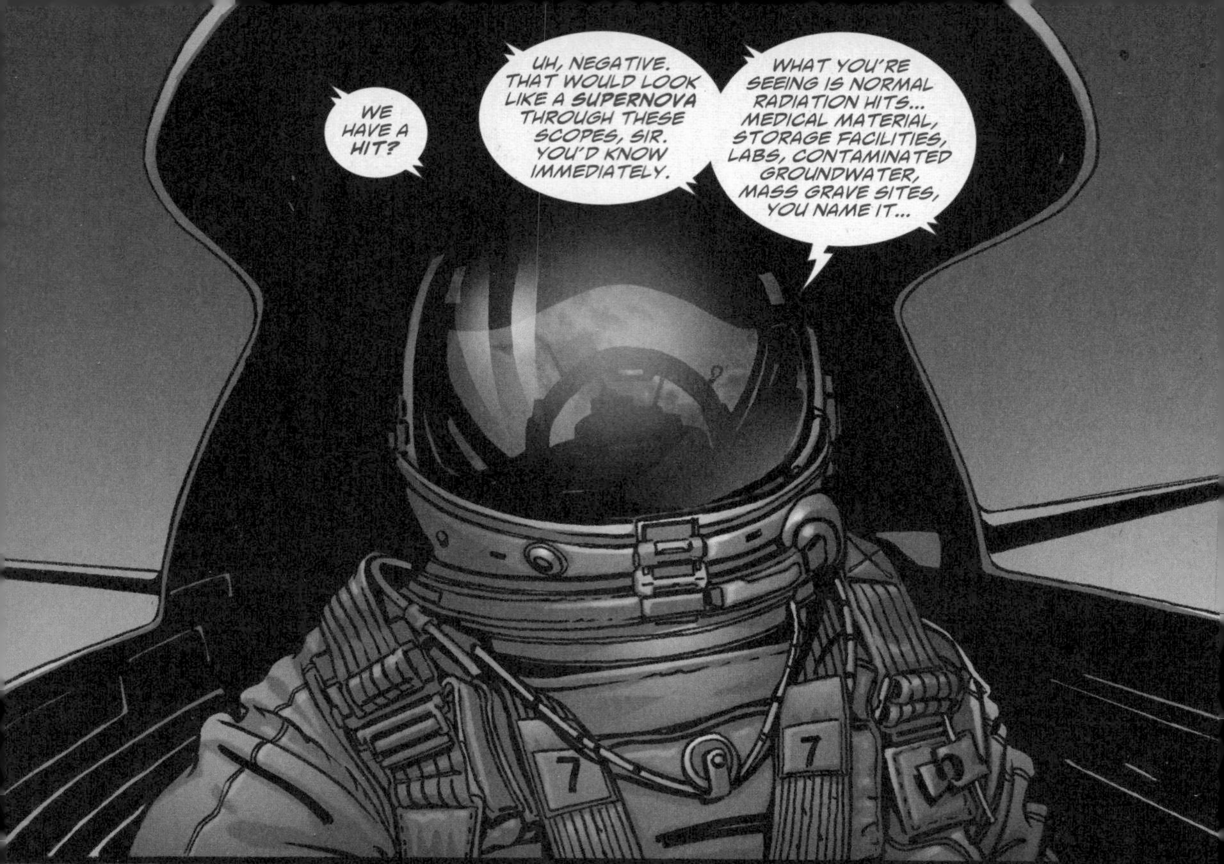
WE HAVE A HIT?
UH, NEGATIVE. THAT WOULD LOOK LIKE A SUPERNOVA THROUGH THESE SCOPES, SIR. YOU'D KNOW IMMEDIATELY.
WHAT YOU'RE SEEING IS NORMAL RADIATION HITS... MEDICAL MATERIAL, STORAGE FACILITIES, LABS, CONTAMINATED GROUNDWATER, MASS GRAVE SITES, YOU NAME IT...

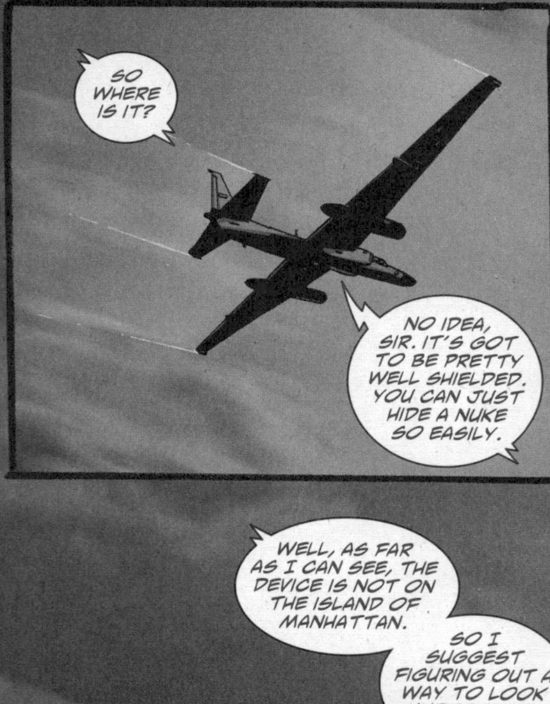
SO WHERE IS IT?
NO IDEA, SIR. IT'S GOT TO BE PRETTY WELL SHIELDED. YOU CAN JUST HIDE A NUKE SO EASILY.

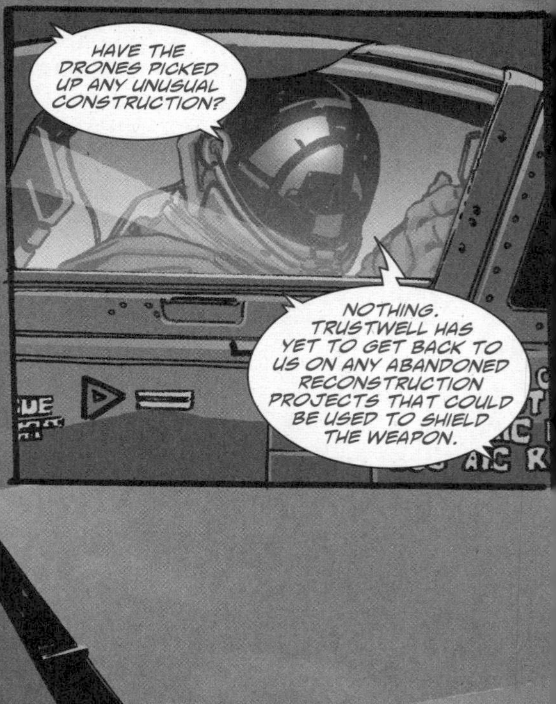
HAVE THE DRONES PICKED UP ANY UNUSUAL CONSTRUCTION?
NOTHING. TRUSTWELL HAS YET TO GET BACK TO US ON ANY ABANDONED RECONSTRUCTION PROJECTS THAT COULD BE USED TO SHIELD THE WEAPON.

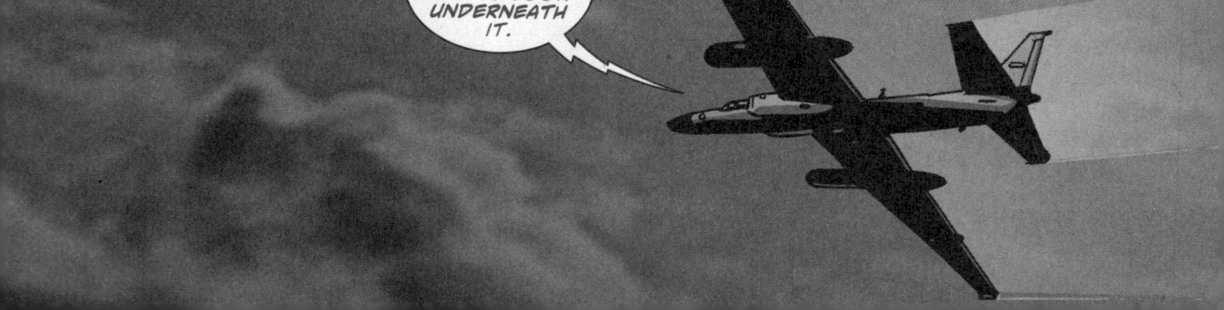
WELL, AS FAR AS I CAN SEE, THE DEVICE IS NOT ON THE ISLAND OF MANHATTAN.
SO I SUGGEST FIGURING OUT A WAY TO LOOK UNDERNEATH IT.

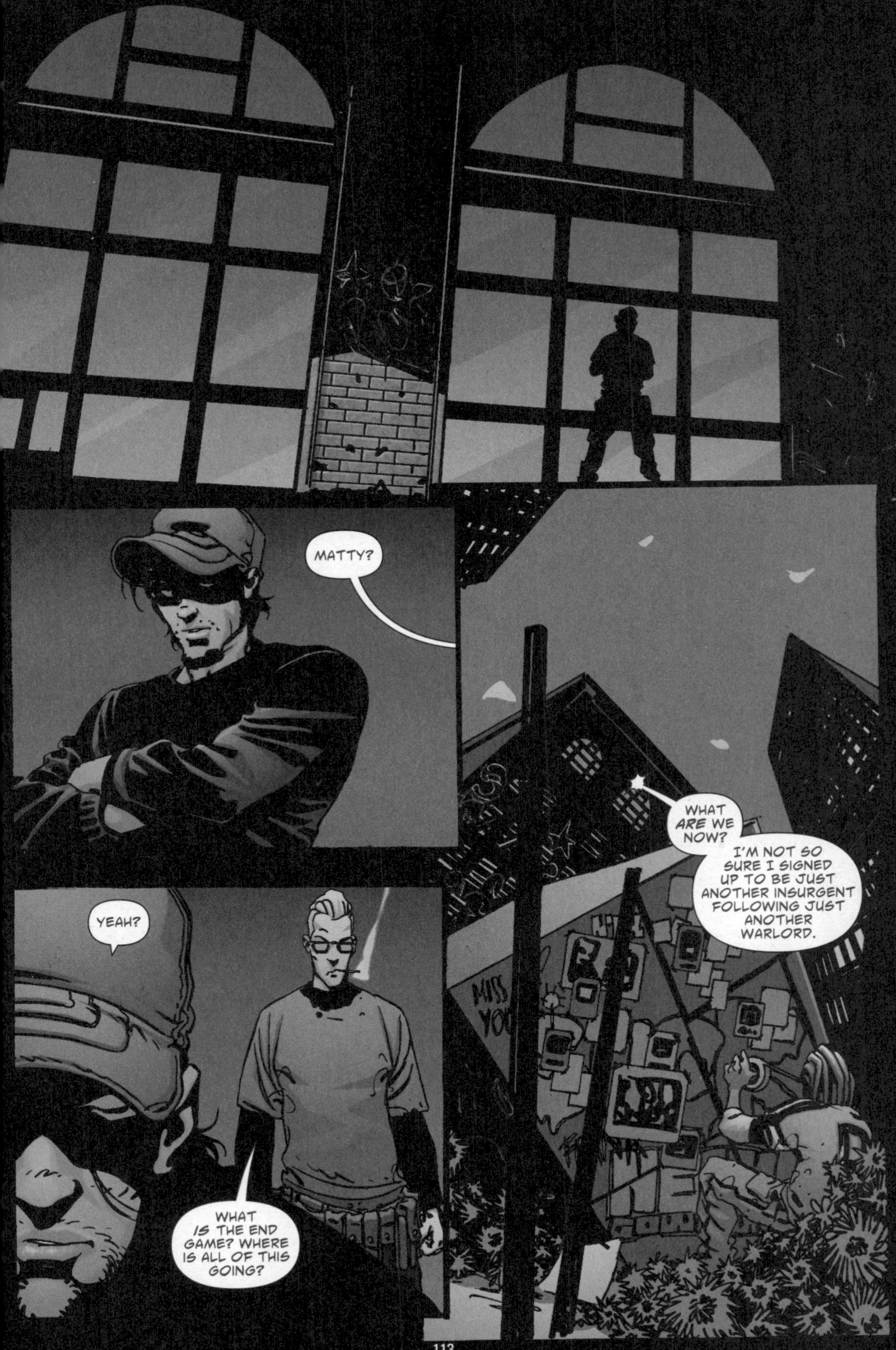
MATTY?
YEAH?
WHAT IS THE END GAME? WHERE IS ALL OF THIS GOING?
WHAT ARE WE NOW?
I'M NOT SO SURE I SIGNED UP TO BE JUST ANOTHER INSURGENT FOLLOWING JUST ANOTHER WARLORD.
MISS YOU

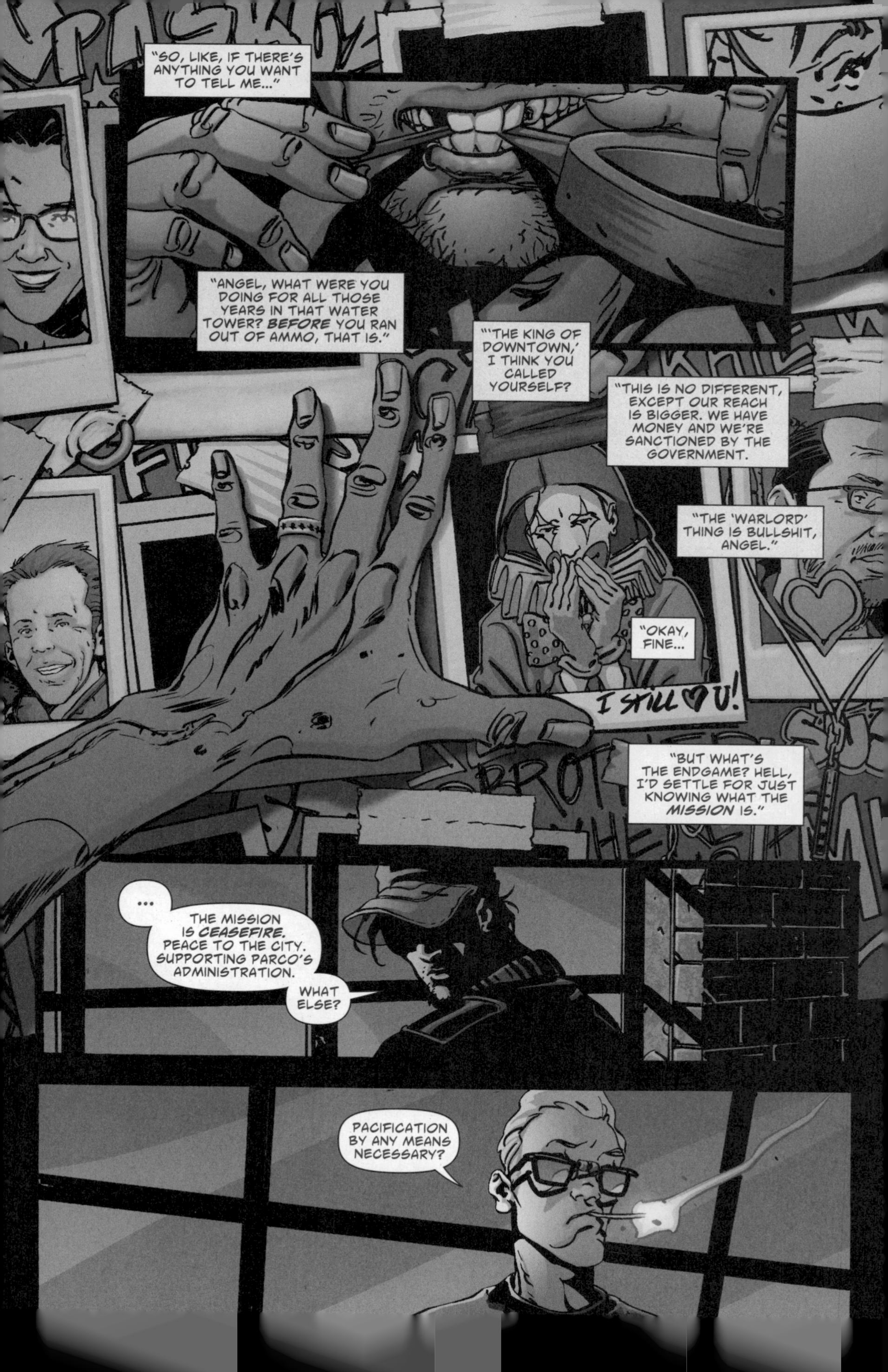
"SO, LIKE, IF THERE'S ANYTHING YOU WANT TO TELL ME..."
"ANGEL, WHAT WERE YOU DOING FOR ALL THOSE YEARS IN THAT WATER TOWER? *BEFORE* YOU RAN OUT OF AMMO, THAT IS."
"'THE KING OF DOWNTOWN,' I THINK YOU CALLED YOURSELF?
"THIS IS NO DIFFERENT, EXCEPT OUR REACH IS BIGGER. WE HAVE MONEY AND WE'RE SANCTIONED BY THE GOVERNMENT.
"THE 'WARLORD' THING IS BULLSHIT, ANGEL."
"OKAY, FINE...
I STILL ♥ U!
"BUT WHAT'S THE ENDGAME? HELL, I'D SETTLE FOR JUST KNOWING WHAT THE *MISSION* IS."
... THE MISSION IS *CEASEFIRE.* PEACE TO THE CITY. SUPPORTING PARCO'S ADMINISTRATION.
WHAT ELSE?
PACIFICATION BY ANY MEANS NECESSARY?

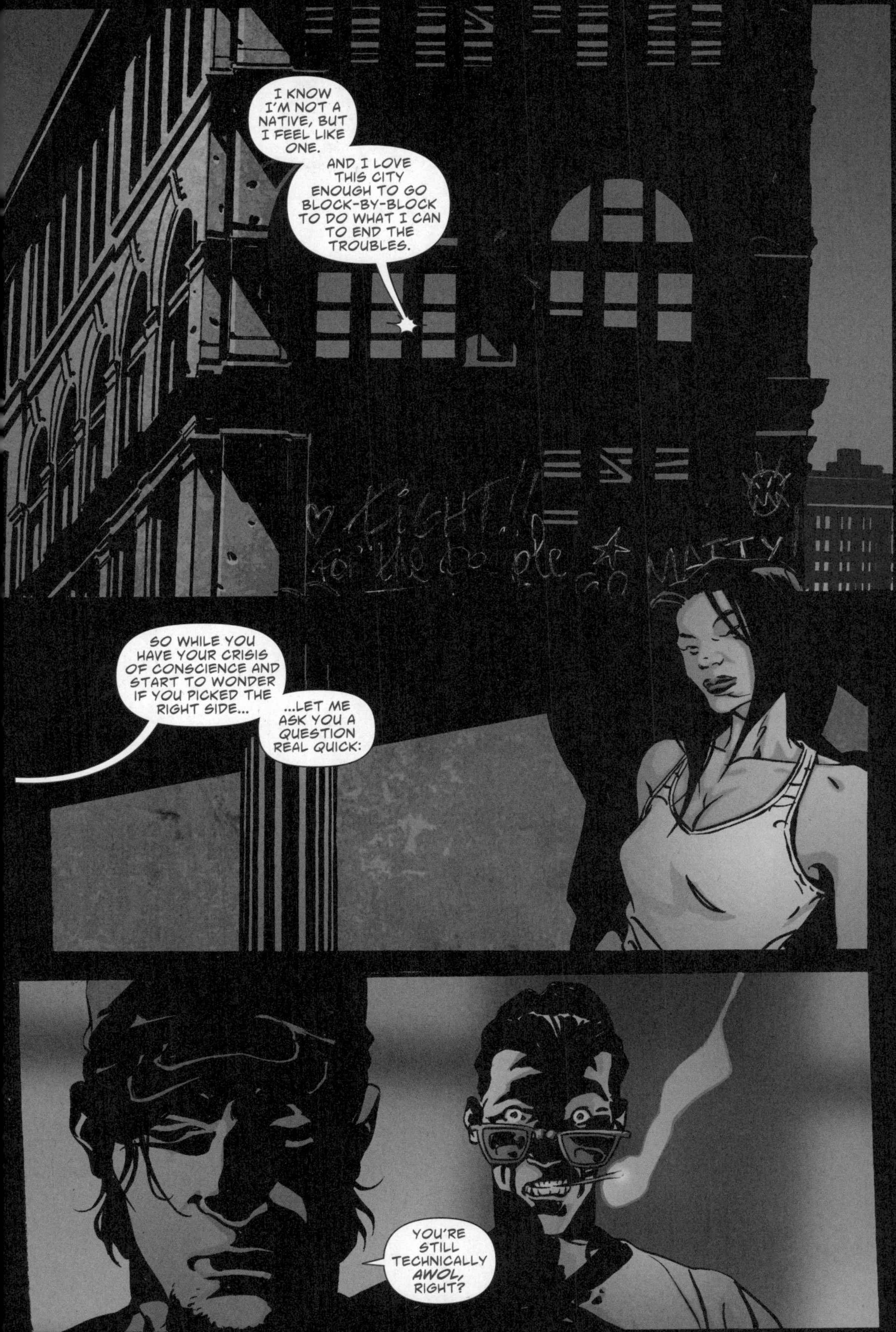
I KNOW I'M NOT A NATIVE, BUT I FEEL LIKE ONE.
AND I LOVE THIS CITY ENOUGH TO GO BLOCK-BY-BLOCK TO DO WHAT I CAN TO END THE TROUBLES.
SO WHILE YOU HAVE YOUR CRISIS OF CONSCIENCE AND START TO WONDER IF YOU PICKED THE RIGHT SIDE...
...LET ME ASK YOU A QUESTION REAL QUICK:
YOU'RE STILL TECHNICALLY *AWOL*, RIGHT?

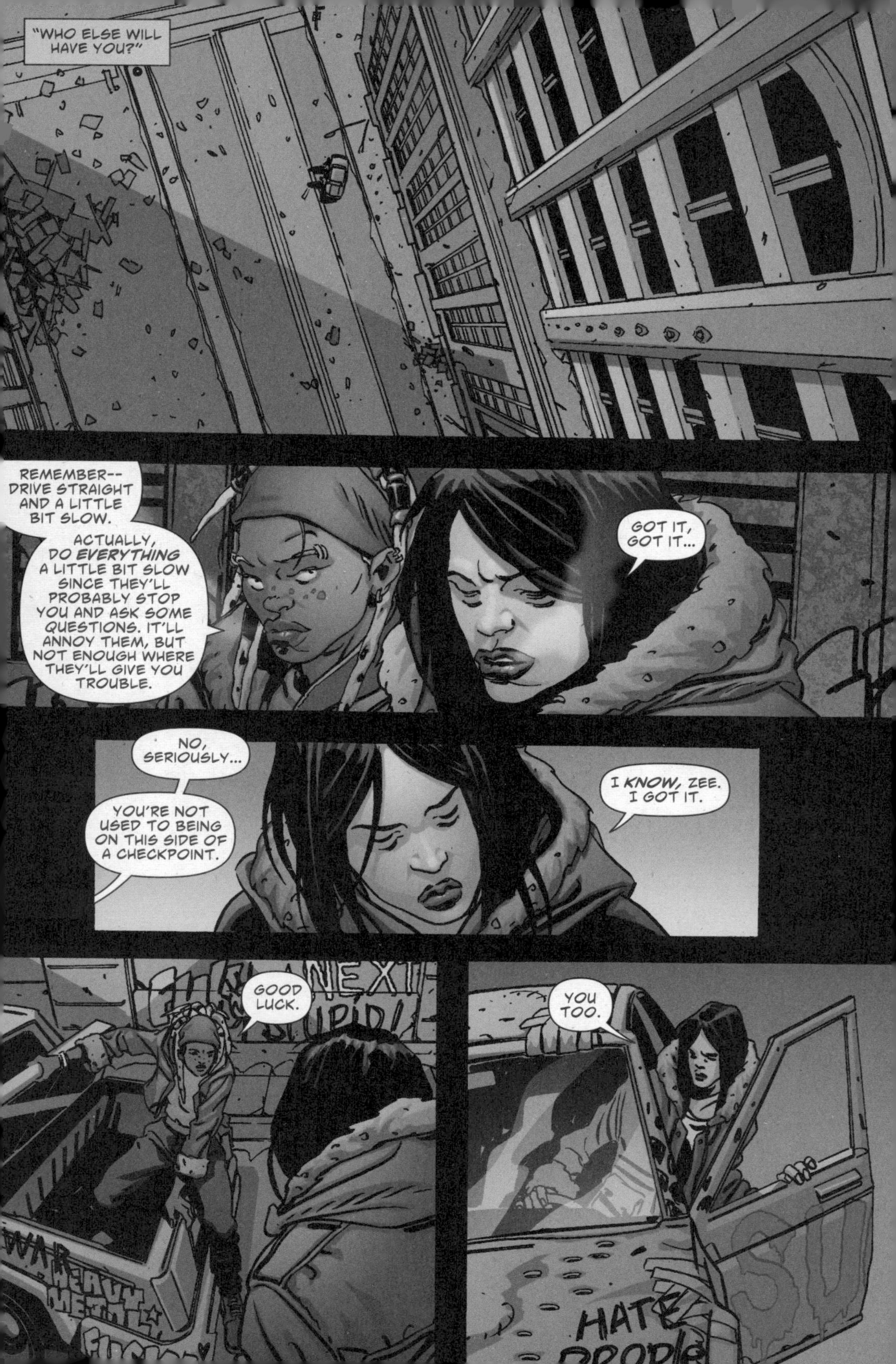
"WHO ELSE WILL HAVE YOU?"
REMEMBER-- DRIVE STRAIGHT AND A LITTLE BIT SLOW.
ACTUALLY, DO *EVERYTHING* A LITTLE BIT SLOW SINCE THEY'LL PROBABLY STOP YOU AND ASK SOME QUESTIONS. IT'LL ANNOY THEM, BUT NOT ENOUGH WHERE THEY'LL GIVE YOU TROUBLE.
GOT IT, GOT IT...
NO, SERIOUSLY...
YOU'RE NOT USED TO BEING ON THIS SIDE OF A CHECKPOINT.
I *KNOW*, ZEE. I GOT IT.
GOOD LUCK.
YOU TOO.
HATE

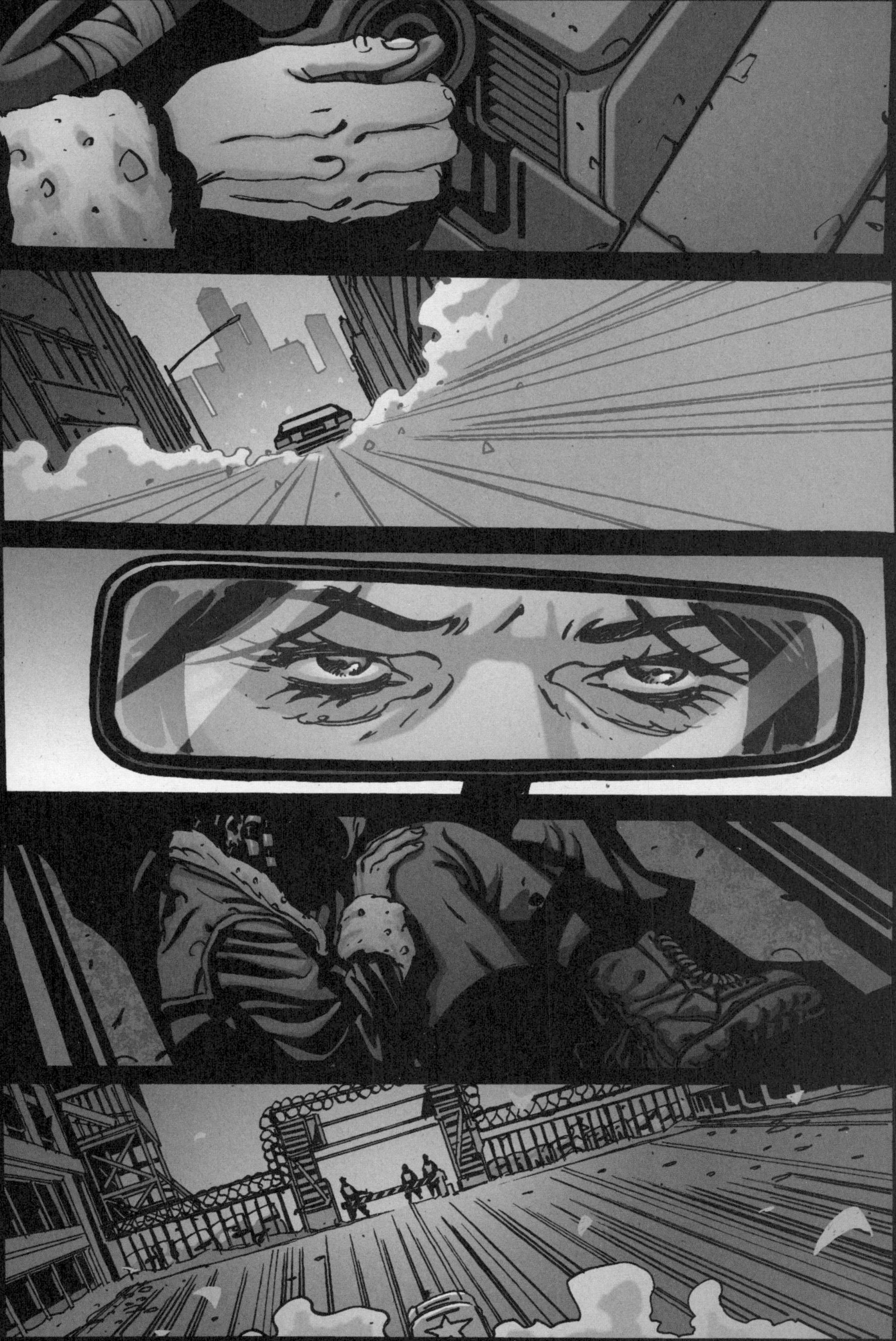

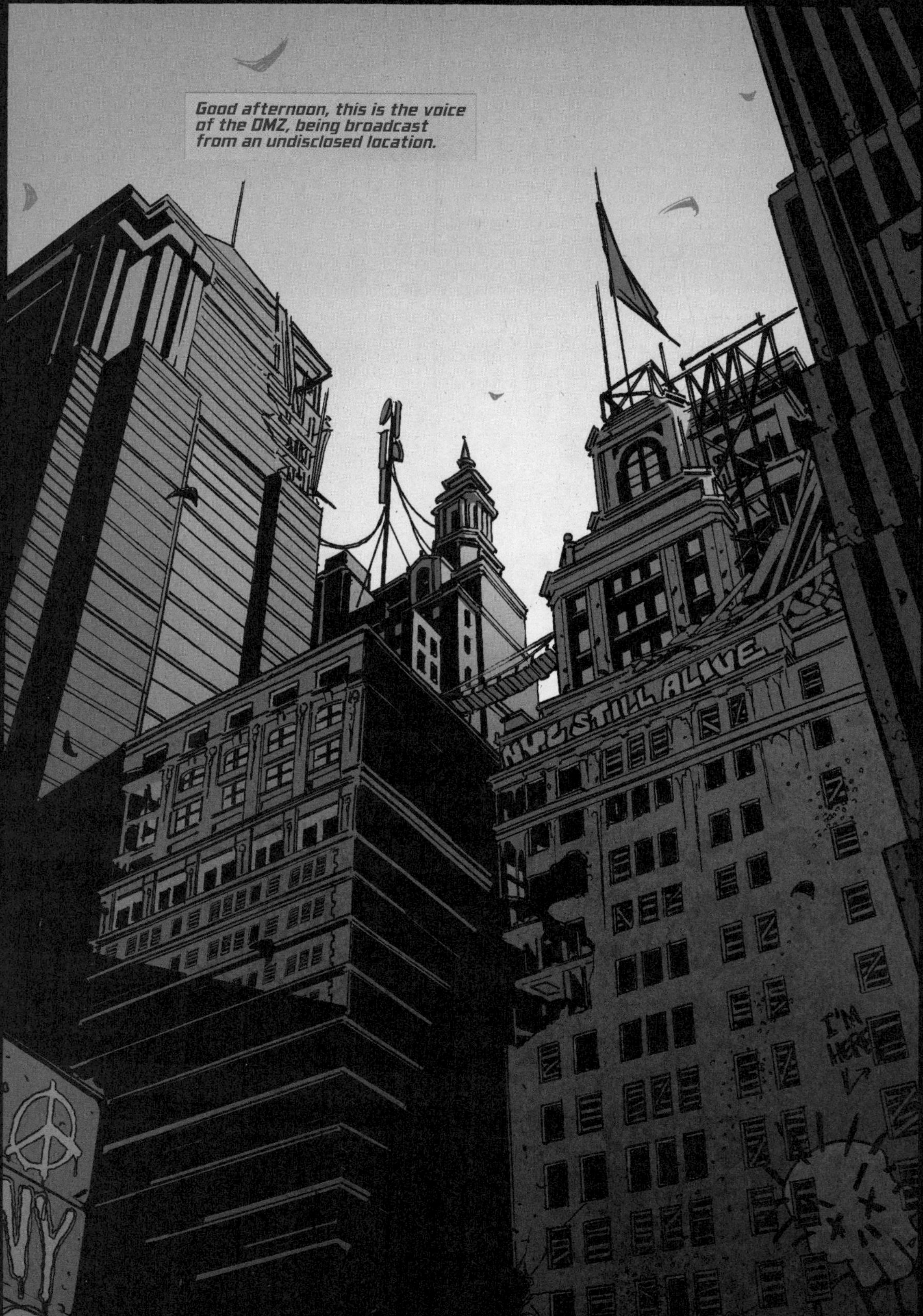
Good afternoon, this is the voice of the DMZ, being broadcast from an undisclosed location.
NYC STILL ALIVE
I'M HERE

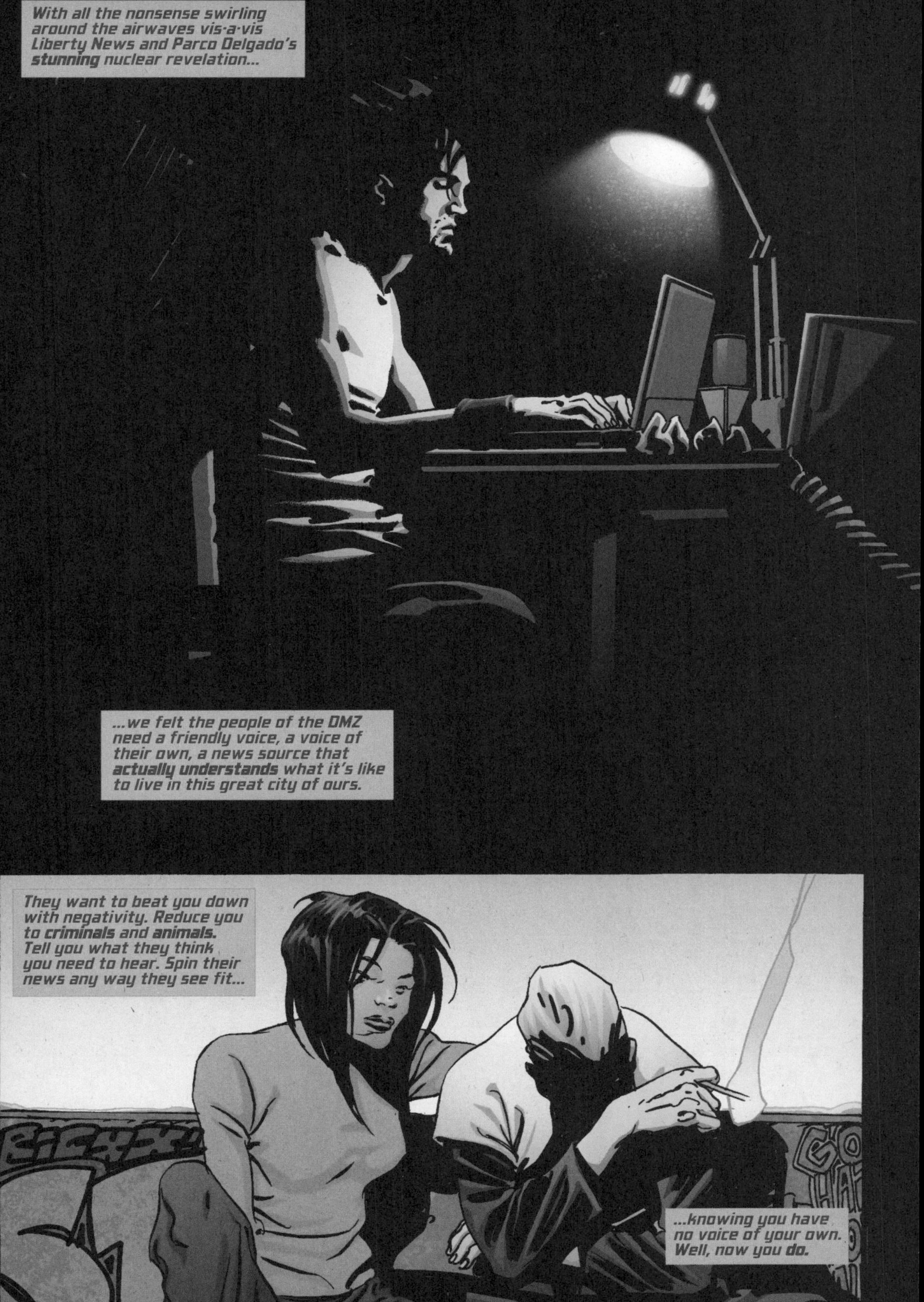
With all the nonsense swirling around the airwaves vis-a-vis Liberty News and Parco Delgado's **stunning** nuclear revelation...
...we felt the people of the DMZ need a friendly voice, a voice of their own, a news source that **actually understands** what it's like to live in this great city of ours.
They want to beat you down with negativity. Reduce you to **criminals** and **animals.** Tell you what they think you need to hear. Spin their news any way they see fit...
...knowing you have no voice of your own. Well, now you **do.**

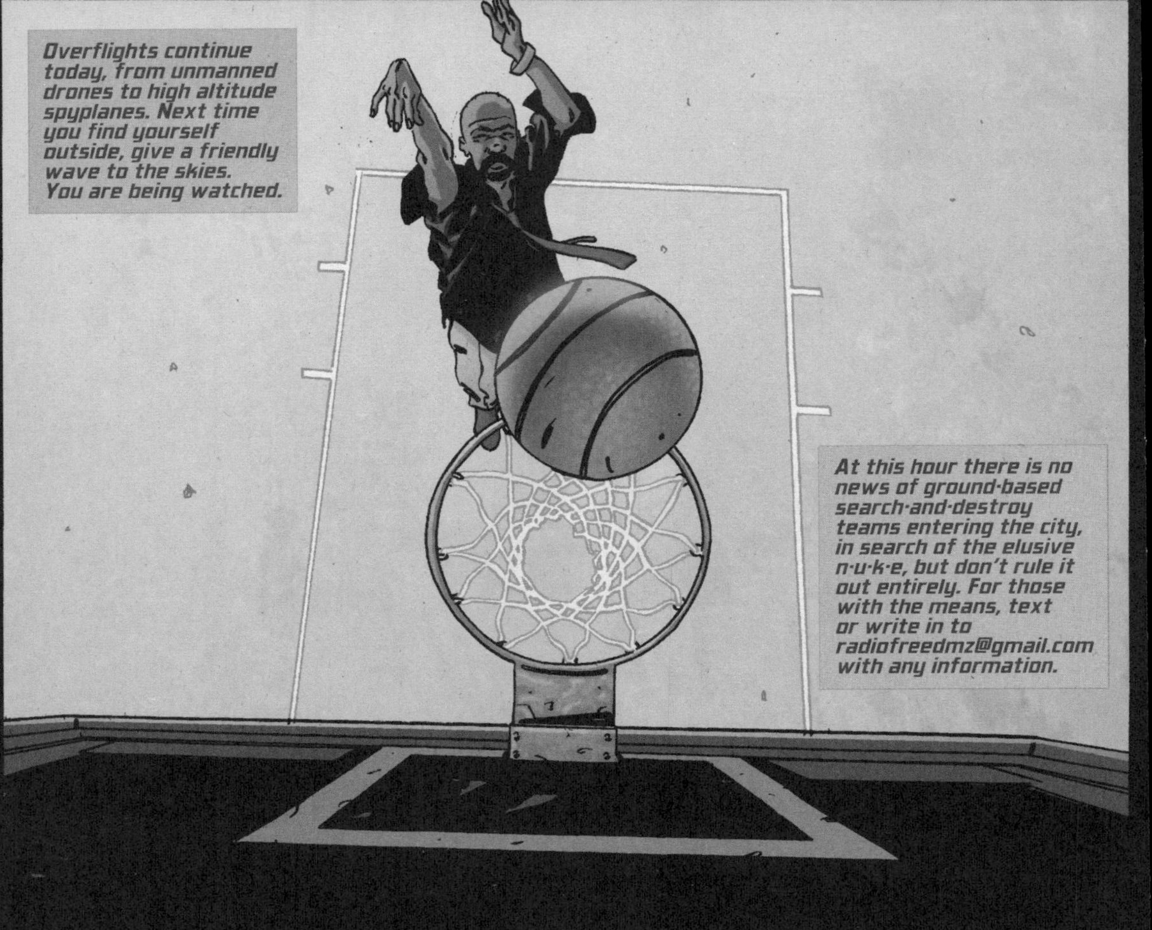
Overflights continue today, from unmanned drones to high altitude spyplanes. Next time you find yourself outside, give a friendly wave to the skies. You are being watched.
At this hour there is no news of ground-based search-and-destroy teams entering the city, in search of the elusive n-u-k-e, but don't rule it out entirely. For those with the means, text or write in to radiofreedmz@gmail.com with any information.

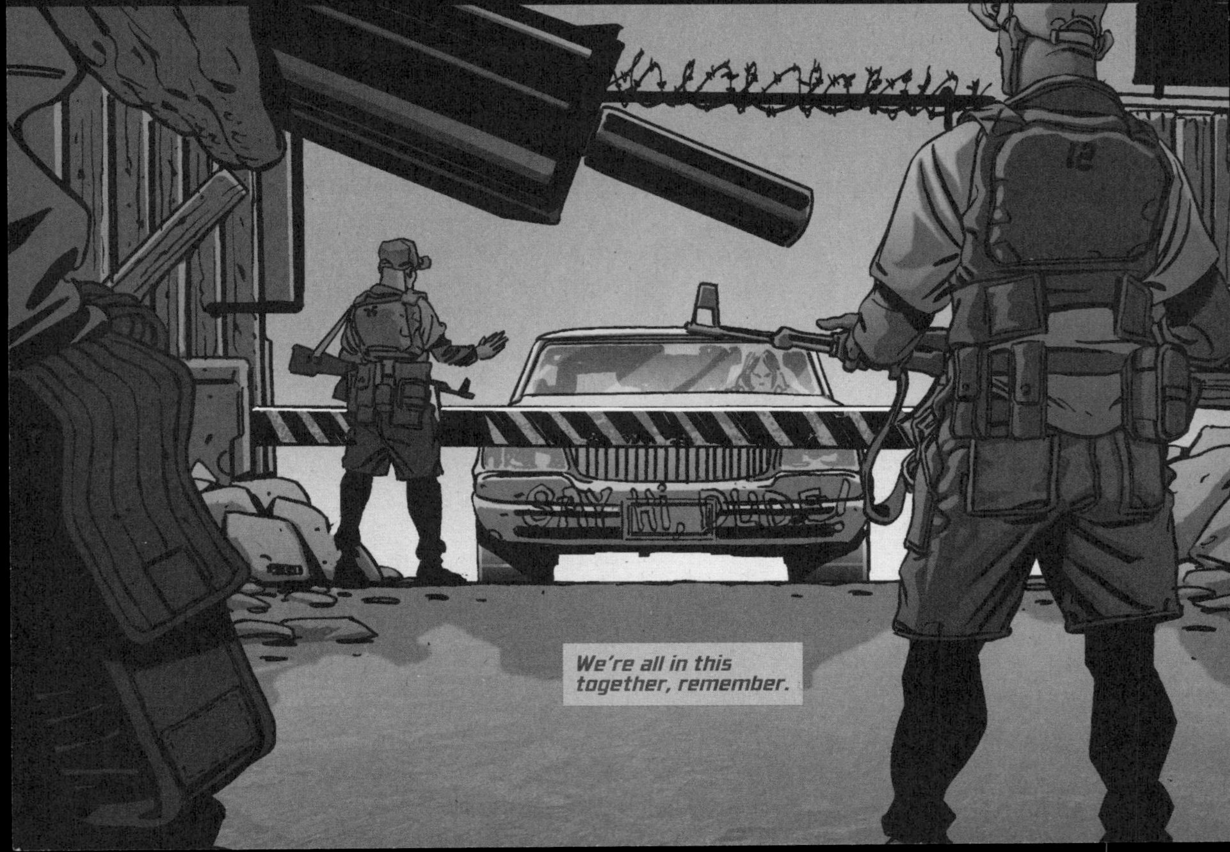
SAY HI, DUDE!
We're all in this together, remember.

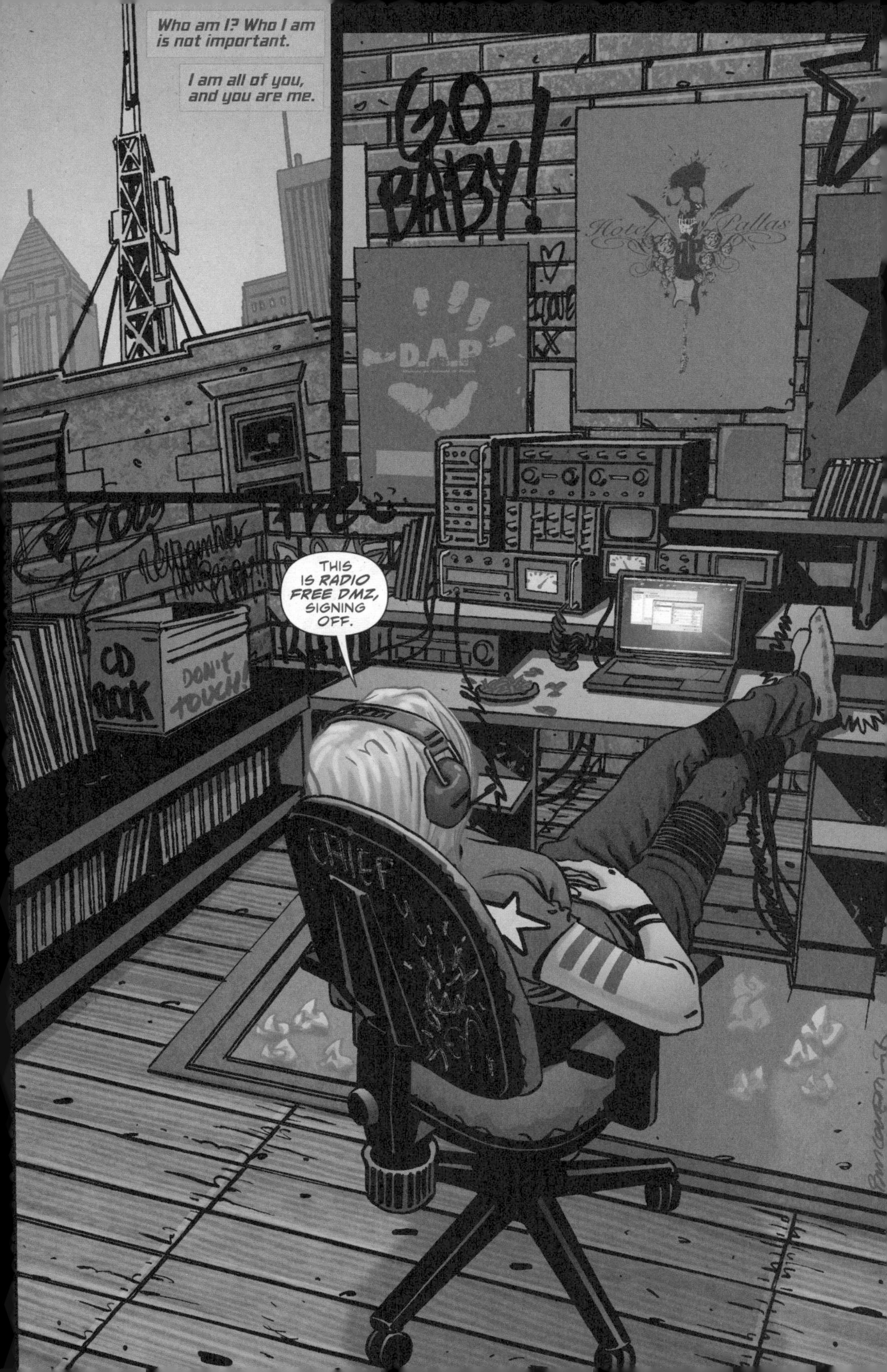
Who am I? Who I am is not important.
I am all of you, and you are me.
GO BABY!
Hotel Pallas
D.A.P
CD ROCK
DON'T TOUCH!
THIS IS RADIO FREE DMZ, SIGNING OFF.
CHIEF

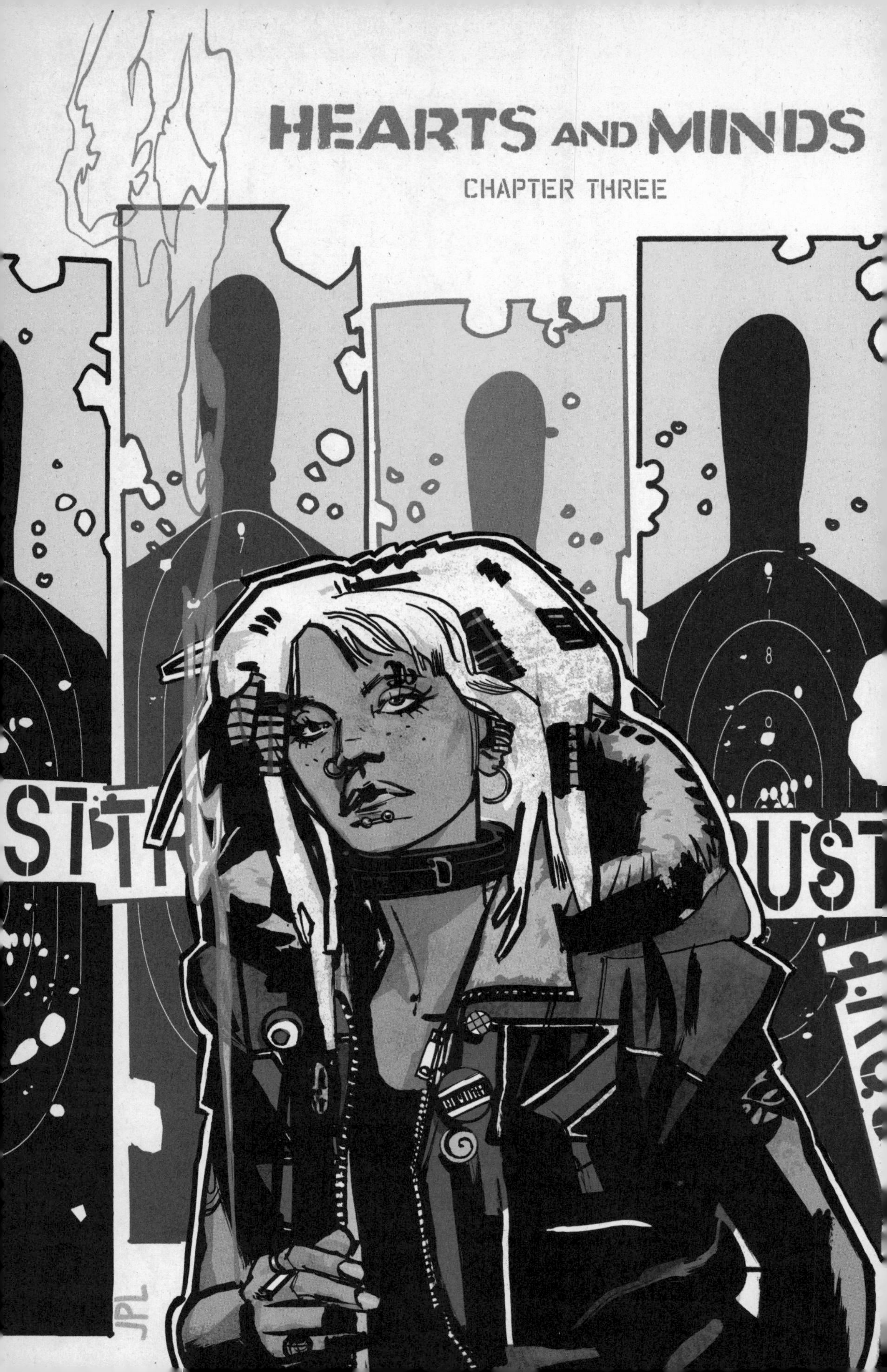
HEARTS AND MINDS
CHAPTER THREE
JPL

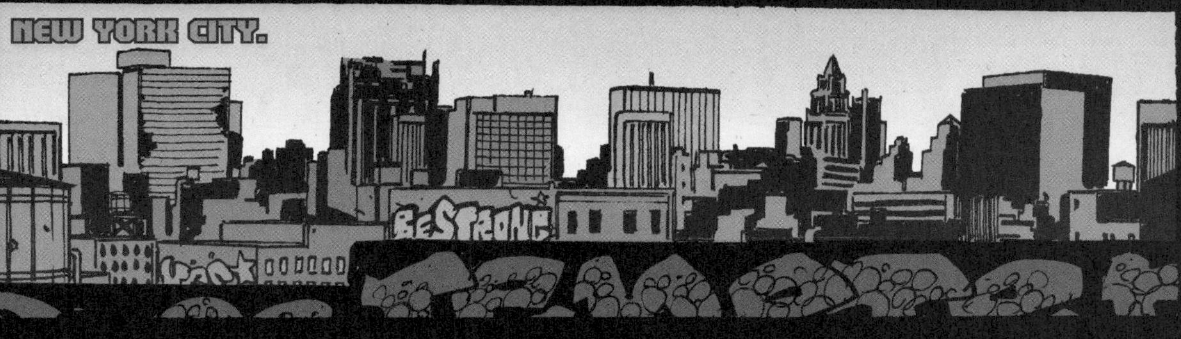
NEW YORK CITY.
BE STRONG

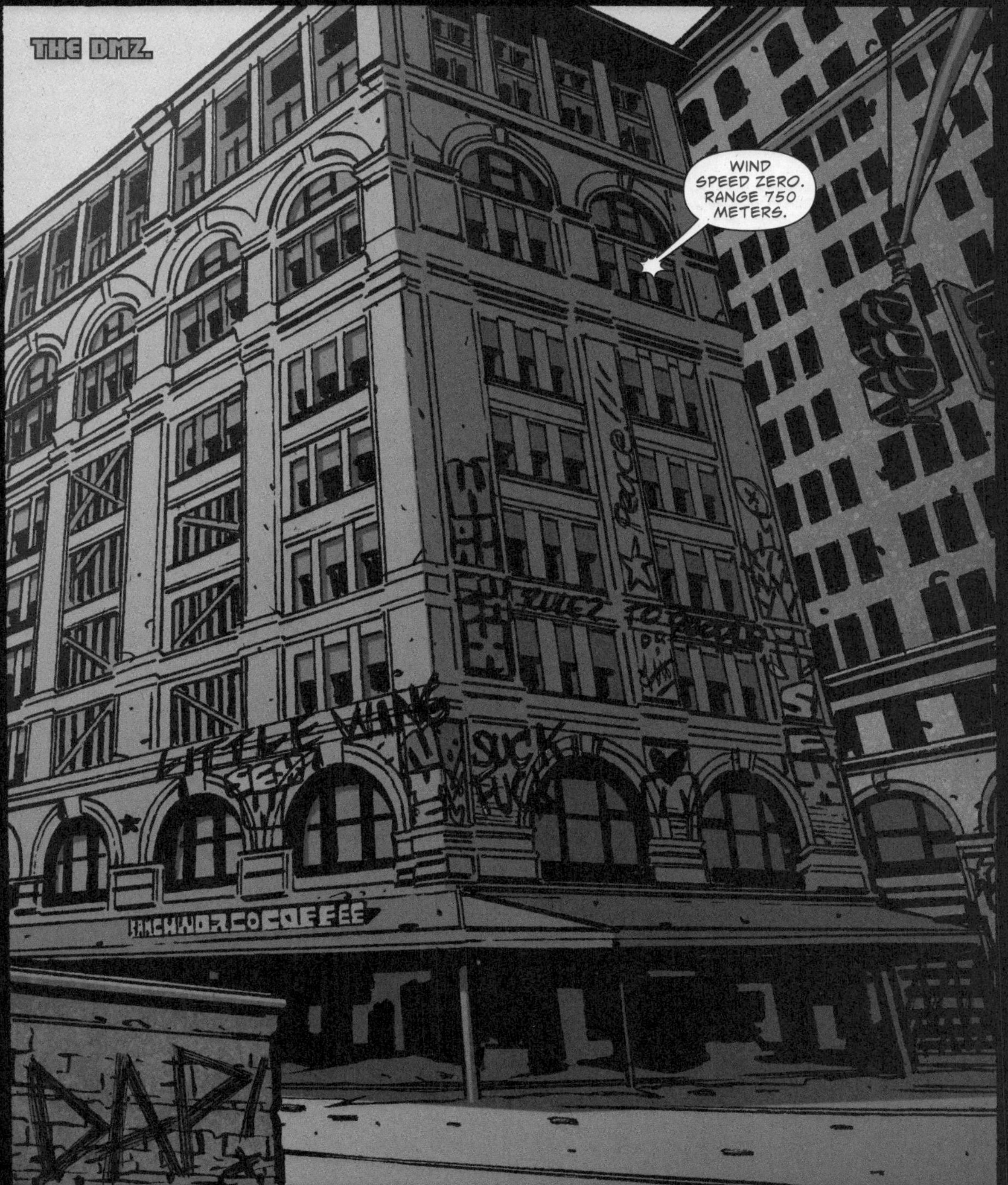
THE DMZ.
WIND SPEED ZERO. RANGE 750 METERS.
SUCK
COFFEE

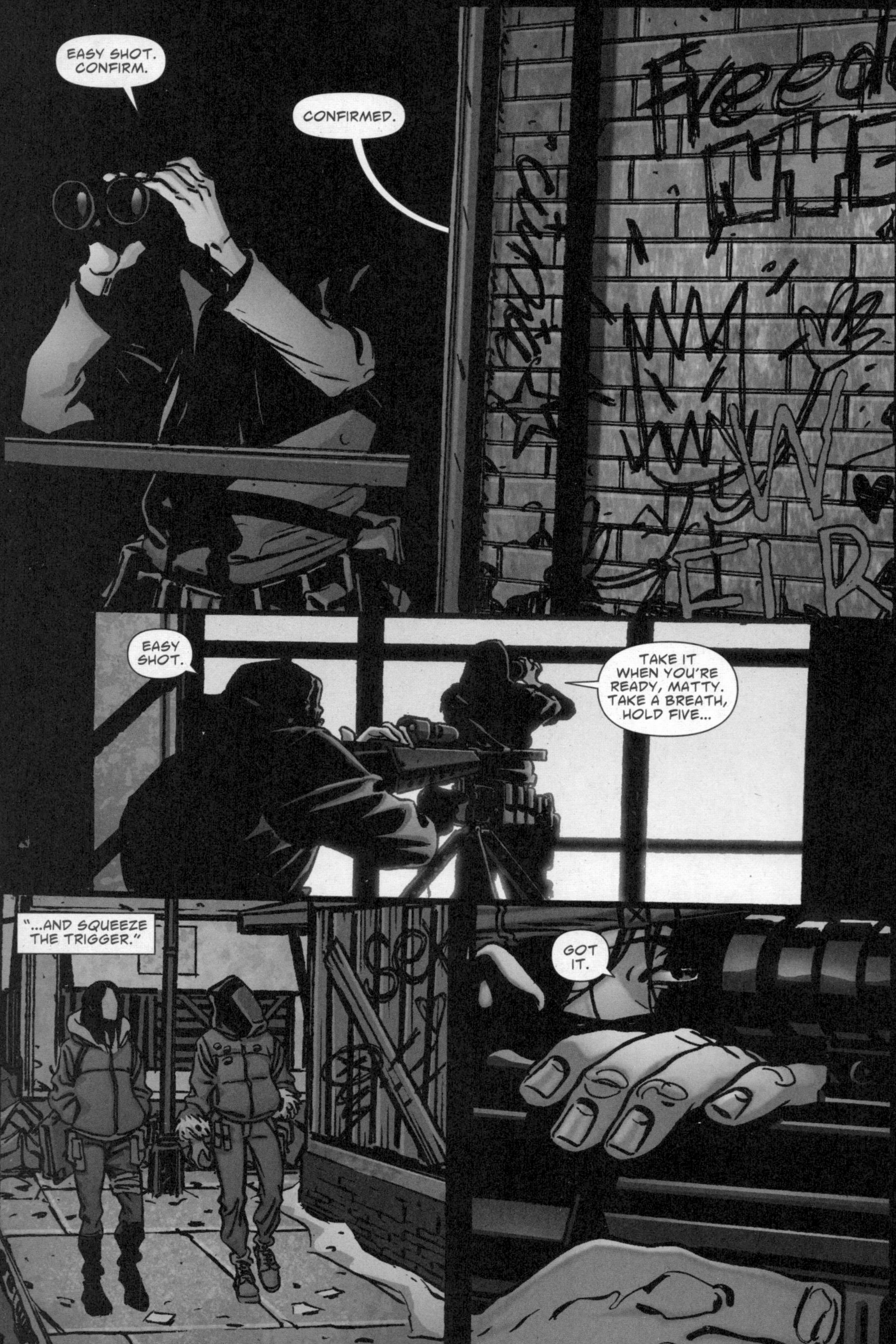
EASY SHOT. CONFIRM.
CONFIRMED.
EASY SHOT.
TAKE IT WHEN YOU'RE READY, MATTY. TAKE A BREATH, HOLD FIVE...
"...AND SQUEEZE THE TRIGGER."
GOT IT.

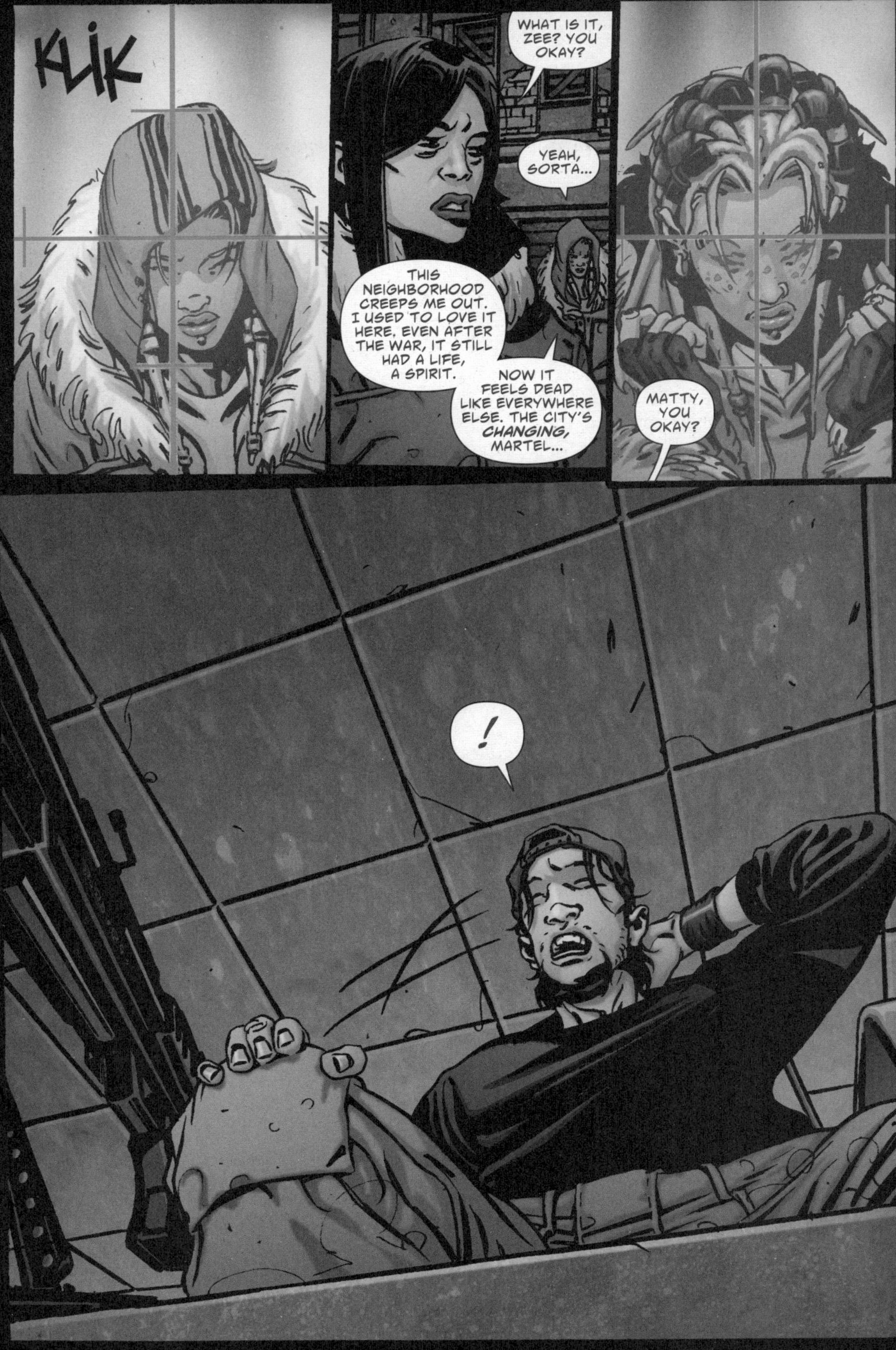
KLIK
WHAT IS IT, ZEE? YOU OKAY?
YEAH, SORTA...
THIS NEIGHBORHOOD CREEPS ME OUT. I USED TO LOVE IT HERE. EVEN AFTER THE WAR, IT STILL HAD A LIFE, A SPIRIT.
NOW IT FEELS DEAD LIKE EVERYWHERE ELSE. THE CITY'S *CHANGING,* MARTEL...
MATTY, YOU OKAY?
!

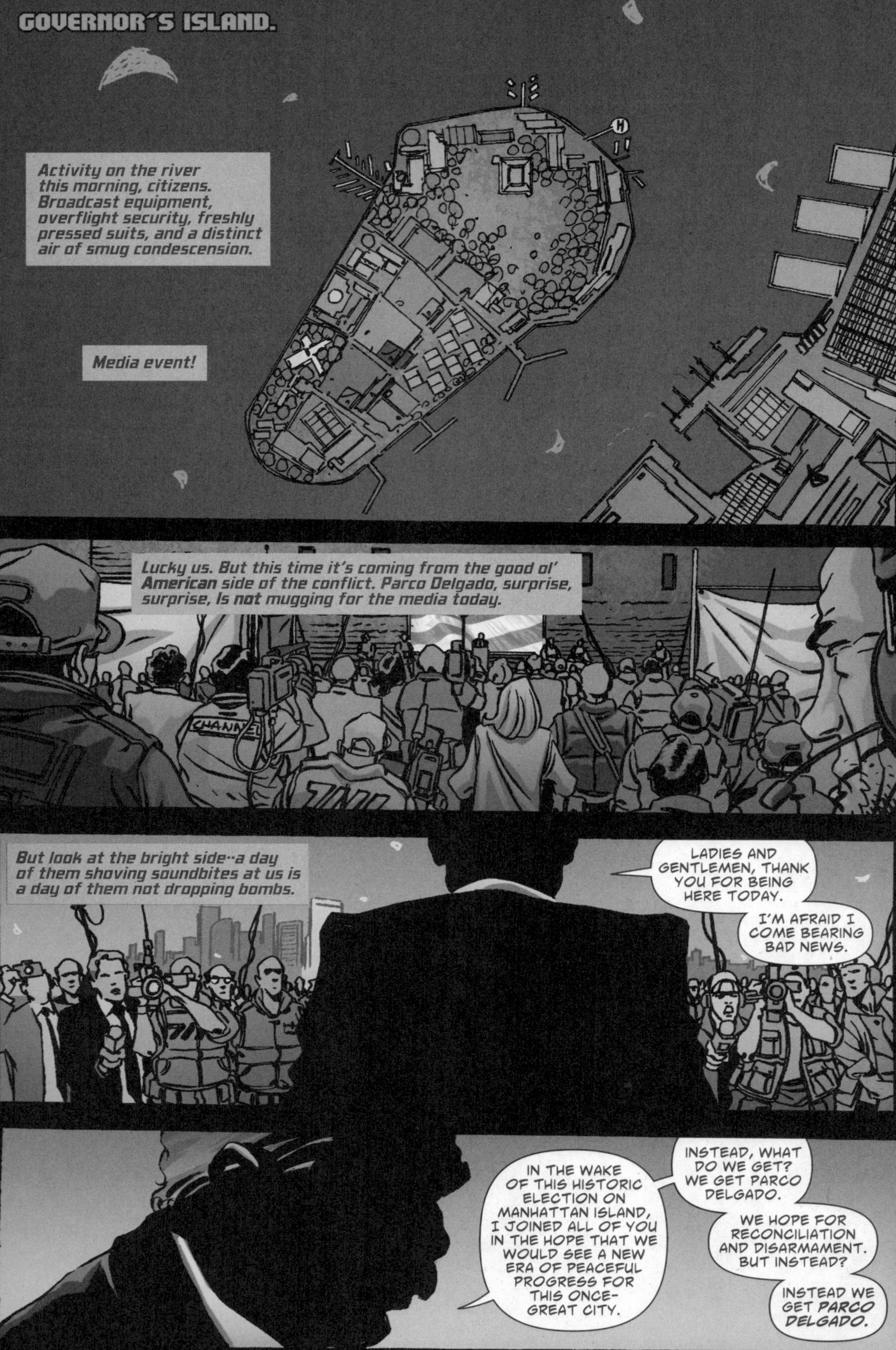
GOVERNOR'S ISLAND.
Activity on the river this morning, citizens. Broadcast equipment, overflight security, freshly pressed suits, and a distinct air of smug condescension.
Media event!
Lucky us. But this time it's coming from the good ol' American side of the conflict. Parco Delgado, surprise, surprise, Is not mugging for the media today.
CHANNEL
But look at the bright side--a day of them shoving soundbites at us is a day of them not dropping bombs.
LADIES AND GENTLEMEN, THANK YOU FOR BEING HERE TODAY.
I'M AFRAID I COME BEARING BAD NEWS.
IN THE WAKE OF THIS HISTORIC ELECTION ON MANHATTAN ISLAND, I JOINED ALL OF YOU IN THE HOPE THAT WE WOULD SEE A NEW ERA OF PEACEFUL PROGRESS FOR THIS ONCE-GREAT CITY.
INSTEAD, WHAT DO WE GET? WE GET PARCO DELGADO.
WE HOPE FOR RECONCILIATION AND DISARMAMENT. BUT INSTEAD?
INSTEAD WE GET PARCO DELGADO.

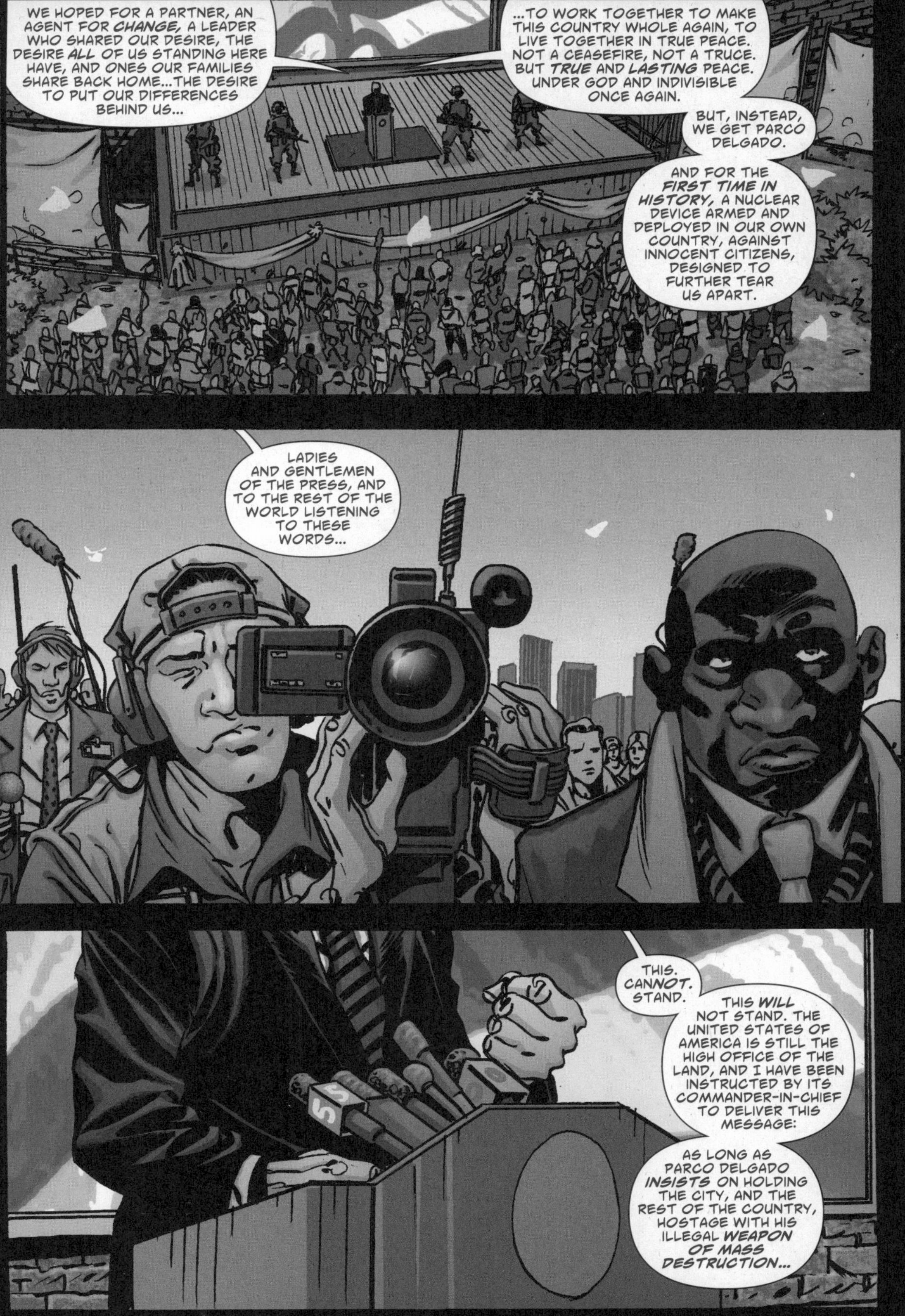
WE HOPED FOR A PARTNER, AN AGENT FOR *CHANGE*, A LEADER WHO SHARED OUR DESIRE, THE DESIRE *ALL* OF US STANDING HERE HAVE, AND ONES OUR FAMILIES SHARE BACK HOME...THE DESIRE TO PUT OUR DIFFERENCES BEHIND US...
...TO WORK TOGETHER TO MAKE THIS COUNTRY WHOLE AGAIN, TO LIVE TOGETHER IN TRUE PEACE. NOT A CEASEFIRE, NOT A TRUCE. BUT *TRUE* AND *LASTING* PEACE. UNDER GOD AND INDIVISIBLE ONCE AGAIN.
BUT, INSTEAD, WE GET PARCO DELGADO.
AND FOR THE *FIRST TIME IN HISTORY*, A NUCLEAR DEVICE ARMED AND DEPLOYED IN OUR OWN COUNTRY, AGAINST INNOCENT CITIZENS, DESIGNED TO FURTHER TEAR US APART.
LADIES AND GENTLEMEN OF THE PRESS, AND TO THE REST OF THE WORLD LISTENING TO THESE WORDS...
THIS. CANNOT. STAND.
THIS *WILL* NOT STAND. THE UNITED STATES OF AMERICA IS STILL THE HIGH OFFICE OF THE LAND, AND I HAVE BEEN INSTRUCTED BY ITS COMMANDER-IN-CHIEF TO DELIVER THIS MESSAGE:
AS LONG AS PARCO DELGADO *INSISTS* ON HOLDING THE CITY, AND THE REST OF THE COUNTRY, HOSTAGE WITH HIS ILLEGAL *WEAPON OF MASS DESTRUCTION*...

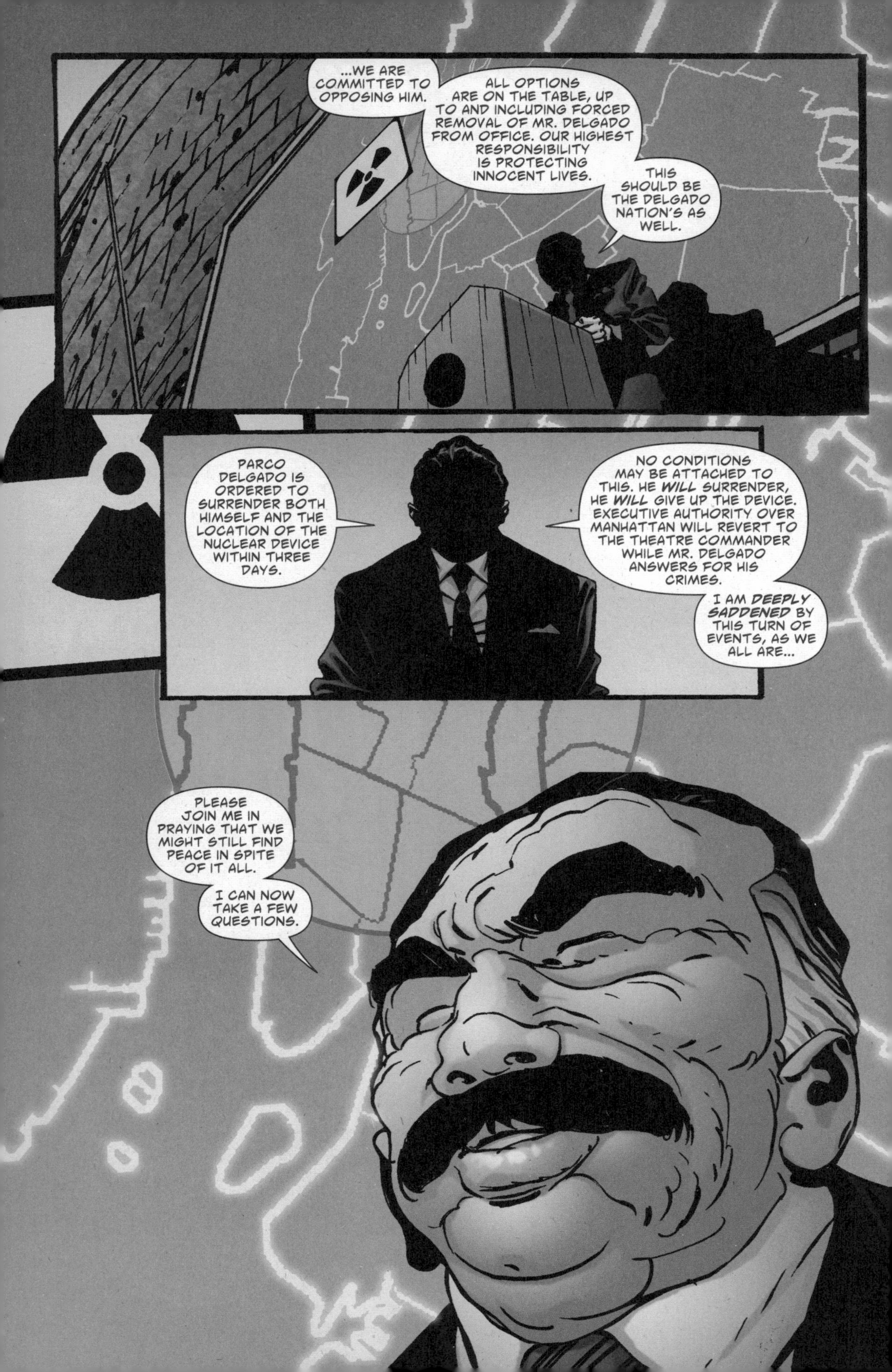
...WE ARE COMMITTED TO OPPOSING HIM.
ALL OPTIONS ARE ON THE TABLE, UP TO AND INCLUDING FORCED REMOVAL OF MR. DELGADO FROM OFFICE. OUR HIGHEST RESPONSIBILITY IS PROTECTING INNOCENT LIVES.
THIS SHOULD BE THE DELGADO NATION'S AS WELL.
PARCO DELGADO IS ORDERED TO SURRENDER BOTH HIMSELF AND THE LOCATION OF THE NUCLEAR DEVICE WITHIN THREE DAYS.
NO CONDITIONS MAY BE ATTACHED TO THIS. HE *WILL* SURRENDER, HE *WILL* GIVE UP THE DEVICE. EXECUTIVE AUTHORITY OVER MANHATTAN WILL REVERT TO THE THEATRE COMMANDER WHILE MR. DELGADO ANSWERS FOR HIS CRIMES.
I AM *DEEPLY SADDENED* BY THIS TURN OF EVENTS, AS WE ALL ARE...
PLEASE JOIN ME IN PRAYING THAT WE MIGHT STILL FIND PEACE IN SPITE OF IT ALL.
I CAN NOW TAKE A FEW QUESTIONS.

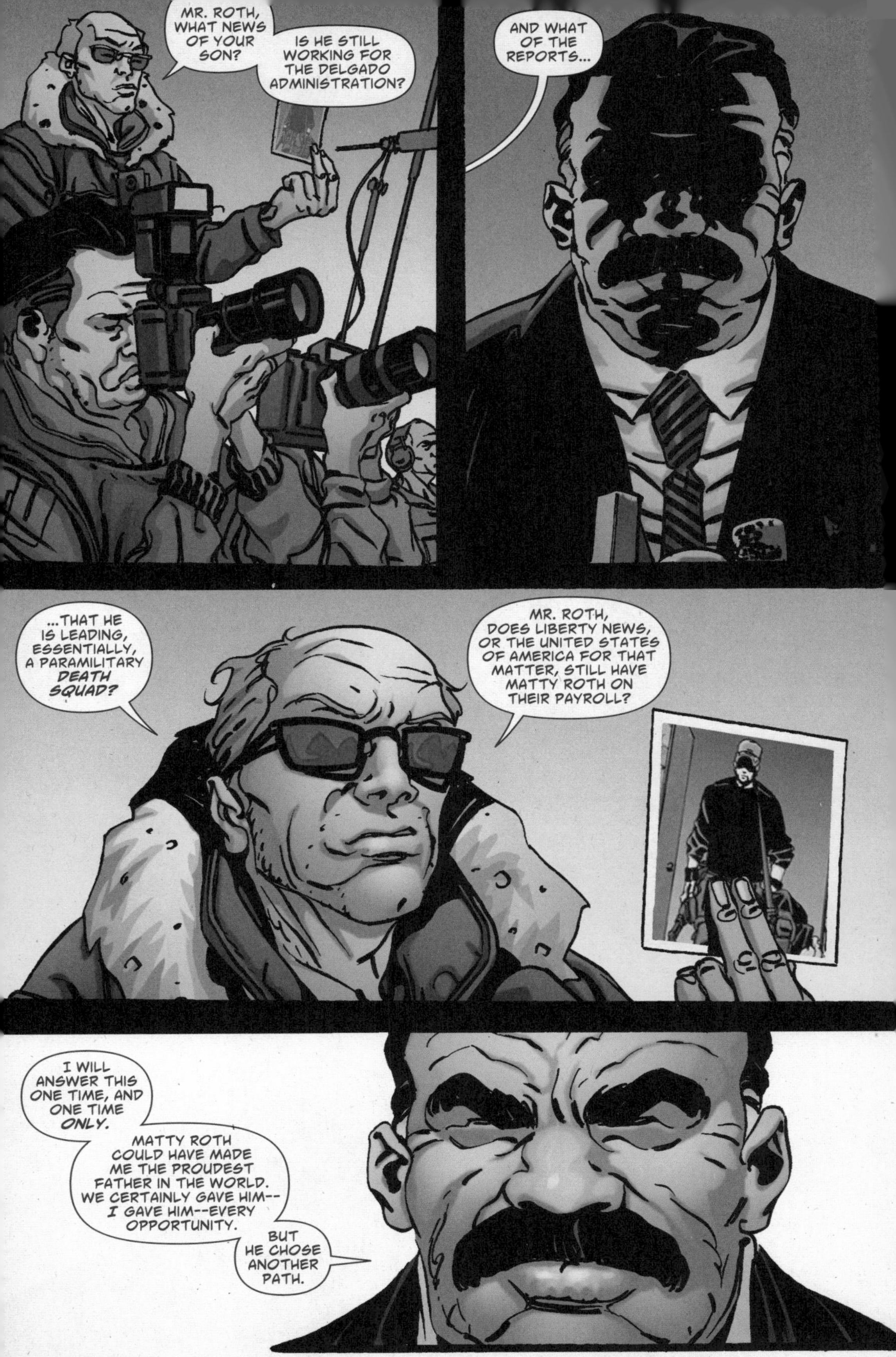
MR. ROTH, WHAT NEWS OF YOUR SON?
IS HE STILL WORKING FOR THE DELGADO ADMINISTRATION?
AND WHAT OF THE REPORTS...
...THAT HE IS LEADING, ESSENTIALLY, A PARAMILITARY *DEATH SQUAD?*
MR. ROTH, DOES LIBERTY NEWS, OR THE UNITED STATES OF AMERICA FOR THAT MATTER, STILL HAVE MATTY ROTH ON THEIR PAYROLL?
I WILL ANSWER THIS ONE TIME, AND ONE TIME *ONLY.*
MATTY ROTH COULD HAVE MADE ME THE PROUDEST FATHER IN THE WORLD. WE CERTAINLY GAVE HIM-- *I* GAVE HIM--EVERY OPPORTUNITY.
BUT HE CHOSE ANOTHER PATH.

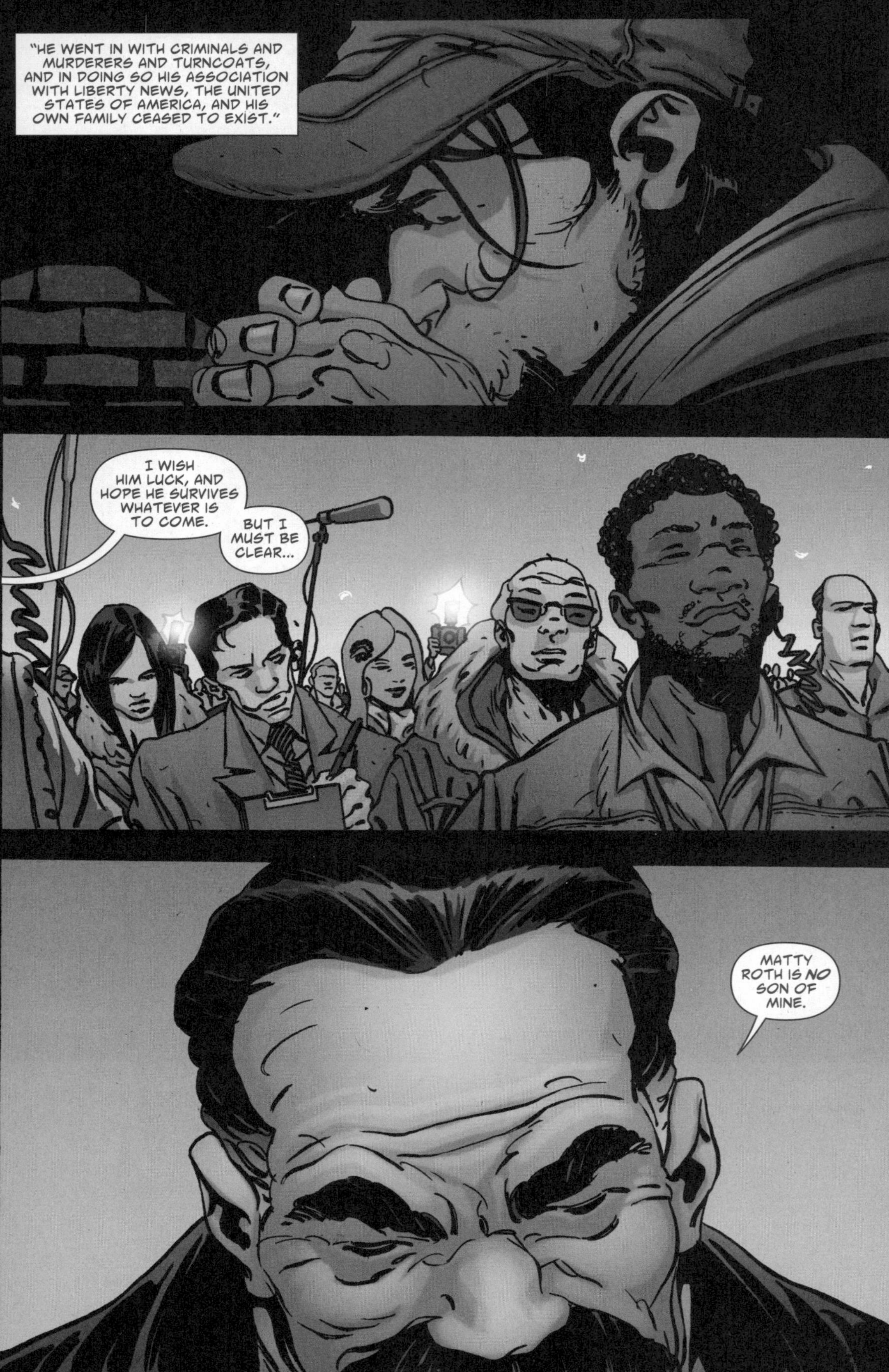
"HE WENT IN WITH CRIMINALS AND MURDERERS AND TURNCOATS, AND IN DOING SO HIS ASSOCIATION WITH LIBERTY NEWS, THE UNITED STATES OF AMERICA, AND HIS OWN FAMILY CEASED TO EXIST."
I WISH HIM LUCK, AND HOPE HE SURVIVES WHATEVER IS TO COME.
BUT I MUST BE CLEAR...
MATTY ROTH IS NO SON OF MINE.

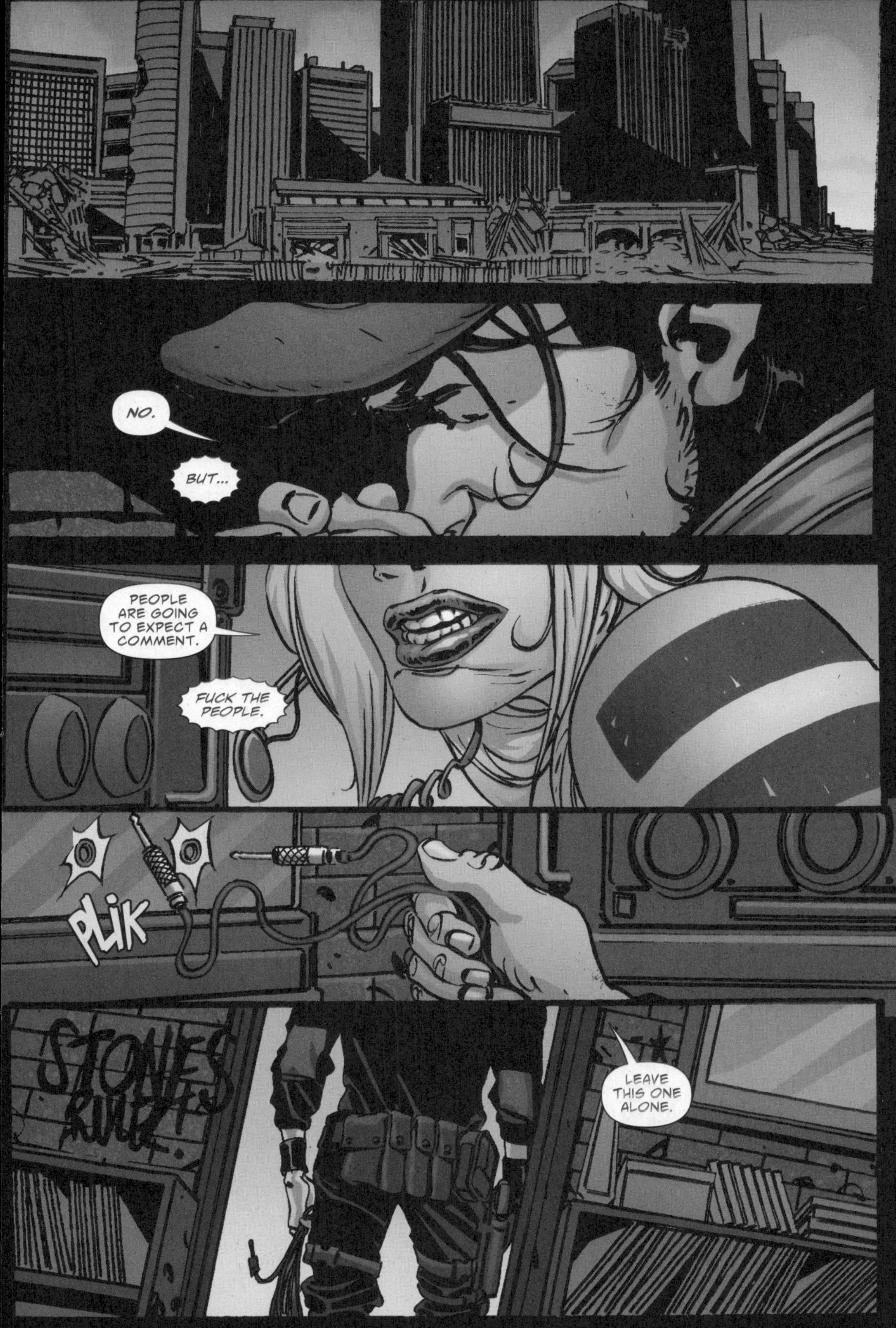
NO.
BUT...
PEOPLE ARE GOING TO EXPECT A COMMENT.
FUCK THE PEOPLE.
PLIK
STONES
LEAVE THIS ONE ALONE.

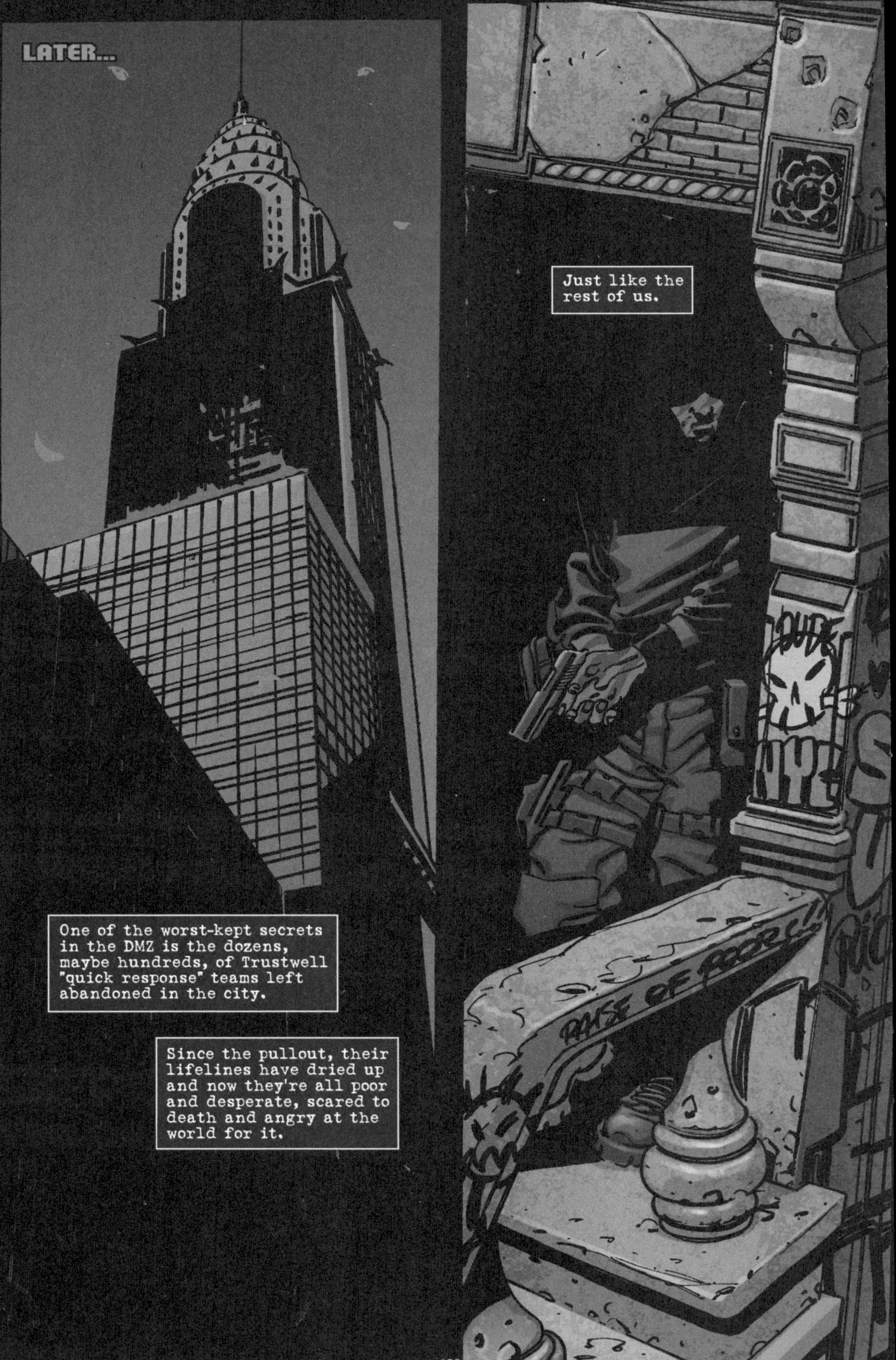
LATER...
One of the worst-kept secrets in the DMZ is the dozens, maybe hundreds, of Trustwell "quick response" teams left abandoned in the city.
Since the pullout, their lifelines have dried up and now they're all poor and desperate, scared to death and angry at the world for it.
Just like the rest of us.

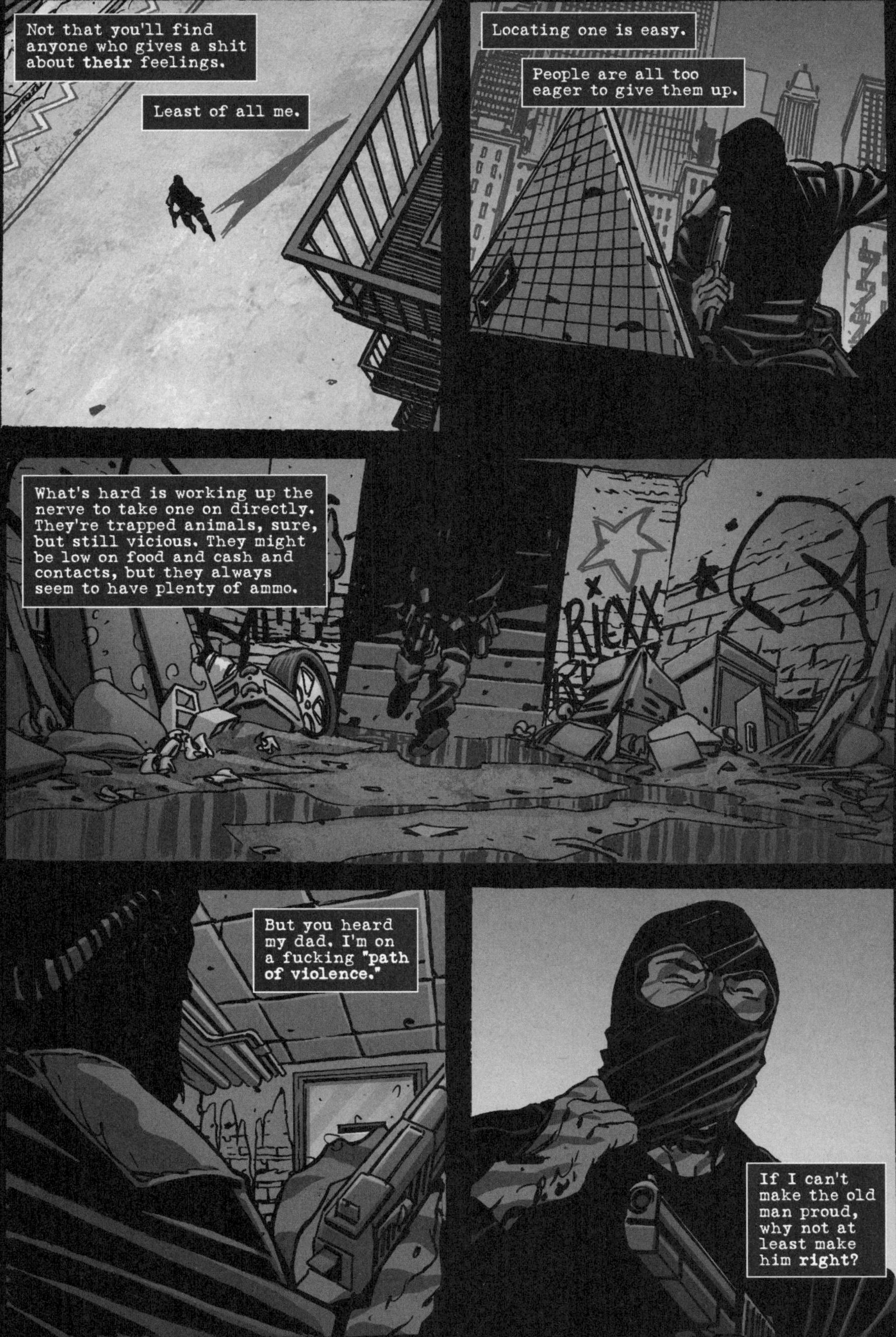
Not that you'll find anyone who gives a shit about **their** feelings.
Least of all me.
Locating one is easy.
People are all too eager to give them up.
What's hard is working up the nerve to take one on directly. They're trapped animals, sure, but still vicious. They might be low on food and cash and contacts, but they always seem to have plenty of ammo.
RICKX
But you heard my dad. I'm on a fucking **"path of violence."**
If I can't make the old man proud, why not at least make him **right?**

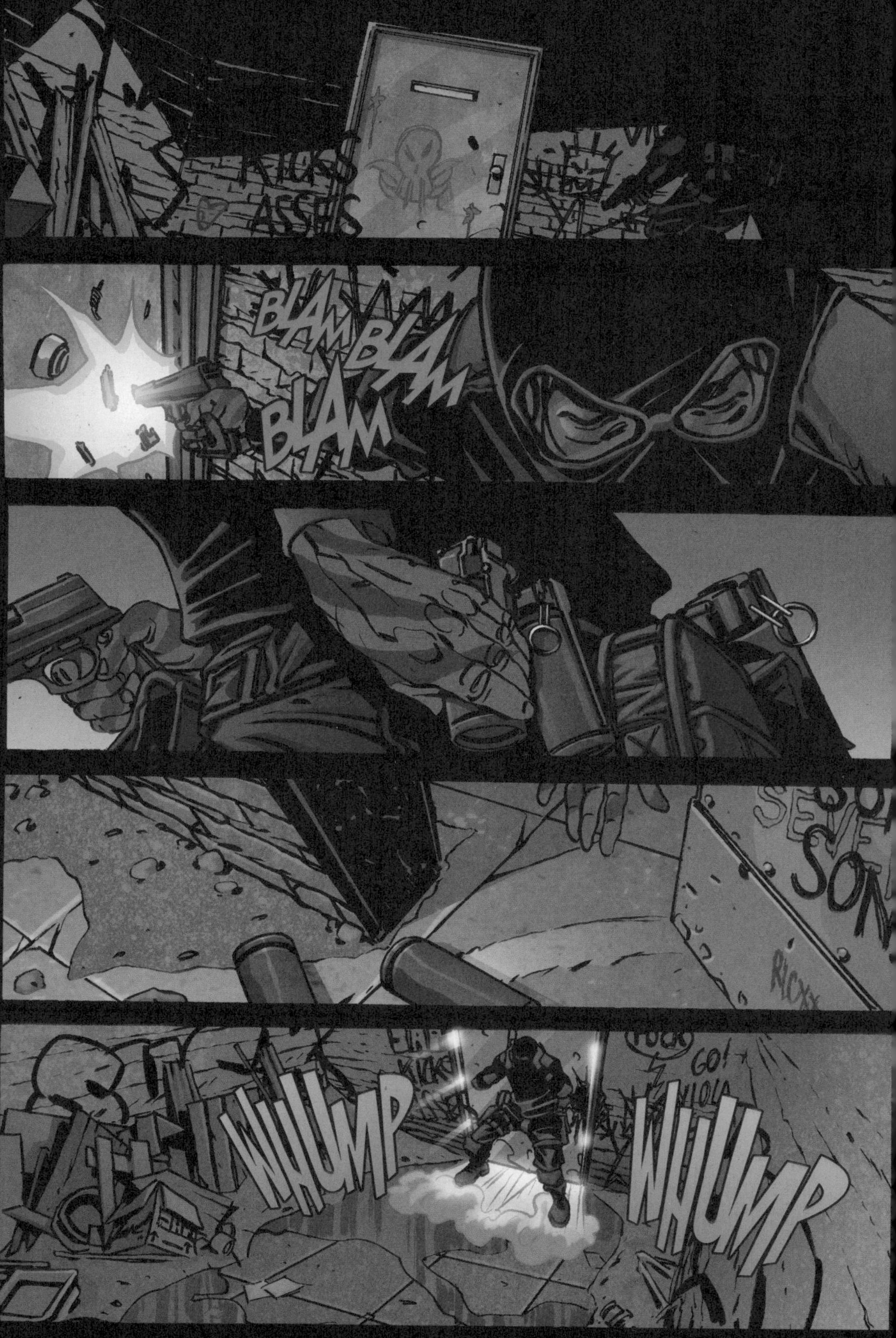
BLAM BLAM
BLAM
WHUMP
WHUMP

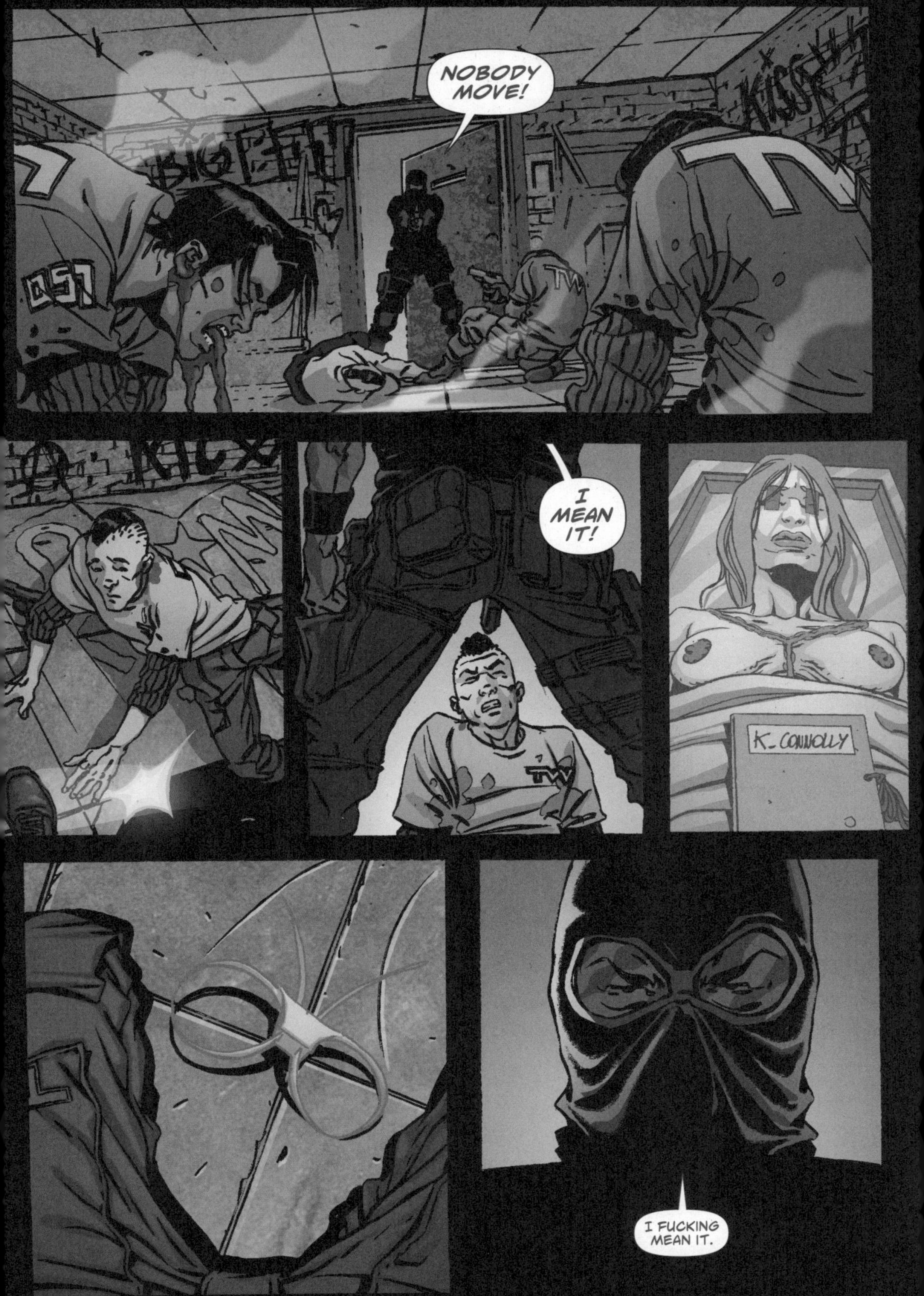

NOBODY MOVE!
BIG PETU
KISS
I MEAN IT!
K_CONNOLLY
I FUCKING MEAN IT.

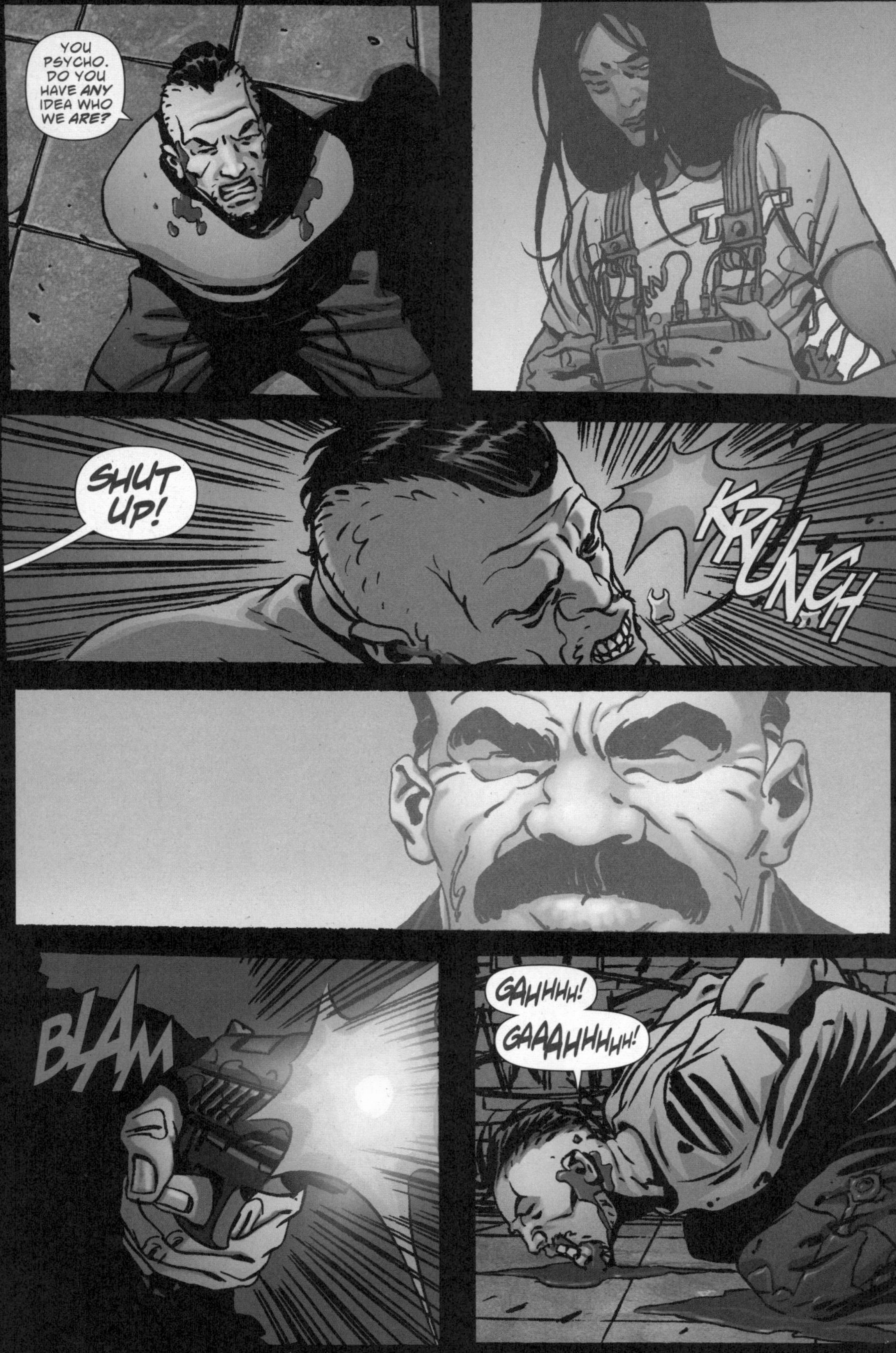
YOU PSYCHO. DO YOU HAVE ANY IDEA WHO WE ARE?
SHUT UP!
KRUNCH
BLAM
GAHHHH! GAAAHHHHH!

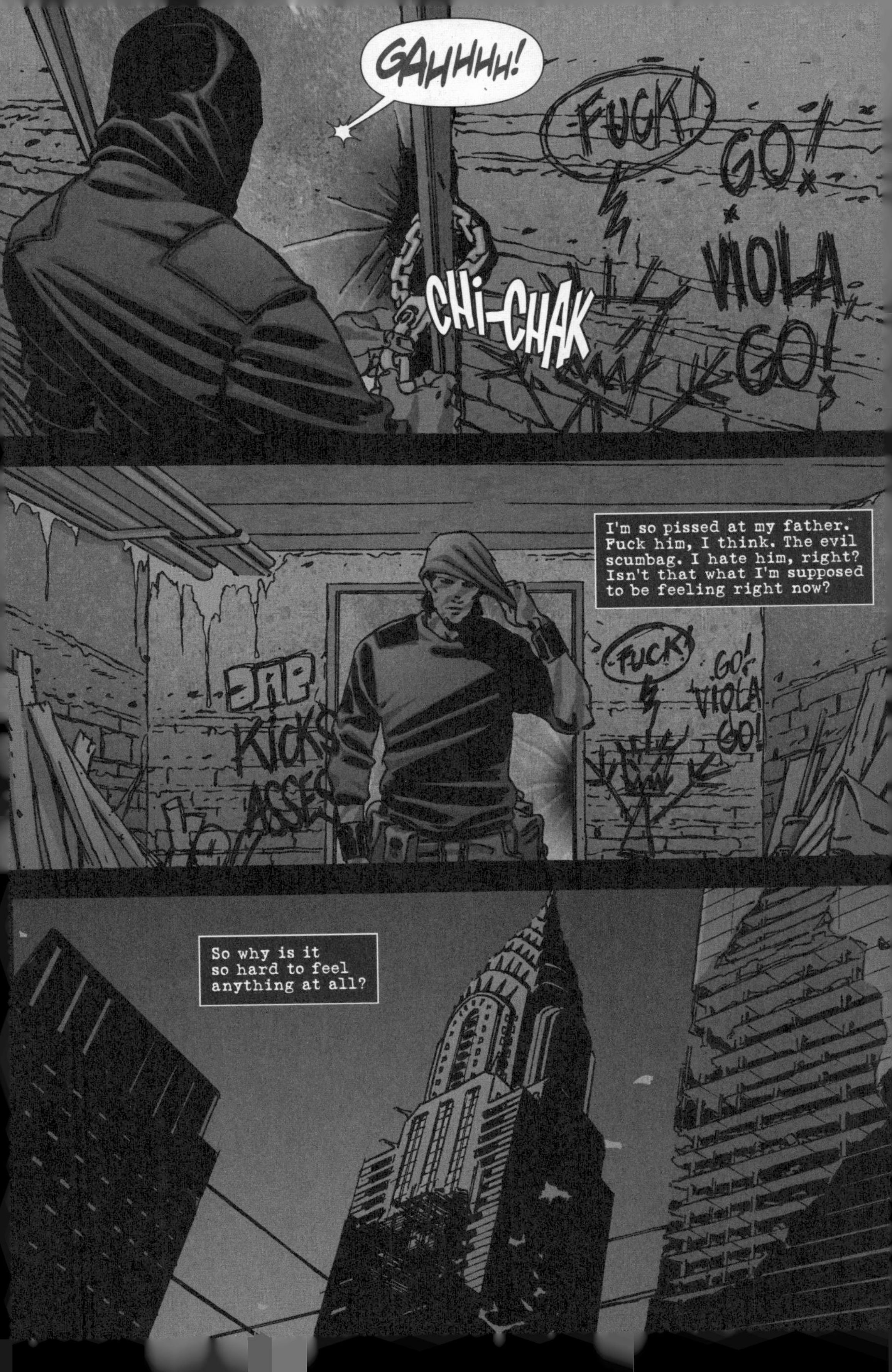
GAHHHH!
CHI-CHAK
FUCK!
GO! VIOLA GO!
I'm so pissed at my father. Fuck him, I think. The evil scumbag. I hate him, right? Isn't that what I'm supposed to be feeling right now?
KICKS
FUCK
GO! VIOLA GO!
So why is it so hard to feel anything at all?

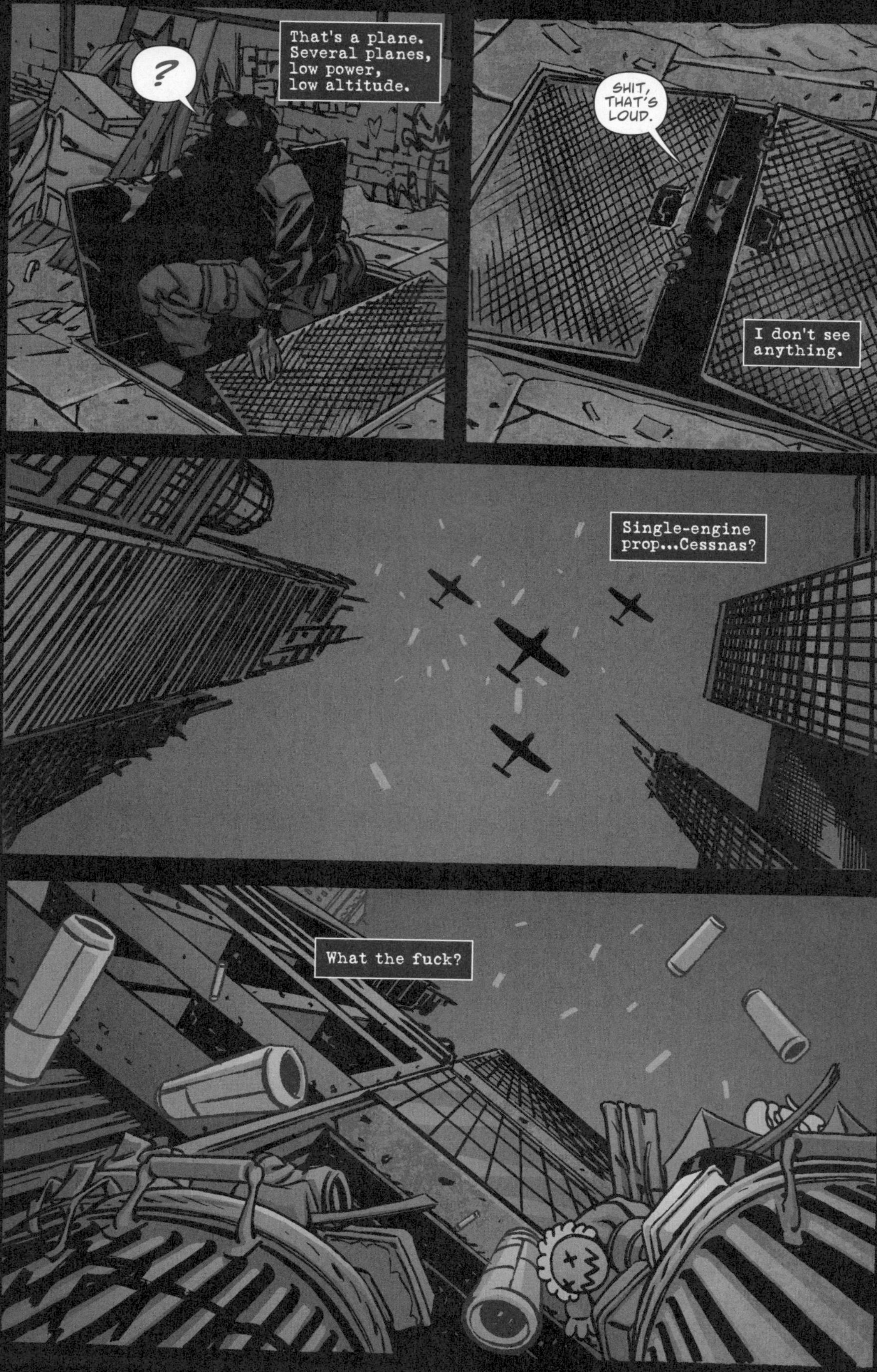

?
That's a plane. Several planes, low power, low altitude.
SHIT, THAT'S LOUD.
I don't see anything.
Single-engine prop...Cessnas?
What the fuck?

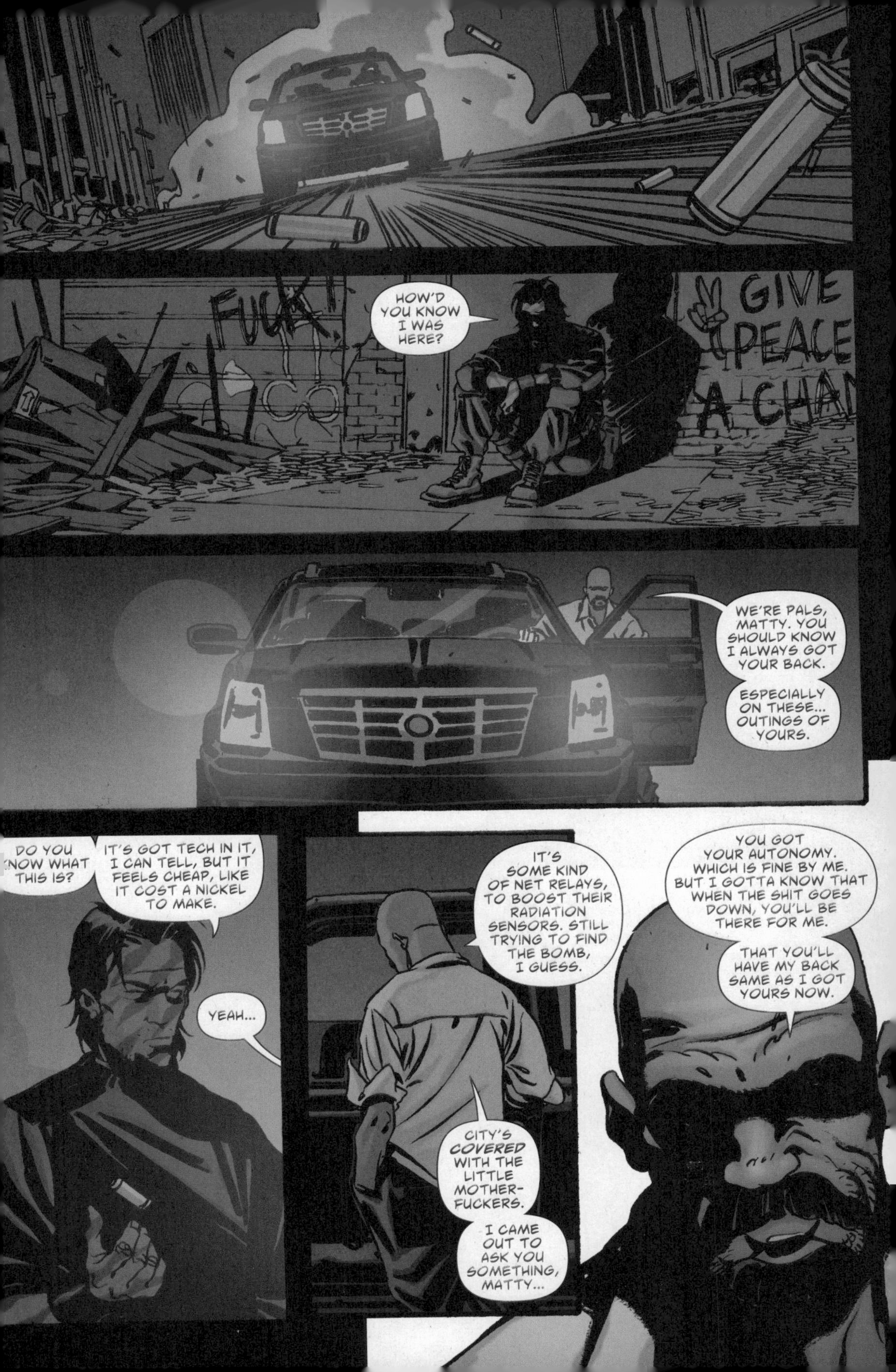
FUCK!
GIVE PEACE A CHAN
HOW'D YOU KNOW I WAS HERE?
WE'RE PALS, MATTY. YOU SHOULD KNOW I ALWAYS GOT YOUR BACK.
ESPECIALLY ON THESE... OUTINGS OF YOURS.
DO YOU KNOW WHAT THIS IS?
IT'S GOT TECH IN IT, I CAN TELL, BUT IT FEELS CHEAP, LIKE IT COST A NICKEL TO MAKE.
YEAH...
IT'S SOME KIND OF NET RELAYS, TO BOOST THEIR RADIATION SENSORS. STILL TRYING TO FIND THE BOMB, I GUESS.
CITY'S *COVERED* WITH THE LITTLE MOTHER-FUCKERS.
I CAME OUT TO ASK YOU SOMETHING, MATTY...
YOU GOT YOUR AUTONOMY. WHICH IS FINE BY ME. BUT I GOTTA KNOW THAT WHEN THE SHIT GOES DOWN, YOU'LL BE THERE FOR ME.
THAT YOU'LL HAVE MY BACK SAME AS I GOT YOURS NOW.

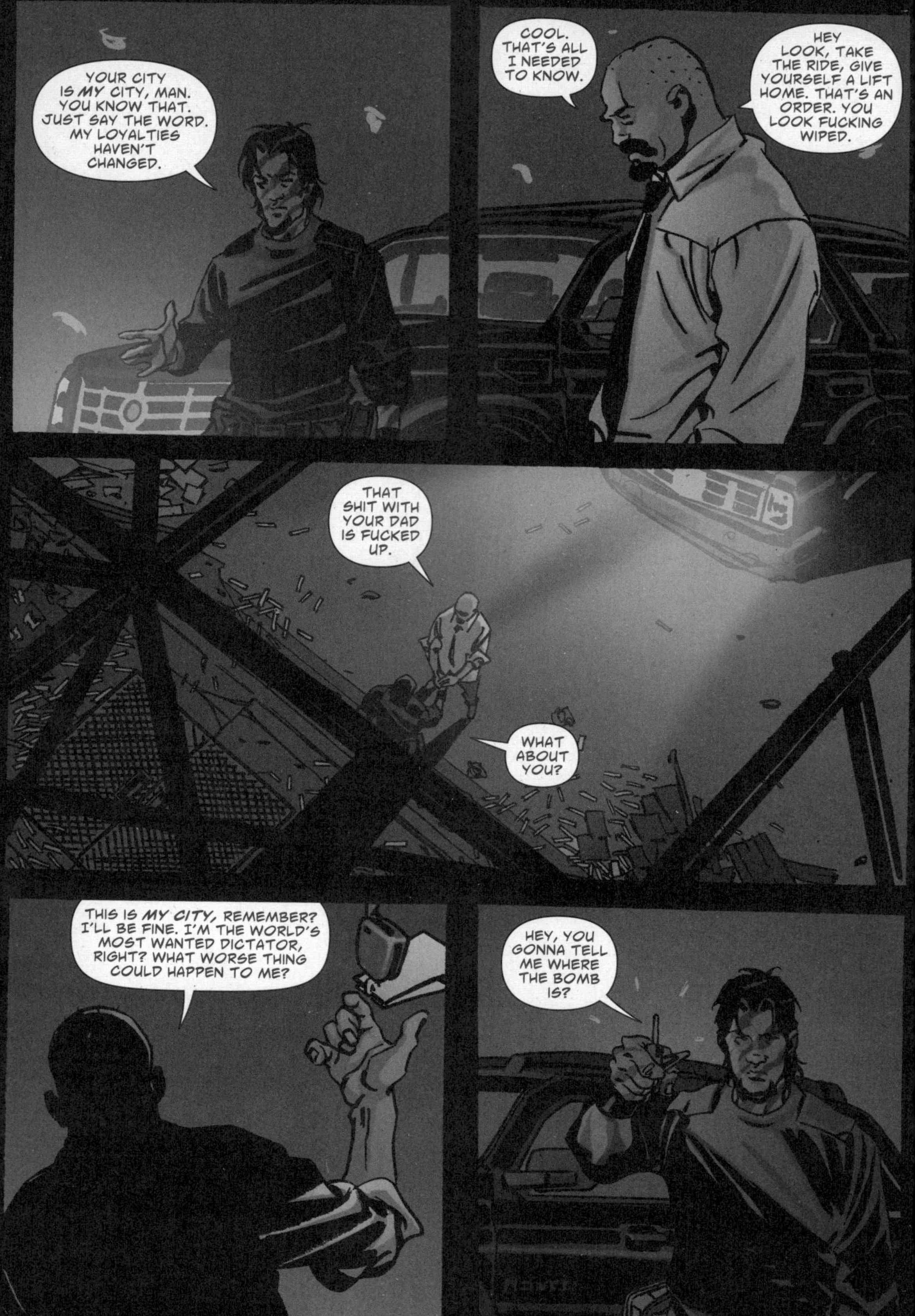
YOUR CITY IS MY CITY, MAN. YOU KNOW THAT. JUST SAY THE WORD. MY LOYALTIES HAVEN'T CHANGED.
COOL. THAT'S ALL I NEEDED TO KNOW.
HEY LOOK, TAKE THE RIDE, GIVE YOURSELF A LIFT HOME. THAT'S AN ORDER. YOU LOOK FUCKING WIPED.
THAT SHIT WITH YOUR DAD IS FUCKED UP.
WHAT ABOUT YOU?
THIS IS MY CITY, REMEMBER? I'LL BE FINE. I'M THE WORLD'S MOST WANTED DICTATOR, RIGHT? WHAT WORSE THING COULD HAPPEN TO ME?
HEY, YOU GONNA TELL ME WHERE THE BOMB IS?

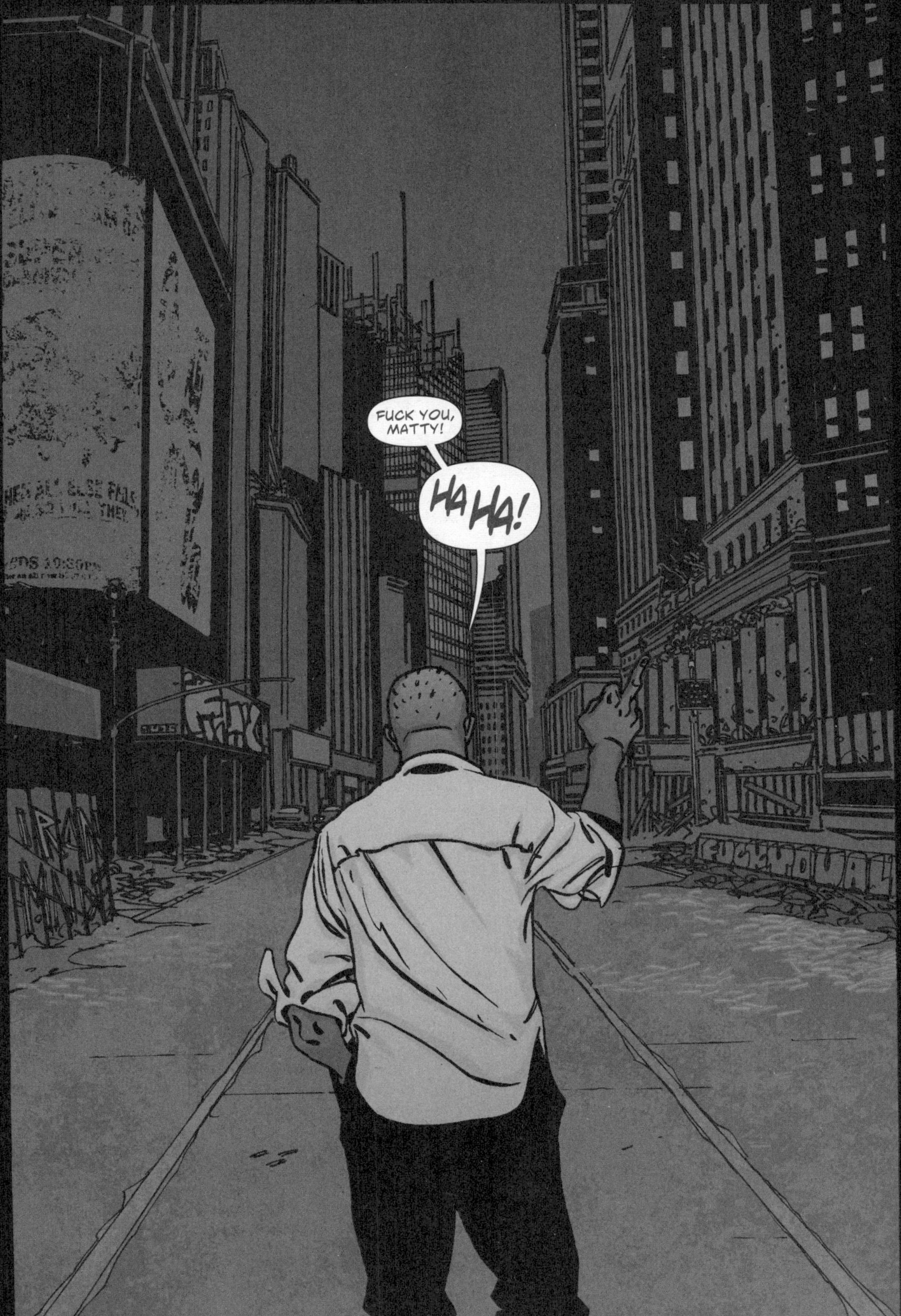
FUCK YOU, MATTY!
HA HA!

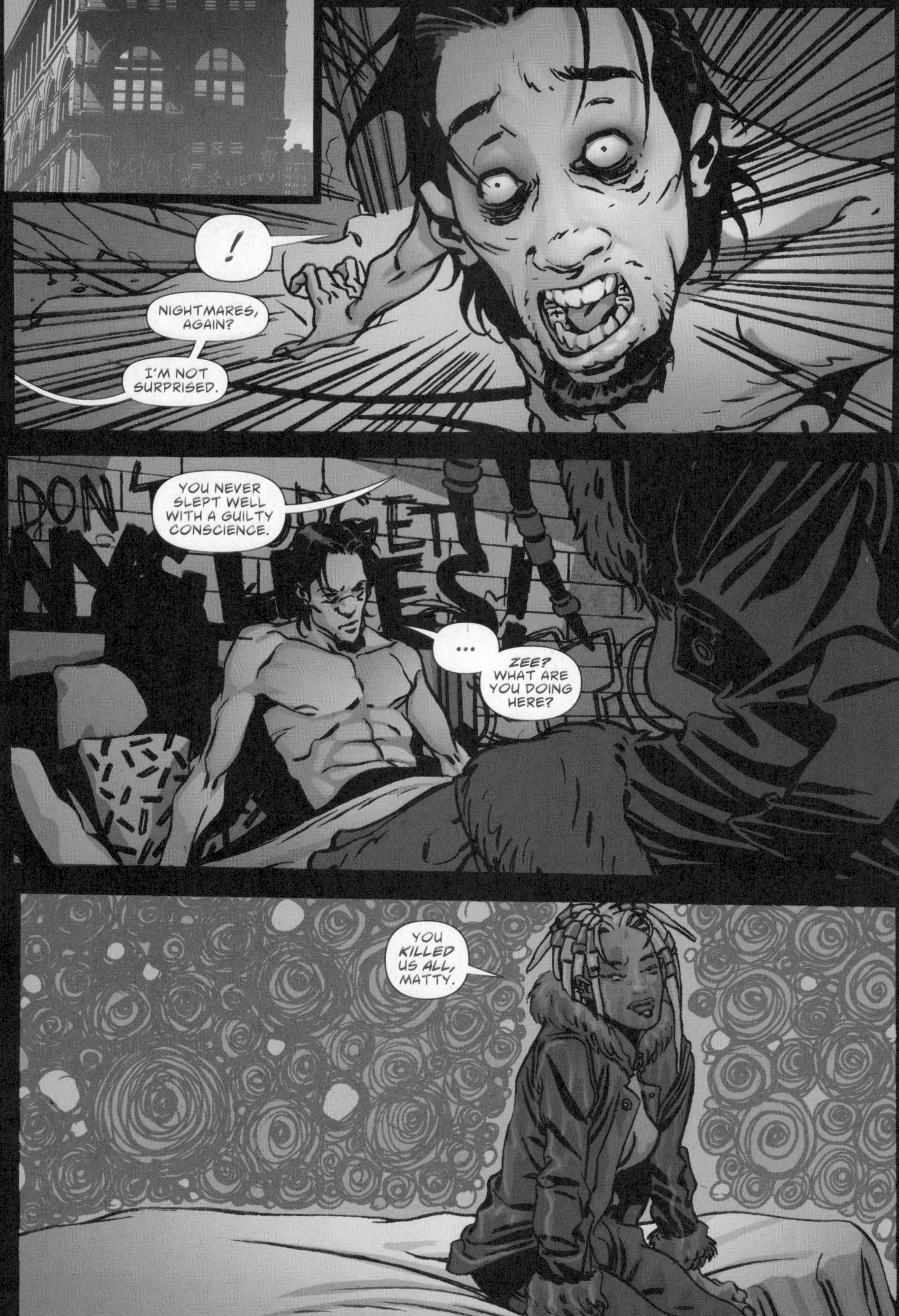
!
NIGHTMARES, AGAIN?
I'M NOT SURPRISED.
YOU NEVER SLEPT WELL WITH A GUILTY CONSCIENCE.
...
ZEE? WHAT ARE YOU DOING HERE?
YOU KILLED US ALL, MATTY.

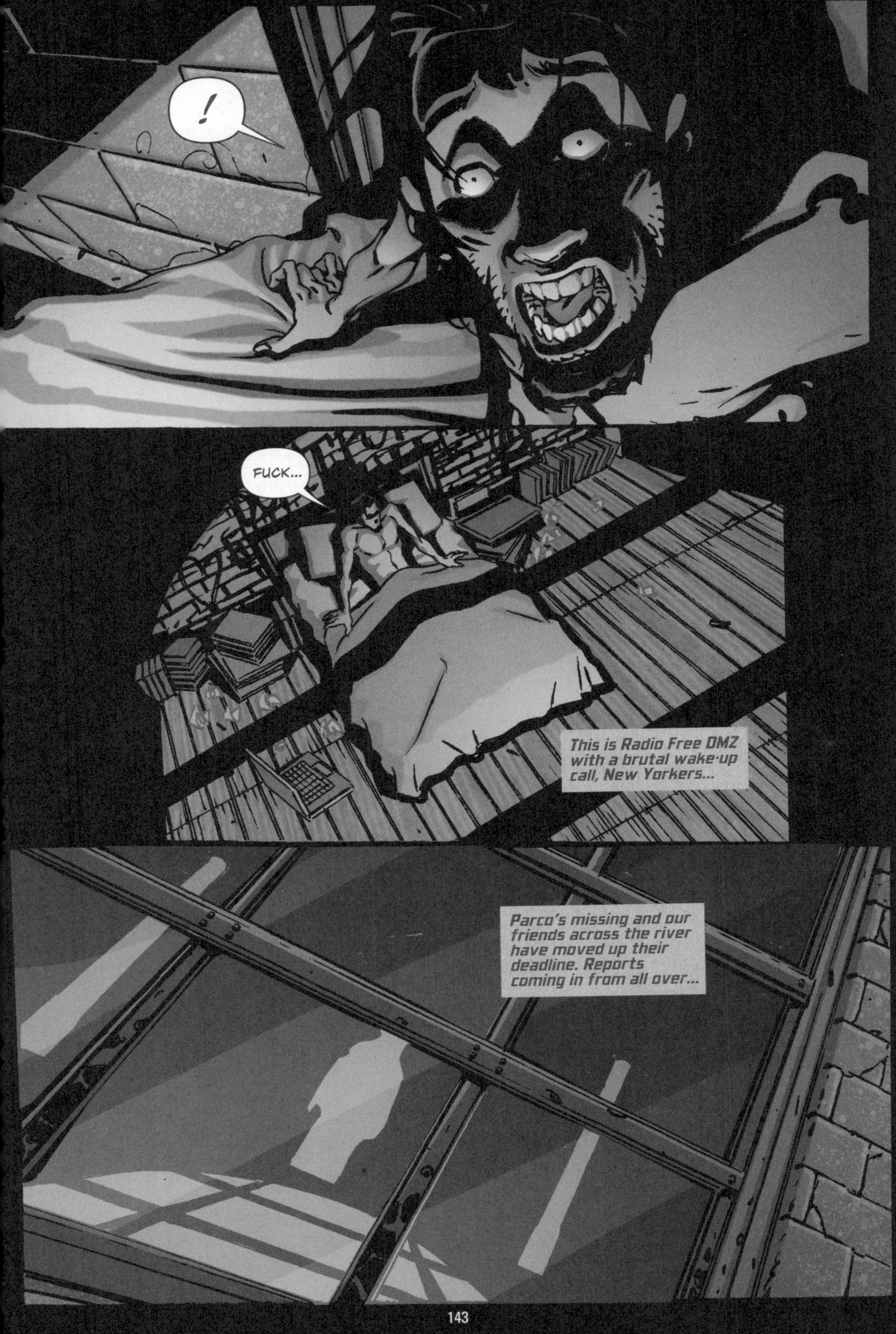

!
FUCK...
This is Radio Free DMZ with a brutal wake-up call, New Yorkers...
Parco's missing and our friends across the river have moved up their deadline. Reports coming in from all over...

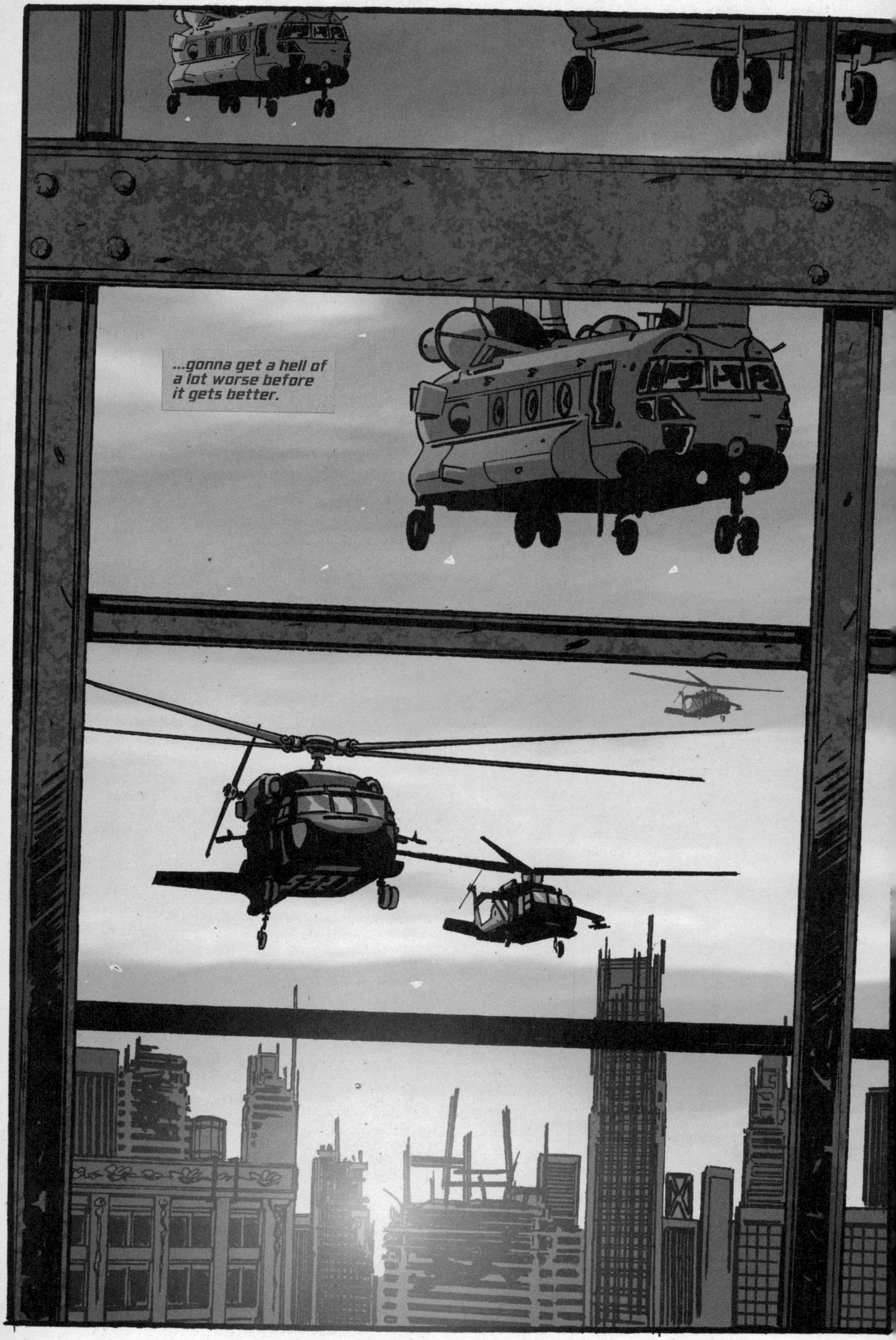
...gonna get a hell of a lot worse before it gets better.

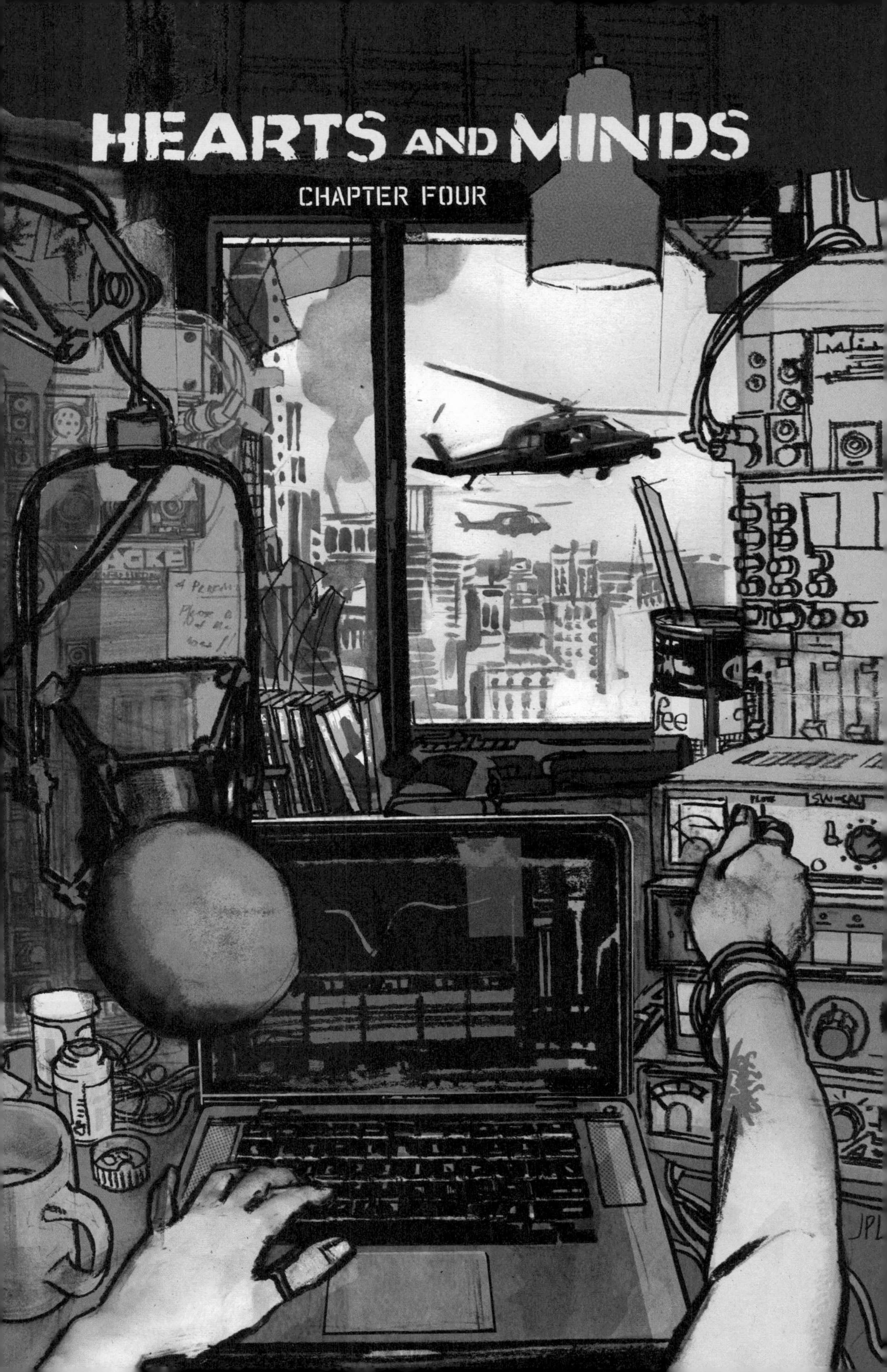
HEARTS AND MINDS
CHAPTER FOUR
JPL

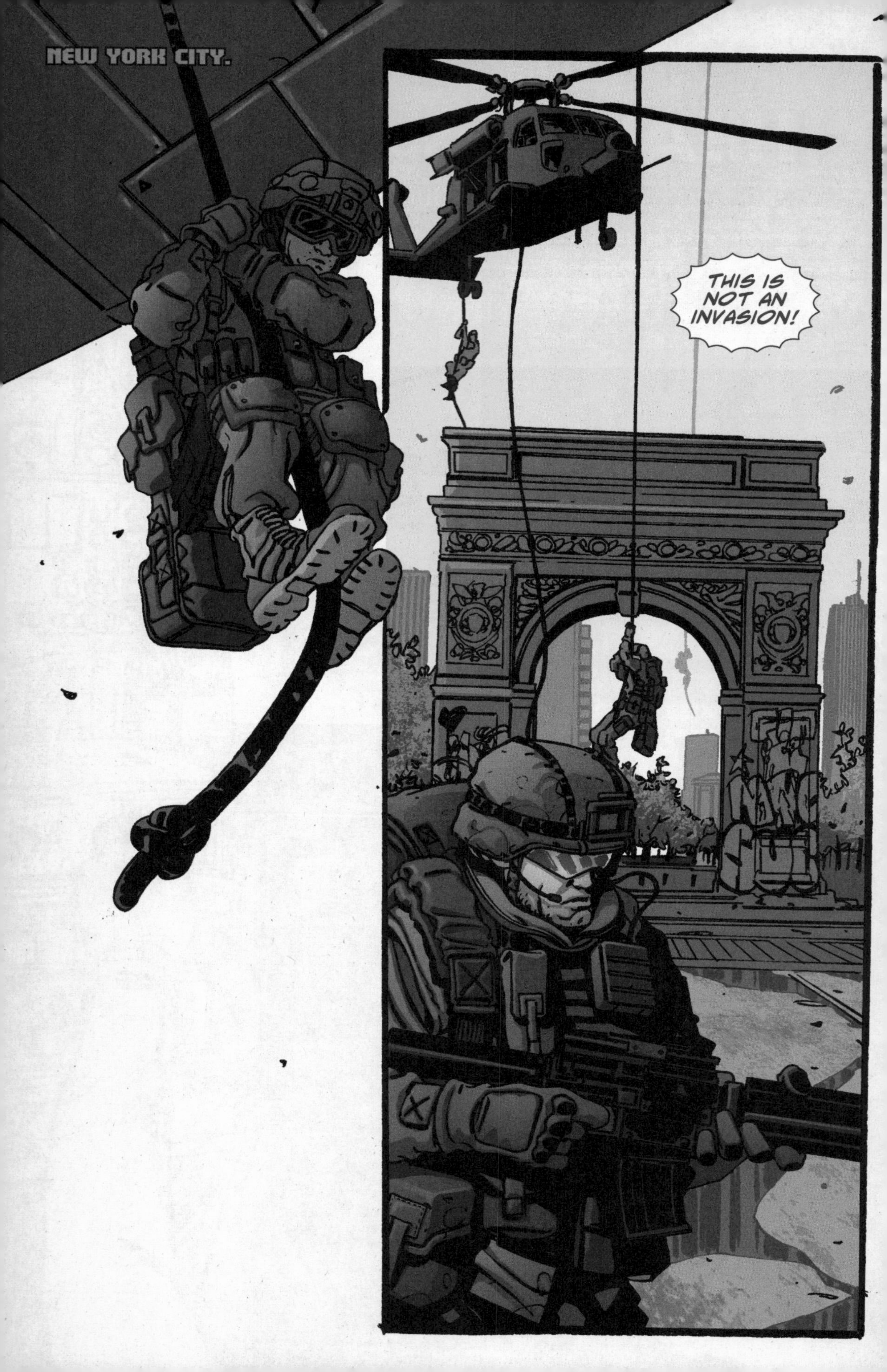
NEW YORK CITY.
THIS IS NOT AN INVASION!

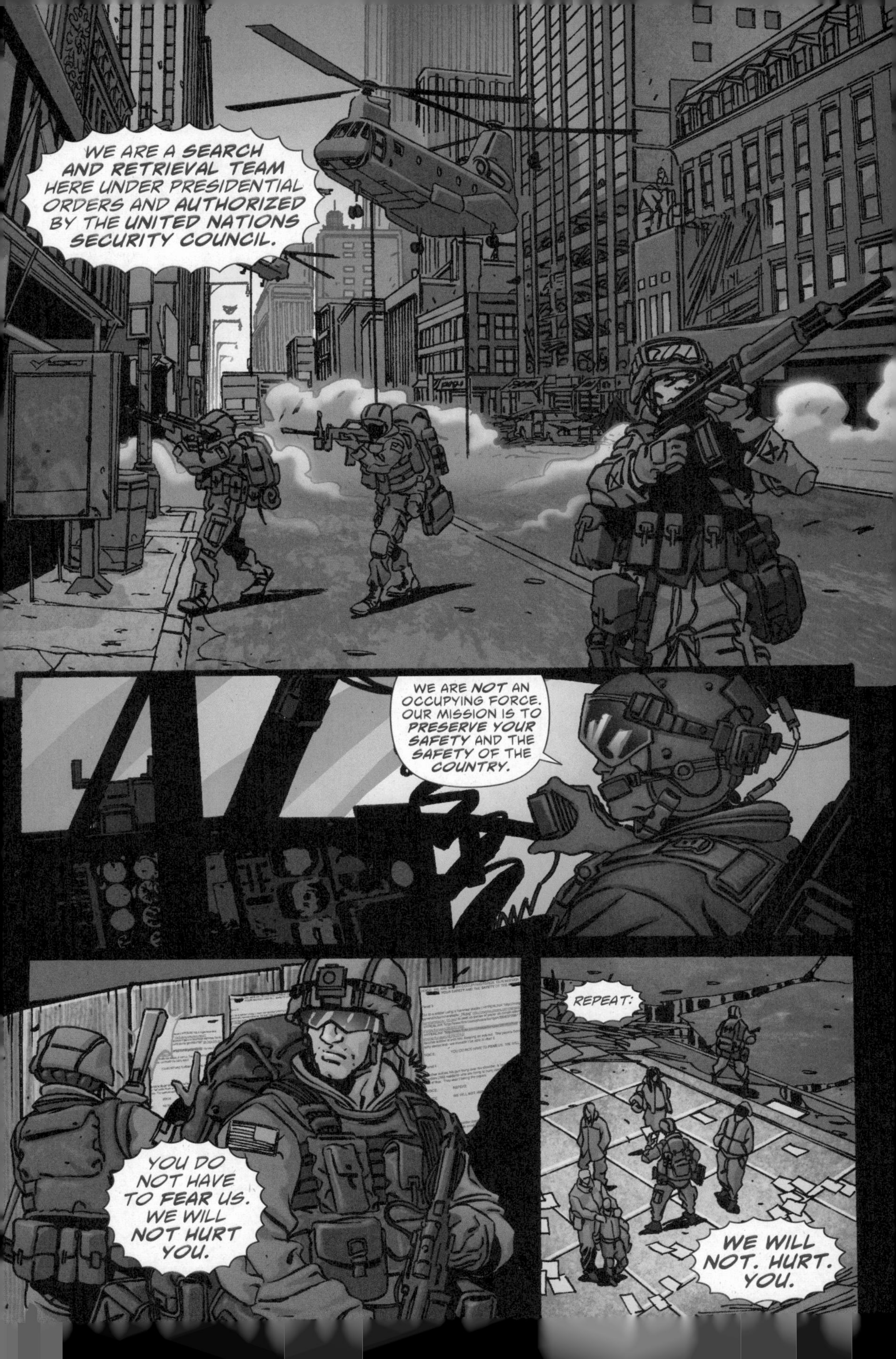
WE ARE A SEARCH AND RETRIEVAL TEAM HERE UNDER PRESIDENTIAL ORDERS AND AUTHORIZED BY THE UNITED NATIONS SECURITY COUNCIL.
WE ARE NOT AN OCCUPYING FORCE. OUR MISSION IS TO PRESERVE YOUR SAFETY AND THE SAFETY OF THE COUNTRY.
YOU DO NOT HAVE TO FEAR US. WE WILL NOT HURT YOU.
REPEAT:
WE WILL NOT. HURT. YOU.

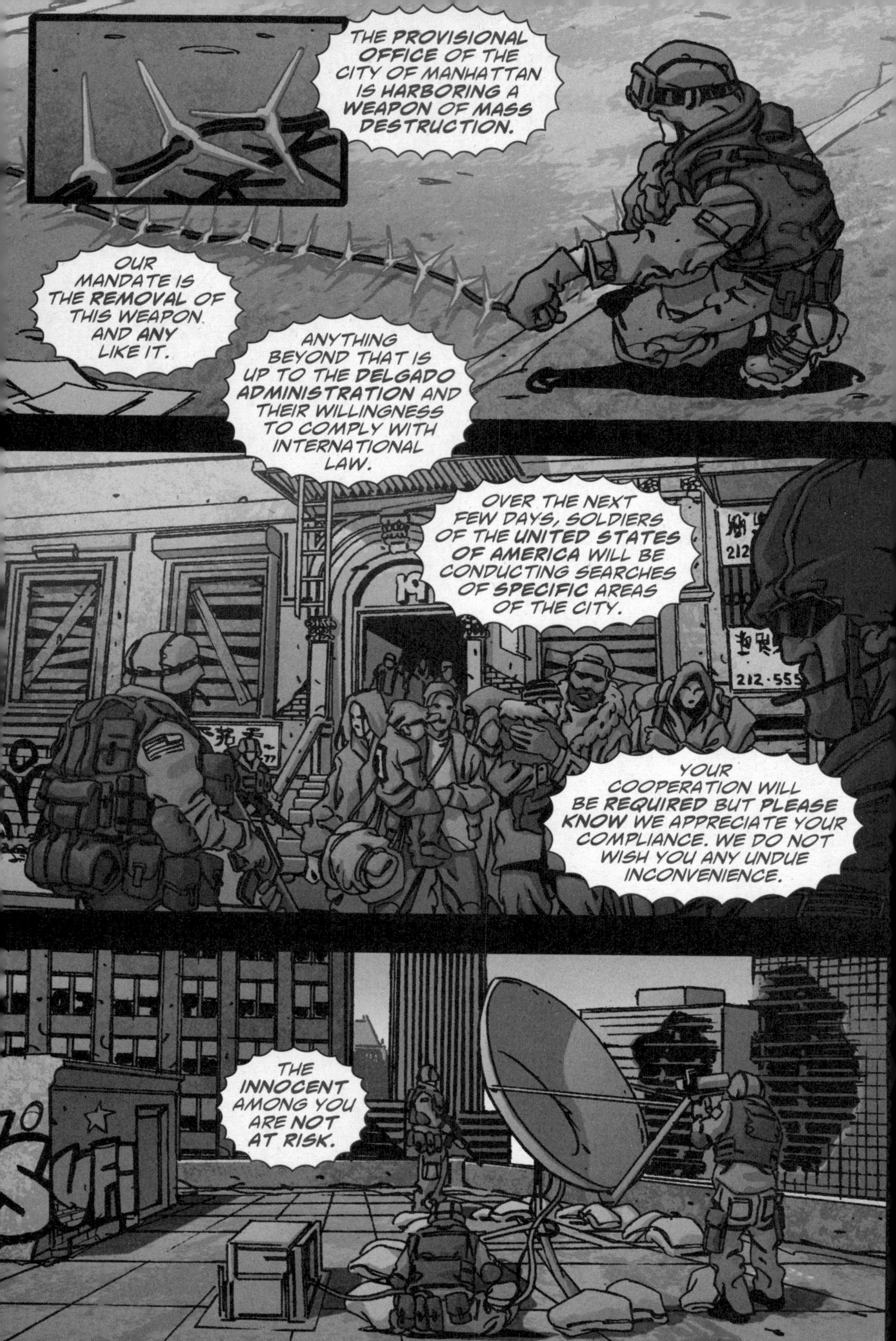

THE PROVISIONAL OFFICE OF THE CITY OF MANHATTAN IS HARBORING A WEAPON OF MASS DESTRUCTION.
OUR MANDATE IS THE REMOVAL OF THIS WEAPON AND ANY LIKE IT.
ANYTHING BEYOND THAT IS UP TO THE DELGADO ADMINISTRATION AND THEIR WILLINGNESS TO COMPLY WITH INTERNATIONAL LAW.
OVER THE NEXT FEW DAYS, SOLDIERS OF THE UNITED STATES OF AMERICA WILL BE CONDUCTING SEARCHES OF SPECIFIC AREAS OF THE CITY.
YOUR COOPERATION WILL BE REQUIRED BUT PLEASE KNOW WE APPRECIATE YOUR COMPLIANCE. WE DO NOT WISH YOU ANY UNDUE INCONVENIENCE.
THE INNOCENT AMONG YOU ARE NOT AT RISK.

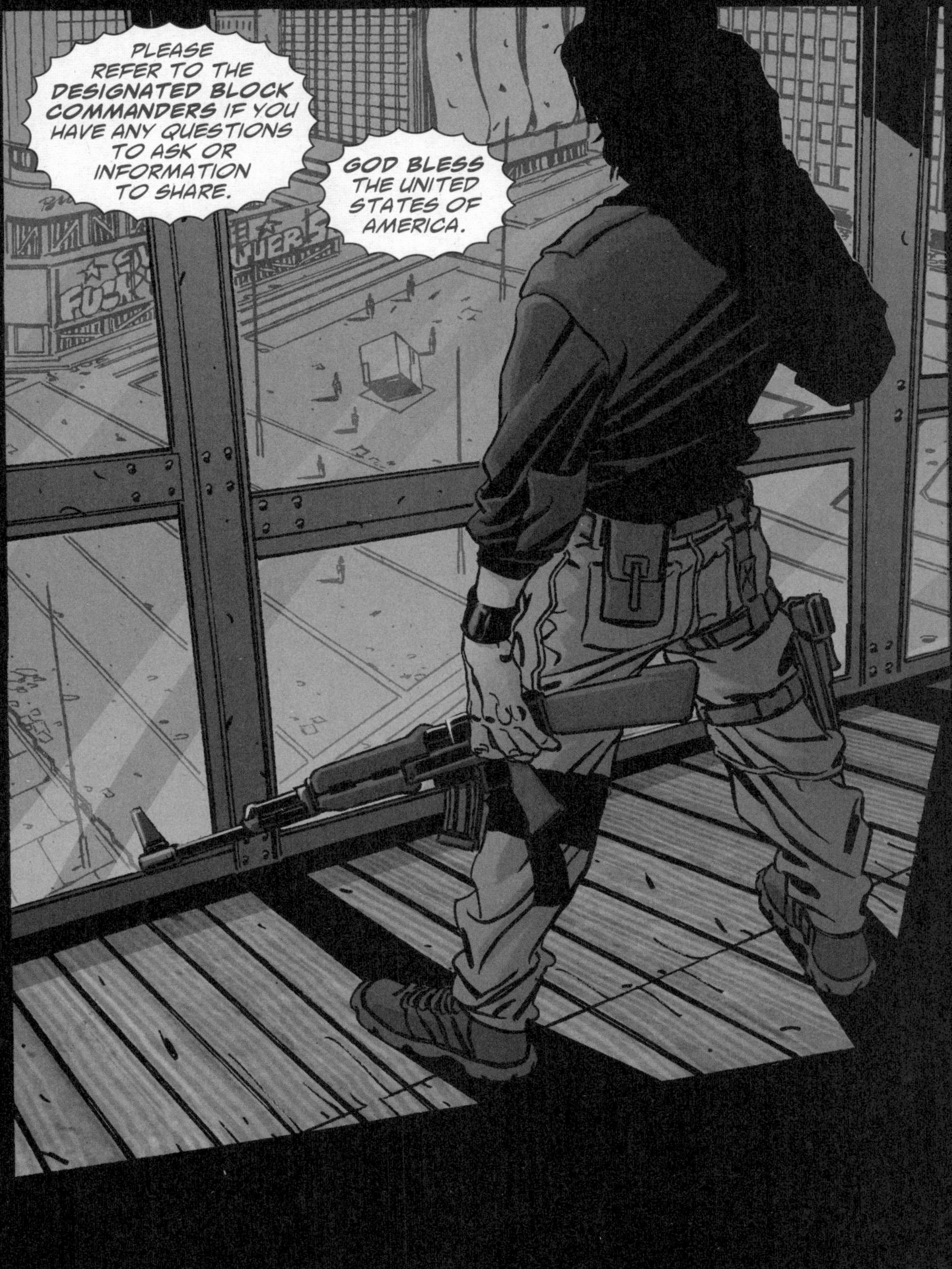
PLEASE REFER TO THE DESIGNATED BLOCK COMMANDERS IF YOU HAVE ANY QUESTIONS TO ASK OR INFORMATION TO SHARE.
GOD BLESS THE UNITED STATES OF AMERICA.

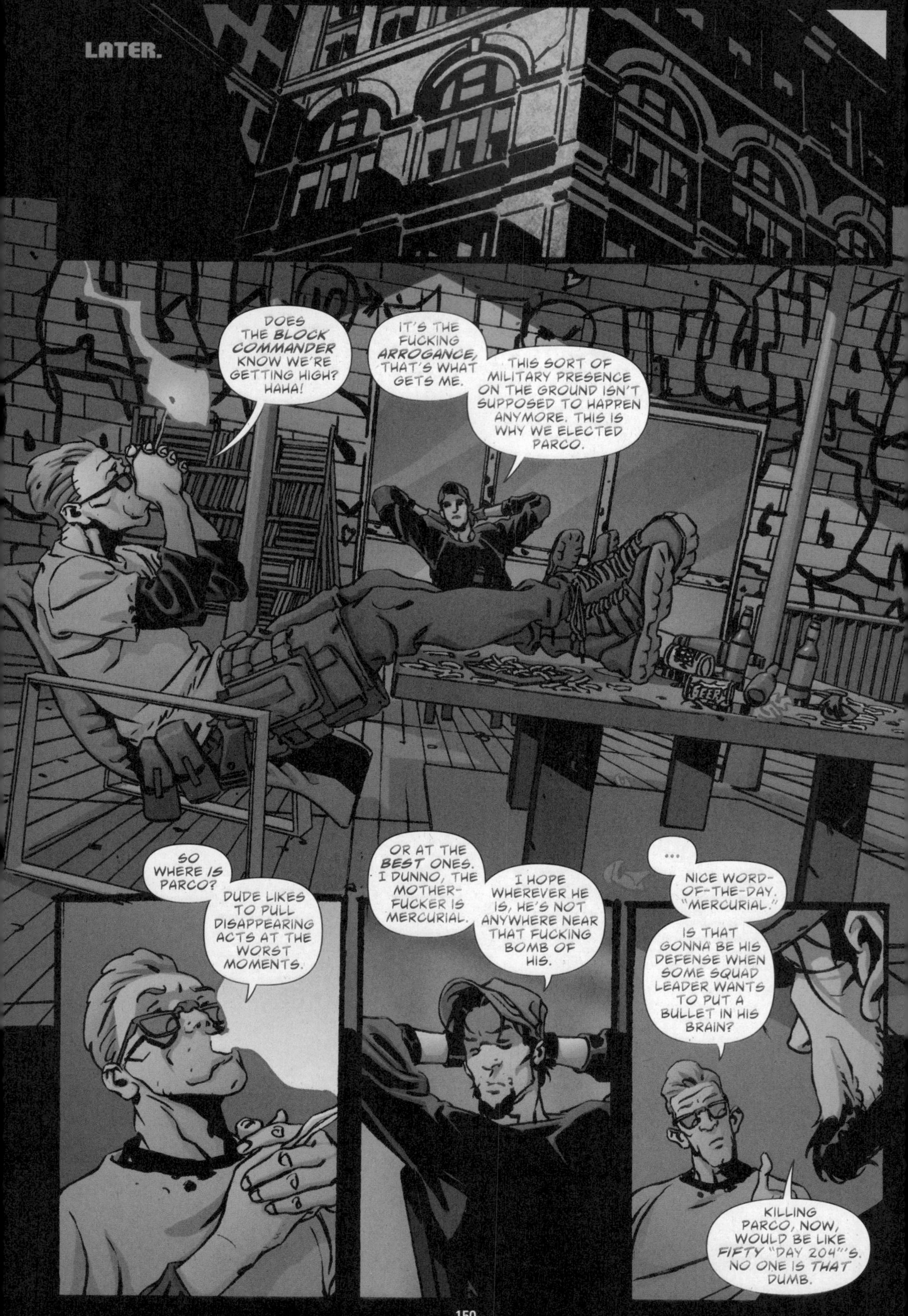
LATER.
DOES THE BLOCK COMMANDER KNOW WE'RE GETTING HIGH? HAHA!
IT'S THE FUCKING ARROGANCE, THAT'S WHAT GETS ME.
THIS SORT OF MILITARY PRESENCE ON THE GROUND ISN'T SUPPOSED TO HAPPEN ANYMORE. THIS IS WHY WE ELECTED PARCO.
SO WHERE IS PARCO?
DUDE LIKES TO PULL DISAPPEARING ACTS AT THE WORST MOMENTS.
OR AT THE BEST ONES. I DUNNO, THE MOTHER-FUCKER IS MERCURIAL.
I HOPE WHEREVER HE IS, HE'S NOT ANYWHERE NEAR THAT FUCKING BOMB OF HIS.
...
NICE WORD-OF-THE-DAY. "MERCURIAL."
IS THAT GONNA BE HIS DEFENSE WHEN SOME SQUAD LEADER WANTS TO PUT A BULLET IN HIS BRAIN?
KILLING PARCO, NOW, WOULD BE LIKE FIFTY "DAY 204"'S. NO ONE IS THAT DUMB.

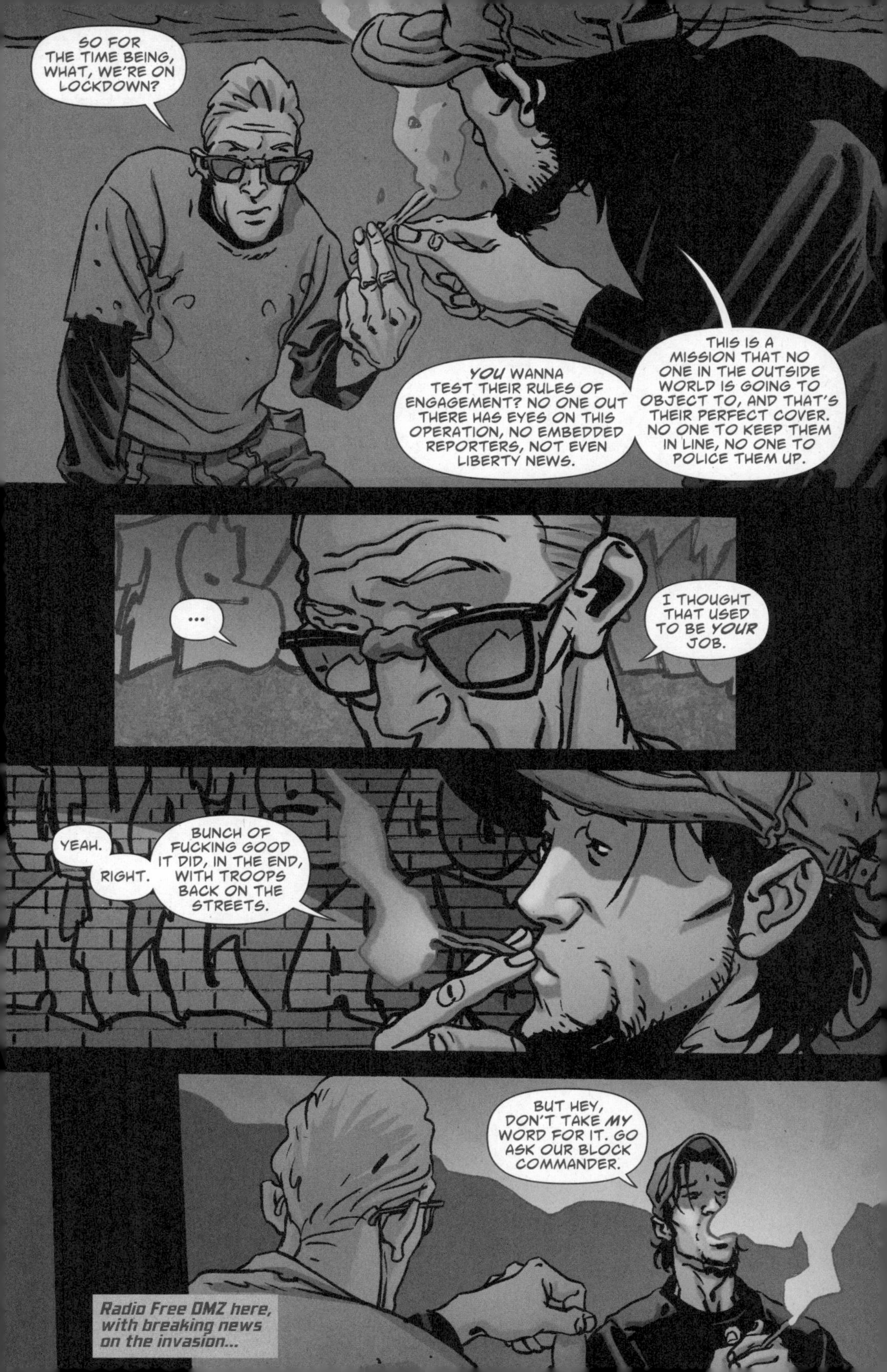
SO FOR THE TIME BEING, WHAT, WE'RE ON LOCKDOWN?
THIS IS A MISSION THAT NO ONE IN THE OUTSIDE WORLD IS GOING TO OBJECT TO, AND THAT'S THEIR PERFECT COVER. NO ONE TO KEEP THEM IN LINE, NO ONE TO POLICE THEM UP.
YOU WANNA TEST THEIR RULES OF ENGAGEMENT? NO ONE OUT THERE HAS EYES ON THIS OPERATION, NO EMBEDDED REPORTERS, NOT EVEN LIBERTY NEWS.
...
I THOUGHT THAT USED TO BE *YOUR* JOB.
YEAH.
RIGHT.
BUNCH OF FUCKING GOOD IT DID, IN THE END, WITH TROOPS BACK ON THE STREETS.
BUT HEY, DON'T TAKE *MY* WORD FOR IT. GO ASK OUR BLOCK COMMANDER.
Radio Free DMZ here, with breaking news on the invasion...

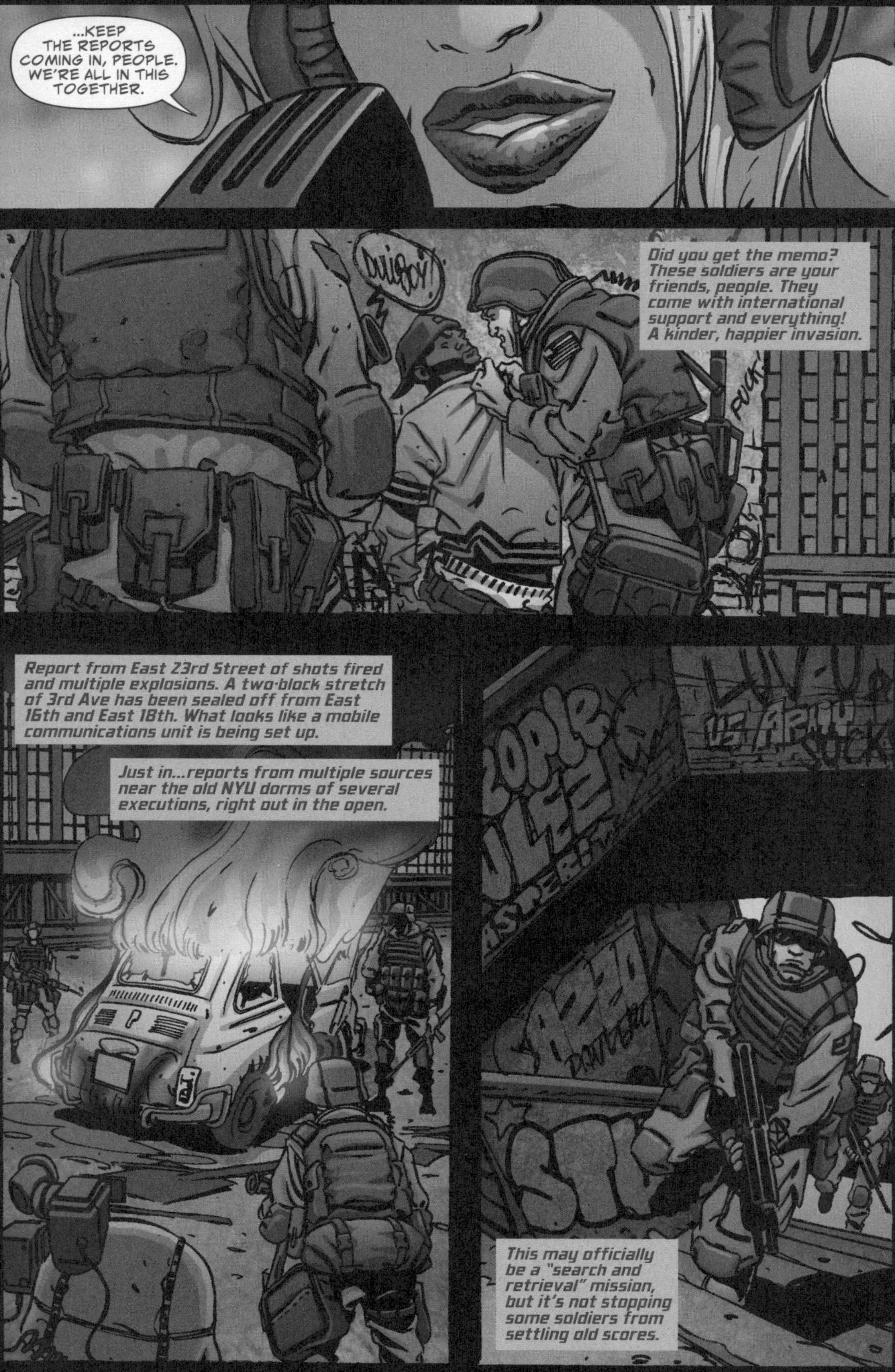
...KEEP THE REPORTS COMING IN, PEOPLE. WE'RE ALL IN THIS TOGETHER.
Did you get the memo? These soldiers are your friends, people. They come with international support and everything! A kinder, happier invasion.
Report from East 23rd Street of shots fired and multiple explosions. A two-block stretch of 3rd Ave has been sealed off from East 16th and East 18th. What looks like a mobile communications unit is being set up.
Just in...reports from multiple sources near the old NYU dorms of several executions, right out in the open.
This may officially be a "search and retrieval" mission, but it's not stopping some soldiers from settling old scores.

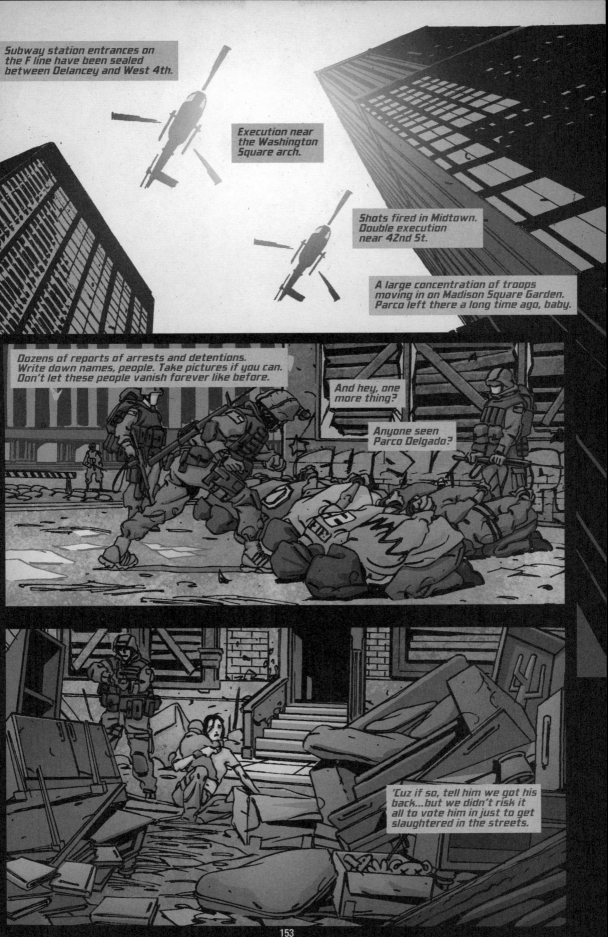

Subway station entrances on the F line have been sealed between Delancey and West 4th.

Execution near the Washington Square arch.

Shots fired in Midtown. Double execution near 42nd St.

A large concentration of troops moving in on Madison Square Garden. Parco left there a long time ago, baby.

Dozens of reports of arrests and detentions. Write down names, people. Take pictures if you can. Don't let these people vanish forever like before.

And hey, one more thing?

Anyone seen Parco Delgado?

'Cuz if so, tell him we got his back...but we didn't risk it all to vote him in just to get slaughtered in the streets.

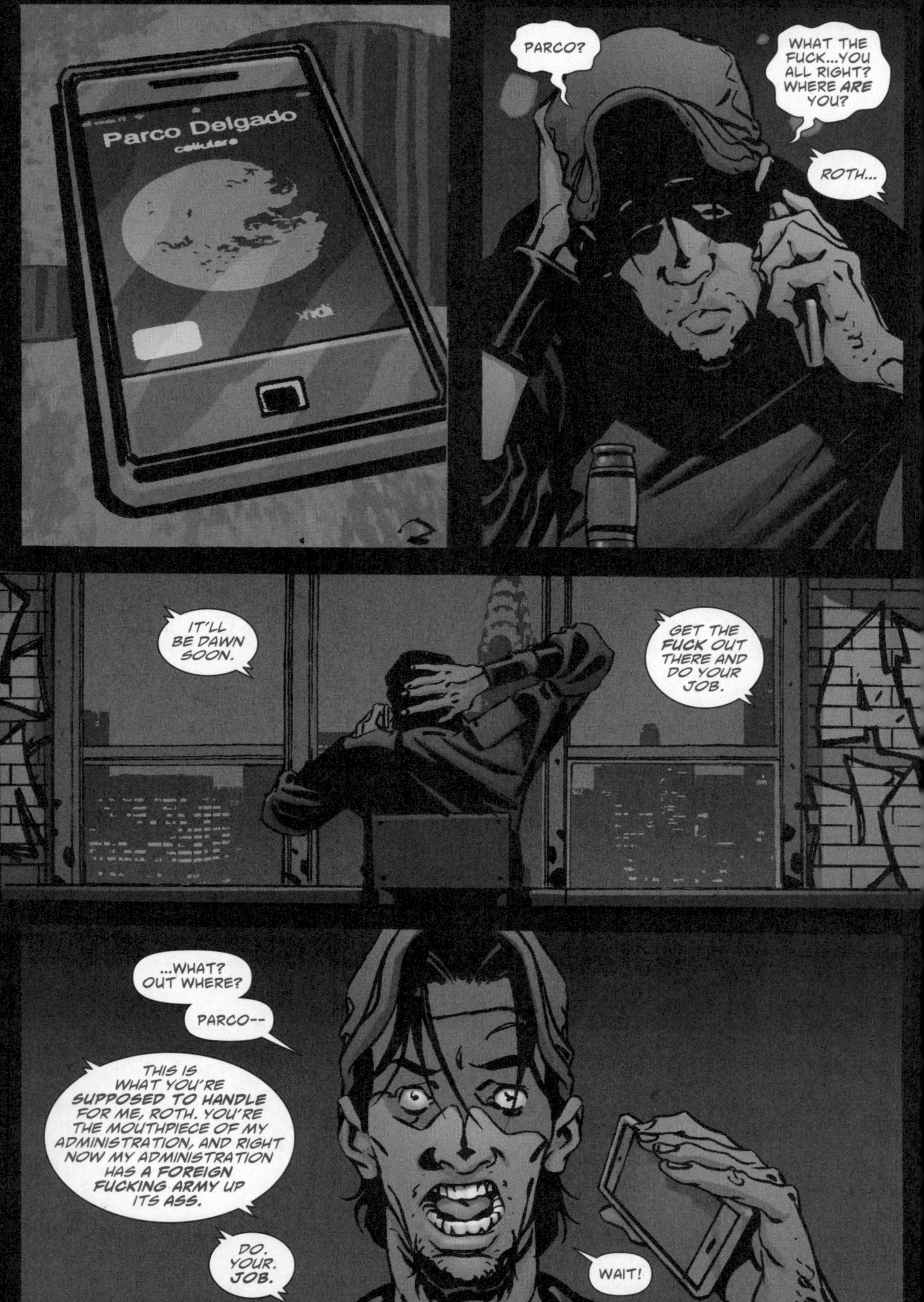
Parco Delgado
cellulare
PARCO?
WHAT THE FUCK...YOU ALL RIGHT? WHERE ARE YOU?
ROTH...
IT'LL BE DAWN SOON.
GET THE FUCK OUT THERE AND DO YOUR JOB.
...WHAT? OUT WHERE?
PARCO--
THIS IS WHAT YOU'RE SUPPOSED TO HANDLE FOR ME, ROTH. YOU'RE THE MOUTHPIECE OF MY ADMINISTRATION, AND RIGHT NOW MY ADMINISTRATION HAS A FOREIGN FUCKING ARMY UP ITS ASS.
DO. YOUR. JOB.
WAIT!

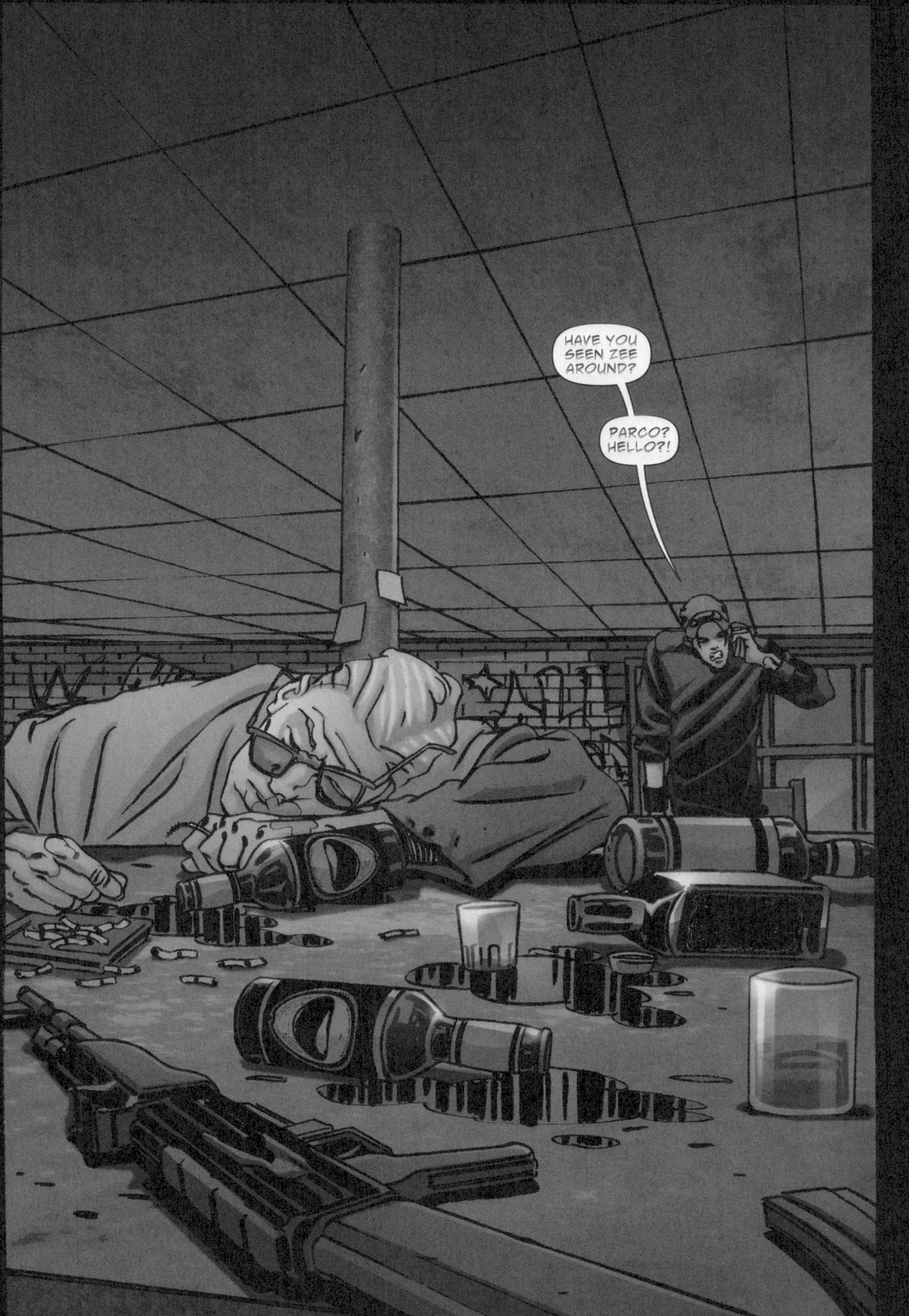
HAVE YOU SEEN ZEE AROUND?
PARCO? HELLO?!

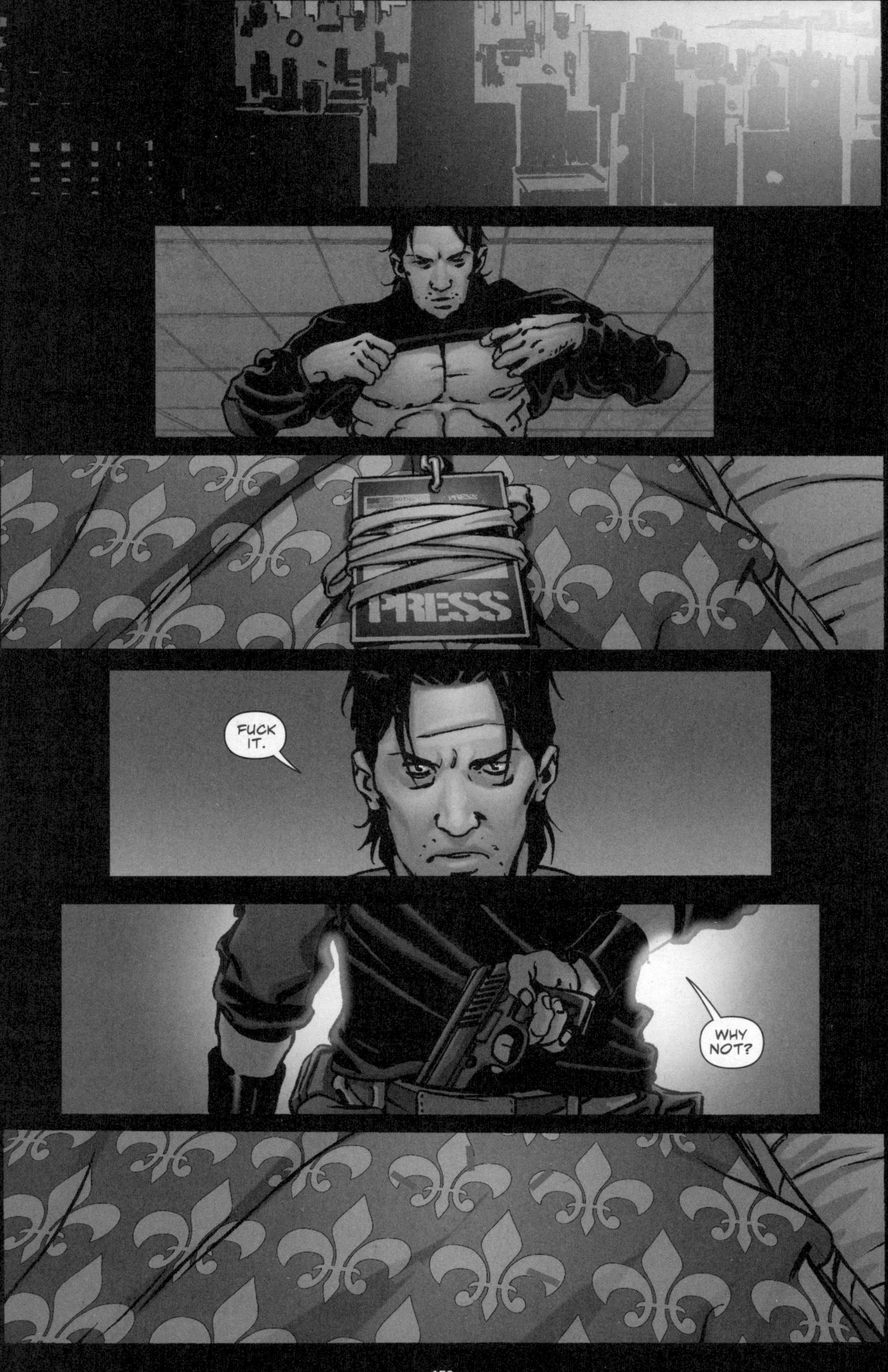
PRESS
PRESS
FUCK IT.
WHY NOT?

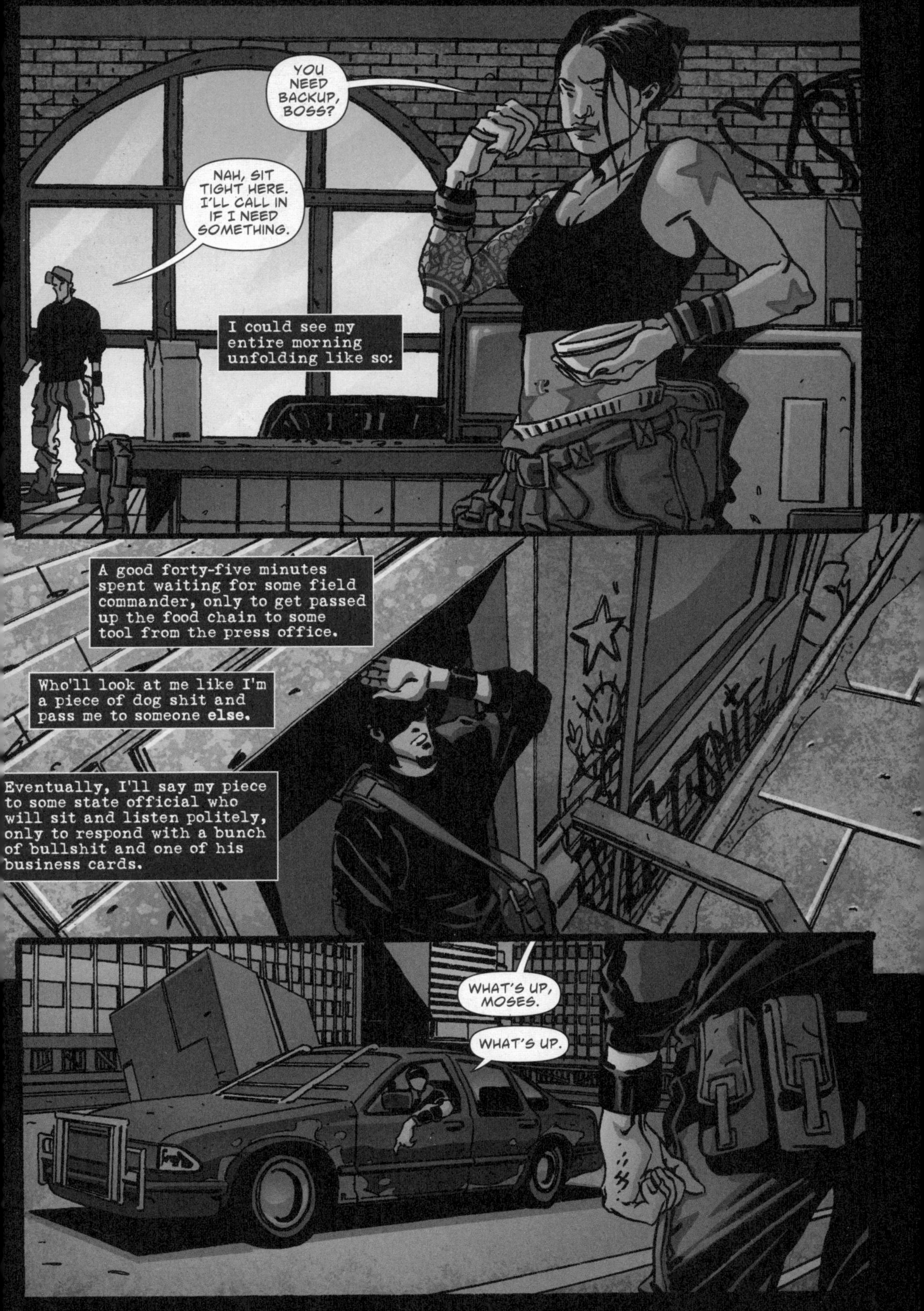
YOU NEED BACKUP, BOSS?
NAH, SIT TIGHT HERE. I'LL CALL IN IF I NEED SOMETHING.
I could see my entire morning unfolding like so:
A good forty-five minutes spent waiting for some field commander, only to get passed up the food chain to some tool from the press office.
Who'll look at me like I'm a piece of dog shit and pass me to someone **else**.
Eventually, I'll say my piece to some state official who will sit and listen politely, only to respond with a bunch of bullshit and one of his business cards.
WHAT'S UP, MOSES.
WHAT'S UP.

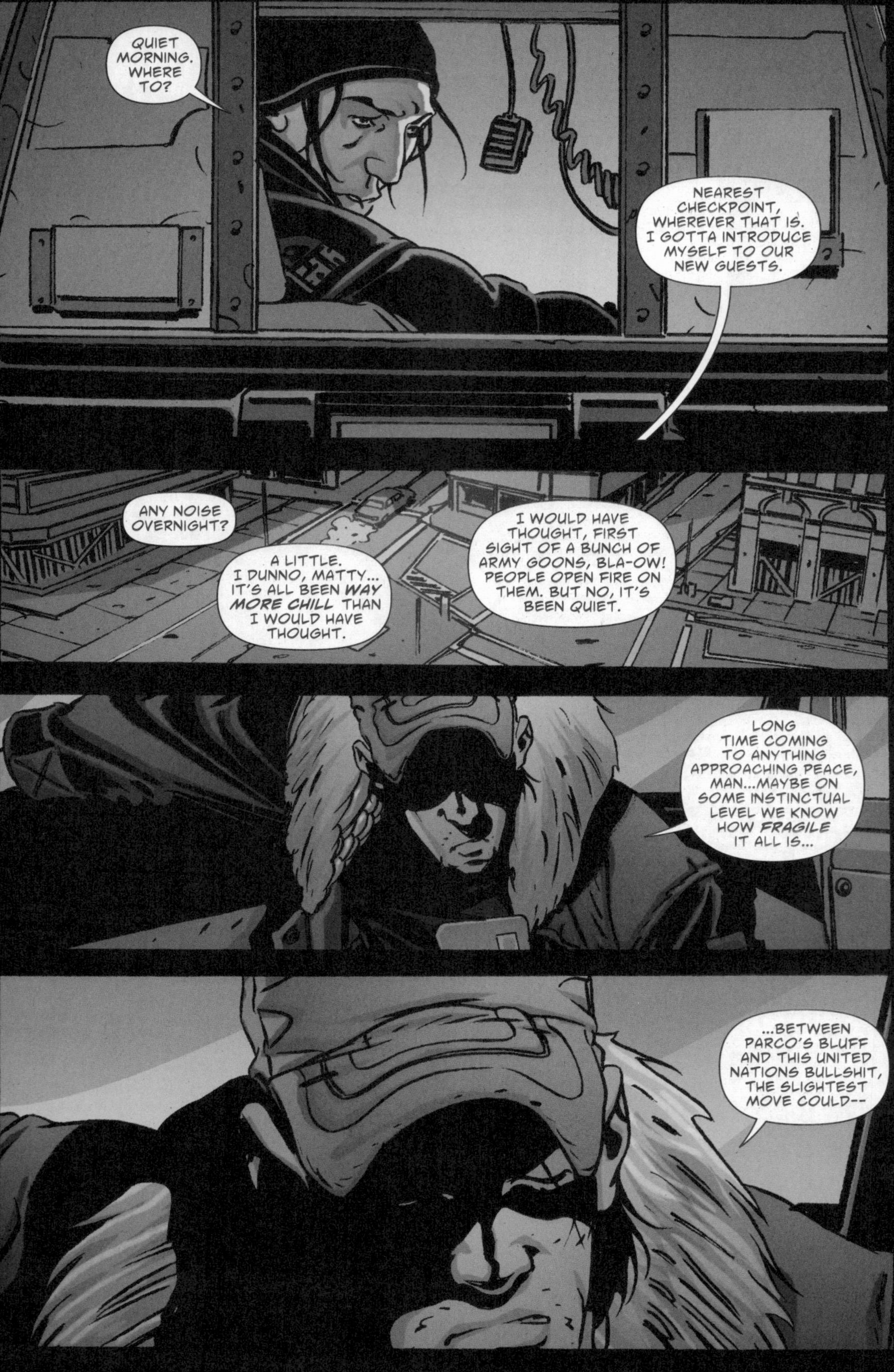
QUIET MORNING. WHERE TO?
NEAREST CHECKPOINT, WHEREVER THAT IS. I GOTTA INTRODUCE MYSELF TO OUR NEW GUESTS.
ANY NOISE OVERNIGHT?
A LITTLE. I DUNNO, MATTY... IT'S ALL BEEN *WAY MORE CHILL* THAN I WOULD HAVE THOUGHT.
I WOULD HAVE THOUGHT, FIRST SIGHT OF A BUNCH OF ARMY GOONS, BLA-OW! PEOPLE OPEN FIRE ON THEM. BUT NO, IT'S BEEN QUIET.
LONG TIME COMING TO ANYTHING APPROACHING PEACE, MAN...MAYBE ON SOME INSTINCTUAL LEVEL WE KNOW HOW *FRAGILE* IT ALL IS...
...BETWEEN PARCO'S BLUFF AND THIS UNITED NATIONS BULLSHIT, THE SLIGHTEST MOVE COULD--

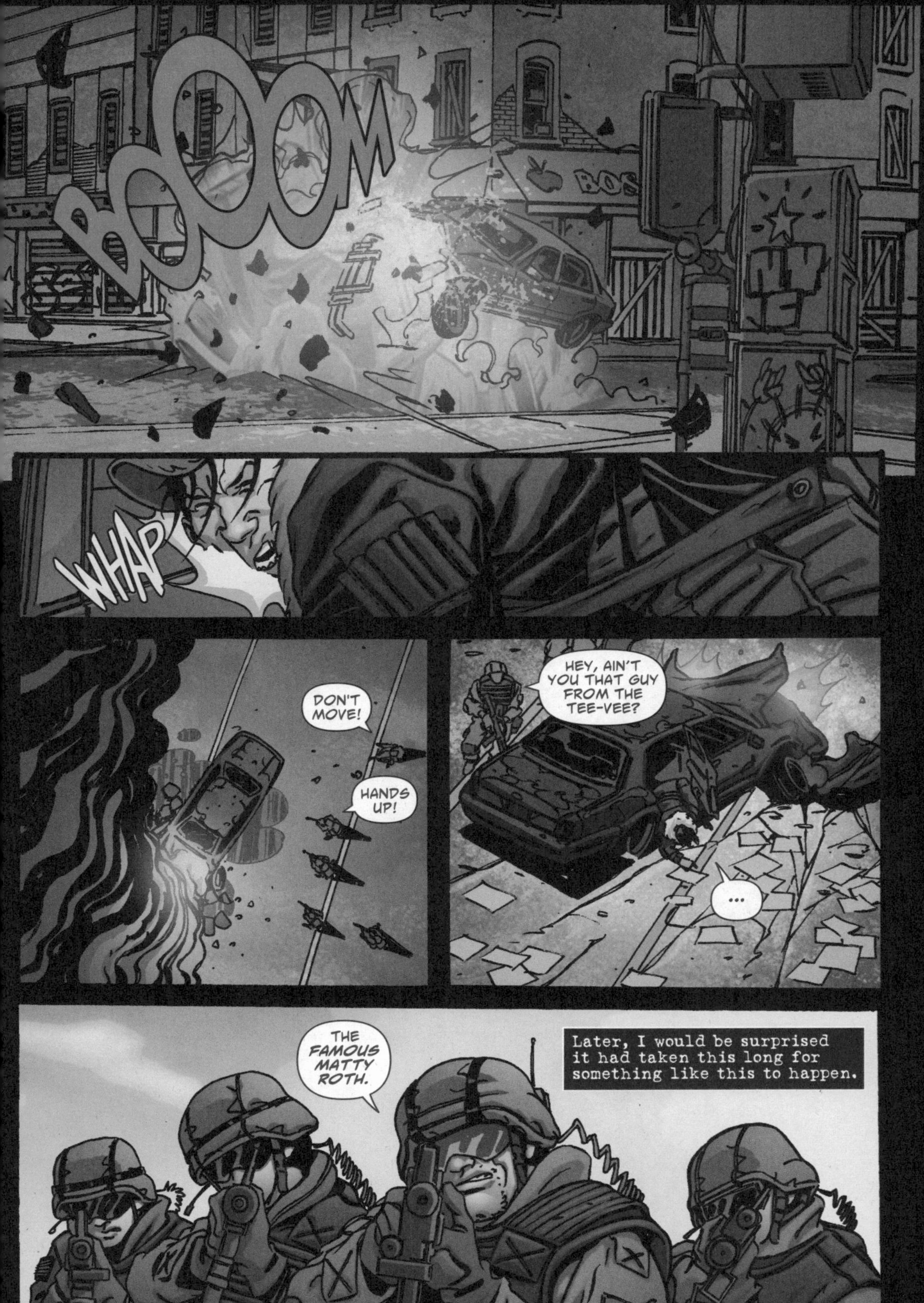
BOOOM
WHAP
DON'T MOVE!
HANDS UP!
HEY, AIN'T YOU THAT GUY FROM THE TEE-VEE?
...
THE FAMOUS MATTY ROTH.
Later, I would be surprised it had taken this long for something like this to happen.

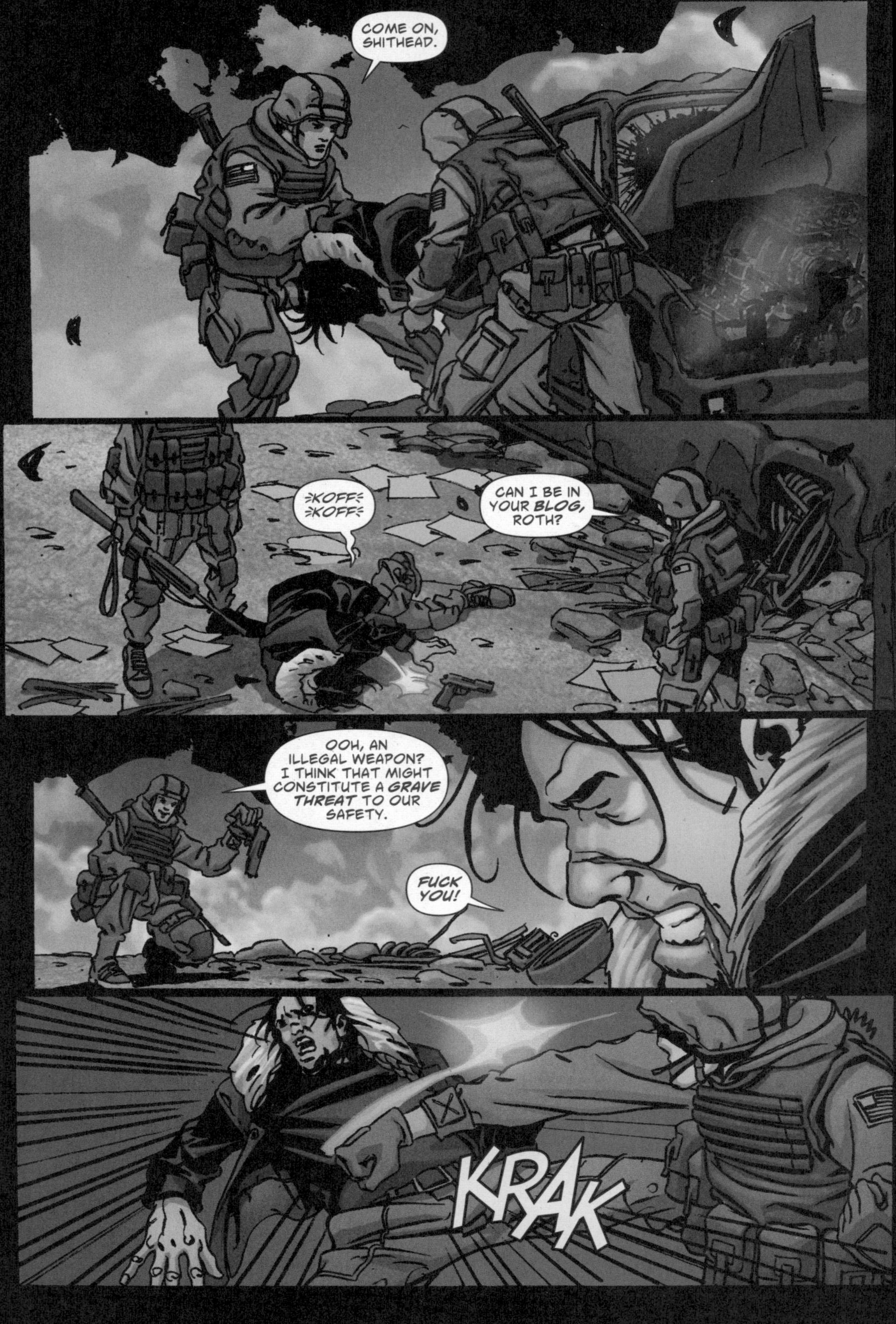
COME ON, SHITHEAD.
KOFF *KOFF*
CAN I BE IN YOUR *BLOG*, ROTH?
OOH, AN ILLEGAL WEAPON? I THINK THAT MIGHT CONSTITUTE A *GRAVE THREAT* TO OUR SAFETY.
FUCK YOU!
KRAK

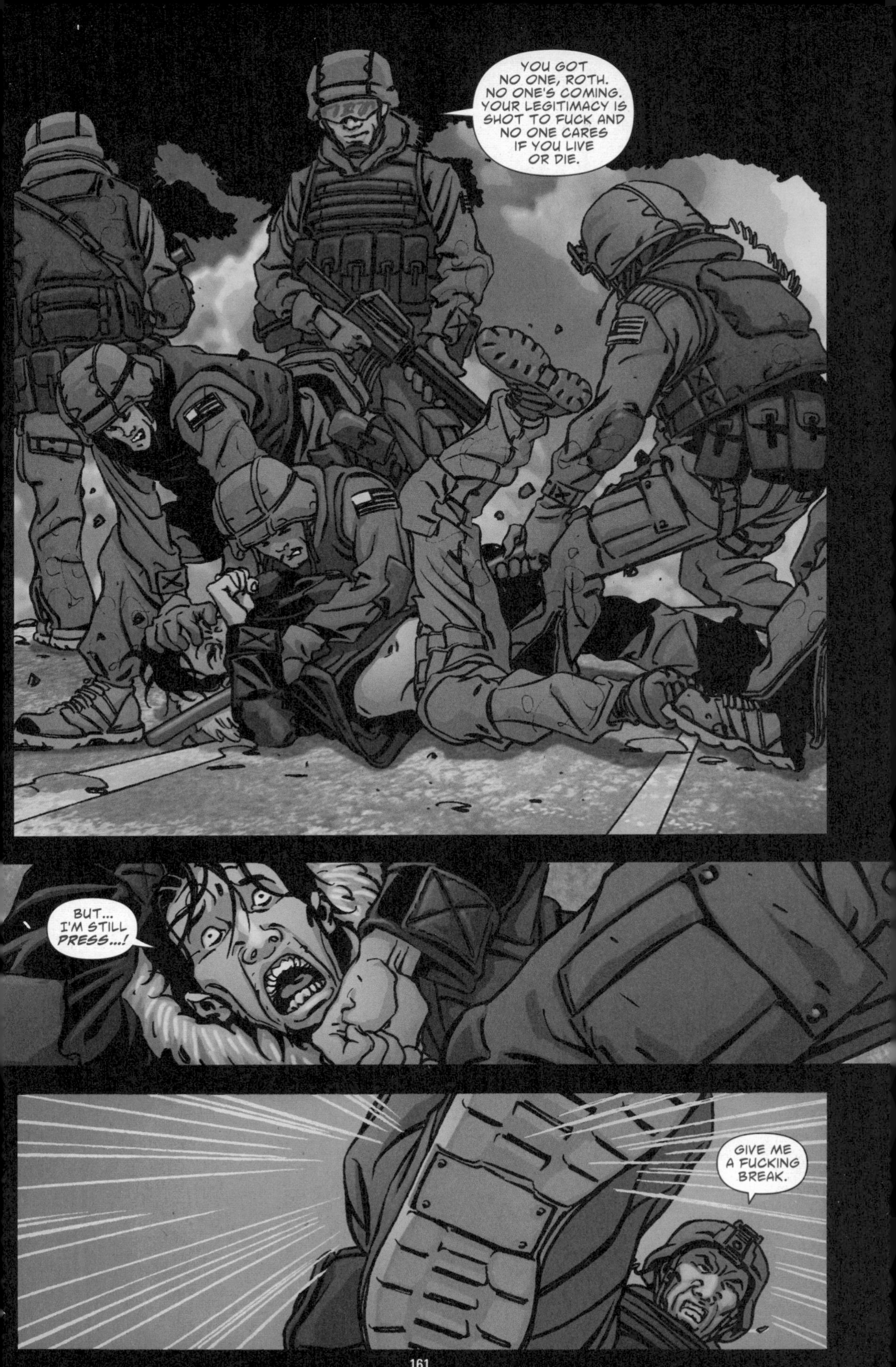
YOU GOT NO ONE, ROTH. NO ONE'S COMING. YOUR LEGITIMACY IS SHOT TO FUCK AND NO ONE CARES IF YOU LIVE OR DIE.
BUT... I'M STILL *PRESS*...!
GIVE ME A FUCKING BREAK.

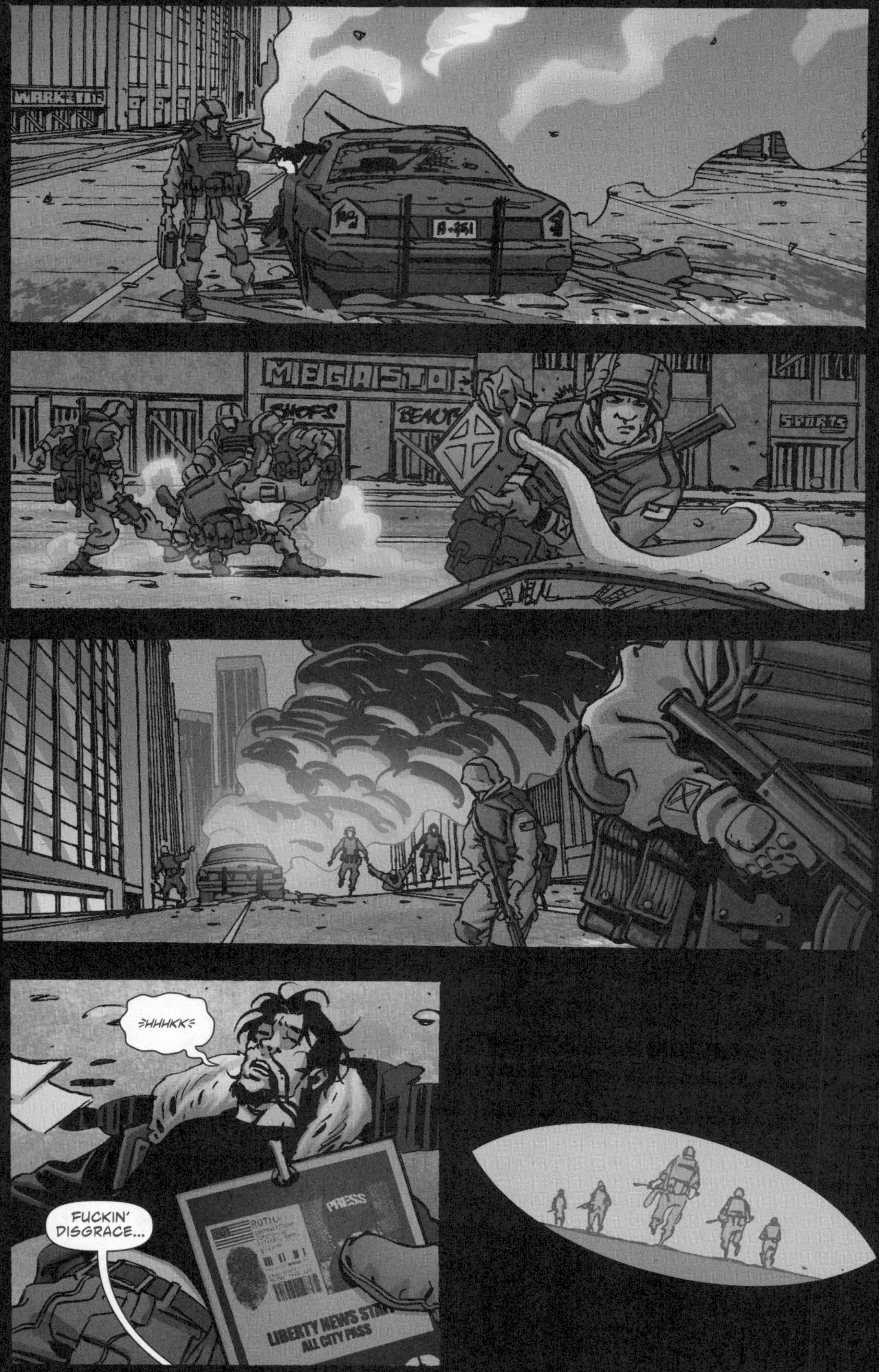
SHOPS
SPORTS
HHHKK
PRESS
ROTH
ALL CITY PASS
FUCKIN' DISGRACE...

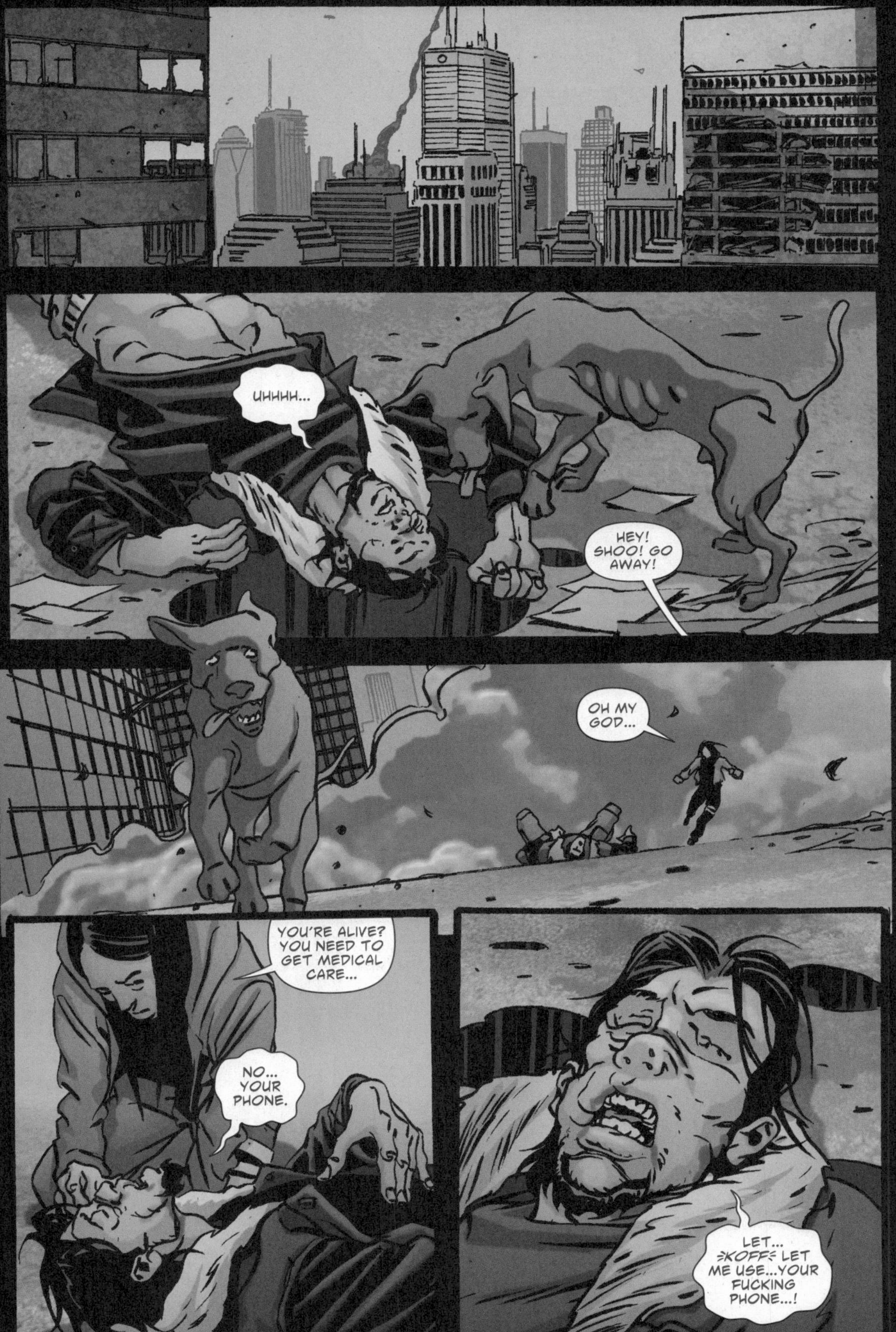
UHHHH...
HEY! SHOO! GO AWAY!
OH MY GOD...
YOU'RE ALIVE? YOU NEED TO GET MEDICAL CARE...
NO... YOUR PHONE.
LET... =KOFF= LET ME USE...YOUR FUCKING PHONE...!

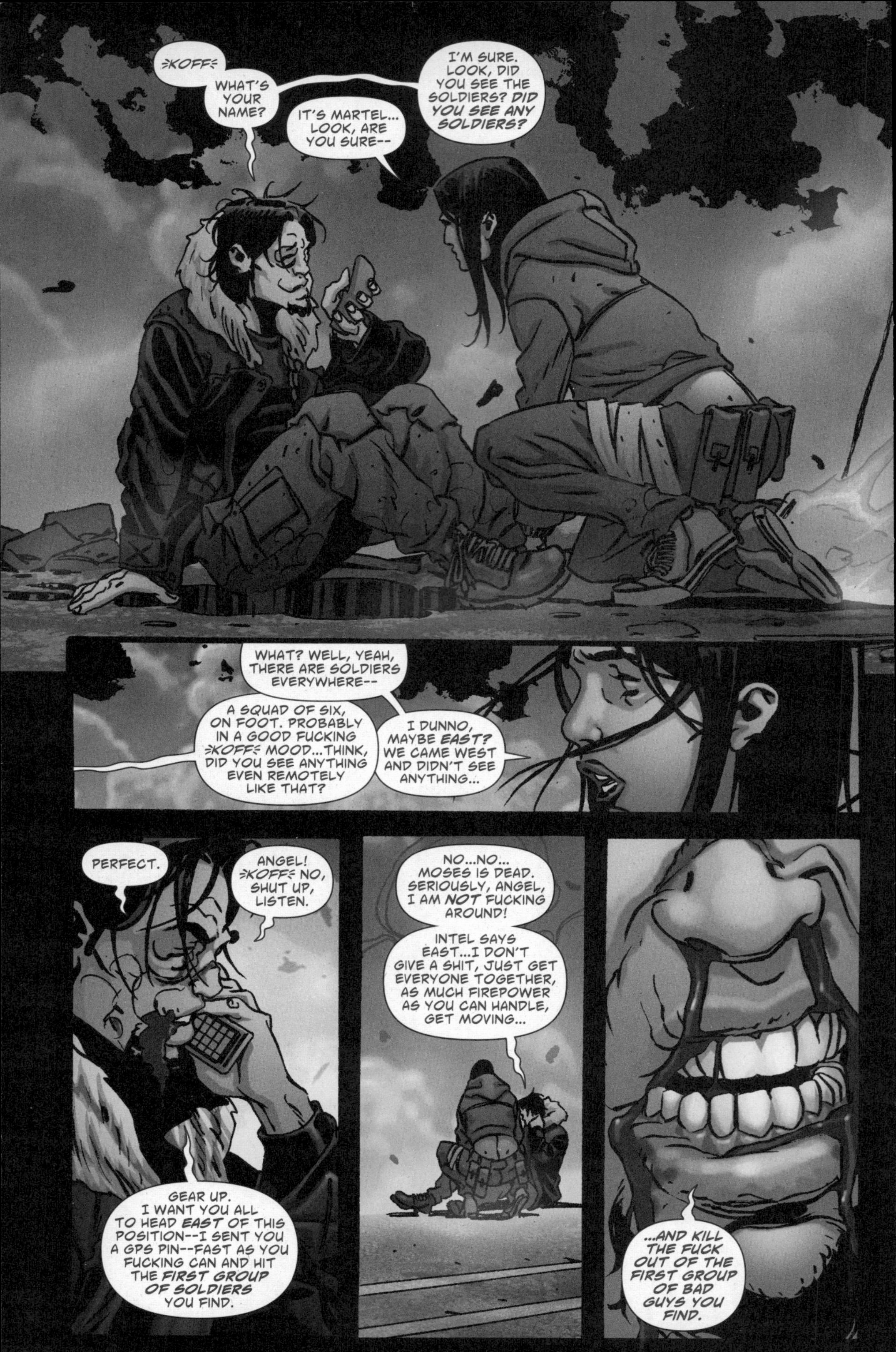

⁼KOFF⁼
WHAT'S YOUR NAME?
IT'S MARTEL... LOOK, ARE YOU SURE--
I'M SURE. LOOK, DID YOU SEE THE SOLDIERS? DID YOU SEE ANY SOLDIERS?
WHAT? WELL, YEAH, THERE ARE SOLDIERS EVERYWHERE--
A SQUAD OF SIX, ON FOOT. PROBABLY IN A GOOD FUCKING ⁼KOFF⁼ MOOD...THINK, DID YOU SEE ANYTHING EVEN REMOTELY LIKE THAT?
I DUNNO, MAYBE EAST? WE CAME WEST AND DIDN'T SEE ANYTHING...
PERFECT.
ANGEL! ⁼KOFF⁼ NO, SHUT UP, LISTEN.
GEAR UP. I WANT YOU ALL TO HEAD EAST OF THIS POSITION--I SENT YOU A GPS PIN--FAST AS YOU FUCKING CAN AND HIT THE FIRST GROUP OF SOLDIERS YOU FIND.
NO...NO... MOSES IS DEAD. SERIOUSLY, ANGEL, I AM NOT FUCKING AROUND!
INTEL SAYS EAST...I DON'T GIVE A SHIT, JUST GET EVERYONE TOGETHER, AS MUCH FIREPOWER AS YOU CAN HANDLE, GET MOVING...
...AND KILL THE FUCK OUT OF THE FIRST GROUP OF BAD GUYS YOU FIND.

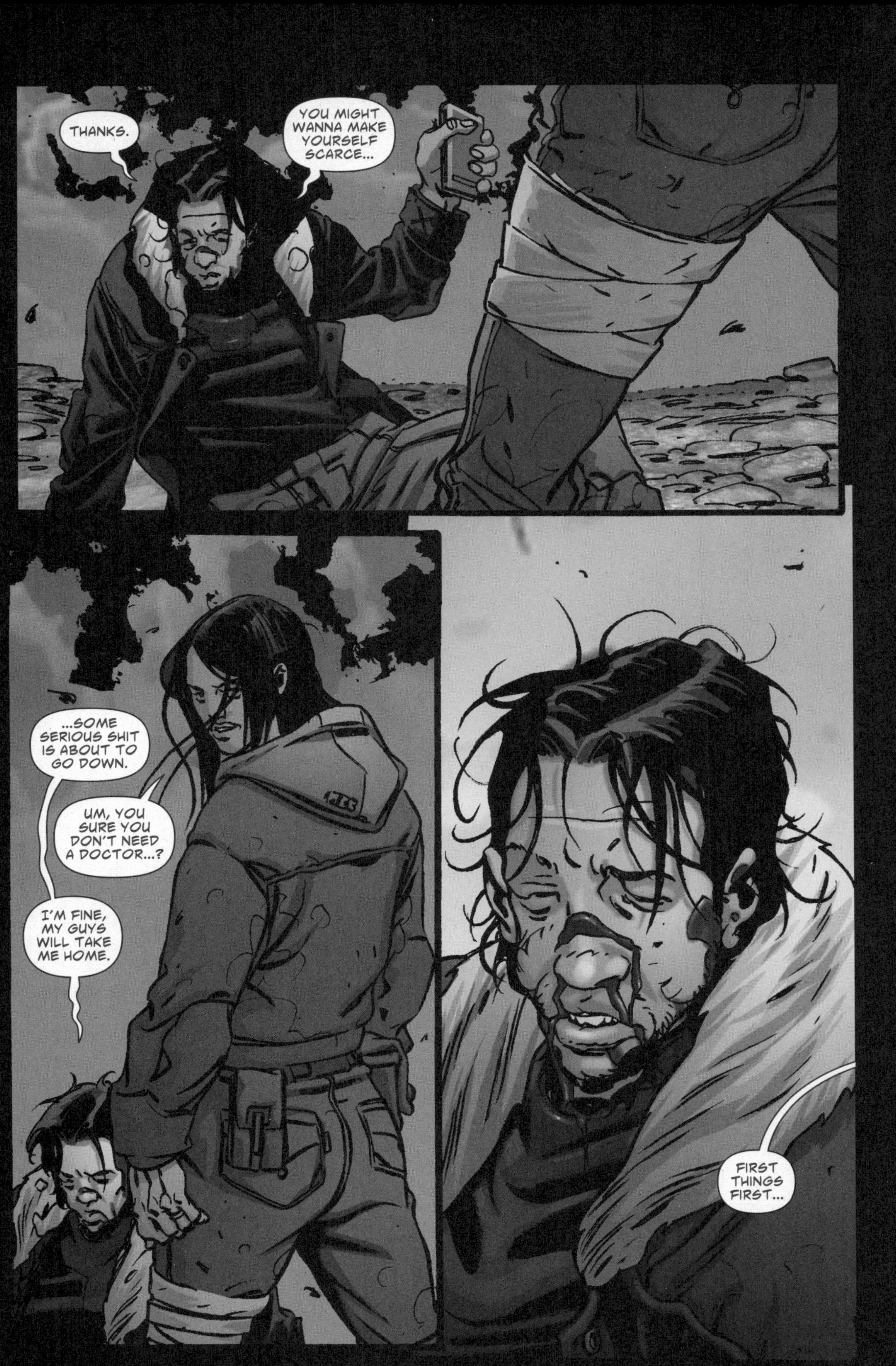
THANKS.
YOU MIGHT WANNA MAKE YOURSELF SCARCE...
...SOME SERIOUS SHIT IS ABOUT TO GO DOWN.
UM, YOU SURE YOU DON'T NEED A DOCTOR...?
I'M FINE, MY GUYS WILL TAKE ME HOME.
FIRST THINGS FIRST...

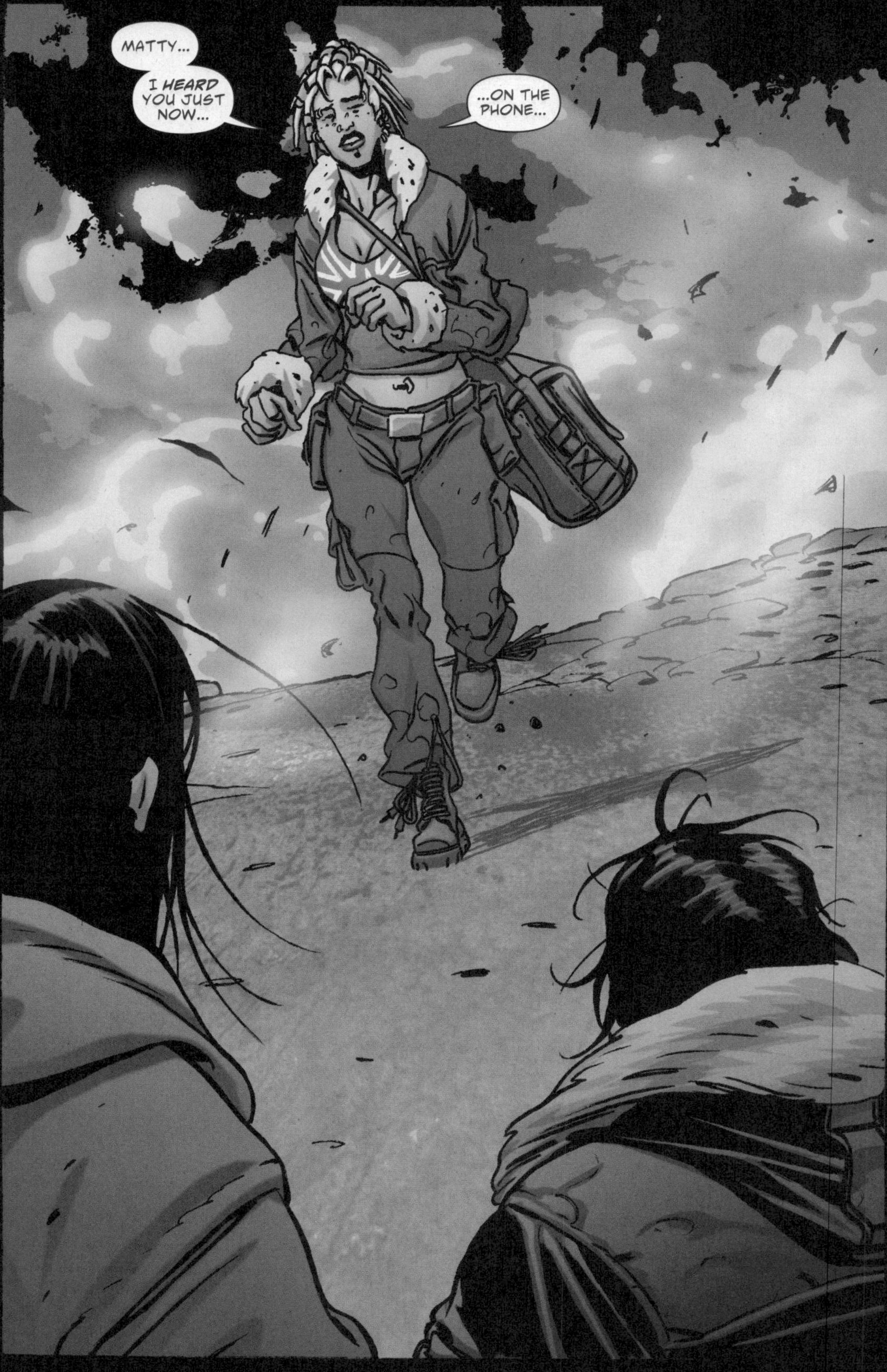
MATTY...
I HEARD YOU JUST NOW...
...ON THE PHONE...

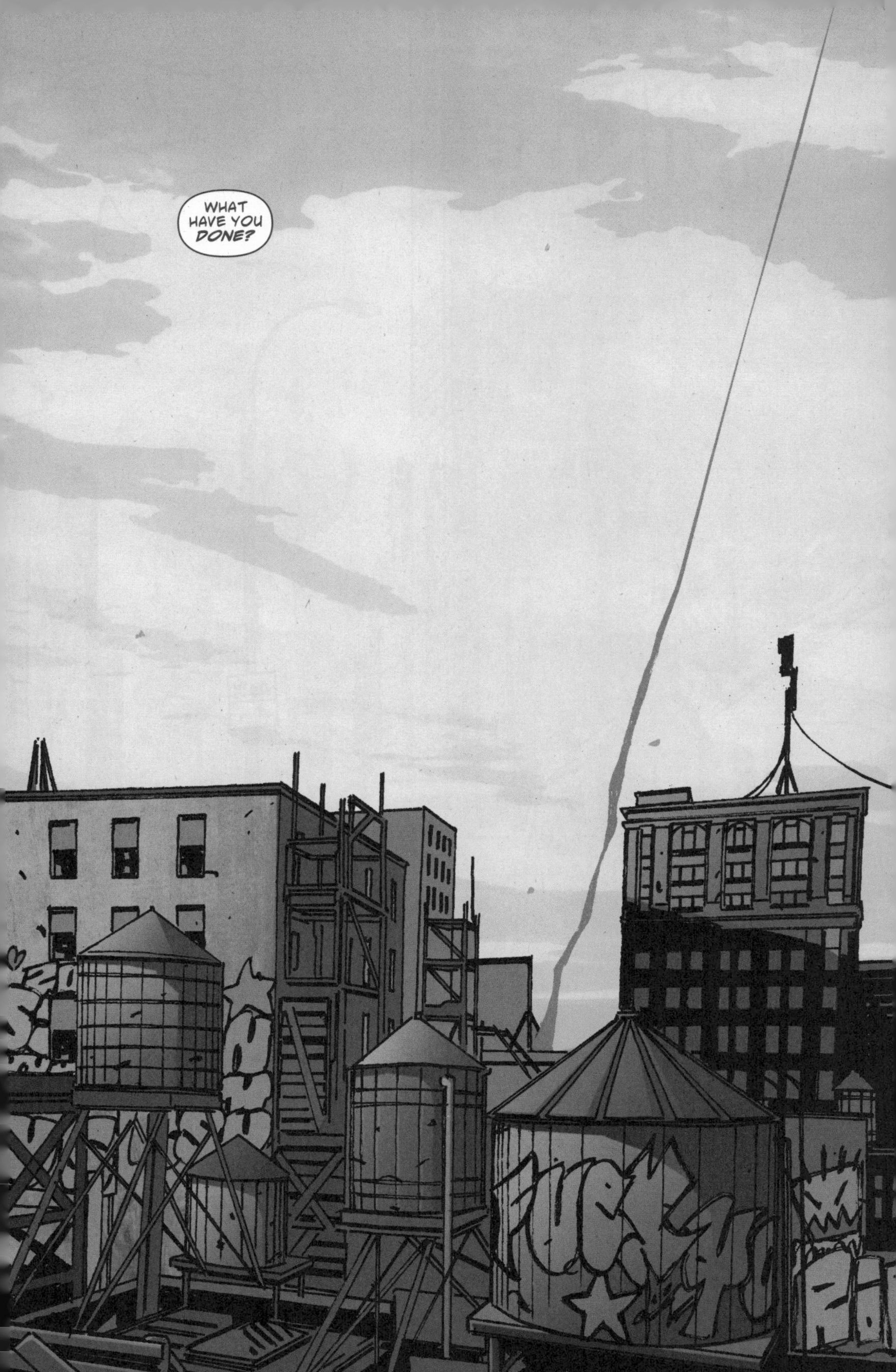
WHAT HAVE YOU DONE?

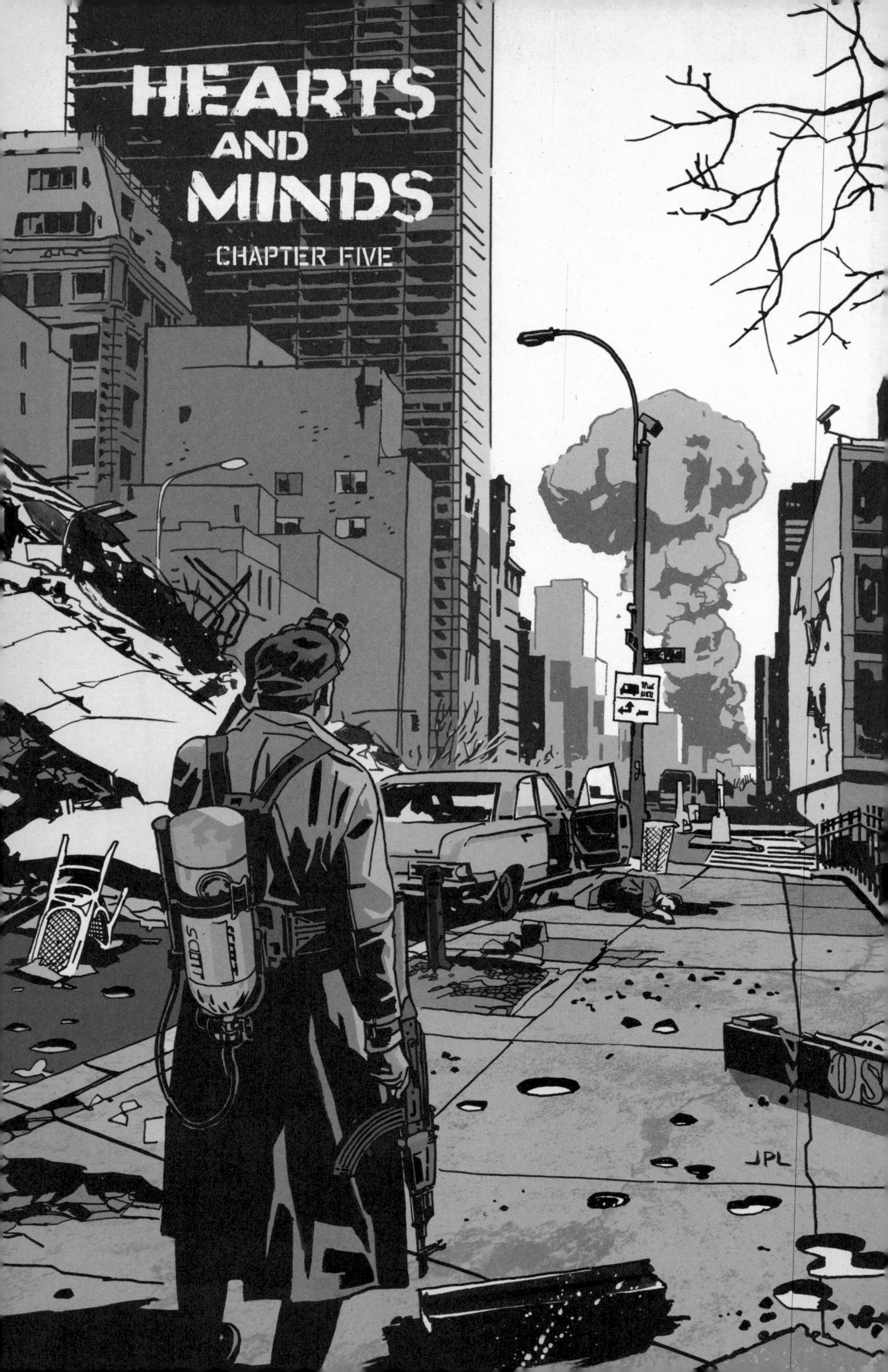
HEARTS
AND
MINDS
CHAPTER FIVE
JPL

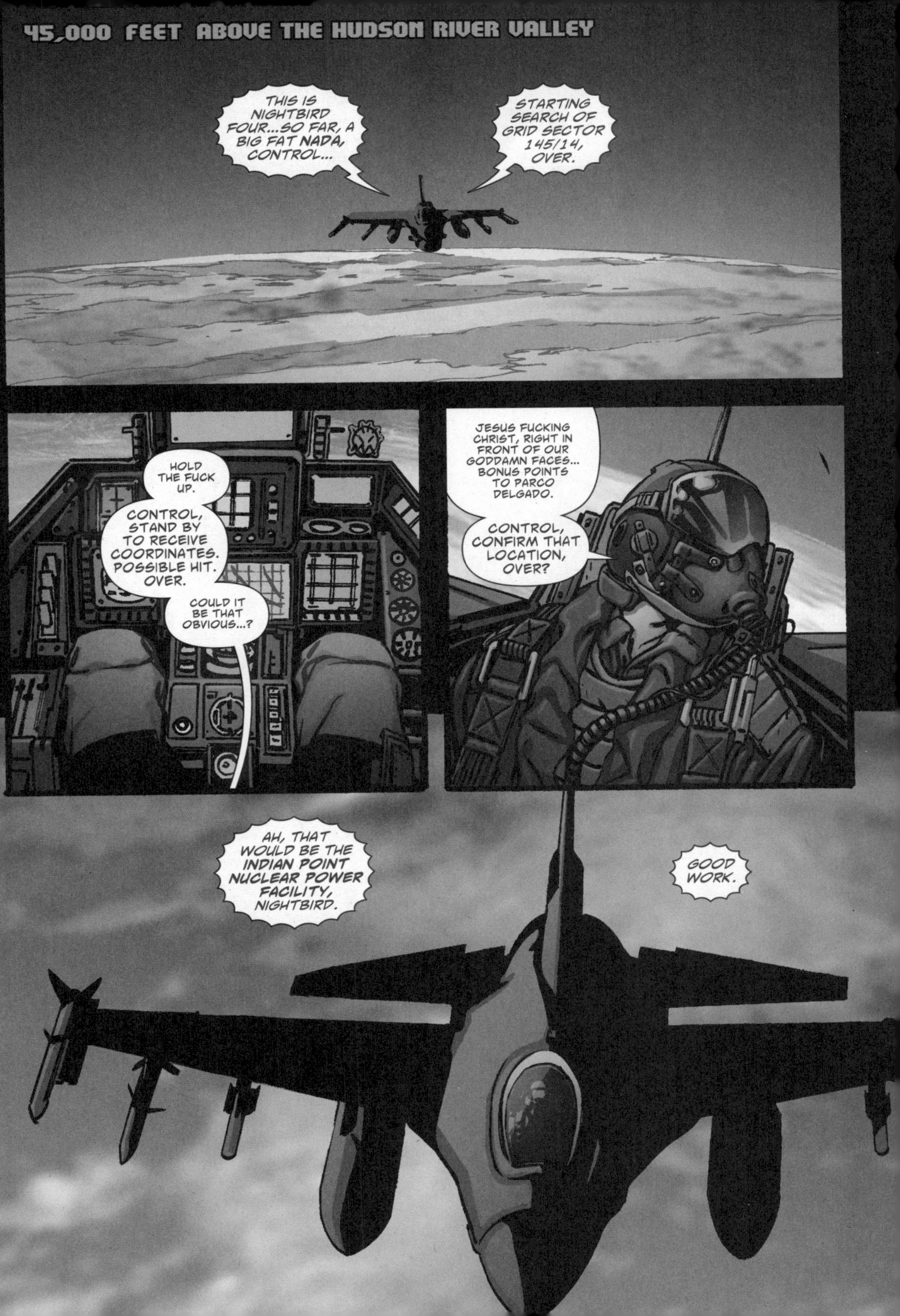
45,000 FEET ABOVE THE HUDSON RIVER VALLEY
THIS IS NIGHTBIRD FOUR...SO FAR, A BIG FAT NADA, CONTROL...
STARTING SEARCH OF GRID SECTOR 145/14, OVER.
HOLD THE FUCK UP.
CONTROL, STAND BY TO RECEIVE COORDINATES. POSSIBLE HIT. OVER.
COULD IT BE THAT OBVIOUS...?
JESUS FUCKING CHRIST, RIGHT IN FRONT OF OUR GODDAMN FACES... BONUS POINTS TO PARCO DELGADO.
CONTROL, CONFIRM THAT LOCATION, OVER?
AH, THAT WOULD BE THE INDIAN POINT NUCLEAR POWER FACILITY, NIGHTBIRD.
GOOD WORK.

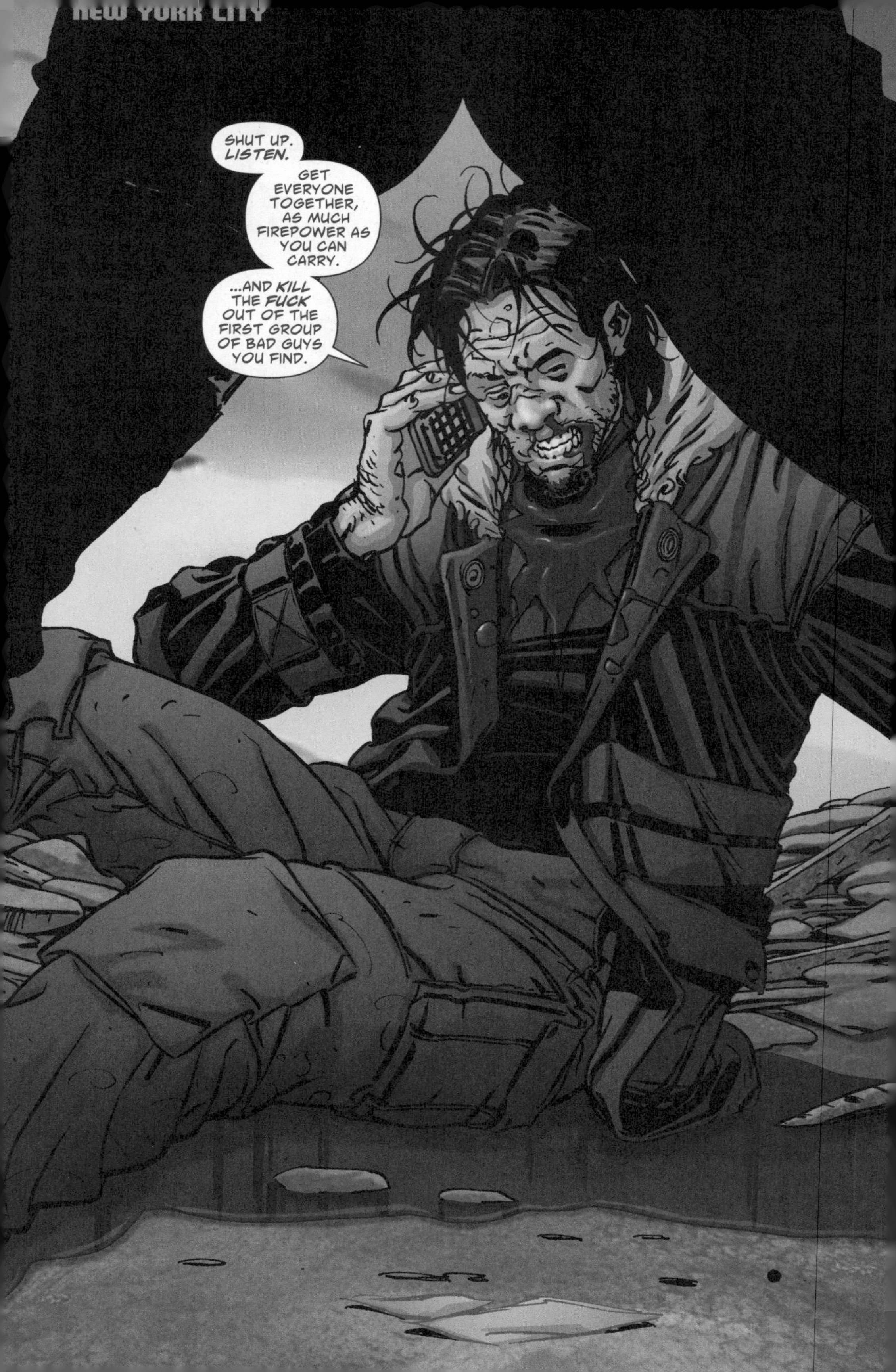
NEW YORK CITY
SHUT UP. LISTEN.
GET EVERYONE TOGETHER, AS MUCH FIREPOWER AS YOU CAN CARRY.
...AND KILL THE FUCK OUT OF THE FIRST GROUP OF BAD GUYS YOU FIND.

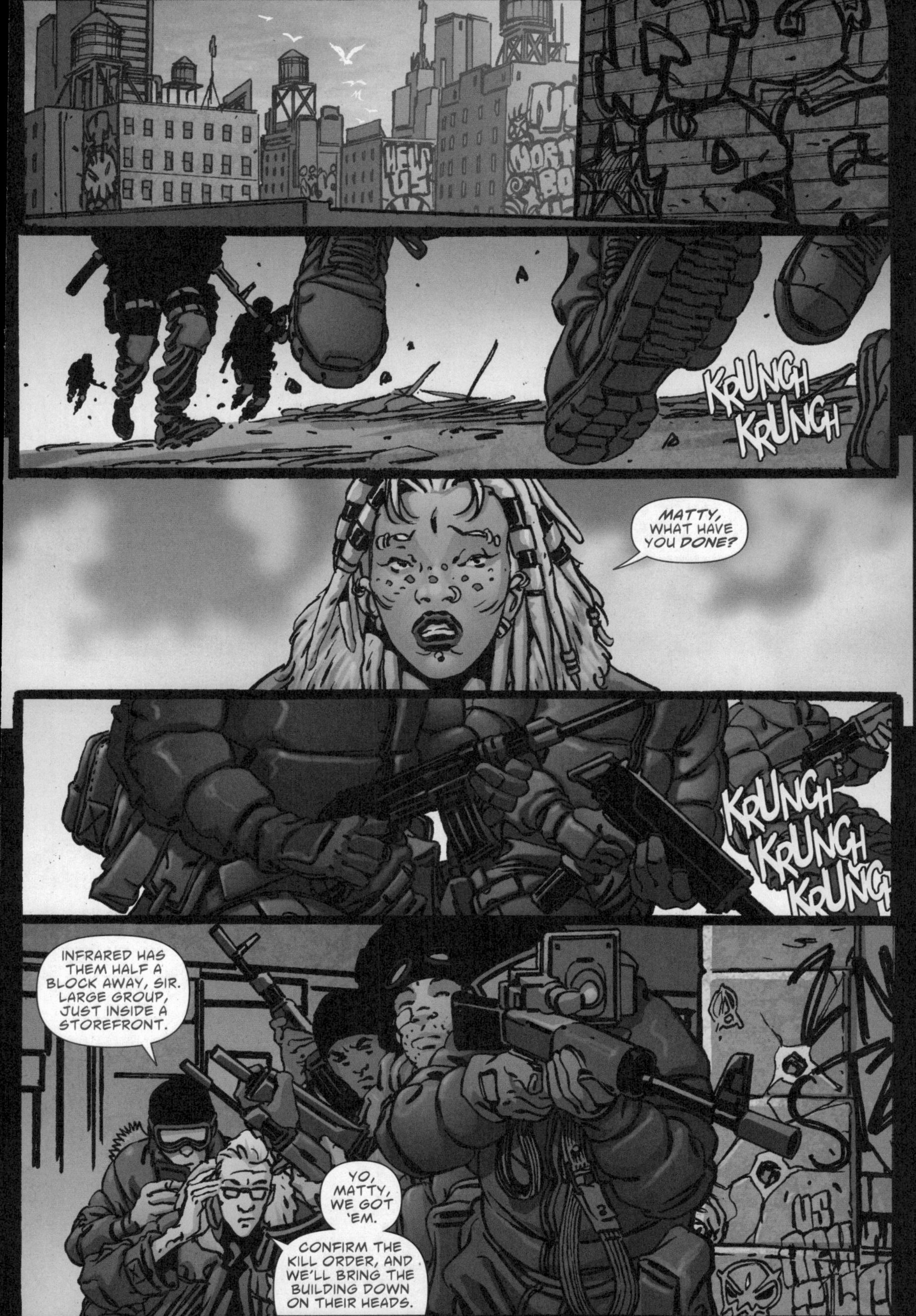
KRUNCH KRUNCH
MATTY, WHAT HAVE YOU DONE?
KRUNCH KRUNCH KRUNCH
INFRARED HAS THEM HALF A BLOCK AWAY, SIR. LARGE GROUP, JUST INSIDE A STOREFRONT.
YO, MATTY, WE GOT 'EM.
CONFIRM THE KILL ORDER, AND WE'LL BRING THE BUILDING DOWN ON THEIR HEADS.

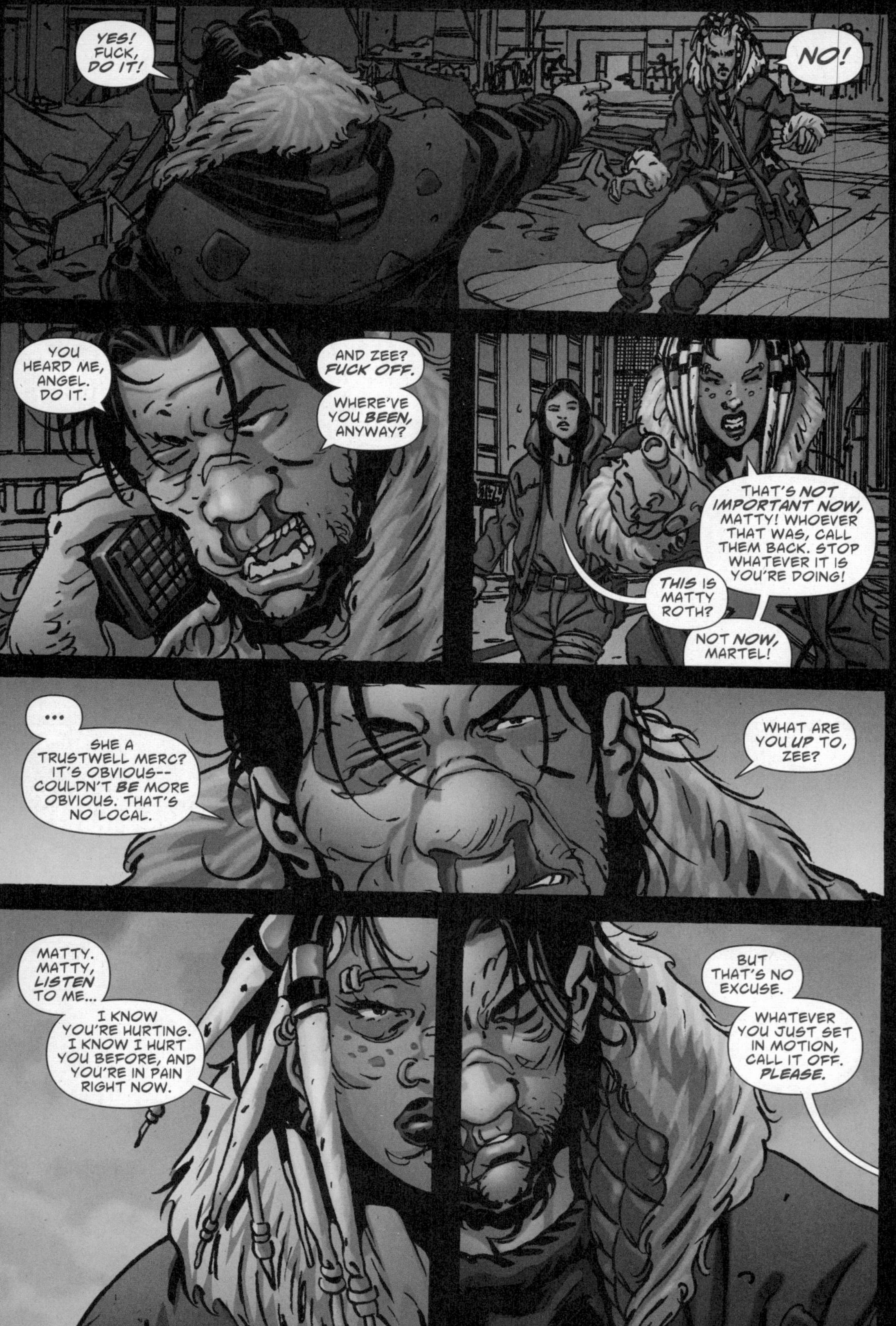
YES! FUCK, DO IT!
NO!
YOU HEARD ME, ANGEL. DO IT.
AND ZEE? FUCK OFF.
WHERE'VE YOU BEEN, ANYWAY?
THAT'S NOT IMPORTANT NOW, MATTY! WHOEVER THAT WAS, CALL THEM BACK. STOP WHATEVER IT IS YOU'RE DOING!
THIS IS MATTY ROTH?
NOT NOW, MARTEL!
...
SHE A TRUSTWELL MERC? IT'S OBVIOUS--COULDN'T BE MORE OBVIOUS. THAT'S NO LOCAL.
WHAT ARE YOU UP TO, ZEE?
MATTY. MATTY, LISTEN TO ME...
I KNOW YOU'RE HURTING. I KNOW I HURT YOU BEFORE, AND YOU'RE IN PAIN RIGHT NOW.
BUT THAT'S NO EXCUSE.
WHATEVER YOU JUST SET IN MOTION, CALL IT OFF. PLEASE.

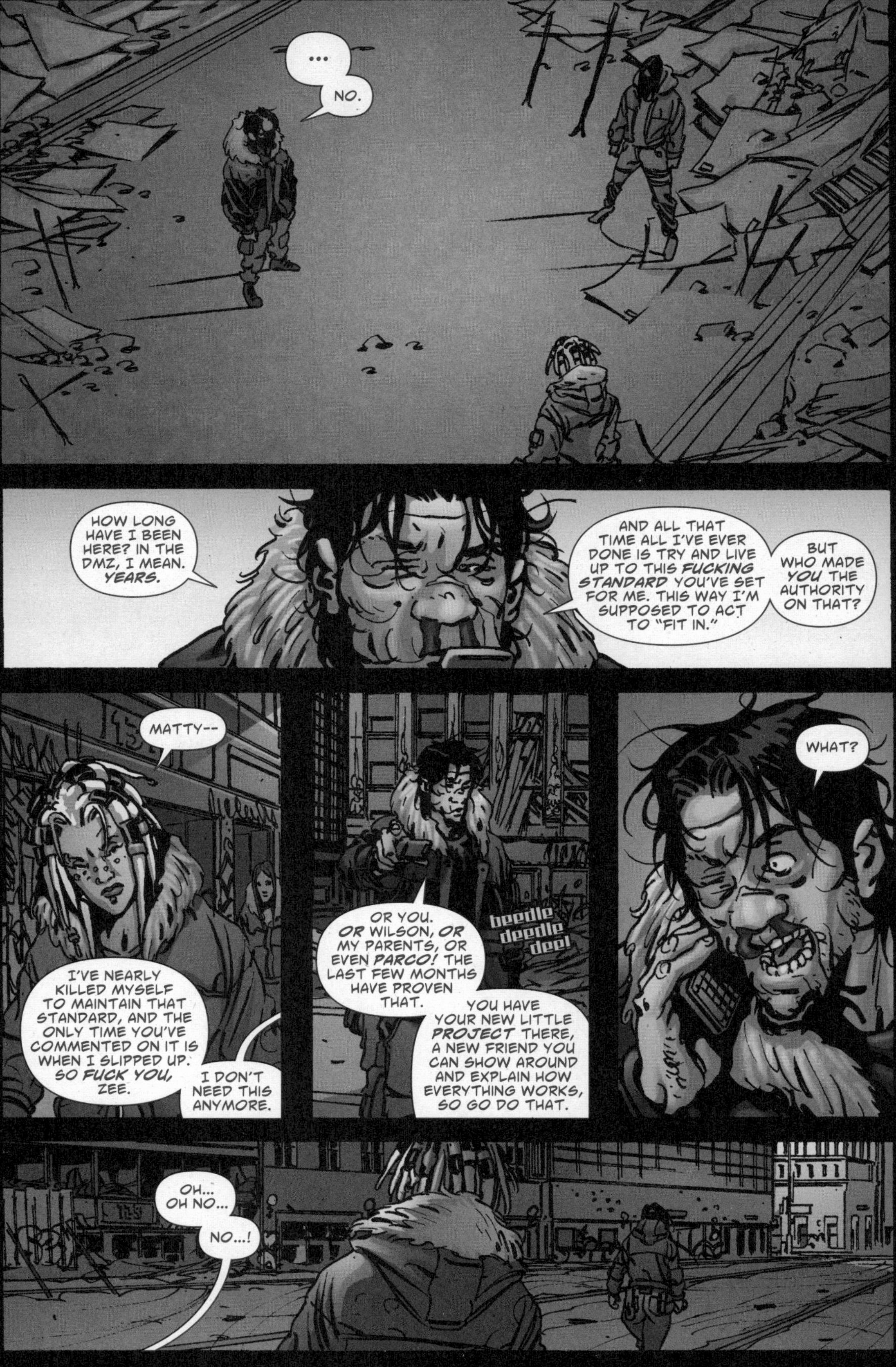
...
NO.
HOW LONG HAVE I BEEN HERE? IN THE DMZ, I MEAN. YEARS.
AND ALL THAT TIME ALL I'VE EVER DONE IS TRY AND LIVE UP TO THIS FUCKING STANDARD YOU'VE SET FOR ME. THIS WAY I'M SUPPOSED TO ACT TO "FIT IN."
BUT WHO MADE YOU THE AUTHORITY ON THAT?
MATTY--
OR YOU. OR WILSON, OR MY PARENTS, OR EVEN PARCO! THE LAST FEW MONTHS HAVE PROVEN THAT.
beedle deedle dee!
WHAT?
I'VE NEARLY KILLED MYSELF TO MAINTAIN THAT STANDARD, AND THE ONLY TIME YOU'VE COMMENTED ON IT IS WHEN I SLIPPED UP. SO FUCK YOU, ZEE.
I DON'T NEED THIS ANYMORE.
YOU HAVE YOUR NEW LITTLE PROJECT THERE, A NEW FRIEND YOU CAN SHOW AROUND AND EXPLAIN HOW EVERYTHING WORKS, SO GO DO THAT.
OH... OH NO...
NO...!

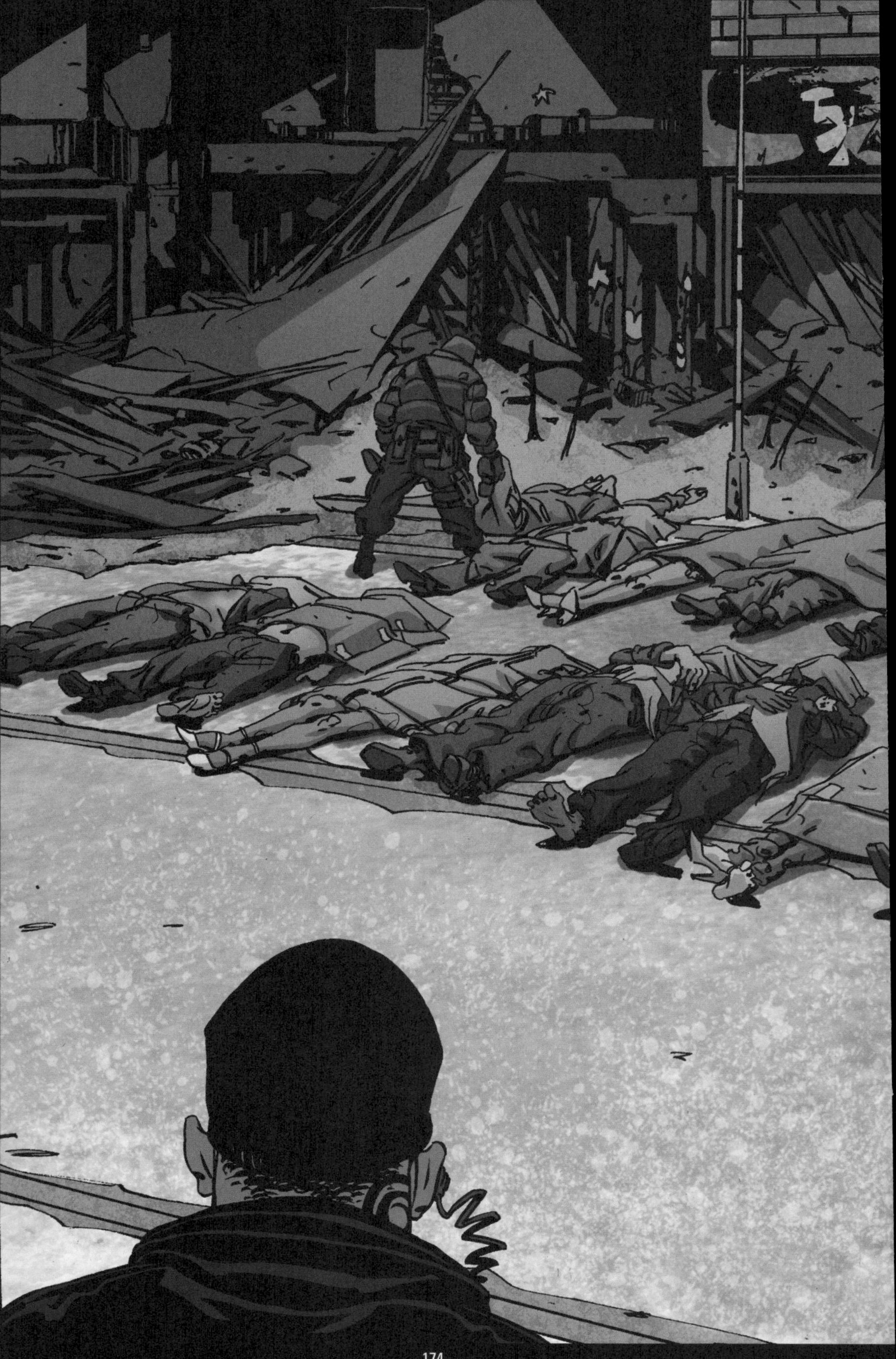

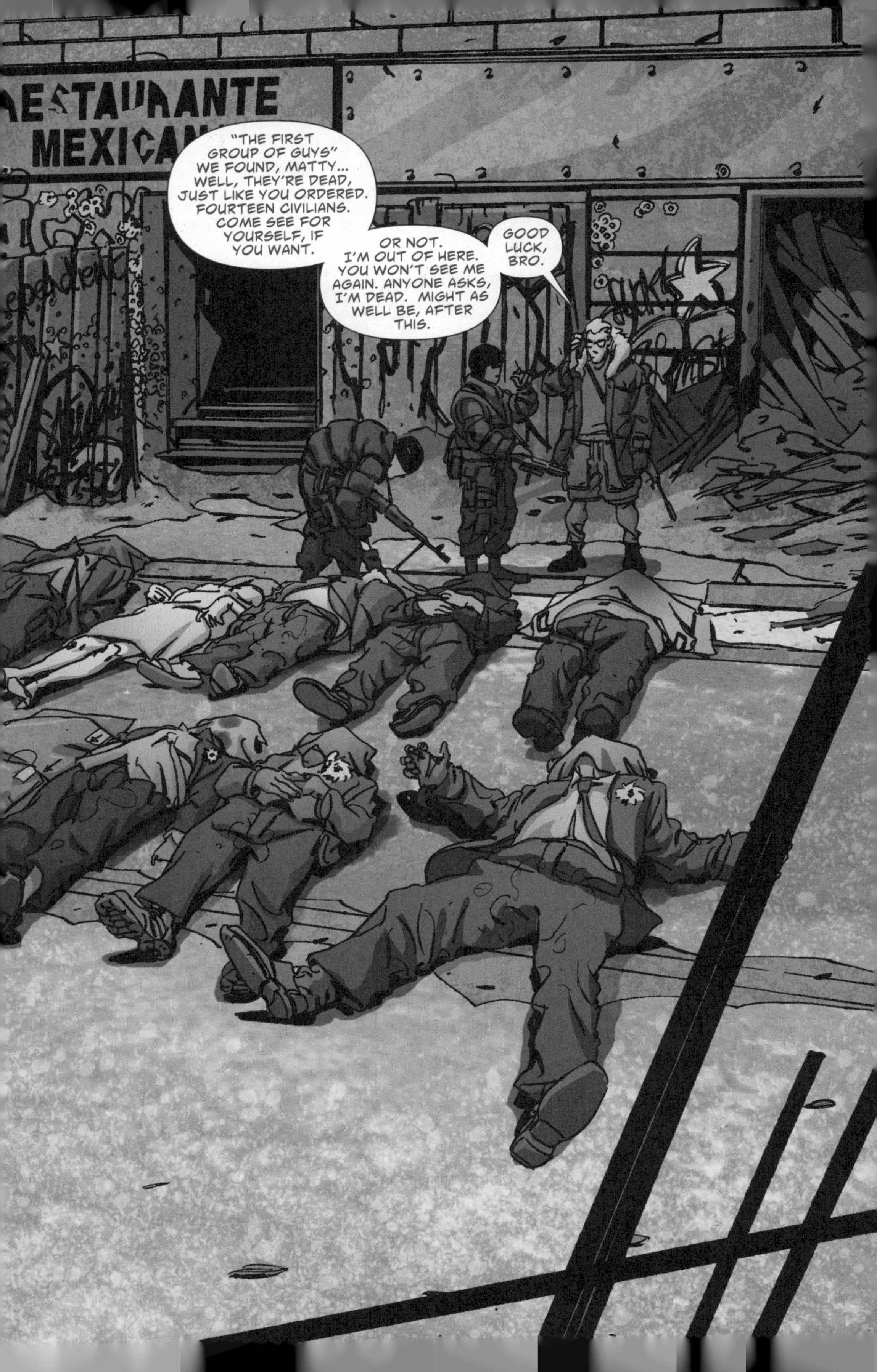
RESTAURANTE MEXICAN
"THE FIRST GROUP OF GUYS" WE FOUND, MATTY... WELL, THEY'RE DEAD, JUST LIKE YOU ORDERED. FOURTEEN CIVILIANS. COME SEE FOR YOURSELF, IF YOU WANT.
OR NOT. I'M OUT OF HERE. YOU WON'T SEE ME AGAIN. ANYONE ASKS, I'M DEAD. MIGHT AS WELL BE, AFTER THIS.
GOOD LUCK, BRO.

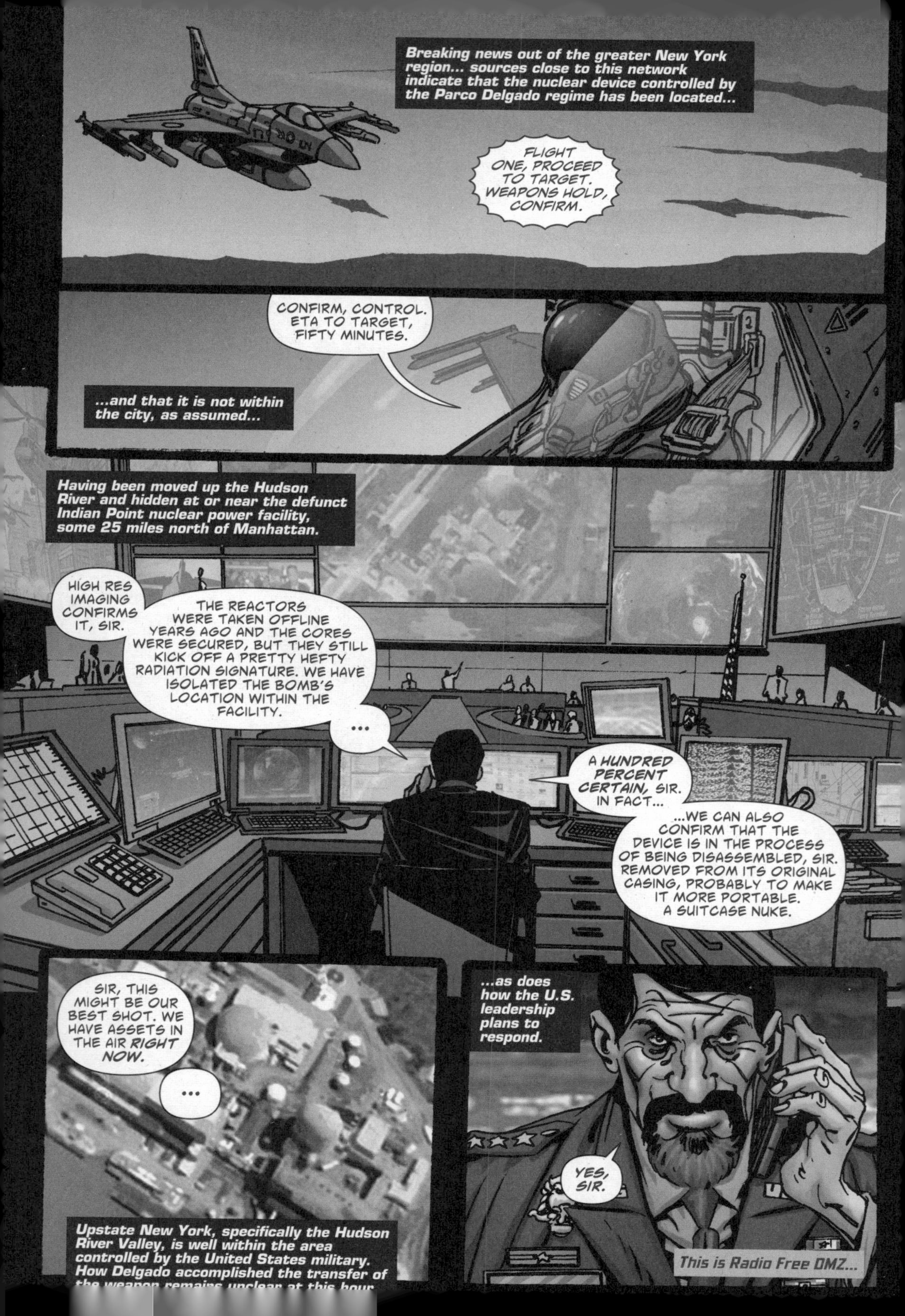
Breaking news out of the greater New York region... sources close to this network indicate that the nuclear device controlled by the Parco Delgado regime has been located...
FLIGHT ONE, PROCEED TO TARGET. WEAPONS HOLD, CONFIRM.
CONFIRM, CONTROL. ETA TO TARGET, FIFTY MINUTES.
...and that it is not within the city, as assumed...
Having been moved up the Hudson River and hidden at or near the defunct Indian Point nuclear power facility, some 25 miles north of Manhattan.
HIGH RES IMAGING CONFIRMS IT, SIR.
THE REACTORS WERE TAKEN OFFLINE YEARS AGO AND THE CORES WERE SECURED, BUT THEY STILL KICK OFF A PRETTY HEFTY RADIATION SIGNATURE. WE HAVE ISOLATED THE BOMB'S LOCATION WITHIN THE FACILITY.
...
A HUNDRED PERCENT CERTAIN, SIR. IN FACT...
...WE CAN ALSO CONFIRM THAT THE DEVICE IS IN THE PROCESS OF BEING DISASSEMBLED, SIR. REMOVED FROM ITS ORIGINAL CASING, PROBABLY TO MAKE IT MORE PORTABLE. A SUITCASE NUKE.
SIR, THIS MIGHT BE OUR BEST SHOT. WE HAVE ASSETS IN THE AIR RIGHT NOW.
...
Upstate New York, specifically the Hudson River Valley, is well within the area controlled by the United States military. How Delgado accomplished the transfer of
...as does how the U.S. leadership plans to respond.
YES, SIR.
This is Radio Free DMZ...

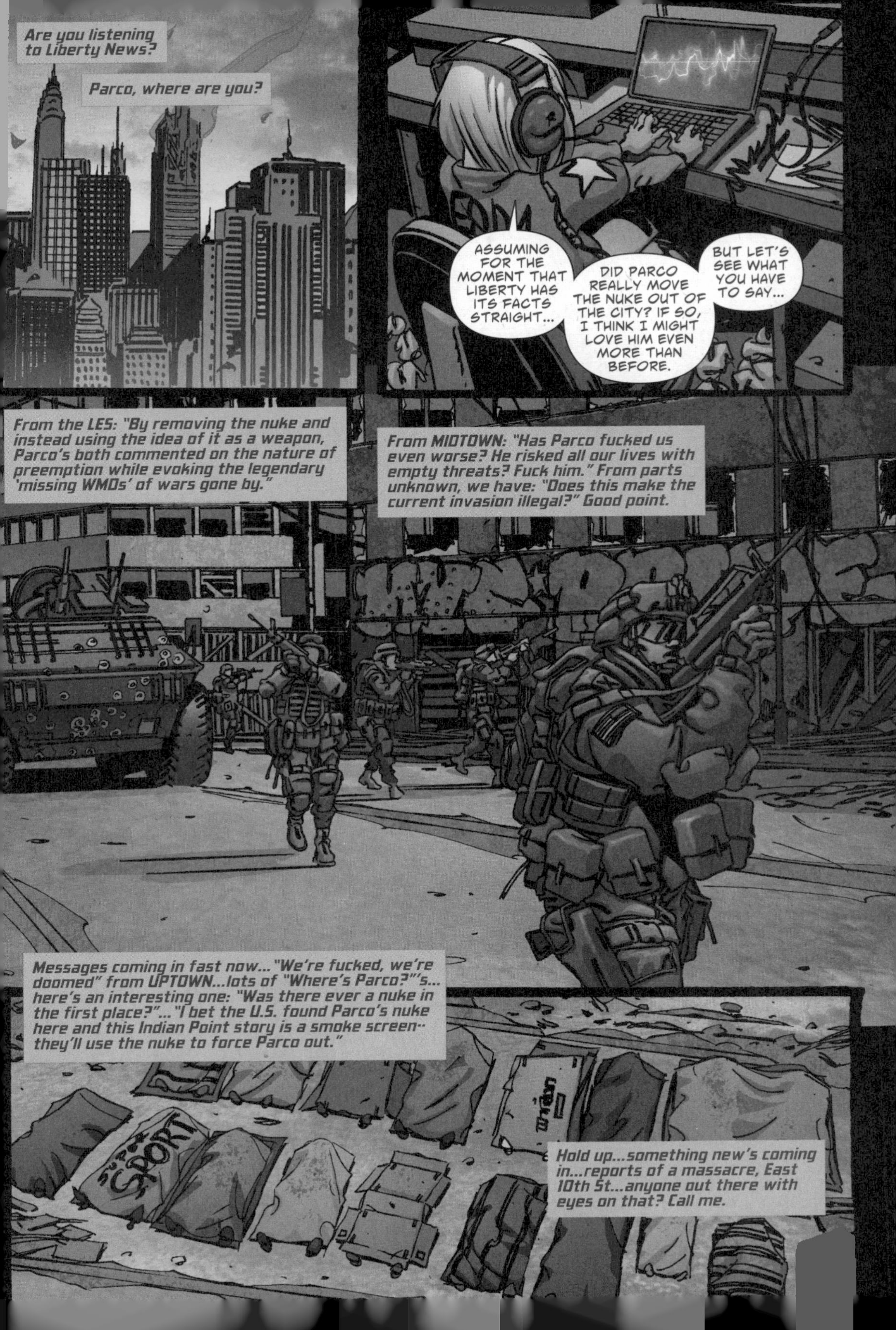

Are you listening to Liberty News?
Parco, where are you?
ASSUMING FOR THE MOMENT THAT LIBERTY HAS ITS FACTS STRAIGHT...
DID PARCO REALLY MOVE THE NUKE OUT OF THE CITY? IF SO, I THINK I MIGHT LOVE HIM EVEN MORE THAN BEFORE.
BUT LET'S SEE WHAT YOU HAVE TO SAY...
From the LES: "By removing the nuke and instead using the idea of it as a weapon, Parco's both commented on the nature of preemption while evoking the legendary 'missing WMDs' of wars gone by."
From MIDTOWN: "Has Parco fucked us even worse? He risked all our lives with empty threats? Fuck him." From parts unknown, we have: "Does this make the current invasion illegal?" Good point.
Messages coming in fast now... "We're fucked, we're doomed" from UPTOWN...lots of "Where's Parco?"'s... here's an interesting one: "Was there ever a nuke in the first place?"... "I bet the U.S. found Parco's nuke here and this Indian Point story is a smoke screen-- they'll use the nuke to force Parco out."
SUPER SPORT
Hold up...something new's coming in...reports of a massacre, East 10th St...anyone out there with eyes on that? Call me.

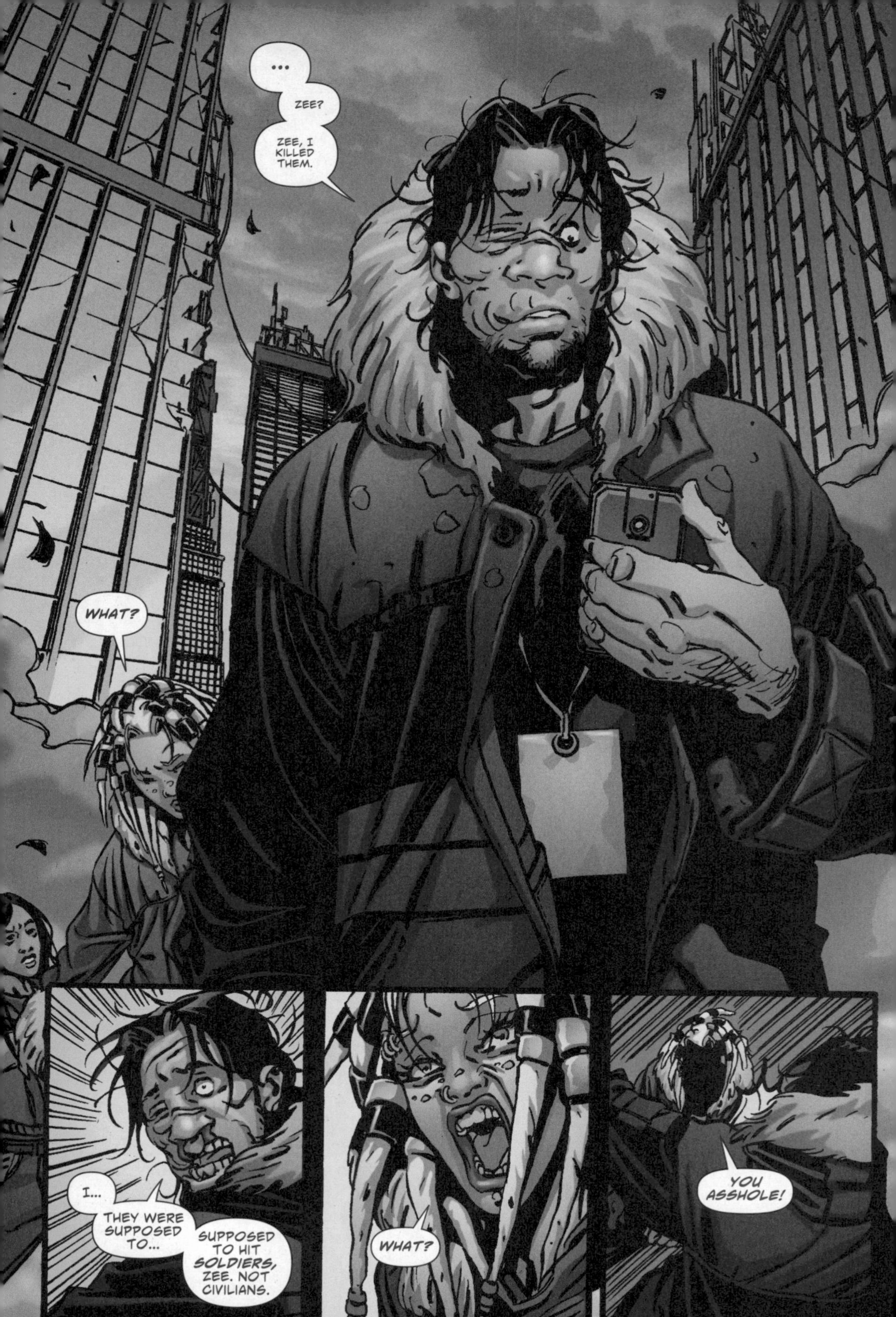
...
ZEE?
ZEE, I KILLED THEM.
WHAT?
I...
THEY WERE SUPPOSED TO...
SUPPOSED TO HIT *SOLDIERS,* ZEE. NOT CIVILIANS.
WHAT?
YOU ASSHOLE!

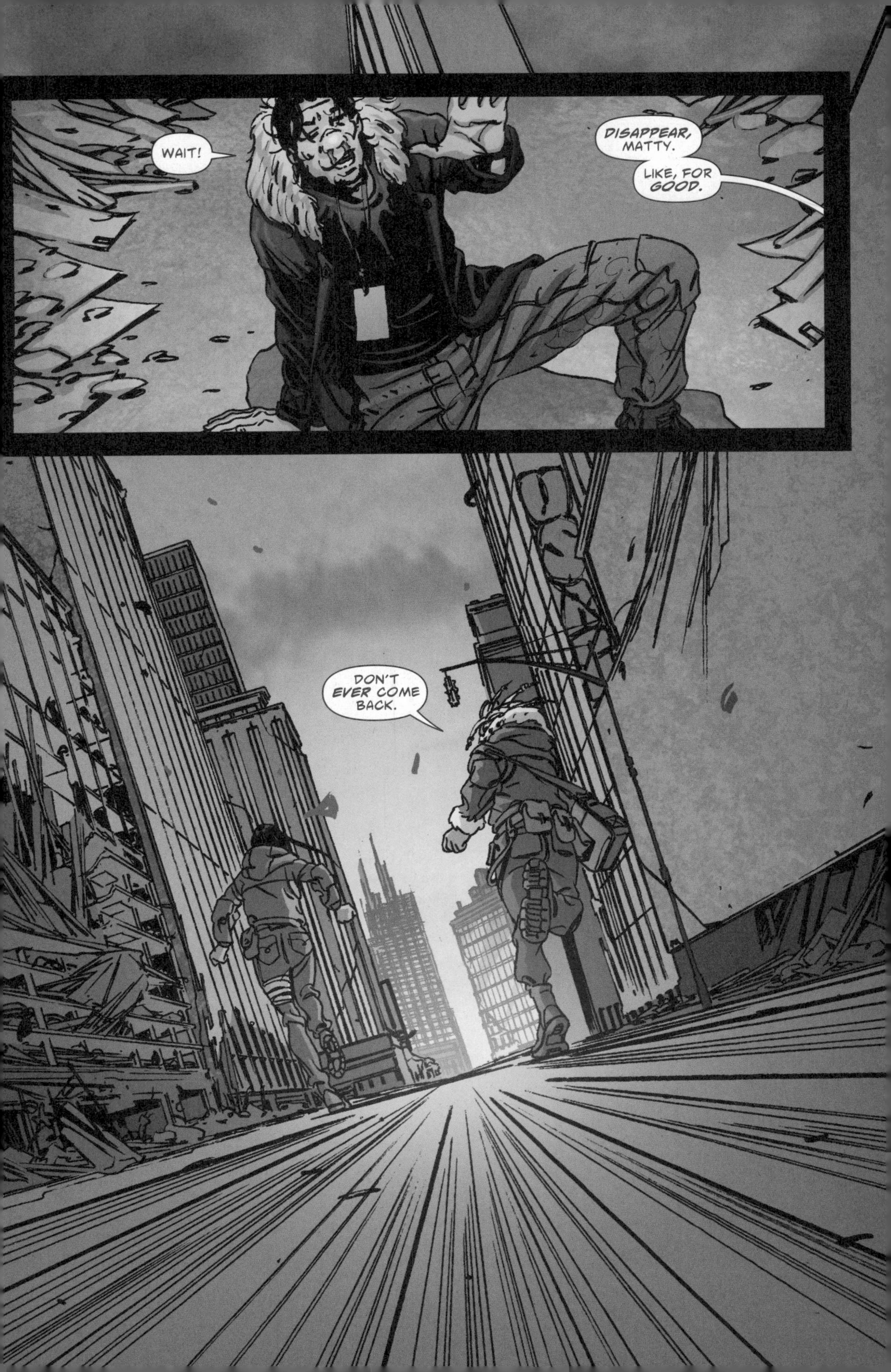

WAIT!
DISAPPEAR, MATTY.
LIKE, FOR GOOD.
DON'T EVER COME BACK.

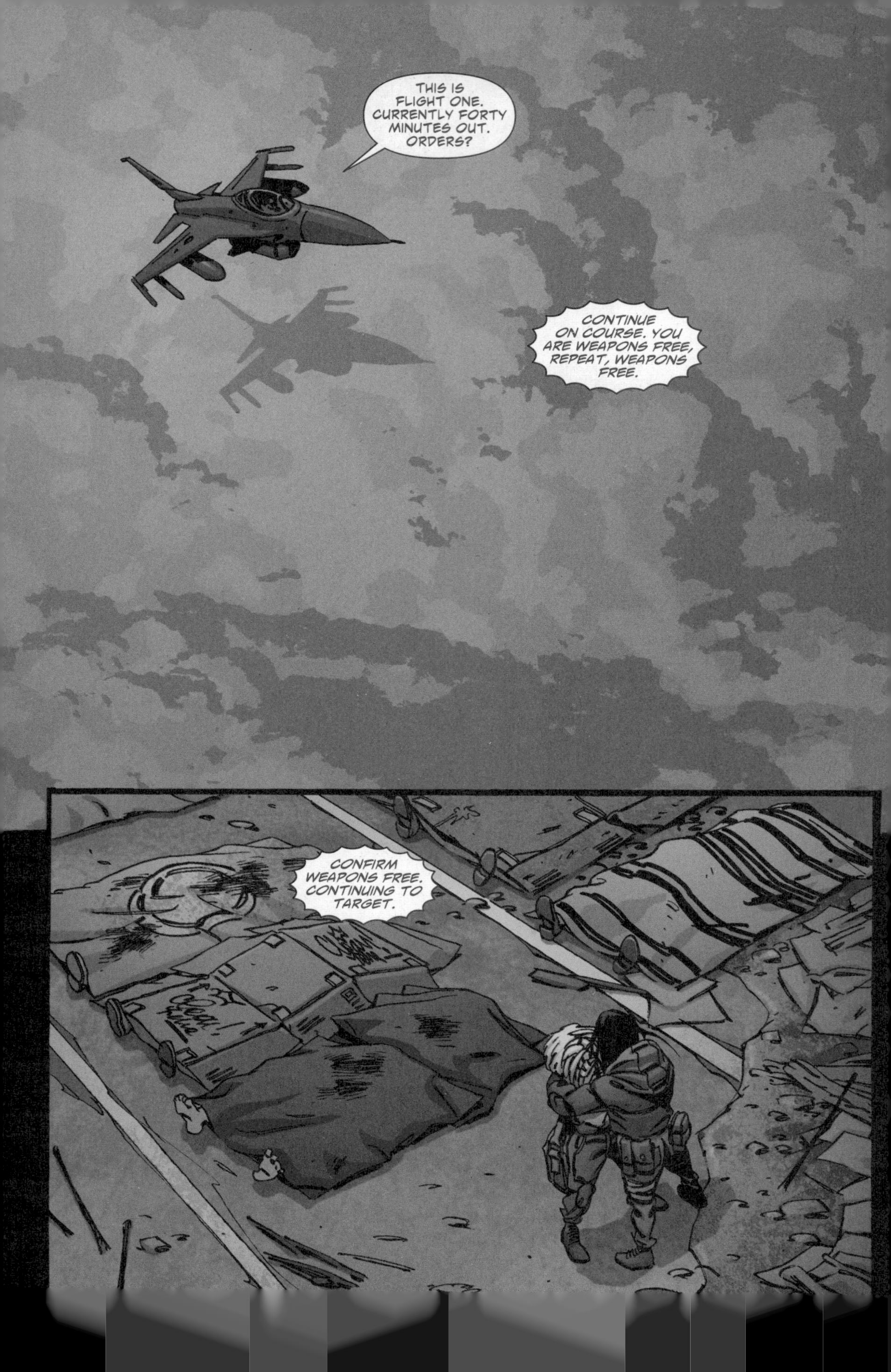
THIS IS FLIGHT ONE. CURRENTLY FORTY MINUTES OUT. ORDERS?
CONTINUE ON COURSE. YOU ARE WEAPONS FREE, REPEAT, WEAPONS FREE.
CONFIRM WEAPONS FREE. CONTINUING TO TARGET.

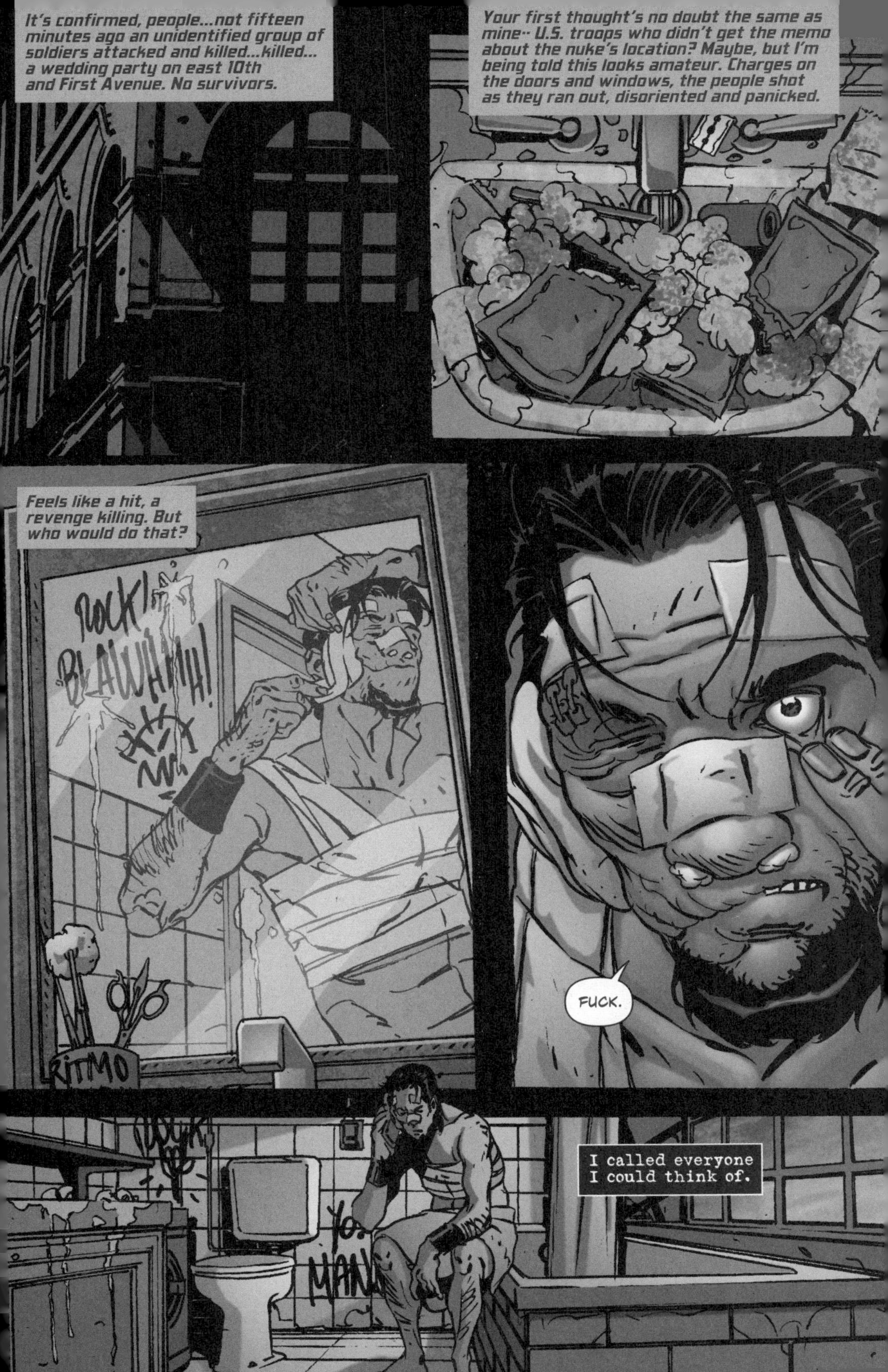
It's confirmed, people...not fifteen minutes ago an unidentified group of soldiers attacked and killed...killed... a wedding party on east 10th and First Avenue. No survivors.
Your first thought's no doubt the same as mine-- U.S. troops who didn't get the memo about the nuke's location? Maybe, but I'm being told this looks amateur. Charges on the doors and windows, the people shot as they ran out, disoriented and panicked.
Feels like a hit, a revenge killing. But who would do that?
FUCK.
I called everyone I could think of.

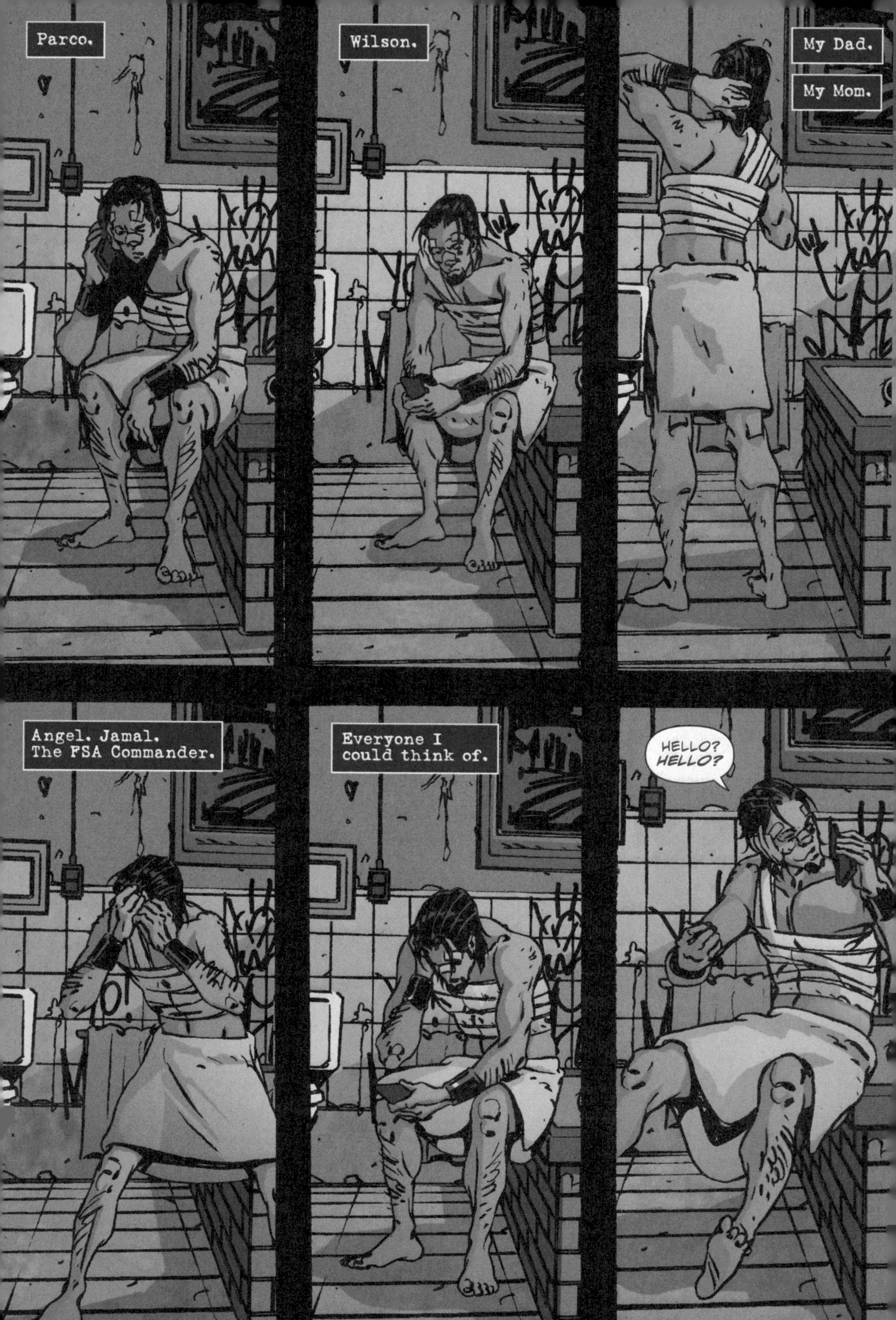
Parco.
Wilson.
My Dad.
My Mom.
Angel. Jamal.
The FSA Commander.
Everyone I
could think of.
HELLO?
HELLO?

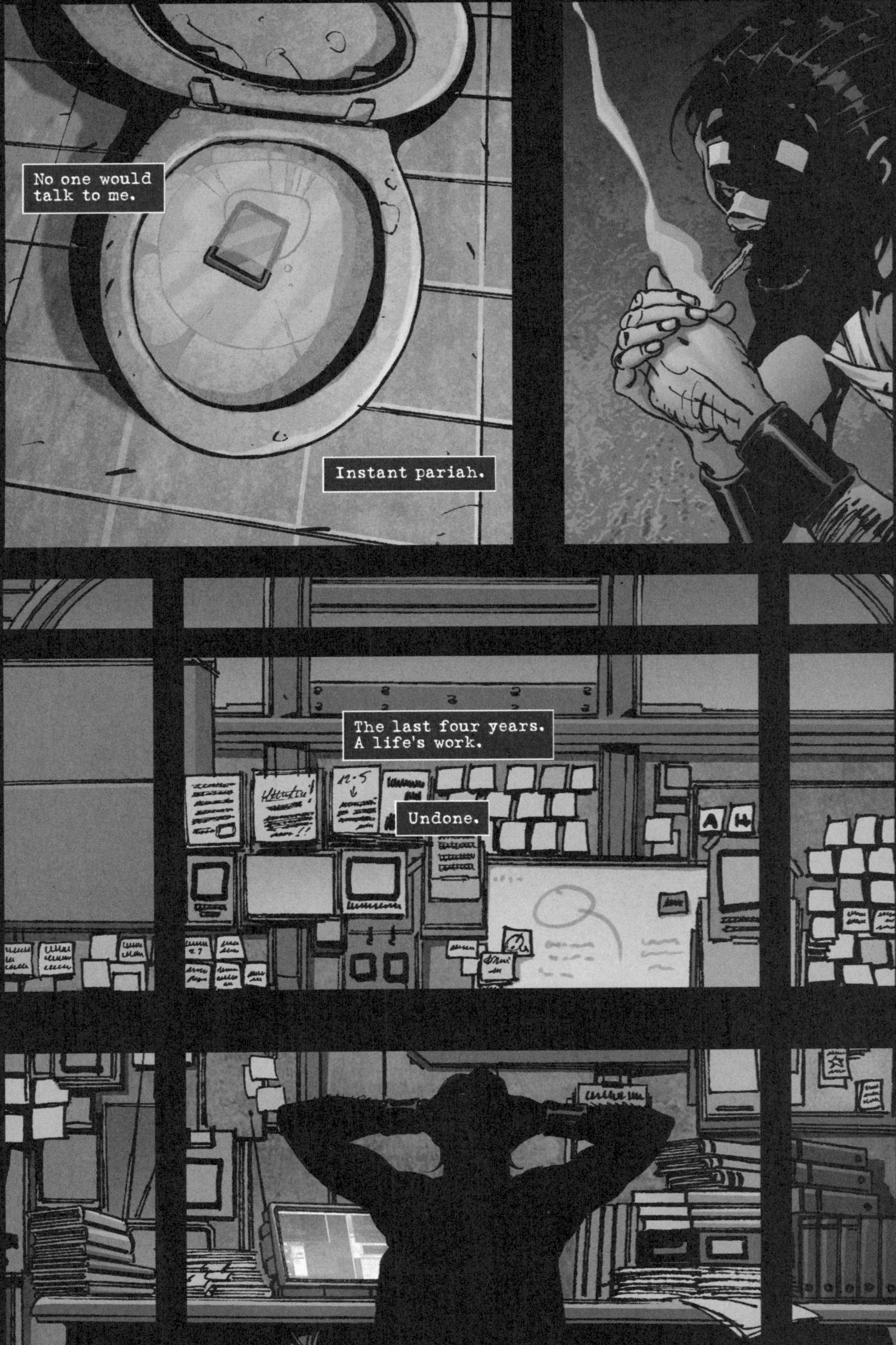
No one would talk to me.
Instant pariah.
The last four years. A life's work.
Undone.

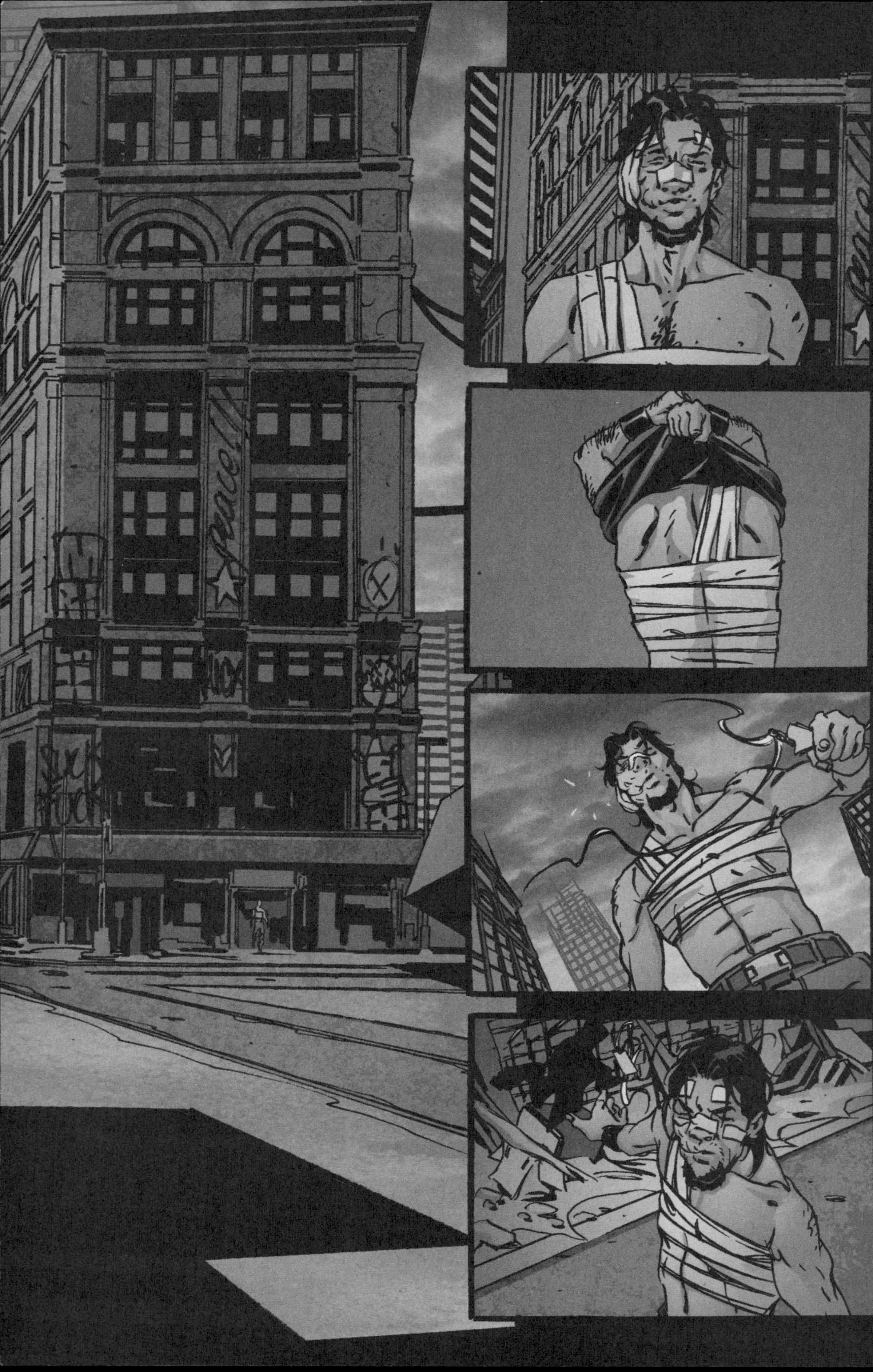
peace!

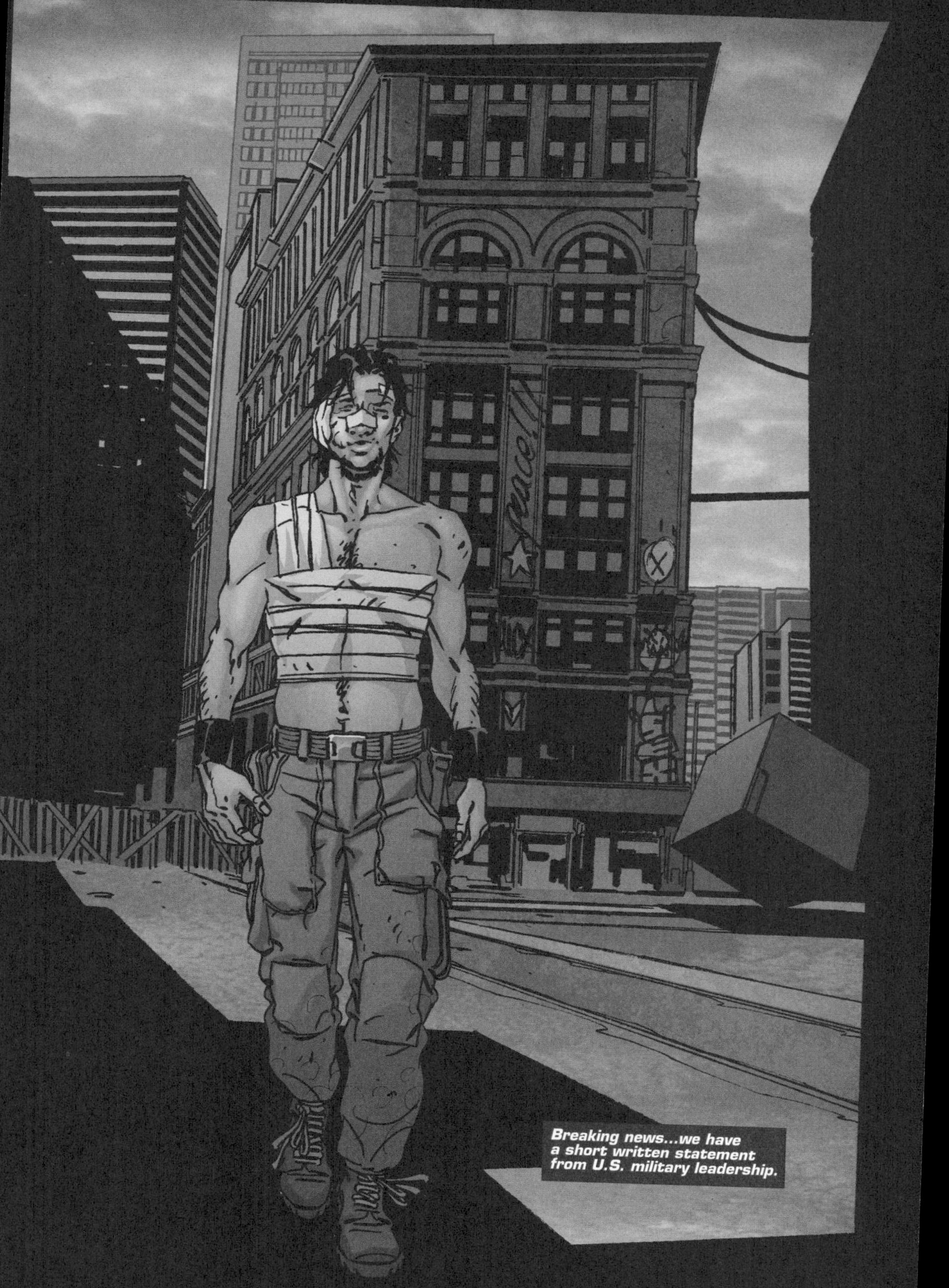
Breaking news...we have a short written statement from U.S. military leadership.

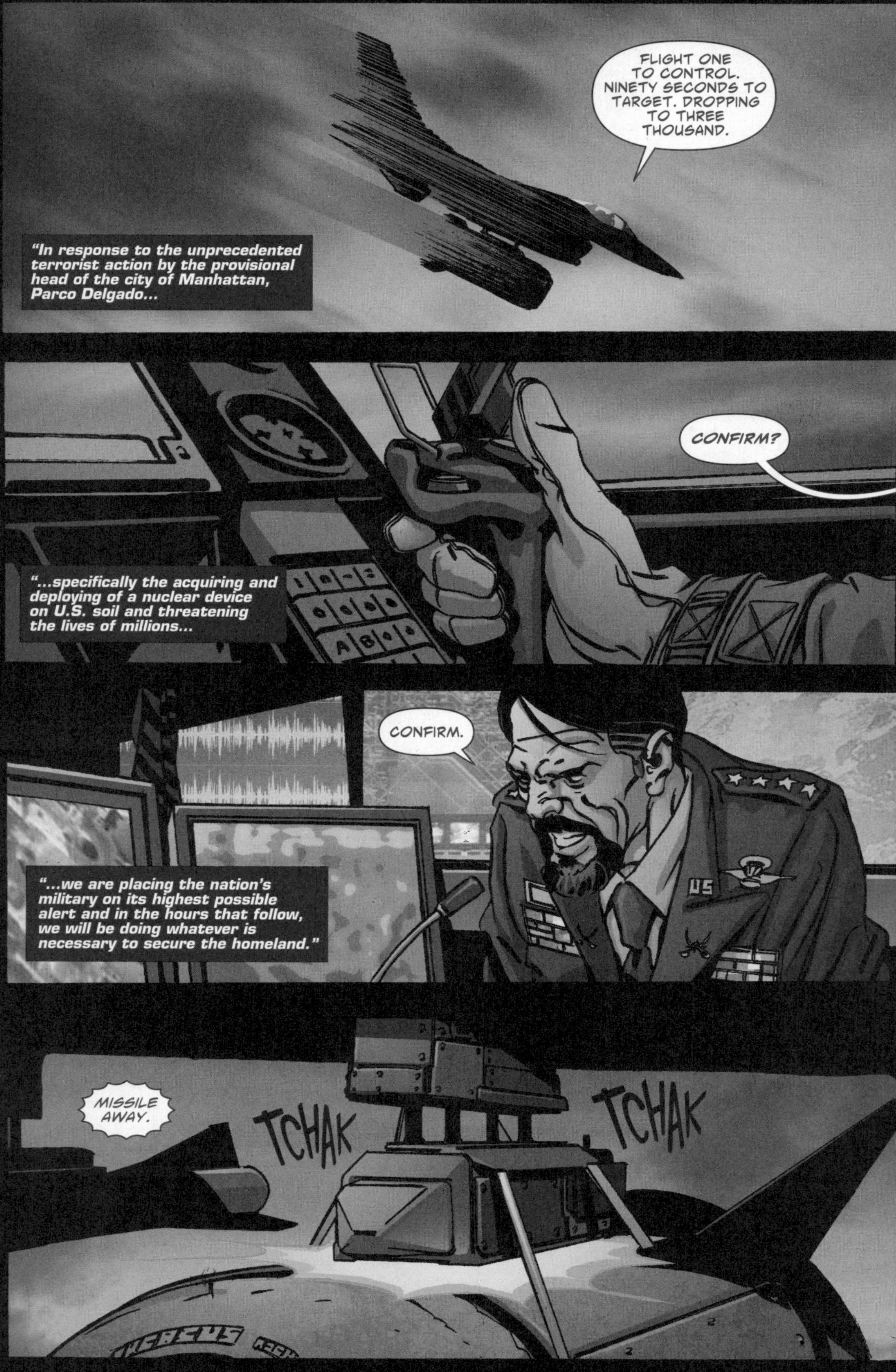
FLIGHT ONE TO CONTROL. NINETY SECONDS TO TARGET. DROPPING TO THREE THOUSAND.
"In response to the unprecedented terrorist action by the provisional head of the city of Manhattan, Parco Delgado...
CONFIRM?
"...specifically the acquiring and deploying of a nuclear device on U.S. soil and threatening the lives of millions...
CONFIRM.
"...we are placing the nation's military on its highest possible alert and in the hours that follow, we will be doing whatever is necessary to secure the homeland."
MISSILE AWAY.
TCHAK
TCHAK

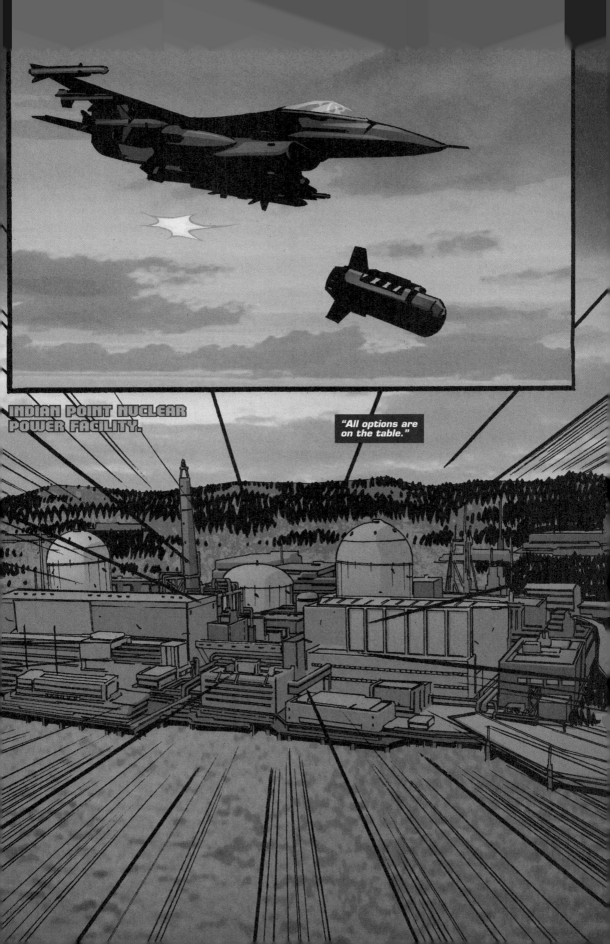

INDIAN POINT NUCLEAR POWER FACILITY.

"All options are on the table."

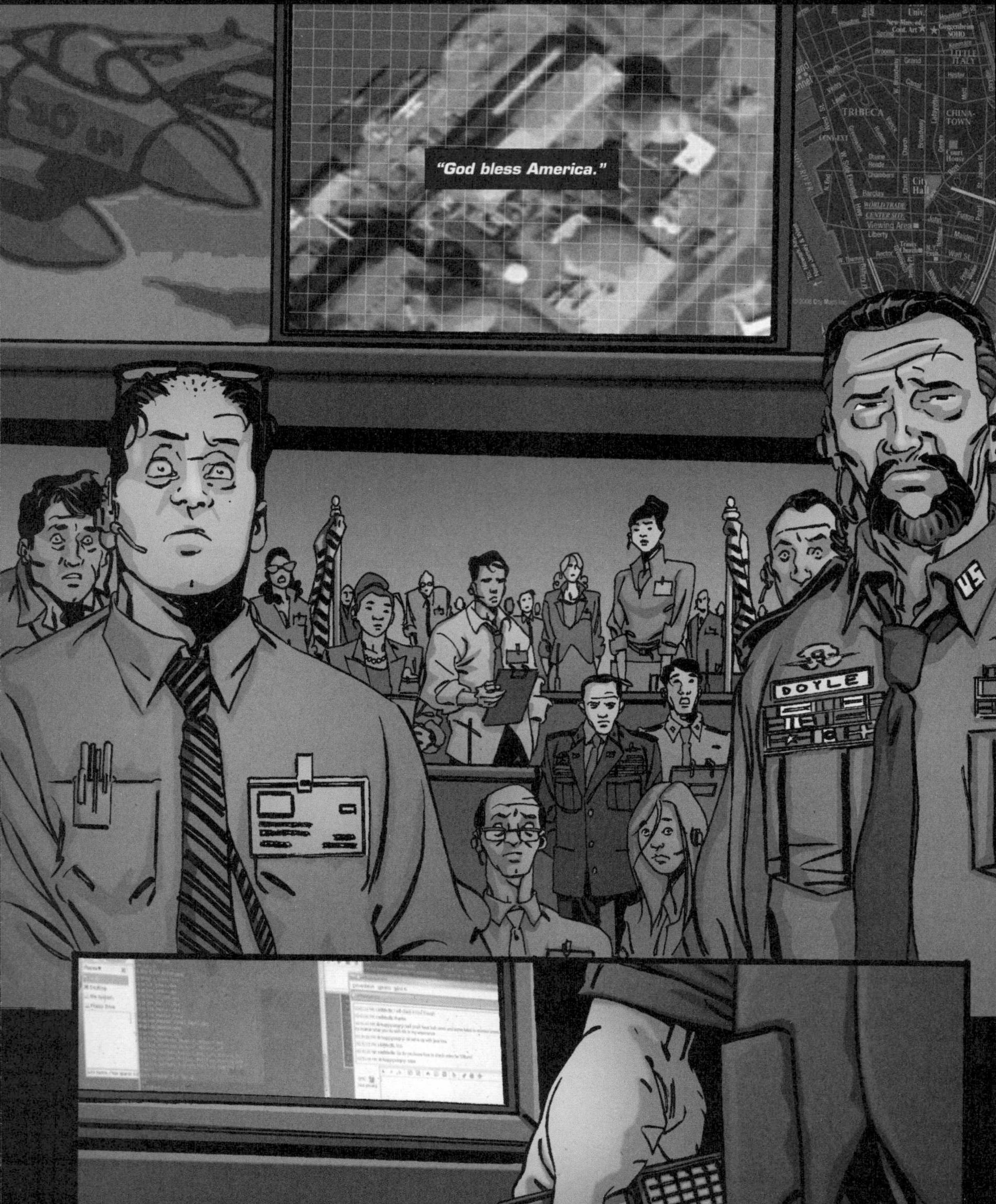
"God bless America."
TRIBECA
CHINA-TOWN
LITTLE ITALY
DOYLE
US

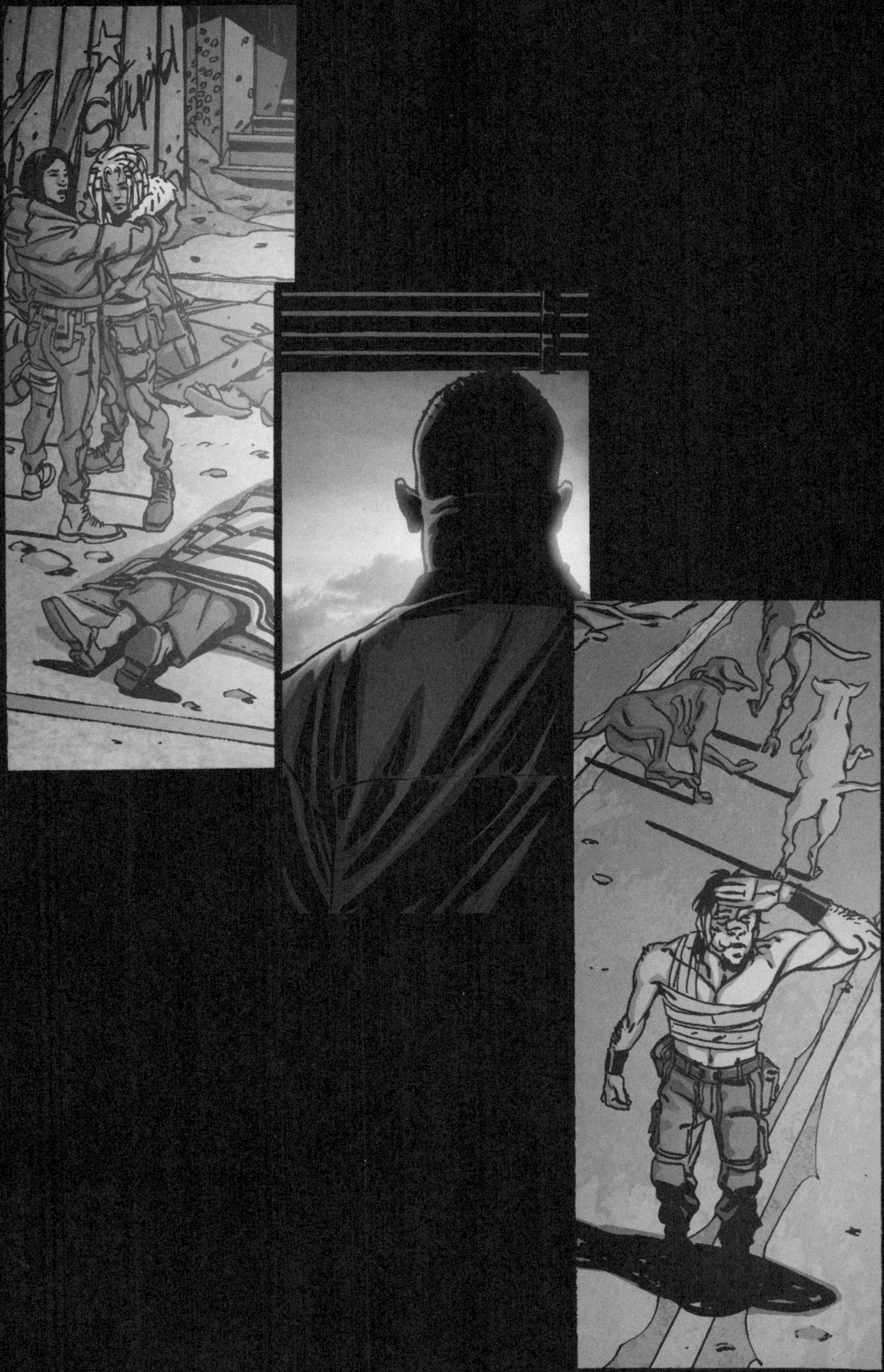
Stupid

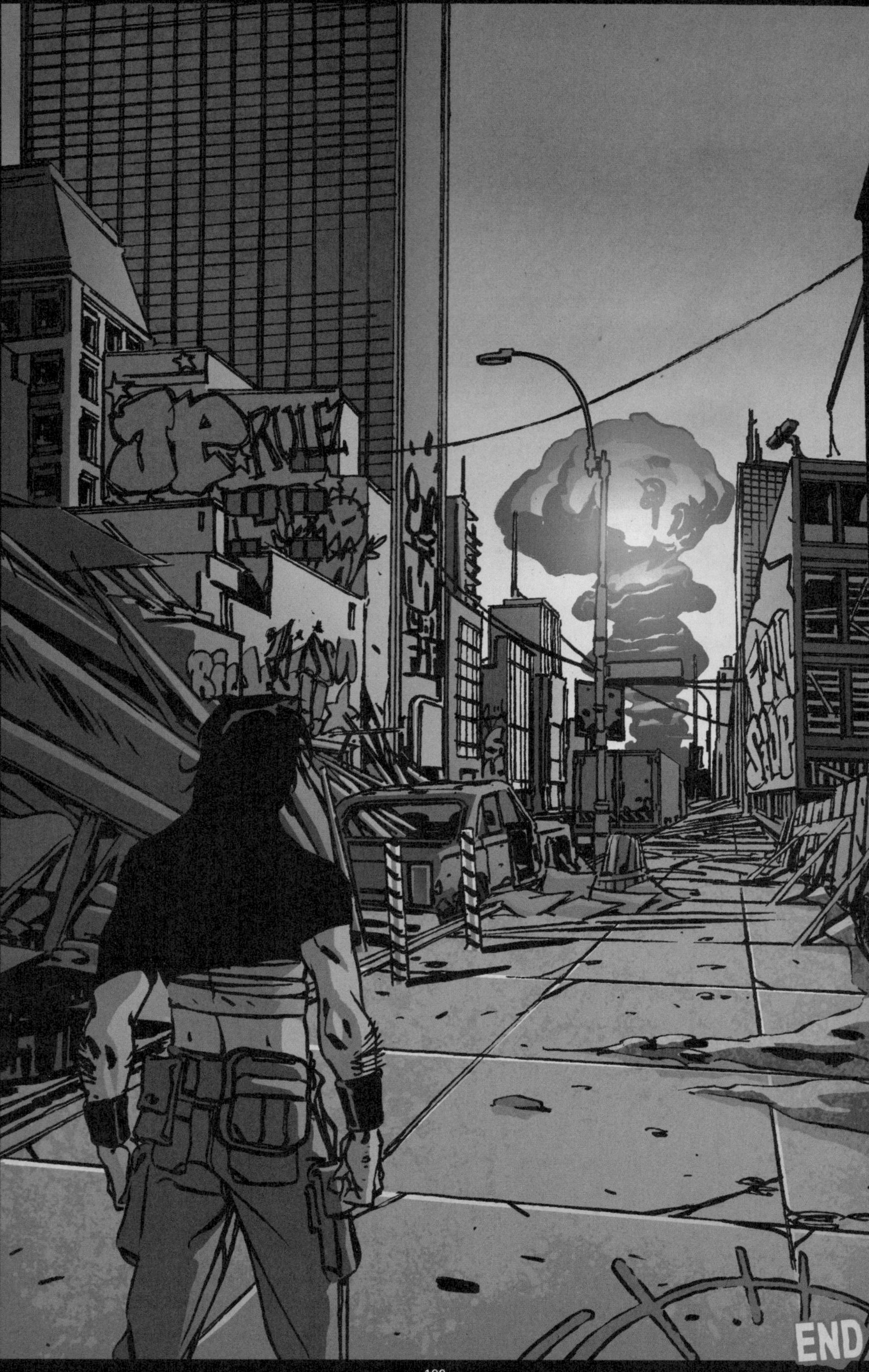
END

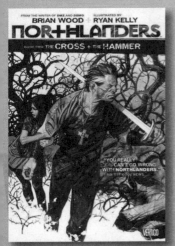
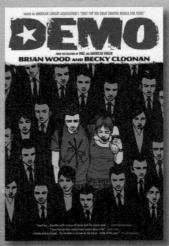

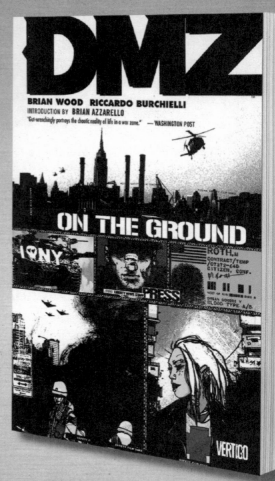

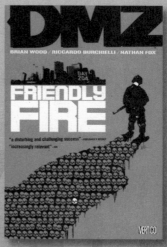